Freedom of Expression as Self-Restraint

Freedom of Expression as Self-Restraint

MATTHEW H. KRAMER
University of Cambridge

OXFORD
UNIVERSITY PRESS

OXFORD
UNIVERSITY PRESS

Great Clarendon Street, Oxford, OX2 6DP,
United Kingdom

Oxford University Press is a department of the University of Oxford.
It furthers the University's objective of excellence in research, scholarship,
and education by publishing worldwide. Oxford is a registered trade mark of
Oxford University Press in the UK and in certain other countries

First Edition published in 2021

Published in the United States of America by Oxford University Press
198 Madison Avenue, New York, NY 10016, United States of America

British Library Cataloguing in Publication Data

Data available

Library of Congress Control Number: 2020948081

ISBN 978–0–19–886865–1

DOI: 10.1093/oso/9780198868651.001.0001

Printed and bound by
CPI Group (UK) Ltd, Croydon, CR0 4YY

To the memory of John Gardner (1965–2019)
and
To the memory of Liu Xiaobo (1955–2017)

Preface

I have presented some small portions of this book as lectures at several venues: Cambridge University's Apotheosis Society in May 2019; University College London in July 2019; the University of Hildesheim in November 2019; and King's College London in January 2020. I am very grateful to the people who hosted me on those occasions (Edward Young, Jeffrey King, Richard Bellamy, Stefani Brusberg-Kiermeier, and Christoph Kletzer), and I am likewise grateful to the attendees for their stimulating feedback.

I owe special thanks to the following people, who each provided extensive and insightful comments on one or more of the chapters: Ian Carter, Rowan Cruft, Michael Ezra, Jelena Gligorijevic, and Christopher Kutz. Also valuable were remarks from Karamvir Chadha, Patrick Duggan, Michael Foran, and Rae Langton. Reports from the Oxford University Press's two anonymous readers were salutarily perceptive.

Jamie Berezin and Brianne Bellio and their colleagues at the Oxford University Press have been most helpful at every stage, in line with what I have come to expect from the OUP.

The final stages of my work on this book have occurred during a worldwide public-health catastrophe. In such a time, I am especially grateful to the Catering and Housekeeping and Maintenance and Portering staff of Churchill College, Cambridge for their support (with particular thanks to David Oakley, the College's Catering Manager).

One of the two people to whose memory this book is dedicated, John Gardner, was a friend of mine—and a champion of the values of liberal democracy—who died of oesophageal cancer at the age of 54. I never met the other dedicatee, Liu Xiaobo, but I long admired his courage and tenacity in pursuit of the ideals of liberal democracy against a tyranny that is ferociously opposed to those ideals. Before and since his death, his endeavors have been paralleled by the struggles of quite a few of his compatriots in mainland China and in Hong Kong. I am proud to co-dedicate a book on freedom of expression to him and implicitly to them.

Matthew H. Kramer
Cambridge, England
August 2020

Contents

1
Introduction: Philosophical Preliminaries

At a time when the values of liberal democracy are frequently under attack both in lofty intellectual settings and in the politics of despotism and demagoguery, this book argues that the principle of freedom of expression—one of the cornerstones of liberal democracy—is always and everywhere binding. Every system of governance that exists in any era is morally obligated to abide by that principle in all circumstances. By contending that the sway of the principle of freedom of expression is indeed exceptionless, I will be affirming that that principle is absolute. However, the nature and implications of its absoluteness will have to be expounded carefully. Absolutism in the domain of freedom of expression is sometimes construed (by its opponents) as the thesis that no type or instance of communicative conduct can ever legitimately be prohibited by a system of governance.[1] As will become apparent, that extravagant thesis is not what this book will be advancing. Rather, the principle of freedom of expression imposes absolute restrictions on the purposes—the ends and means—that can legitimately be pursued by a system of governance through any measures that prohibit types or instances of communicative conduct. Those moral restrictions on governmental purposes are unyielding, but they are consistent with laws which pursue morally permissible purposes and which nonetheless forbid certain types or instances of communications.

In Chapters 2 and 3, this book will elaborate the principle of freedom of expression in depth and will explore its implications. Chapter 4 will unfold a complex justification for the status of that principle as one of the absolutes of political morality, by showing how it relates to the paramount responsibility of every system of governance. Chapters 5 and 6 will then defend the principle of freedom of expression against some powerful assaults upon it that have been mounted in recent years by Rae Langton and other feminist philosophers and by Jeremy Waldron; those chapters will investigate the especially controversial topics of pornography and hateful extremism. My final chapter will briefly conclude the volume by mulling over a few of the procedural issues that arise in the implementation of the principle of freedom of expression through the operations of legal systems.

This opening chapter is a prolegomenon to the rest of the book, as it elucidates a number of complicated philosophical matters that will be invoked at various

[1] For a notorious example of this kind of interpretation, see Bork 1971, 21. For some correctives, see Baker 2012, 57–8 n1; Ely 1975, 1500; Frantz 1963, 751; Jacobson 2004, 49–50; Linde 1969, 1285–6; Meiklejohn 1948, 18–19.

Freedom of Expression as Self-Restraint. Matthew H. Kramer, Oxford University Press (2021). © Matthew H. Kramer.
DOI: 10.1093/oso/9780198868651.003.0001

junctures hereafter. Although this volume will engage quite frequently with American constitutional law—which, under the heading of the First Amendment to the U.S. Constitution, has developed an extraordinarily rich set of doctrines and distinctions pertaining to freedom of expression—it is not a work of constitutional theory. Rather, it is a work of political philosophy. Notwithstanding that the principle of freedom of expression which I explore and commend is convergent with the First Amendment on some significant points, it is a precept of political morality rather than of American constitutional law. It is incumbent as a moral principle on every system of governance, rather than solely on the system of governance in the United States. Whether or not its requirements have been given effect in law (or in a society's conventional morality) to any considerable degree in this or that jurisdiction, it is morally binding there as well as in all other jurisdictions. Moreover, on some points its requirements are markedly different from those of the First Amendment. Thus, although the principle of freedom of expression is often illuminated by the ideas and categories that have been developed under the auspices of the First Amendment, it is also a basis for critiques of some of those ideas and categories. My endeavor to expound and vindicate that principle is a philosophical undertaking.

As a work of philosophy, this book quite frequently draws on philosophical concepts that are not distinctively associated with debates over freedom of expression. Those concepts are of course applicable to such debates, but also extend far beyond them into numerous other matters of political and moral and legal philosophy. Having treated of most of those other matters at length elsewhere, I will here merely outline some of the key notions that pertain to them. In this chapter, which is devoted to the task of delineating those notions, the aim is to smooth the way into the subsequent chapters by clarifying the philosophical technicalities that will surface in them from time to time. Let us begin with the property of absoluteness, to which this chapter has already prominently adverted.

1.1 Weak Absoluteness versus Strong Absoluteness

In debates over the principle of freedom of expression, one of the frequent points of controversy is whether the moral constraints established by that principle are absolute. Such a question is in need of disambiguation, however. It might be asking whether those moral constraints are always and everywhere binding in all possible worlds, or it might be asking whether the stringency of those ever-binding constraints is always and everywhere greater than the stringency of any duties that might conflict with them. Whereas the former version of the question is about weak absoluteness, the latter version is about strong absoluteness. Although an affirmative answer to the former version of the question is entailed by an affirmative answer to the latter version, there is no entailment between affirmative answers in the other direction. Strong absoluteness entails weak absoluteness, but not vice versa.

Any weakly absolute moral principle WM is binding always and everywhere in all possible worlds. No circumstances, however exigent, can ever negate or diminish the demands of such a principle. Nonetheless, although WM is irrepressibly binding in all possible situations, it can be locked in conflicts with competing moral requirements. Moreover, in some imaginable circumstances, the competing moral requirements are more stringent than WM with which they conflict. In such circumstances, compliance with WM would be even more gravely wrong than a contravention of it. Still, any contravention of WM is indeed a contravention—that is, a moral wrong—and it will thus trigger remedial obligations. (Of course, if WM is formidably stringent, there might never materialize any actual situation in which a transgression of WM would be less gravely wrong than compliance therewith. Nevertheless, so long as there *could* arise some context in which such a transgression would be the lesser of two wrongs, WM is only weakly absolute rather than strongly absolute.)

If a moral principle is strongly absolute, it is not only binding at all times in all places in all possible worlds; in addition, it is always more stringent than any possible countervailing moral requirements. Of course, the absoluteness of that principle in this strong sense is perfectly consistent with the possibility of countervailing moral requirements that militate against compliance with the principle. In other words, a strongly absolute moral obligation can be locked in conflicts with competing moral obligations that are inferior in their stringency. Although those latter obligations are indeed less stringent, they impose genuine moral demands that will give rise to remedial duties if they are left unfulfilled.[2]

Now, when this book maintains that the principle of freedom of expression is absolute, it is contending that that principle is weakly absolute. As has been declared in the book's opening paragraph, exceptionlessness—rather than anything stronger—is the property which I ascribe to the principle of freedom of expression when I defend it as a moral absolute. Pressingly stringent though the requirements imposed by that principle are, there is no suggestion herein that those requirements are always and everywhere of greater stringency than is every moral obligation that might conflict with them.

[2] For some longer ruminations on the distinction between weak absoluteness and strong absoluteness, see Kramer 2014, 8–9.

1.2 Moral Conflicts, Permissibility, and Stringency

In my explication of the properties of weak absoluteness and strong absoluteness, I have referred at several junctures to conflicts between moral duties. Like many other philosophers, I use the phrase "moral conflict" to denote any situation in which someone is under a moral duty to φ and is simultaneously under a moral duty not to φ. (The variable "φ" stands for any verb or verbal phrase that refers to any action or omission.) Again like many other philosophers, I additionally use the phrase "moral conflict" to denote any situation in which the contents of the clashing duties are contraries rather than contradictories. Such a situation arises when someone is under a moral duty to do *x* and is simultaneously under a moral duty to do *y*, where (i) doing *x* is logically inconsistent with doing *y* and (ii) not doing *x* is logically consistent with not doing *y*. Though the clashing duties within a moral conflict can perfectly well coexist, they can never be jointly fulfilled; the fulfillment of either of them entails the non-fulfillment of the other.

Slightly more involuted is the matter of moral permissibility. Crucial here is a distinction between two broad types of permissibility, which can best be approached through a distinction between two main kinds of moral duties.[3] An overtoppingly stringent moral requirement exceeds in stringency all the moral duties with which it conflicts, or is not in conflict with any other moral duties. A non-overtoppingly stringent moral requirement *R* does not exceed in stringency all the moral duties that conflict with it. (Any competing moral requirements might be equal in importance to *R*, or they might exceed it in importance, or they might be insusceptible to any determinate comparisons with it because of problems of incommensurability.)

Now, through this dichotomy between overtoppingly stringent and non-overtoppingly stringent duties, we can differentiate between weak permissibility and strong permissibility:

> **Weak Permissibility**. Some person *X* is morally permitted to perform some action *q* if and only if *X* is not under any overtoppingly stringent moral obligation to not perform *q*.[4]

X can be weakly permitted to perform *q* while being under a non-overtoppingly stringent moral obligation to not perform *q*. In that respect, weak permissibility differs from strong permissibility.

[3] For some more expansive accounts of the distinction between strong permissibility and weak permissibility, see Kramer 2014, 4–7; 2016, 165–8. Throughout this book, I use the terms "permissible" and "legitimate" (and the terms "permissibility" and "legitimacy") interchangeably. I also use the terms "duty" and "obligation" and "requirement" interchangeably. Whenever I use "responsibility" as a count noun rather than as a mass noun, it too is synonymous with "duty" and "obligation" and "requirement."

[4] To avoid ambiguities in my prose, my placement of "not" will create some ugly split infinitives at several junctures in this discussion.

> **Strong Permissibility.** *X* is morally permitted to perform *q* if and only if *X* is neither under an overtoppingly stringent moral obligation to not perform *q* nor under a non-overtoppingly stringent moral obligation to not perform *q*.

X is strongly permitted to perform *q* if and only if *X* is under no moral obligation whatsoever to not perform *q*. Note that the proposition "*X* is strongly permitted to perform *q*" entails the proposition "*X* is weakly permitted to perform *q*," but not vice versa.

Whenever this book uses the term "permissible" or "legitimate" (or "permissibility" or "legitimacy") without any qualification, it is invoking the notion of permissibility in the strong sense. Consequently, the term "impermissible" or "illegitimate" is to be understood as "not strongly permissible." That is, I generally assume that some action or policy *q* is morally impermissible for a system of governance unless that system is under no moral obligation whatsoever to not undertake *q*. Moreover, the adjectives "wrong" and "impermissible" are interchangeable throughout this book; a course of conduct is morally wrong unless it does not contravene any moral duties.

In these first two sections of this chapter, I have adverted repeatedly to the property of deontic stringency. That property can be understood in several ways (Kamm 2007, 248–68), and a choice among them is not necessary for my purposes in this book. By any reckoning, deontic stringency is a measure of the moral importance of a duty. Still, worth indicating here is the conception of stringency that implicitly underlies my numerous invocations of that notion. The stringency of a moral duty is given by the onerousness or sizeableness of the step(s) required in order to remedy a contravention of the duty. If the remedial obligations engendered by wholesale violations of some duty D_1 are heavier than the remedial obligations engendered by wholesale violations of some other duty D_2, then D_1 is more stringent than D_2.[5]

1.3 Deontology versus Consequentialism

As will be emphasized at many junctures in this book, my account of the principle of freedom of expression is strongly deontological. Hence, another point of preliminary clarification that is requisite here is the distinction between deontology and consequentialism. That distinction can be drawn in more than one way, and elsewhere I have indeed drawn it in two main ways (Kramer 2014, 20–4). For the purposes of this book, however, the most general and straightforward demarcation between deontology and consequentialism is perfectly sufficient on its own.

[5] This conception of stringency is integrally connected to the account of moral rights which I have propounded in Kramer 2004, 249–94.

That demarcation is centered on the basic moral import—the moral permissibility or impermissibility—of certain modes of conduct (Kramer 2014, 20–1). A deontological moral theory holds that some modes of conduct are morally impermissible regardless of the benignity of the consequences that are likely to flow from the occurrence of any such modes of conduct. If somebody is under a deontological duty not to perform some action *q*, then his performance of *q* is wrong regardless of how valuable the state of affairs ensuing from his performance of *q* might be. That is, every deontological duty proscribes some course of conduct even if one's adoption of that course of conduct in particular circumstances would yield much better consequences than one's refraining therefrom.

While deontologists ascribe consequence-independent moral statuses to various types of actions and omissions, consequentialists of course maintain that the moral character of any type or instance of conduct is fully determined by the causal consequences that will probably or actually flow therefrom.[6] In the eyes of the latter theorists, no type or instance of conduct is ever endowed with any inherent moral import. Instead, every action or omission derives its moral import from the effects with which it is causally associated. Accordingly, as John Finnis has aptly remarked, a proponent of any consequentialist doctrine "holds himself ready to do *anything*" (Finnis 1980, 121, emphasis in original). According to the consequentialists, there are no principled limits on the range of actions that can legitimately be undertaken in sundry circumstances. The breadth or narrowness of that range will depend entirely on the results that are likely to follow causally from each of the multitudinous modes of conduct that might be adopted by people in any number of contexts. No mode of conduct, however abhorrent it may be, is unconditionally disallowed by the reckoning of a consequentialist theory. The only thing unconditionally disallowed by such a reckoning is the inconduciveness of one's behavior to the attainment of a maximally good state of affairs—where maximal goodness is gauged with reference to the desideratum or set of desiderata commended by the theory.

As is evident, this distinction between deontology and consequentialism is directly relevant to the matter of moral absolutes. Whereas the only moral absolute that is postulated by consequentialists is a prohibition on impeding the maximal attainment of some fundamental desideratum or set of desiderata, any full-blown deontologists affirm that some specified moral prohibitions are binding always and everywhere irrespective of the likely consequences of compliance therewith. In particular, deontologists affirm that each such specified prohibition is binding even when some contraventions of it will serve to lower greatly the overall frequency with which it is contravened. Insofar as anyone contends that some mode

[6] I am of course here assuming that the types or instances of conduct are identified without reference to the desideratum or set of desiderata pursued by any consequentialist theory that is under consideration.

of conduct is always and everywhere morally wrong—and, thus, insofar as anyone maintains that the forbiddenness of such conduct is a moral absolute—he or she is a deontologist. (Note that the absoluteness integral to deontological prohibitions is exceptionlessness—weak absoluteness—rather than the stronger property of invariably supreme stringency.)

1.4 Physical Freedom versus Deontic Freedom

In a book on freedom of expression, the nature of freedom is obviously a matter of great importance. Although quite a few distinctions would have to be drawn in a full-length account of that nature,[7] the chief dichotomy for the purposes of this book is between physical freedom and deontic freedom. In a nutshell, on which I will briefly expand here, that dichotomy is between freedoms as abilities and freedoms as permissions.

Someone is physically free to φ if and only if she is able to φ—that is, if and only if she is not prevented from φ-ing either by internal incapacities or by external obstacles. Her being physically free to φ does not entail her φ-ing, since she might choose not to φ; but her being physically free to φ entails that, if she carefully endeavors to φ, she will indeed φ. By contrast, someone is physically not free to φ if and only if she is not able to φ. She is physically *un*free to φ if and only if her being physically not free to φ is causally attributable to some actions or dispositions-to-perform-actions on the part of some other person(s).

In the preceding paragraph's terse remarks on physical freedoms and unfreedoms, which I have elsewhere elaborated and defended at great length, the key concepts are modal rather than deontic. That is, they concern what *can* or *cannot* occur, rather than what *should* or *should not* occur. They concern what each person is *able* or *unable* to do, rather than what each person is *permitted* or *forbidden* to do. Being physically free to φ consists in being able to φ—whether or not one actually chooses to φ—and being physically not free to φ consists in being unable to φ. Whereas the antithesis of being physically free to φ is being prevented from φ-ing, the antithesis of being physically not free to φ is being unprevented from φ-ing. Note that "physically" is not to be understood here in contrast with "mentally" or "psychologically." Unless someone is psychologically able to φ, he or she is not able to φ and is therefore not physically free to φ. Hence, "physically" includes "psychologically," as physical freedoms (in the relevant sense of "physical") are always partly constituted by psychological abilities. Instead of being contrasted with "mentally" or "psychologically," "physically" is to be understood in contrast

[7] For a full-length account, see Kramer 2003. See also Carter 1999; Kramer 2010; and Carter, Kramer, and Steiner 2007. Throughout this book, I use the terms "freedom" and "liberty" (and the terms "freedoms" and "liberties") interchangeably.

with "deontically." (Although "physically" is in contrast with "deontically," it is not in contrast with "normatively." As will be noted in §1.5.3 below, legal powers to alter legal relationships and moral powers to alter moral relationships are abilities rather than permissions. Hence, they too are classifiable as physical freedoms in contradistinction to deontic freedoms.)

Deontic freedoms are permissions rather than abilities. They consist not in unpreventedness but instead in permittedness or unforbiddenness. If somebody is deontically free to φ, then he is allowed to φ by any applicable authoritative norms such as legal mandates or moral principles or institutional rules. Conversely, if somebody is deontically *un*free to φ, then he is prohibited from φ-ing by one or more of those authoritative norms. When we ask whether somebody is deontically free to φ, we are not asking whether he is *capable* of φ-ing; we are asking whether he is *entitled* to φ. Thus, the antithesis of being deontically free to φ is being forbidden to φ, and the antithesis of being deontically unfree to φ is being under no obligation to abstain from φ-ing.

Physical liberty and deontic liberty diverge in a number of respects that derive in various ways from the basic modal/deontic difference—the difference between abilities and permissions—that has just been recounted (Kramer 2003, 60–75). Most obvious among the dissimilarities between the concept of physical freedom and the concept of deontic freedom is their extensional non-equivalence. That is, a person will often be deontically free to φ without being physically free to φ, and vice versa. For example, although I am both legally and morally permitted to run a one-mile race under four minutes, I am not physically able to do so; my deontic liberty to run at that speed is not accompanied by a corresponding physical liberty. Conversely, although I am physically able to assault unprovokedly the person standing ahead of me in a queue, I am neither legally nor morally permitted to do so. My physical freedom to commit the assault is not accompanied by any corresponding deontic freedom. Permissibility and ability can coincide and very frequently do coincide, but they likewise frequently diverge.

Of course, the extensional non-equivalence and the several other contrarieties between physical liberty and deontic liberty should not induce us to overlook the many affinities between them. For one thing, as has just been stated, the two types of freedom very frequently converge extensionally; people are often able to do things which they are permitted to do, and they are often permitted to do things which they are able to do. Moreover, liberty of each type consists in an absence of constraints. Though the constraints that negate abilities are different in sundry ways from the constraints that negate permissions, unconstrainedness is the essence of deontic freedom just as it is of physical freedom. Freedom of each type consists in opportunities.

Both kinds of freedom will figure prominently in this book, though deontic freedom and unfreedom will figure especially saliently. As will be argued in support of the central thesis of this book, systems of governance are always morally obligated to refrain from imposing legal constraints on communicative activities qua communicative activities—which is to say that this book's central thesis is concerned with the deontic unfreedom (moral unfreedom) of any system of governance to impose deontic unfreedoms (legal unfreedoms) on citizens in their communicative endeavors.[8] Also crucial, however, are *physical* freedoms to engage in communicative activities. Any system of governance is morally obligated to refrain from eliminating such freedoms for certain purposes, and is also morally obligated to keep hecklers and hostile audiences from eliminating such freedoms in some circumstances. We shall encounter these freedom-pertaining matters again and again in the chapters that follow.

1.5 The Hohfeldian Analysis

Somewhat over a century ago, the American jurist Wesley Hohfeld propounded an analysis of legal positions that has remained enormously influential to the present day.[9] Hohfeld differentiated among four main kinds of entitlements that are commonly designated as "rights," and he sought to highlight their distinctness. Among those four categories are deontic liberties. (Hohfeld concentrated on legal positions, but most aspects of his analysis are equally applicable to moral positions. Beyond the scope of the present book are the aspects of the Hohfeldian analysis that are not straightforwardly transferable from the legal domain to the moral domain.)

Hohfeld's analysis of legal entitlements and their correlates is encapsulated in the following table:

HOHFELDIAN TABLE OF LEGAL POSITIONS

ENTITLEMENTS	**claim (or claim-right)**	**liberty**	**power**	**immunity**
CORRELATES	duty	no-right	liability	disability

[8] Here and elsewhere throughout this book, I use the word "citizens" expansively to denote private individuals (including public officials in their capacities as private individuals). That word is not limited to the people in any jurisdiction who are full members of the polity there. It extends also to residents who are not such members. The operative contrast is not between citizens and other residents, but is instead between citizens and people who are acting in their capacities as officials.

[9] Hohfeld's main law-review articles were collected posthumously in Hohfeld 1923. Especially germane are the first two chapters in that book. I have elsewhere expounded the Hohfeldian analysis in some of my many essays on rights. See especially Kramer 1998, 7–60, 101–11; 2001, 73–89; 2008, 415–17; 2019a.

Each of the four positions in the top half of the table is an entitlement that is correlated with a position in the lower half of the table. Correlativity in the Hohfeldian sense is biconditional entailment; the existence of any Hohfeldian entitlement with a certain content entails the existence of the correlative position with the same content, and vice versa. For example, Joe's claim-right to be paid $10 by Sally entails Sally's duty to pay $10 to Joe, and vice versa. Neither an entitlement with a certain content nor its correlate with that same content can ever exist without the other. Each exists if and only if the other exists.

One major logical relationship exhibited in the Hohfeldian table, then, is that of correlativity (biconditional entailment) between the two positions in each of the four columns of the table. In addition are some logical relationships between the two columns on the left-hand side of the table, and between the two columns on the right-hand side. Whereas the positions diagonally across from each other on the left-hand half of the table are logical duals, the positions diagonally across from each other on the right-hand half are logical contradictories.

A terse elucidation of the distinction between duals and contradictories is advisable here. Consider, for example, the proposition "Sally bears a duty to pay $10 to Joe" and the proposition "Sally is at liberty not to pay $10 to Joe." The former proposition is true if and only if the negation of the latter proposition is true. Each proposition is the negation of the other, and the content of the deontic predicate (that is, the content of the duty or liberty) in each proposition is the negation of the content of the deontic predicate in the other proposition. These twofold instances of negation, the negation of the proposition and the negation of the predicated content, are characteristic of logical duals.

By contrast, the diagonal opposites on the right-hand side of Hohfeld's table are contradictories rather than duals. Thus, for example, "Peter is liable to undergo a certain change X in his legal relations brought about by Melanie" is the contradictory of "Peter is immune from undergoing that change X in his legal relations brought about by Melanie." The former proposition is true if and only if the negation of the latter proposition is true, but the content of the normative predicate (that is, the content of the liability or immunity) in each proposition is the same as the content of the normative predicate in the other proposition.

1.5.1 Claim-Rights and Duties

Because the Hohfeldian framework is indispensable for a precise understanding of the principle of freedom of expression, a brief column-by-column conspectus will be salutary here—starting, of course, with the claim-right/duty axis. A *claim-right* confers deontic protection on its holder against the interference or uncooperativeness of some other person(s). Interference and uncooperativeness are both understood very broadly here to encompass the countless ways in which the actions or omissions of some person(s) can harm or disadvantage some other person(s). Anyone who bears a *duty* correlative to a specified claim-right is required by some norm(s) to behave in accordance with the content of the claim-right, whether that content calls for non-interference or for cooperativeness. Thus, to return to the example above, the fact that Joe has a claim-right to be paid $10 by Sally is something that endows him with deontic protection (legal or moral protection, for example) against her withholding of the payment of $10. As the bearer of the duty correlative to his claim-right, Sally is required by some norm(s) to behave in accordance with the content of the claim-right by paying $10 to Joe.

As has been indicated, the protection bestowed by a claim-right on its holder is deontic rather than physical. Hence, Joe's claim-right to be paid $10 by Sally is not in itself a physical constraint on Sally's latitude. However, if a claim-right is legal or institutional, it will usually be backed up with the prospect of enforcement in the event of noncompliance with its requirements. That prospect of enforcement does serve as a physical constraint on the latitude of the duty-bearer, not typically by eliminating certain physical freedoms discretely *ab initio* but instead typically by eliminating the ability of the duty-bearer to exercise certain physical freedoms in conjunction with certain other physical freedoms. Given that a duty-bearer will be subjected to a legal sanction at some time t_2 for having exercised a specified physical freedom (athwart her duty) at some earlier time t_1, and given that the imposition of the sanction will deprive the duty-bearer of some physical freedoms that could otherwise have been exercised by her at t_2, the duty-bearer is not able to exercise both the specified physical freedom at t_1 and the physical freedoms that will be removed by the sanction at t_2. For example, if Sally declines to pay $10 to Joe at the time when her payment is due, and if a legal sanction will subsequently be imposed on her for her breach of the legal duty which she has owed to Joe, she is not able to exercise both her physical freedom to withhold the payment of $10 and any physical freedoms that will be removed from her by the imposition of the legal sanction. Accordingly, although the legal claim-right held by Joe vis-à-vis Sally or the correlative legal duty owed by her to him is not in itself a physical constraint on her latitude, the prospect of legal enforcement that will be triggered in the event of her noncompliance with his claim-right (and with her own correlative duty) is such a physical constraint.

1.5.2 Liberties and No-Rights

The holder of a Hohfeldian *liberty* is free of any duty to some other person(s), with regard to the act or omission or state of affairs covered by the liberty. Suppose that Agnes is legally at liberty vis-à-vis Fred to visit her grandmother on Saturday morning. In that case, she does not owe Fred any legal duty not to visit her grandmother on Saturday morning. She might owe Fred a moral duty not to visit her grandmother on Saturday morning, or she might owe Tom a legal duty not to visit her grandmother at that time, or she might not be physically capable of visiting her grandmother at that time; nonetheless she is legally at liberty vis-à-vis Fred to visit her grandmother on Saturday morning, if and only if she does not owe him any legal duty to refrain from visiting her grandmother at that time.

Correlative to any liberty is a *no-right* concerning the conduct or the state of affairs covered by the liberty, though the bearer of the no-right may well be at liberty to stymie the occurrence of that conduct or that state of affairs. If Agnes vis-à-vis Fred is legally at liberty to visit her grandmother on Saturday morning, then Fred vis-à-vis Agnes bears a legal no-right with regard to her visiting her grandmother on Saturday morning. Given that the liberty and the no-right are correlative, the content of each is the same as the content of the other. Consequently, the content of the no-right is the negation of the content of the claim-right that is negated by the no-right (just as the content of the correlative liberty is the negation of the content of the duty that is negated by the liberty). Fred vis-à-vis Agnes bears a no-right with regard to her visiting her grandmother on Saturday morning, if and only if he does not have any claim-right to her not visiting her grandmother at that time.

The entry in Hohfeld's table that has most frequently been neglected in discussions of his overall analytical framework is the no-right. Doubtless, one reason for the relative dearth of scrutiny accorded to no-rights is that Hohfeld devised a hyphenated neologism to designate them. Each of the other positions in the Hohfeldian table is designated by a term with a solid grounding in everyday discourse and juristic discourse—though Hohfeld greatly precisified and regimented each of those terms for his analysis, by attaching a univocal or nearly univocal meaning to each of them—whereas the hyphenated term "no-right," in contrast with the unhyphenated phrase "no right," does not have any comparable grounding either in ordinary discourse or in juristic discourse. That neologism is almost never employed by anyone outside the confines of discussions of Hohfeld's categories, and it is often not employed even within those confines. (In such discussions, sentences that use the everyday phrase "no right" are often employed in lieu of sentences that use the arcane hyphenated term "no-right." As I have recounted elsewhere—in Kramer 2019a—the logic of that phrase is very different from the logic of the hyphenated term.)

In line with what has been mentioned above, the bearer of a no-right concerning some other person's φ-ing can be at liberty to prevent the exercise of the other person's liberty to φ. Suppose that William and Audrey are competing against each other as the two participants in a one-mile race. William is at liberty to win the race by outrunning Audrey, and she is at liberty to win the race by outrunning him. If William exercises his liberty to win the race, he will thereby have prevented Audrey from exercising her liberty to win the race. Likewise, of course, if Audrey exercises her liberty to win the race, she will thereby have prevented William from exercising his liberty to win. Each participant in the race holds claim-rights against the other participant's adoption of sundry unfair tactics (such as pushing or tripping or stabbing or shooting), but neither participant holds a claim-right against being outrun by the other. Hence, in this situation as in any relevantly cognate situation, somebody's no-right with regard to some other person's φ-ing is accompanied by a liberty to thwart that other person from φ-ing.

1.5.3 Powers and Liabilities

A Hohfeldian *power* is an ability to alter other legal or moral positions (including other Hohfeldian powers). For example, if Samuel holds some legal powers to gain ownership of certain items of merchandise from Julia through his purchasing of them at her shop, his exercise of those powers will have altered his own legal positions and Julia's legal positions. He will have endowed himself with legal liberties to use the purchased items, and with legal claim-rights against various types of impediments to his possession and use of those items, and with legal powers to transfer ownership of the items to other people, and with legal immunities against being divested of these other legal entitlements. He will likewise have imposed upon himself a legal duty to refrain from taking back nonconsensually the money which he has paid to Julia at her shop.

A Hohfeldian *liability* is a position of susceptibility to changes in one's legal or moral positions through the exercise of a power by oneself or by somebody else. In the example broached in the preceding paragraph, Samuel and Julia have borne legal liabilities that correlate with the legal powers which they respectively exercise when Julia sells some goods to Samuel at her shop. Samuel has borne a legal liability to undergo the acquisition of legal claim-rights against interference with his retention of the purchased items of merchandise, and he has similarly borne legal liabilities to undergo the acquisition of the other legal entitlements with which he has vested himself through his payment of money for those items. At the same time, he has borne a legal liability to incur the legal duty which he now owes to Julia: the duty to abstain from taking back nonconsensually the money that he has paid to her. His legal liabilities have been correlated with the legal powers which he has exercised and the legal powers which Julia has exercised through her act of transferring ownership of the goods to him in return for his payment.

Although the Hohfeldian use of the term "liability" corresponds to one way (or one set of ways) in which "liability" is employed in quotidian discourse, that term in such discourse is most often used negatively to denote something that is disadvantageous. For instance, the statement "His presence on the team was a liability" is a declaration that somebody's membership of a team was detrimental on balance. By contrast, a Hohfeldian liability can be either advantageous or disadvantageous for its bearer; the class of advantageous Hohfeldian liabilities is no less expansive than the class of disadvantageous Hohfeldian liabilities. For example, when Michael presents his friend Alice with an elegant new dress as a gift, his power to endow her with ownership of the dress has been correlated with her liability to become so endowed. Her bearing of that liability has clearly redounded to her benefit rather than to her detriment. Much the same is true, *mutatis mutandis*, of innumerable other Hohfeldian liabilities.

Commensurately, Hohfeldian powers can be either beneficial or detrimental for their holders. The class of disadvantageous Hohfeldian powers is no less expansive than the class of advantageous Hohfeldian powers.[10] For example, if Bartholomew has kicked Martha in a situation where he is not thereby defending himself or somebody else, he has exercised some legal powers to alter his own legal positions and the legal positions of certain other people such as law-enforcement officers; he has saddled himself with liabilities to undergo arrest and other measures of enforcement, and he has invested certain people with legal powers and legal liberties to resort to such measures. Bartholomew has furthermore placed himself under a liability to be sued successfully by Martha, and he has invested her with legal powers and legal liberties to pursue tort-law proceedings successfully against him. His holding of the several legal powers which he has exercised through his performance of a criminal and tortious action is something that has redounded to his detriment rather than to his benefit. Again, much the same is true (*mutatis mutandis*) of countless other legal powers.

Finally, let us note—as a follow-up to what has been mentioned fleetingly in §1.4 above—that Hohfeldian powers are abilities and are therefore classifiable as physical freedoms in contradistinction to deontic freedoms. Whereas the categories that make up the left-hand side of the Hohfeldian table are deontic, the categories on the right-hand side of the table are non-deontically normative. (Although all deontic concepts are normative, not all normative concepts are deontic.) Thus, although normative powers are obviously different from physical powers in the ordinary sense of "physical," both normative powers and physical powers are abilities. Thus, both are rightly classifiable as physical freedoms—because the term "physical" in the phrase "physical freedoms" is used not in the relatively narrow ordinary sense but instead as a synonym of "modal." One facet of the distinction between deontic freedoms and physical freedoms, then, is the distinction between Hohfeldian liberties and Hohfeldian powers. It is one facet of the contrast between freedoms as permissions and freedoms as abilities.

[10] In this very respect, Hohfeld's conception of legal powers is different from the conceptions propounded by some other legal philosophers such as H.L.A. Hart. See Kramer 2018, 36–7.

1.5.4 Immunities and Disabilities

As the negation of a liability, an *immunity* is a position of insusceptibility to the bringing about of any normative changes that are precluded by the immunity. Whenever a legal or moral immunity is possessed by someone vis-à-vis some other party, any attempt by that other party to exercise a legal or moral power in order to produce the change(s) covered by the immunity will be unavailing. Correlative to any immunity is a *disability* with the same content. If Andrew holds an immunity vis-à-vis Rachel against her cancellation of the debt of £500 which she owes to him, then Rachel bears a disability vis-à-vis Andrew with regard to her canceling of that debt. An attempt by her to exercise a power of cancellation will be fruitless.

Commentators on Hohfeld's analysis of legal positions tend to say rather little about immunities and disabilities, but immunity/disability relationships are in fact of immense importance—specifically for a book on freedom of expression, and also more broadly. Many of the entitlements conferred by so-called bills of rights are immunities, and the bestowal of immunities on citizens is the paramount effect of the First Amendment to the American Constitution. Although the wording of the First Amendment with reference to freedom of expression ("Congress shall make no law . . . abridging the freedom of speech, or of the press") could have been construed as primarily duty-imposing, it has in fact been construed as predominantly immunity-conferring. That is, instead of being interpreted as imposing legal duties on the Congress to refrain from enacting laws that abridge people's communicative liberties in certain ways, the First Amendment has been interpreted as bestowing legal immunities on Americans which shield them against Congressional legislation that would abridge such liberties in the disallowed ways.[11] Whereas the American courts do not levy sanctions on the Congress for enacting laws that are at odds with the First Amendment, they hold that those laws—or the relevant provisions of those laws—are invalid. In other words, the courts hold that the Congress by enacting such laws has gone beyond the scope of its legislative powers. Those laws are within the ambit of the disability imposed on the Congress by the First Amendment, and are therefore of no effect. In general, the free-speech guarantee under the American Constitution is implemented principally through immunity/disability relationships rather than principally through claim-right/duty relationships. (We shall explore this point further in subsequent chapters, especially Chapters 2 and 7.)

Apart from the role of immunities and disabilities in the effectuation of the First Amendment's free-speech guarantee—and in the effectuation of various other

[11] For the past nine decades, the U.S. Supreme Court has deemed the First Amendment's free-speech guarantee to be applicable not only to the Congress but also to state legislatures (through the Fourteenth Amendment). My reason for omitting any mention of the state legislatures in the brief discussion in the text is simply that I can thereby avoid cumbersome prose.

constitutional guarantees—immunities are crucial for securing the existence and continuity of other legal positions. For example, if Melanie has a legal claim-right against being punched in the face by Luke, and if she holds no legal immunities against being divested of that claim-right by Luke through countless elementary means (such as his looking at her or his smiling at her or his uttering of some mundane phrase), then her claim-right is almost entirely hollow. Indeed, if she holds no legal immunity against being divested of that claim-right through Luke's clenching of his fist or through his movement of his arm toward her face, we shall have to conclude that she does not hold such a claim-right at all. Given that in such circumstances Melanie can be deprived of her legal claim-right by precisely the sorts of movements of Luke's body that would be involved in his contravening the claim-right, her legal protection against being punched in the face by Luke would be indistinguishable from her not having any legal protection against such misconduct by him. Consequently, the very existence of her claim-right in any meaningful sense is dependent on its being accompanied by sundry immunities against the extinguishing of that claim-right.

This role of immunities in securing the existence and continuity of other entitlements is pervasive and vital, yet it is almost always taken for granted rather than made explicit. Still, like the presence of oxygen in the atmosphere of Earth—which is necessary for the continued existence of human beings, but which is mostly taken for granted in everyday life—the aforementioned role of immunities is no less important for going so often unnoticed. Immunities are central not only to freedom of expression but also to the sway of legal and moral positions more generally.

1.6 The Causal/Constitutive Distinction

A final preliminary matter to be covered by this chapter pertains to a dichotomy that will surface at numerous junctures in this book: the dichotomy between causal relationships and constitutive relationships. On the one hand, the general character of causation is an involuted topic which I have tackled at length elsewhere (Kramer 2003, 277–85, 297–303, 344–6) and which lies beyond the purview of the present book. On the other hand, my chief concern here is to differentiate between causal connections and constitutive connections. For that purpose, we do not need to delve into the technicalities of the account of causation which I have elaborated in some of my previous work. Rather, we should simply note the major feature of causal relationships that sets them apart from constitutive relationships. When events or facts are causally related to each other, they are logically distinct. Instead of being connected by ties of logical indisseverability, they are connected through laws of nature that are ascertainable empirically by physicists and chemists and biologists and other scientists. Those laws of nature conjoin events or facts causally in the operations of the material world.

Constitutive relationships are very different.[12] Some event or fact X is constituted by some event or fact Y if and only if (1) Y, in combination with all the prevailing circumstances other than any causal laws of nature, logically entails X; and (2) without Y, the prevailing circumstances other than any causal laws of nature would not logically entail X. Whereas laws of nature are the foundations of causal relationships, they do not play any role in tying events or facts together constitutively. If one event or fact constitutes another, the two of them are linked conceptually or logically rather than through the operations of the material world.

Suppose for example that John and Tony are the sole competitors in a two-mile race, and that John finishes the race ahead of Tony without having transgressed any rules of the competition. His having finished ahead of Tony, in combination with all the prevailing circumstances other than any causal laws, logically entails his having won the race. Indeed, his having finished ahead of Tony—in combination with all the prevailing circumstances other than any causal laws—amounts to his having won the race. Among the prevailing circumstances, of course, are the rules of the race which specify the conditions for winning. Likewise among those prevailing circumstances is the fact that John has not contravened any of the applicable rules.

In this scenario, John's having finished the race ahead of Tony and his having won the race are not two separate events that are each to be counted in an overall tally of entities that exist and events that have occurred. Rather, they are one and the same event under two somewhat different descriptions. As I have said above, John's having finished the race ahead of Tony amounts to his having won the race. Hence, we would be guilty of double counting if we were to include both the winning and the finishing ahead of Tony as items in a register of events that have occurred. Only the latter item is to be included. In this situation, the constitutive relationship between John's finishing the race ahead of Tony and his winning the race is aptly classifiable as a relationship of reducibility.

However, not every constitutive relationship is a relationship of reducibility. For instance, let us here ponder the multitude of communicative actions and dispositions over time that cumulatively constitute a natural language such as English. In combination with the prevailing circumstances other than any causal laws, the communicative actions and dispositions of the users of the language (including their actions of compiling dictionaries and grammatical treatises, for example) are collectively constitutive of the language and of its sundry syntactical and semantic rules. Should we conclude, then, that those rules of syntax and semantics are not to be counted in any overall reckoning of entities that exist and events that occur? Given that the multifarious communicative actions and dispositions of the users of the language are to be counted in such a reckoning, would we be guilty

[12] In this paragraph and the next few paragraphs, I draw quite heavily (with many modifications) on Kramer 2018, 25–7.

of double counting if we also included the syntactic and semantic rules that are constituted by those actions and dispositions? As should be evident, the answer to each of these questions is negative. Although the communicative actions and shared dispositions of the users of a language do constitute the language's semantic and syntactic rules in the sense that has been specified here, they are also oriented toward those rules—for the rules guide and structure the very actions and dispositions that sustain them.[13] We would be missing the reciprocality of this dynamic of constitutiveness and guidance if we declined to include the rules of syntax and semantics along with the communicative actions and dispositions in an overall tally of entities that exist and events that occur. Whereas John's finishing ahead of Tony and John's winning the race are one and the same event under slightly different descriptions, the communicative actions and dispositions of the users of a language are not exactly the same things as the rules of syntax and semantics that are constituted by those actions and dispositions. Hence, the constitutive relationship between the actions and dispositions on the one hand and the rules on the other hand is not aptly classifiable as a relationship of reducibility. (Of course, the rules of syntax and semantics are abstract normative entities rather than material entities. They are immanent in the communicative practices of which they are the normative structure and lodestars. They guide those practices not by serving as causal mechanisms but instead by serving as foci for the exercise of people's linguistic competences. Still, in any satisfactory overall reckoning of entities that exist and events that occur, we have to take account of normative entities as well as of material entities.[14])

1.7 A Terse Conclusion

Although this chapter has sought at several junctures to indicate some of the ways in which the philosophical concepts introduced herein can contribute to a theory of freedom of expression, those concepts are salient as well in a vast number of other domains. They bear crucially on the topic of freedom of expression, but they are not *peculiarly* associated with that topic. This book has begun with them as philosophical preliminaries so that my subsequent chapters can draw upon them without having to expound them at any length; instead, the expositions and

[13] When I say that the actions and dispositions are oriented toward the rules and guided by them, I am not implying that all or most of the competent users of the relevant language would be able to articulate the rules in any precise fashion. Even while not being able to formulate the rules with any precision, people can be guided by them through steady adherence to them. One adheres to the rules not only through one's implicit applications of them in one's own speaking and writing, but also through one's tendency to recognize when they have been infringed by other people.

[14] For a defense of this assertion about the reality of normative entities, see Kramer 2018, 28–31.

arguments in those subsequent chapters can concentrate on matters that are more specifically associated with the topic of freedom of expression.

In the following chapters of this book, the argumentation will of course remain on a philosophical level of abstraction. As has been emphasized already, this book is a work of philosophy—political and moral philosophy—rather than a work of constitutional theory or social science. Still, henceforward the focus will lie squarely on the principle of freedom of expression and on the knotty problems to which it pertains. Even in Chapter 4, which includes some general ruminations on the fundamental moral responsibilities of every system of governance, those ruminations are directly serviceable for the chapter's endeavor to explain why the principle of freedom of expression is always and everywhere binding as a precept of political morality; the justification which this book supplies for that principle is embedded in a broader account of the fundaments of liberal democracy and thus a broader account of the proper role for any system of governance in a society. Accordingly, as we move on now to Chapter 2, this book will shift from mulling over some preliminaries (vital preliminaries) and will proceed to grapple sustainedly with the intricacies of the principle of freedom of expression.

2
Components of a Theory of Freedom of Expression

Though a system of governance in any society can legitimately prohibit or restrict or disadvantage certain modes of communication, it cannot ever legitimately prohibit or restrict or disadvantage them qua modes of communication. Such a rough-hewn statement of the principle of freedom of expression might initially seem quite simple, but the appearance of simplicity is deceptive. As this chapter and indeed the rest of this book will reveal, numerous aspects of the principle of freedom of expression stand in need of elucidation and defense. Whereas the present chapter is concerned chiefly with the task of elucidation, the subsequent chapters are primarily concerned with the task of defense. Still, there is obviously no tidy division between those tasks; the clarificatory discussions in this chapter are aimed at vindicating the principle on which they shed light, and my efforts to uphold that principle in the subsequent chapters will do so partly by sharpening my account of its contours and implications.

Let us proceed, then, to contemplate some of the complexities surrounding the principle of freedom of expression. Although many of the expositions in this chapter will be amplified and precisified in subsequent chapters, they will provide the indispensable basis from which my further elaboration and defense of the principle of freedom of expression can be developed. We should start here by considering what counts as expression or communication.

2.1 What is Expression or Communication?

In the philosophical and legal literature on freedom of expression, the phrases "freedom of expression," "freedom of speech," "freedom of communication," and "free speech" are very often used interchangeably. I too will generally use those phrases interchangeably, but in my next section we shall ponder some ambiguities in them—ambiguities that pertain partly to the distinction drawn by Chapter 1 between freedoms as abilities and freedoms as permissions. In this section, however, the focus lies on the prior question of what is to be classified as expression or communication.

In ordinary usage, the noun "speech" is typically narrower in its extension than are the nouns "expression" and "communication." It is frequently understood to

Freedom of Expression as Self-Restraint. Matthew H. Kramer, Oxford University Press (2021). © Matthew H. Kramer.
DOI: 10.1093/oso/9780198868651.003.0002

encompass only oral linguistic utterances. However, when "speech" is an element of the phrases "freedom of speech" and "free speech," it is normally more capacious in its extension—on a par with the terms "expression" and "communication." For example, it is normally then understood to encompass writing and also to encompass various forms of non-linguistic expression such as gestures and dances and marches and artistic creations and musical compositions. Thus, although this book will much more frequently employ the terms "expression" and "communication" than the term "speech," it is not thereby signaling that the phrases "freedom of speech" and "free speech" are somehow dubious or that they are construed here any differently from the phrases "freedom of expression" and "freedom of communication."

Notwithstanding the interchangeability of the aforementioned phrases, we are left with the task of pinning down what expression or communication is. In everyday discourse, the term "expression" is sometimes used more broadly on its own than when it is an element of the phrase "freedom of expression." For example, in sentences such as "His heavy perspiration was an expression of his nervousness" or "His alcoholism is an expression of his despair over the human condition," the word "expression" is being used to mean "manifestation." To express an attitude in this broad sense is to evince or exhibit it. Now, although the term "expression" in this capacious sense includes the meanings attached to that term in the somewhat narrower sense that is operative in the phrase "freedom of expression," it is too wide-ranging for the purposes of this book. In most circumstances, sweating because of one's anxiety and imbibing alcohol excessively because of one's desolation are not expressive or communicative activities in any sense relevant to a theory of freedom of expression.[1] A somewhat narrower conception of expression or communication is requisite here.

2.1.1 The Structure of Expression or Communication

In a standard instance of expression or communication, at least one addressor and at least one addressee are involved. What is communicated from the addressor(s) to the addressee(s) can be a message expressed in propositional form, but it can equally well be something more nebulous such as a sentiment or an outlook or a mood. Chief among the differences between a mere manifestation of an attitude and a standard instance of expression or communication is that an addressor who engages in such a standard instance intends to have the addressee(s) recognize both the content of what is being communicated and also the intention to convey that content. Typically, someone who perspires because of nervousness is

[1] This point has been made well in Schauer 1982, 50–2. See also Raz 1994, 146; Shiffrin 2014, 112–14. For some conflations of the broad sense and the narrower sense of "expression" (or of "communication"), see Bollinger 1986, 62, 63, 115–16.

not intending thereby to divulge the anxiousness of his outlook to others and is not intending to have anyone else perceive in him a communicative intention of that kind. By contrast, somebody who addresses someone else with the utterance "I am really nervous" is typically intending to have the addressee discern (1) a propositional message about the addressor's state of mind, (2) that state of mind itself, and (3) the addressor's intention to convey those other communicative contents.

2.1.1.1 Communications without Addressors

Now, of course, there are numerous instances of expression or communication that are far less straightforward than the standard instances that have just been sketched. Although at least some of the elements outlined in the preceding paragraph will be present in any act of expression or communication, not every such act will comprise all of those elements. For example, as Larry Alexander has contended (2005, 8–9), an instance of expression or communication can occur—in unusual circumstances—in the absence of any genuine addressor and thus in the absence of any intention of an addressor to communicate something to somebody else. Alexander adduces a scenario in which people watch sunsets because they believe that various subversive messages are being conveyed to them through the patterns in the sky by angels or by other supralunary authorities, and he likewise adverts to the hackneyed scenario in which a thousand monkeys press randomly on typewriter keys and manage to produce a treatise full of incendiary vituperation directed against the injustices of the prevailing system of governance. If the officials in that system were to enact laws that prohibit people from trying to glimpse messages in the heavens by watching sunsets, or if those officials were to enact laws that prohibit people from reading the treatise produced by the monkeys, they would be contravening the principle of freedom of expression. Each of these scenarios involves communication or expression which is covered by that principle, even though in neither scenario is there any genuine addressor of what has been communicated.

As Alexander suggests, the key to the occurrence of the communication or expression in each of these cases is the role of the addressees. In the scenario where people watch sunsets, they believe that there are genuine addressors of messages conveyed to them from the skies, and they believe that those addressors harbor communicative intentions of the kinds that have been delineated in the penultimate paragraph above. In the scenario of the revolutionary tract composed through the typing of the monkeys, by contrast, any readers of the tract who accept that it did emerge through such random typing will not think that any genuine addressors or communicative intentions have been involved in its production. Nevertheless, in each of these thought-experiments there are some addressees and some messages (or other communicative contents) with which the addressees engage. Even in the absence of any genuine addressors or perceived addressors, the interpretive efforts of addressees to come to grips with messages or other communicative contents are properly classified under the rubric of "expression" or "communication"—where the breadth of that rubric is gauged for the purpose of ascertaining what is covered by the principle of freedom of expression.

Moreover, given that the thought-experiment pertaining to the monkeys is vastly more far-fetched than the thought-experiment pertaining to the viewers of sunsets, we can conclude that any non-fanciful instance of communication or expression involves either some genuine addressor(s) or some perceived addressor(s). Indeed, even when the readers of the monkeys' treatise are told of its origins, they will almost certainly doubt the veracity of what they have been told. Thus, in the scenario of the monkeys as well as in the scenario of the sunsets, the addressees will presume that the messages received by them have emanated from some addressor(s).

2.1.1.2 Communications without Other Addressees

Alexander is correct when he highlights the pivotal role of addressees in instances of communication that do not involve any genuine addressors. However, he goes too far when he suggests that every instance of expression or communication comprises some addressee(s) other than any addressor from whom the expression or communication has issued: "Freedom of expression would appear to require the presence of an audience capable of understanding the ideas [or sentiments or outlook] the speaker intends to express" (Alexander 2005, 10). Frederick Schauer has articulated a similar view about the indispensability of the presence of some addressee(s): "Without communicative intent, a communicated message, and a recipient of the communication there is no complete communicative act, and no occasion to talk about freedom of speech" (1982, 98).

Although Alexander and Schauer diverge on the question whether an actual communicative intention is necessary for the occurrence of an act of communication, they agree that the presence of some addressee(s) is necessary. On that point of agreement, they are both mistaken. For one thing, many of the utterances of any typical person are to himself or herself (Redish 1992, 30–1; Shiffrin 2014, 83, 93). Diaries, private reflections, and self-motivational exhortations are just some of the forms that can be taken by such utterances. Any such utterance does have an addressee, of course, but the addressee is not distinct from the addressor. Perhaps Alexander and Schauer would allow that self-directed communications are indeed communications, since without inconsistency they can endorse that point while cleaving to the notion that the presence of some addressee(s) is essential for the status of any instance of conduct as an act of expression or communication. Nevertheless, their insistence on the latter notion is more generally misguided.[2]

[2] That notion resembles some claims by Jennifer Hornsby and Rae Langton—about the role of "uptake" in speech-act philosophy—which I will contest in Chapter 5. There I will accept that certain types of communicative actions, such as warnings and refusals, cannot take place as such if the addressees of those communications are altogether absent. To accept as much, however, is not to imply that the

Suppose that Barbara engages on her own in a séance during which she makes numerous statements to several dead people whose spirits she presumes to have conjured up through her clairvoyant powers. Although her statements lack any genuine addressees, they are straightforwardly classifiable as acts of expression or communication. They are covered by the principle of freedom of expression. Much the same is true of statements made by Charlie to his wife when—unbeknownst to him—she has exited the house and is unable to hear anything that he is saying to her. No addressee is present to hear those utterances by Charlie, but they are instances of expression or communication. Similarly, if Patricia intones some prayers to God or to various gods while she is worshipping by herself, the fact that her petitionary utterances lack any genuine addressees is no basis for denying that they are instances of expression or communication. They are covered by the moral principle of freedom of expression as much as by any moral principle that protects freedom of religious observances.

Except in the present paragraph and the next paragraph, this book will take "expression" and "communication"—and "expressive" and "communicative"—to be interchangeable terms. However, we should note here *en passant* that some interjections without addressees are perhaps better labeled as "expressive" than as "communicative." For example, suppose that Ken while alone has injured his foot by dropping something onto it, and that he exclaims "Ouch" (with or without accompanying expletives) in response. Such an interjection might not be aimed at communicating anything to anyone, not even to Ken himself. It might instead be simply a way of venting his frustration and easing his pain. Similarly, suppose that Isabella while alone has come upon a grand sight and that she exclaims "Wow" or "My, oh my" in response. Rather than being aimed at communicating any message or sentiment or outlook to any addressee—even to Isabella herself—her interjection might simply be a way of giving voice to her sense of wonder. Exclamations akin to those of Ken and Isabella are perhaps not idiomatically designated as instances of communication, but they are instances of expression. They fall within the ambit of the principle of freedom of expression. They do more than simply manifest some sentiments; they articulate those sentiments.

When utterances without addressees are appositely classifiable as instances of communication or expression—like the utterances of Barbara and Charlie and Patricia in the penultimate paragraph above—they are aimed at conveying messages or sentiments or outlooks to addressees, even though no addressees are present to engage with the utterances. When utterances without addressees are idiomatically classifiable as instances of expression but perhaps not as instances of communication (like the utterances of Ken and Isabella in the last paragraph

utterances which constitute the attempted warnings or refusals are unclassifiable as acts of expression or communication at all. (For another example of the view taken by Alexander and Schauer, see Raz 1994, 146.)

above), they are not aimed at conveying anything to the addressors themselves or to any other addressees. In either case, utterances without any addressees are nonstandard. There is a clear sense in which the statement quoted from Schauer is correct in declaring that an utterance without any addressee(s) is "no complete communicative act." Even when an addressor of some utterances is knowingly alone, she herself will normally be an addressee of those utterances. At any rate, even when the interjections or other utterances of someone are addressed neither to herself nor to anyone else, they are instances of expression and are therefore covered by the principle of freedom of expression.

2.1.2 The Distinctiveness of Communication or Expression

In the litigation that has proliferated over many decades under the First Amendment to the American Constitution, one abiding problem has lain in pinning down the distinctiveness of communication or expression. An approach commonly taken over the years, both by jurists and by scholars, has been to differentiate between communication and conduct—or between communicative conduct and non-communicative conduct.[3] The idea has been that the First Amendment's protections extend only to communicative activities and not to non-communicative activities.

Such a demarcation has seemed particularly needful in cases where communications are carried out through means other than words. In what is often labeled as "symbolic speech," people convey certain messages or sentiments or allegiances not by speaking or writing some words but by performing some non-linguistic actions. For example, protesters against a war conducted by the United States might go beyond the chanting of slogans and might proceed to shred some American flags or (in bygone days) to burn their American draft cards. Quite a few jurists and scholars have hoped to differentiate between communicative activities and non-communicative activities in order to explain why sundry instances of symbolic speech lie within or outside the scope of the First Amendment. They would presumably reason similarly about the scope of the moral principle of freedom of expression.

Neither in relation to the First Amendment's constitutional guarantee nor in relation to the moral principle of freedom of expression, however, is such an approach tenable. Jurists and scholars enamored of such an approach have aspired to determine whether any particular instance of symbolic speech is predominantly

[3] Among those who have relied on such a distinction are Antony 2017, 72; Emerson 1963, 880–1, 931–4, *et passim*; Kagan 1993, 884; Schauer 1982, 98–9. Among those who have eschewed such a distinction are De Montigny 1992, 37, 43, 45; Douglas 1995, 172–3, 181–2; Ely 1975, 1494–6; Harel 2012, 308–10; Langton 2009, 28; Post and Molnar 2012, 24; Rawls 1993, 345 n56; Rubenfeld 2001, 782–3; 2002a, 41; Scanlon 1972, 207–8; 1979, 521–2; Strossen 1990, 542–3 n295.

expression or predominantly action. Specifically with reference to the burning of a draft card as a form of protest against the Vietnam War, John Hart Ely contended nearly half a century ago that the hopes of those jurists and scholars were forlorn:

> But burning a draft card to express opposition to the draft is ... 100% action and 100% expression. It involves no conduct that is not at the same time communication, and no communication that does not result from conduct. Attempts to determine which element "predominates" will therefore inevitably degenerate into question-begging judgments about whether the activity should be protected. (Ely 1975, 1495)

We can behold vividly the misguidedness of the approach which Ely assailed, when we glance at an argument by Schauer in his landmark book on freedom of expression. Schauer there refers to the American case of *Davis v Norman*, which arose from some events in the state of Arkansas in the mid-1970s. After Keith Davis had been killed in a collision while he was driving a truck at high speed to escape from a pursuing police car, his father—who blamed the police for the death—placed the wrecked truck on the lawn of his house as a way of protesting against what the father perceived as an abuse of the police's authority. Under the terms of a local ordinance that prohibited the unenclosed storage of ruined motor vehicles, the father was served with a notice to remove the wrecked truck from his lawn. He explained to the local authorities that he was displaying the truck on his property as a statement of protest against the high-handedness of the police, and he submitted that his display was an instance of symbolic speech for which he could claim the protection of the First Amendment. His appeals against the seizure and removal of the vehicle from his lawn were dismissed by the federal courts that ultimately ruled on the matter.

Concurring with the outcome of the litigation, Schauer maintains that the display of the demolished truck was not a form of communication or expression and was thus not covered by the First Amendment at all. He first offers a loose approximation of his position on the matter: "[W]here a method of communication is so unconventional as to be incapable of understanding by recipients of that communication, then there is no communicative content and thus no justification for deploying the Free Speech Principle" (Schauer 1982, 98). Lest the initial statement of his position be construed too expansively, Schauer proceeds to tighten it as follows: "[T]he Free Speech Principle [includes] any method of communication even remotely capable of transmitting a message. The demolished automobile may properly be excluded, but the reason is not simply that it is not communicative, but that it is not even remotely communicative" (98–9). As a response to *Davis v Norman*, this reasoning by Schauer is peculiarly inapposite. Quite evident from the judgment in that case by the U.S. Court of Appeals for the Eighth Circuit is that the message conveyed by Mr Davis through his display of the ruined truck was understood perfectly well by the members of his community. Nobody can plausibly claim that Mr Davis's graphic method of communicating his fury over the actions of the police was excluded from the scope of the principle of freedom of expression (or from the scope of the First Amendment) on the ground that it was "incapable of understanding by recipients of that communication." *A fortiori*, nobody can plausibly claim that that method of communication was excluded on the ground that it was not "even remotely capable of transmitting a message." The perils of trying to determine whether any instance of symbolic speech should be placed in a "communicative" pigeonhole or in a "non-communicative" pigeonhole—perils against which Ely admonished his readers—are well revealed by the inadequacy of Schauer's analysis. What we can accurately say about the display of the wrecked vehicle by Mr Davis is that, although it was straightforwardly a mode of communication (with a clear-cut message that was apprehended by the addressees to whom it was intentionally transmitted), it took the form of conduct that would normally be non-communicative. Schauer's pigeonholing approach cannot do justice to the complexity of such a mode of communication.[4]

Anticipating my elaboration of the principle of freedom of expression later in this chapter, we can find a highly promising approach to this matter in the judgment of the Eighth Circuit Court of Appeals. Instead of trying to resolve the case by classifying the display of the truck as either "communicative" or "non-communicative," the Court recognized that both of those labels were applicable. It then enquired into the terms and animating purposes of the ordinance that forbade the unenclosed storage of ruined or abandoned motor vehicles. On the one hand, the prohibition imposed by that ordinance was applicable to the display of the truck by Mr Davis; it was therefore applicable to at least one instance of communicative conduct. On the other hand, neither on the surface of its wording nor in its underlying purpose was the ordinance directed against Mr Davis's conduct (or any other instance of conduct) *as an act of communication*. Neither the general communicative character nor the specific communicative content of the display of the demolished truck contributed in any way to bringing the display within the interdictory ambit of the ordinance. That ordinance did not discriminate between communicative and non-communicative instances of unenclosed storage, and its purposes—readily ascribable to it on the basis of its preamble and its legislative history—were not concerned at all with preventing the occurrence of communications. (Those purposes were focused on considerations of public health and safety and aesthetics.) Of course, had there been in Mr Davis's community a longstanding or widespread practice of using the ruins of automobiles symbolically

[4] Given that I am criticizing Schauer here, I should note that elsewhere he wisely and robustly declares that we should "avoid the hopeless search for a predominant feature, either speech or conduct, in the wide range of cases when communicative intent is coupled with conduct other than talking or writing" (Schauer 1981, 279 n67).

for communication, the Court would have had good reasons for ascribing to the ordinance an expression-restricting purpose. However, given that there was no evidence of any such practice, the purposes discernible from the ordinance's preamble and legislative history could safely be taken at face value. Thus, although the ordinance did extend to some acts of communication such as that of Mr Davis, it did not extend to them qua acts of communication. It was therefore consistent with the principle of freedom of expression.

Notwithstanding that the Court's approach with its focus on the purposes of the ordinance was clearly superior to Schauer's pigeonholing approach, there is one respect in which the Court did not carry its enquiry far enough. We can see what was missing, if we look at Jed Rubenfeld's laconic distillation of the ways in which any instance of communicative conduct might be subjected to legal penalties qua act of communication:

> A person made liable under a prohibitory law is punished *for* speaking if and only if: (1) the law makes the fact that he was communicating an element of the prohibited offense; (2) the legislative purpose was to target speech even though the prohibition is speech-neutral on its face; or (3) the law was selectively enforced to target speech. If none of these three conditions holds, then the person will have no free speech claim at all, no matter how expressive his words or actions were. (Rubenfeld 2001, 784, emphasis in original)

Worth noting briefly, as an aside, is a matter on which this chapter will later expand. That is, Rubenfeld in this passage is concentrating specifically on criminal prohibitions. Criminal prohibitions are of immense significance as means by which any system of governance can restrict people's communicative activities, but (as will be observed later) they are not the only such means. Other types of penalties and disadvantages can also restrict those activities. Indeed, the case of *Davis v Norman*—which Rubenfeld does not discuss at all—itself involved one of those other measures. Instead of being punished for his display of the ruined truck, Mr Davis was served with a notice to remove the truck from his lawn.

Still, Rubenfeld's pithy summary can easily be amplified to include those other measures of restriction. Here his summary is especially important because it indicates a crux which the Eighth Circuit Court of Appeals left unaddressed. Although the terms and purposes of the municipal ordinance in *Davis v Norman* were unexceptionable, we cannot tell (from the Court's judgment) whether the invocation of the ordinance by the local authorities in response to Mr Davis's display of the demolished truck was similarly beyond reproach. Among the people in the local community who understood the message imparted by the display were the police. They were undoubtedly displeased by the harsh criticism of them which Mr Davis communicated through his positioning of the truck on his lawn. Hence, in the absence of any further evidence on the question, we have ample grounds for wondering whether the ordinance was being applied selectively against him to squelch that criticism. If the effectuation of the ordinance was indeed selective in that fashion, then the issuance of a removal directive to Mr Davis transgressed the principle of freedom of expression (and the First Amendment) even though the ordinance itself was consistent with that principle.

At any rate, although the Eighth Circuit Court of Appeals neglected to ponder the matter that has just been broached, its judgment was otherwise sound. The Court rightly eschewed any pigeonholing approach, and focused its attention instead on the question whether the ordinance was directed against any acts of communication qua acts of communication. Such a question, expanded to inquire about the implementation of any laws or policies as well as about their terms and purposes, is *mutatis mutandis* what we should be asking whenever we seek to determine whether a system of governance has abided by the principle of freedom of expression or not. (To know what counts as an act of communication, we should have recourse to what has been said about standard instances and nonstandard instances of communication in §2.1.1 above.)

2.1.3 Low-Value Expression?

In many of the writings by American jurists and legal scholars on the First Amendment, and in many of the writings by philosophers on versions of the principle of freedom of expression, there have been efforts to differentiate between low-value modes and high-value modes of expression.[5] The idea has been that, because some kinds of communication are worthier than others, the full moral protection of the principle of freedom of expression—or the full legal protection of the First Amendment—extends only to the worthier kinds. In this way of thinking, the less valuable modes of communication are more susceptible to being legitimately restricted by any system of governance.

Such a way of thinking has become common in much of contemporary American constitutional law. It was articulated prominently by the U.S. Supreme Court in 1942 in the case of *Chaplinsky v New Hampshire* (a case that gave rise to the "fighting words" doctrine, which—as we shall see in Chapters 3, 5, and 6—can be defended without any reliance on the low-value/high-value distinction), and

[5] For some excellent discussions of this matter, see Rubenfeld 2001, 798–801, 822–6. For others who are likewise wary of the idea that the degree of protection conferred by the principle of freedom of expression (or by the First Amendment) is dependent on the "social value" of various types of communications, see Bollinger 1986, 182; Buchanan 1979, 557–9; Meiklejohn 1961, 262–3; Scanlon 1979, 541–2. For some writings that are more receptive to the prospect of differential degrees of protection, see Abrams 2012, 117–18; 2019, 82; Appiah 2012, 170; Badamchi 2015, 910–11; De Montigny 1992, 48–51; Hornsby 2011, 380, 382; Kagan 1993, 899–900; 1996a, 479–83; Lakier 2015; Meiklejohn 1948, 37–41 *et passim*; Post and Molnar 2012, 12; Rawls 1993, 349–52; Scanlon 1979, 522–3; 2017, 139; Schauer 1982, 175; Shiffrin 2014, 98–102; Stone 1983, 194–6; 2007a, 187; 2007b, 93.

it has taken hold in areas of American constitutional law ranging from the prohibition of obscenity to the regulation of commercial speech. In the philosophical and other scholarly literature on versions of the ideal of freedom of expression, proposals for differential levels of protection have been especially salient among theorists who seek to ground their conclusions on the requirements and character of a democratic polity.[6] In the eyes of most such theorists, freedom of expression pertains chiefly if not exclusively to modes of communication that bear directly on those requirements of collective self-governance; most such theorists would favor full protection for hateful utterances as well as benign utterances on matters of public concern, but would favor an attenuated level of protection for utterances on matters of purely banausic or private concern.

Much could be said against a division between high-value speech and low-value speech in a theory of freedom of expression. For example, the difficulties that will confront judges and administrators in trying to reach decisions by reference to such a division are formidable. However, here the fatal problem afflicting the high-value/low-value dichotomy is that the structure of differential levels of protection is profoundly inconsistent with the principle of freedom of expression which this book will be expounding and defending. As is already evident from my opening chapter, that principle is absolute; it is applicable always and everywhere to all modes of communication. It does not morally exempt all types or instances of communicative activities from governmental restrictions, but it morally disallows all such restrictions that are directed against the communicative character of any of those activities. This limitation, on the nature or purpose of any curb that can legitimately tether people's communications, is operative across the board rather than only in relation to high-value forms of expression. Indeed, as will become especially apparent in Chapter 4, any endeavor to confine the operativeness of the principle of freedom of expression to high-value forms of communication would run directly athwart the fundamental justification for that principle. Such an endeavor would strive to introduce the fine-grained control (over the patterns of discourse in a society) that is antithetical to the ideal of self-restraint which the principle of freedom of expression encapsulates.

Of course, my rejection of the distinction between high-value speech and low-value speech within a theory of freedom of expression does not imply that that distinction is untenable in other contexts. Some types and products of expressive activity are far more valuable than others, by any reasonable

[6] A seminal text in this school of thought was Meiklejohn 1948. In more recent decades, Corey Brettschneider, Owen Fiss, Eric Heinze, Harry Kalven, Robert Post, John Rawls, Cass Sunstein, and James Weinstein have been some of the leading figures in this camp. For two valuable introductions to this democracy-centered approach, see Post 2011 and Weinstein 2011. A version of that approach is central to the constitutional protection of communicative liberties in Australia; for some relevant discussion, see Gelber 2012a, 202–5; 2012b, 63–8. See also Griffiths 2005. I will say more about the democracy-centered theories in Chapter 4.

reckoning. For example, a play by William Shakespeare—even one of his least distinguished plays, such as *The Two Gentlemen of Verona*—is vastly better as a product of expressive activity than is the doggerel in a Christmas card. Nevertheless, although such an evaluative assessment is patently correct, and although countless other evaluative comparisons are likewise correct, they are irrelevant for determining the applicability or inapplicability of the principle of freedom of expression. The absoluteness of the constraints imposed by that principle is obviously not due to the unsustainability or meaninglessness of all evaluative comparisons, given that myriad such comparisons are both meaningful and sustainable. Nor is the absoluteness of those constraints due to the unreliability of governmental officials in arriving at correct evaluative comparisons (though concerns about the unreliability of those officials on such matters are often well-founded). Rather, the principle of freedom of expression is absolute because only thus is its justification realized; only thus is the ideal of freedom of expression as self-restraint realized. With an eye toward that justification, which will be unfurled in Chapter 4, we should recognize that the high-value/low-value division cannot have a place in any satisfactory exposition of this book's topic.

2.1.4 A Trichotomous Distinction

Over the course of four decades—most recently in Schauer 2019a—Schauer, in the context of American constitutional theory and the First Amendment, has sought to underscore a distinction between coverage and protection. His dichotomy is really a trichotomy. He maintains firstly that some communications are not even covered by the First Amendment's free-speech guarantee at all. No question arises about the degree to which they are protected by that guarantee, since they fall outside its scope altogether. Schauer secondly contends that some communications are covered by the First Amendment but are not protected by it. Perhaps, for example, some covered mode of expression would give rise to a clear and present danger of the occurrence of serious criminality if that mode of expression were to be left unrestricted. In that event, although the specified mode of expression is covered by the First Amendment's guarantee—and is therefore exempt from legal or other governmental constraints unless those constraints satisfy a heightened level of scrutiny by the courts—it is not ultimately protected by that guarantee, because the serious danger that would ensue from such a mode of expression is sufficient to render legitimate the imposition of some legal trammels. Finally, in a third category by Schauer's reckoning are the countless types and instances of communication that are not only covered by the First Amendment but also protected by it. Such types and instances are shielded by a stringent level of judicial scrutiny against any laws or policies that would curb them, and there are no grounds for holding that any of those laws or policies will have passed muster under that stringent level of scrutiny.

Even in the context of American constitutional theory, Schauer's trichotomous schema is problematic—both because of its general character and more specifically because of the consequentialist terms in which Schauer elaborates it. As he himself remarks, his trichotomy does not have any solid grounding in the practices and pronouncements of American courts: "The existing approaches to determining coverage thus leave much to be desired, but part of the problem is the reluctance of the courts, especially, to carefully recognize the problem of coverage as a distinct question" (Schauer 2019a, 46). At any rate, whatever may be the pertinence of Schauer's approach in relation to the First Amendment and American constitutional law, it is wholly unsuitable for the context in which I am writing: the context of political philosophy, where the focus of attention is not the First Amendment but is instead a major principle of political morality. As a moral absolute, that principle imposes moral constraints that are always and everywhere binding on systems of governance. As we shall see shortly (and as has been suggested already in this chapter), those constraints limit the range of purposes that can legitimately underpin any laws or policies which impinge on communicative activities. All such activities are covered by the moral principle of freedom of expression, in that no such activities can ever legitimately be restricted for the purposes which are ruled out by that principle. Thus, in relation to the principle of freedom of expression, there is no category that corresponds to the first category in Schauer's schema. There are no uncovered modes of expression.

What might lead a theorist to posit a category of uncovered modes of expression is that the legitimacy of some governmental restrictions on certain modes of expression is manifest—unmistakably manifest—to anyone who is competent to assess such matters. Let us ponder a vivid example. Suppose that Warren and Steve are snarling at each other in an angry altercation, and suppose that Warren exclaims to Steve: "I detest you, and I'm going to convey to you how much I loathe you!" Warren proceeds to punch Steve in the face. Not only is Warren's statement of detestation an instance of communicative conduct, but so too in the circumstances is his act of punching Steve in the face. All the same, the imposition of sanctions on Warren under a law that prohibits the perpetration of battery is patently legitimate. Indeed, given that the invocation of such a law against him is so obviously legitimate, any contestation of it with reference to the principle of freedom of expression would be ludicrous. Precisely because any contestation along those lines would be risible, the likelihood of its occurrence is virtually nil. As Ronald Dworkin has observed, "we need not ask questions when we already know the answer" (1986, 266). Nonetheless, the absence of any such contestation does not imply that Warren's act of punching Steve is uncovered by the principle of freedom of expression. Like any other instance of communicative conduct, Warren's action of punching is covered—in that, if any laws or sanctions were directed against his action because of its communicative character, they would be in contravention of the principle of freedom of expression. However, because every ordinary law that prohibits the perpetration of battery is clearly not directed against any communicative import of the proscribed conduct (and is instead directed against its physically violent and psychologically harmful aspects), the application of such a law to Warren's act of thuggery is straightforwardly consistent with the principle of freedom of expression. A proponent of Schauer's trichotomous schema goes astray in thinking that the straightforward consistency amounts to uncoveredness.

2.2 The Ambiguity of Some Key Phrases

As will become evident in §5.4.4 of Chapter 5, some of the key phrases in this area of political philosophy are commonly understood in multiple ways. As has been noted in §2.1 above, those phrases—"freedom of expression," "freedom of communication," "freedom of speech," "free speech"—are construed in this book (and, usually, in other philosophical writings on these matters) as largely interchangeable. However, their interchangeability extends to their ambiguity; each of those phrases is ambiguous in the same ways. Let us consider here four main ways in which each of those phrases is frequently understood. For the sake of readability, I will concentrate here on the phrase "freedom of expression." However, this discussion will be equally applicable to the phrases "freedom of communication" and "freedom of speech."

In the first place, the phrase "freedom of expression" often refers to the moral principle of freedom of expression. That is, it often denotes a major principle of political morality that deontologically constrains the purposes for which—or the ways in which—any system of governance can legitimately curtail the communicative freedoms and activities of the people in a society. That principle, of course, will be expounded later in this chapter and defended in my subsequent chapters. When the phrase "freedom of expression" is used in this manner, it designates a prescription concerning the proper relationship between a system of governance and the citizenry over whom the system presides.

In a closely related sense, the phrase "freedom of expression" commonly denotes the state of affairs that ensues from compliance by a system of governance with the principle of freedom of expression. Such compliance brings about the relationship—between a system of governance and its populace—for which that principle calls. When the aforementioned phrase is employed in this fashion, it denotes not a prescription but instead the realization or fulfillment of that prescription. In the title of this book, the phrase "freedom of expression" is used in this second sense.

Quite different are the remaining two senses that frequently get attached to that phrase. We return here to my opening chapter's account of the distinction between physical liberty and deontic liberty. On the one hand, the phrase "freedom of expression" commonly denotes the physical and psychological and normative abilities of people to engage in sundry communicative activities. When that phrase is employed in this third sense by theorists who contend that a person's freedom of expression has been restricted or diminished, they are indicating that some of the person's physical or psychological or normative abilities to undertake various communicative activities have been removed by the actions of governmental officials—or by other causes such as the interference of hecklers. Whereas every action or policy that impairs freedom of expression in the second sense above is morally wrong, not every action or policy that impairs somebody's freedom of expression in this third sense is morally wrong.

Finally, in yet another common pattern of usage, the phrase "freedom of expression" refers to certain legal or moral or institutional permissions. Someone who enjoys ample freedom of expression in this fourth sense is legally or morally or institutionally allowed to undertake a wide array of communicative endeavors. Like freedom of expression in the third sense, freedom of expression in this fourth sense is a scalar property. That is, someone's freedom of expression can obtain to varying degrees across any number of historical or societal contexts. Over time or in diverse jurisdictions, a person's legal or moral or institutional permissions to undertake communicative activities can vary in the breadth or narrowness of the range of such activities to which the permissions pertain.

As is manifest, these four ways of explicating the phrase "freedom of expression" are not to be conflated. Chapter 1 has already noted some of the dissimilarities between physical freedom and deontic freedom—and thus between freedom of expression in the third sense and freedom of expression in the fourth sense. Another evident dissimilarity among the four types of freedom of expression is a point that distinguishes the first type from the remaining three types. Whereas freedom of expression in the first sense is not a scalar property, freedom of expression in any of the remaining senses is a scalar property. Freedom of expression of the first kind is an abstract normative entity that always and everywhere obtains as a moral principle. By contrast, freedom of expression of the second kind—the compliance of a system of governance with the requirements incumbent upon it under the principle of freedom of expression—is realized to a greater or lesser degree at any given time in any given society. Similarly, freedom of expression in either the third sense or the fourth sense is a property of individuals or groups which can vary in magnitude among them and which can vary for any particular individual or group over time and across sundry contexts.

Because of the multiple differences among these four types of freedom of expression, the phrase commonly employed to designate each of them can lead to confusion unless it is handled carefully. In this book henceforth, I use the unadorned phrase "freedom of expression" only in its second sense (the sense attached to it in the book's title). When I am talking instead about the moral principle that calls for freedom of expression, I shall use the phrase "principle of freedom of expression." When I am talking about variants of that principle envisioned by other theorists or jurists, I shall use the phrase "versions of the principle of freedom of expression." And when I am talking about the deontic or physical liberties of people to engage in communicative conduct, I use several phrases—such as "communicative liberties" or "communicative freedoms"—that should each be perspicuous. (As has already been implied, §5.4.4 in Chapter 5 is the one portion of this book that is an exception to what has been said in this paragraph. There I again broach some of the ambiguities discussed in this section; accordingly, at that juncture I deliberately use the phrase "freedom of expression" or "free speech" in multiple senses.)

2.3 The Principle of Freedom of Expression

The moral principle of freedom of expression which this book defends is as follows. No system of governance can ever legitimately subject anyone to sanctions or other disadvantages for engaging in communicative conduct, where the rationale for the sanctions or disadvantages is focused on the communicative tenor of the conduct. Every system of governance is morally obligated to refrain from penalizing any communicative activities qua communicative activities. In other words, any restrictions imposed by a system of governance on some communicative activity are morally legitimate only if they have been imposed not because the activity is communicative but instead because it instantiates a type of misconduct whose wrongness is not distinctively communicative.

Heretofore, this chapter has endeavored to clarify what counts as communicative conduct. In need of elucidation now are the other main concepts that are operative in the principle of freedom of expression. Let us start here with the notion of neutrality.

2.3.1 Types of Neutrality

What the principle of freedom of expression requires in any society is that the relationship between the society's system of governance and the communicative activities of its citizens be marked by several types of neutrality. Only insofar as each of those types of neutrality is attained, will a system of governance have exerted the self-restraint that is involved in never directing any penalties or disadvantages against communicative endeavors qua communicative endeavors.

2.3.1.1 Communication-Neutrality

Most general among the ways in which every system of governance should be neutral with regard to the communicative conduct of its citizens is that it should never treat the communicative character of the conduct either as a ground for the imposition of sanctions (or other disadvantages) or as a ground for the conferral of benefits. Under the principle of freedom of expression, the terms and purposes of all governmentally imposed restrictions must conform to this requirement of general communication-neutrality. An insistence on such neutrality has underlain some of the most famous doctrines and distinctions in American constitutional law.

Let us briefly ponder here Oliver Wendell Holmes's famous example of a man who maliciously shouts "Fire" in a crowded theater. Although such an action is communicative, the prohibition of it can be morally legitimate because the action instantiates a type of misconduct whose wrongness is not distinctively communicative. That is, the shouting is an attempt to induce serious public disorder in circumstances where the disorder is very likely to result in deaths or injuries and damage to property. Such an attempt could have been undertaken through non-communicative conduct such as the firing of a gun or (for that matter) the igniting of a fire. Hence, a law that proscribes such misconduct can be—and almost always will be—communication-neutral in its purpose. Such a law, banning the inducement of serious public disturbances, can provide for sanctions without treating the communicative character of this or that instance of the banned misconduct as a ground for the imposition of those sanctions.

Let us also glance here at a distinction to which we shall return in Chapters 5 and 6—the distinction between advocacy and incitement, as it has been drawn by the U.S. Supreme Court in the celebrated 1969 case of *Brandenburg v Ohio*. When somebody's utterances incite other people to engage in serious criminality, her statements are aimed at bringing about some major wrongdoing in circumstances where the imminent occurrence of the wrongdoing is likely as a result of the statements. That is, a communication that amounts to incitement is characterized by three main elements: the intendedness of the link between the communication and some serious misconduct, the imminence of the misconduct, and the likelihood of the occurrence of the misconduct. By contrast, when somebody advocates the perpetration of misconduct but does not commit incitement, at least one of the three elements just specified is missing. A classic example of incitement, to which we shall return in Chapters 5 and 6, is John Stuart Mill's scenario of a fiery speaker who rails against the iniquity of corn-dealers while addressing a mob of angry people who have gathered outside the home of a local corn-dealer (Mill 1956, 67–8). In Mill's scenario, and in other cases of incitement, the utterance of inflammatory statements by a speaker is constitutive of the speaker's participation in the serious and imminent misconduct which the statements are designed and likely to bring about. Because of the proximity between the inciting utterances and the imminent criminality which they are intended to produce, the utterances are subsumed into the criminality as some of the initial stages thereof. Consequently, the imposition of sanctions on Mill's fiery speaker is unequivocally consistent with the principle of freedom of expression. Punishment is administered not because of the communicative character of the speaker's fulminations, but because of their having constituted his direct and deliberate involvement in the perpetration of a lynching. Accordingly, that punishment is communication-neutral.

What the *Brandenburg* criterion for incitement enables us to do, in any context where somebody (like Mill's rabble-rouser) has exhorted people to commit violence or other serious wrongdoing, is to determine whether the exhortations can be penalized in a communication-neutral manner or not. If the utterances in question do meet the *Brandenburg* test for incitement, then a relevant communication-neutral legal prohibition—a prohibition on rioting or vandalism or murder or arson, for example—can be applied to those utterances in a communication-neutral fashion. Contrariwise, if the speaker's declamations do not meet the *Brandenburg* test and are therefore properly classifiable as mere advocacy rather than as incitement, then any sanctions imposed in response to them are not communication-neutral. Even if the legal prohibition that provides for the sanctions is itself communication-neutral (like the prohibition on rioting or vandalism or murder or arson), any application of it to an act of mere advocacy is not communication-neutral. Unlike incitement, mere advocacy is not subsumed into the misconduct for which it calls; it is not sufficiently proximate to that misconduct to be so subsumed. Hence, if it is subjected to legal sanctions, it is subjected as an act of communication rather than as one of the initial stages of the communication-independent misconduct. Administered in such circumstances, the sanctions are not communication-neutral and are thus in violation of the principle of freedom of expression.

2.3.1.2 Two Types of Content-Neutrality

Another type of neutrality required under the principle of freedom of expression is that of content-neutrality, which obtains in two main varieties: neutrality of subject matter and neutrality of viewpoint. We should examine each of those two main varieties in turn.

2.3.1.2.1 Subject-Neutrality

A system of governance that duly abides by the constraint of neutrality of subject matter does not differentiate among the topics that can be broached whenever any general communicative activities are permitted. Helpful here will be a scenario in which this subject-neutrality has been forsaken. Suppose that a local ordinance permits the placing of advertisements (in return for set fees) on the sides and backs of municipal buses, and suppose that the ordinance excludes from this arrangement any advertisements that address politically sensitive topics. That exclusion does not discriminate among viewpoints at all; it applies to any political advertisements irrespective of the points on the political spectrum whence they emanate. Nonetheless, it plainly does discriminate on the basis of subject matter. With regard to a prominent public setting, its purpose is to delimit the range of topics that can be raised by potential communicators and pondered by potential addressees of the communications.

Such a content-specific restriction contravenes the principle of freedom of expression, even though a municipal government could legitimately exclude advertisements altogether from the sides and backs of its buses. What contravenes the principle of freedom of expression is not the extent of the restriction but instead its fine-grainedness. Of course, that feature of the restriction could have been accentuated. For example, instead of excluding all political advertisements, the ordinance might have excluded only advertisements pertaining to abortion or only advertisements pertaining to matters of immigration. Either of those exclusions would have been less wide-ranging than the exclusion of all politically sensitive topics, but—precisely for that reason—either of them would have been more fine-grained as an effort to direct the flow of discourse in a prominent public setting. As will become apparent in Chapter 4, selectivity can be as problematically inimical to freedom of expression as is overbreadth.[7]

2.3.1.2.2 Viewpoint-Neutrality

Arguably even more important than neutrality of subject matter, as an aspect of the compliance by a system of governance with the principle of freedom of expression, is neutrality of viewpoint. Suppose that, instead of excluding all political advertisements from the sides and backs of municipal buses, a local ordinance were to exclude all advertisements that express opposition to the policies of the United Kingdom's Labour Party. Or suppose that, instead of excluding all advertisements that pertain to the matter of abortion, a local ordinance were to exclude all advertisements that call for the outlawing of the practice of abortion. Neither of these examples involves a restriction on the range of topics that can lawfully be addressed in a prominent public setting, but each of them involves a restriction on the range of viewpoints that can lawfully be espoused within that setting. Opponents of the Labour Party or of abortion are not legally allowed to proclaim their views in the form of advertisements on public buses, whereas admirers of the Labour Party and proponents of the "pro-choice" side in controversies over abortion are legally allowed to proclaim their views in such a fashion.

Once again, what makes the exclusions objectionable is their selectivity. A municipal government is not morally obligated to make the sides and backs of public buses available as spaces for advertising, but a policy in favor of making them available as such spaces (in return for paid fees) cannot legitimately discriminate with reference to the viewpoints of would-be advertisers. As will become evident in Chapter 4, the selectivity of such discrimination is particularly deplorable because it deviates so egregiously from the self-restraint that is morally required of

[7] For an illuminating exploration of this point, see Kagan 1992 (a few portions of which are superseded by Kagan 1996a). See also Suk 2012, 146–7.

every system of governance under the principle of freedom of expression. On the one hand, such self-restraint would be grossly abandoned through any sweeping restrictions on communications in contexts where no significant restrictions are morally permissible. For example, if a municipal government were to enact a law that prohibits people from conversing in public parks or in railway stations, its heavy-handed attempt to regiment public discourse would be blatantly in violation of the principle of freedom of expression. On the other hand, not only would departures from subject-neutrality or viewpoint-neutrality be morally illegitimate in the contexts just mentioned, but they would also be morally illegitimate in contexts where some blanket restrictions would be morally legitimate. Just above, we have been pondering a context of the latter kind: whereas a local government can permissibly disallow any advertisements on the sides and backs of its municipal buses, no subject-specific or viewpoint-specific limitations would be morally permissible even in such a setting. As endeavors to control minutely the patterns of public discourse and contemplation, subject-specific and viewpoint-specific prohibitions are often more sharply at variance with the ideal of governmental self-restraint than are prohibitions that sweep indiscriminately. (We shall return to this matter at several junctures in this book, especially in Chapter 4.)

2.3.1.3 Speaker-Neutrality

A further type of governmental impartiality required under the principle of freedom of expression is speaker-neutrality. Although this kind of neutrality is closely related to neutrality of viewpoint, the two are not equivalent. For example, a particular person might be legally prohibited from speaking publicly on a certain issue, even though others who share that person's position on the issue are legally permitted to speak publicly about it. Indeed, a particular person might be legally prohibited from speaking publicly about some matter, even though other people are legally permitted to appear on radio or television to articulate that very person's pronouncements on the matter. Just such a situation obtained in the United Kingdom from 1988 to 1994, when broadcasters throughout the country were legally banned from airing the voices of members of Northern Irish terrorist groups—and members of the political party Sinn Féin—on radio or television (Donohue 2008, 293–4). British broadcasters during that period were legally permitted to employ actors to read out the words that had been uttered by the members of those groups in interviews or in other public statements. Consequently, everything said by the terrorists and their political comrades could legally be aired on radio or television in the United Kingdom, provided that the voices of the terrorists or their comrades were replaced with actors' voices. In such a situation, there was no transgression of content-neutrality by the British system of governance, but there was an obvious transgression of speaker-neutrality.

A point to be emphasized here about the requirement of speaker-neutrality is that it forbids not only the identity-based disadvantaging of a speaker but also any identity-based preferential treatment. This point has sometimes been overlooked even by eminent champions of the values of liberal democracy. For instance, when writing about the egregiously unjust U.S. Supreme Court case in which the Court upheld the conviction of Eugene Debs for speaking against the role of the United States in the First World War, John Rawls lamented that the Court was "little troubled by the constitutional question raised in *Debs*, even though the case involves a leader of a political party, already four times its candidate for the presidency" (1993, 351). Rawls was right to be indignant about the Supreme Court's judgment in the *Debs* case, but he erred in suggesting that the stature of Debs as a politician was a factor which militated against that judgment. The stature of Debs as a politician was irrelevant; no preferential treatment of his utterances was warranted on that ground. Decisive instead was the fact that he with his orations did not deliberately give rise to any clear danger of serious and imminent misconduct. His speeches did not constitute any participation by him in such misconduct, as they amounted to advocacy rather than to incitement. This communication-neutral ground for acquitting Debs is also straightforwardly speaker-neutral. It applies to his orations the same standard—the *Brandenburg* Court's version of the clear-and-present-danger standard—that is applicable to the orations of any other speaker.

2.3.1.4 The Upshot of Neutrality

If and only if a legal mandate partakes of each type of neutrality that has just been adumbrated, it is in conformity with the requirements laid down by the principle of freedom of expression. Though some types or instances of communicative conduct might be prohibited by a mandate that is in conformity with that principle, they are not prohibited because of their distinctively communicative character or content or because of the identities of the people who engage in them. Instead of being prohibited qua acts of communication, those types or instances of conduct are prohibited because they are constitutive of some communication-independent misdeeds. Communication-neutrality and subject-neutrality and viewpoint-neutrality and speaker-neutrality, then, are the hallmarks of laws enacted by a system of governance that exerts the self-restraint involved in the realization of freedom of expression.

Of course—as has been observed in §2.1.2 above—the foregoing types of neutrality are crucial not only in connection with the terms and purposes of the laws that have been enacted by a system of governance, but also in connection with the processes whereby those laws are implemented through the decisions and actions of administrative and adjudicative officials. Even if a statute or some other law is itself impeccably in compliance with the principle of freedom of expression, it might be applied selectively by administrative officials or adjudicative officials in contravention of that principle. We may have encountered an example of such selectivity in §2.1.2, when contemplating the local ordinance in Arkansas that forbade the unenclosed storage of ruined automobiles. Though the terms and purposes of the ordinance were unexceptionably communication-neutral and content-neutral and speaker-neutral, there are quite solid grounds for suspecting that the ordinance was applied selectively to the conduct of Mr Davis in a manner that was neither communication-neutral nor content-neutral. In any event, whatever may be the accuracy or inaccuracy of these surmises about the actions of the police in that Arkansas municipality, the general point here is that the foregoing types of neutrality are required (under the principle of freedom of expression) in processes of administration and adjudication as well as in the outputs of legislation. In relation to any law or policy that is adopted by a system of governance, the principle of freedom of expression is fulfilled only insofar as both the law or policy itself and the implementation of it are characterized by all of the aforementioned types of neutrality.

Before we move on, we should glancingly mull over a matter that will figure saliently in Chapter 4. As is perhaps evident, the several kinds of neutrality required under the principle of freedom of expression are in need of justification. After all, a stance of wholesale communication-neutrality and content-neutrality and speaker-neutrality will carry some significant drawbacks in any number of instances. Let us here briefly return to the municipal ordinance which authorizes the selling of places for advertisements on the sides and backs of public buses but which excludes any advertisements that are expressive of certain viewpoints. If every such ordinance is disallowed, and if strict viewpoint-neutrality is insisted upon, the municipal government may sometimes find itself presented with applications for advertisements from odious groups such as the Ku Klux Klan or the Communist Party. Why should the local officials have to choose between not allowing any advertisements to be placed on buses and leaving open the possibility of occasional advertisements placed by such groups?

A satisfactory answer to this question, and a satisfactory answer to any cognate question about any of the other types of neutrality that are mandatory under the principle of freedom of expression, will amount to a full-scale justification of that principle. Chapter 4 will present such a justification. For now, in anticipation of that later chapter, we should simply seek to gain a rough sense of the focus that is appropriate for the justification that will be advanced there. We can gain such a sense if we reflect afresh here on what has already been said about the difference between the extent of a restriction and the selectivity of a restriction.

If the best justification for the principle of freedom of expression were to be centered on the provision of opportunities for addressors (speakers and writers and composers and artists and so forth) to impart their ideas and sentiments, we would be hard pressed to explain why selective restrictions on communications are frequently more problematic than wholesale restrictions. After all, the opportunities for expression available to addressors are curtailed by the latter restrictions far more extensively than by the former restrictions. We would face comparable difficulties if the best justification for the principle of freedom of expression were instead centered on ensuring that potential addressees (listeners and readers and viewers) enjoy ample access to the articulated ideas and feelings and hopes of other people. Selective restrictions impinge on such access less severely than do sweeping restrictions. Nor will we be able to account for the moral disparity between selective curbs and blanket curbs if we try to vindicate the principle of freedom of expression by concentrating on a societal desideratum such as the promotion of knowledge. Whereas the pursuit of such a desideratum would typically be badly hindered by any wide-ranging curbs on communicative activities, it could typically be furthered rather than hampered by some curbs that are suitably selective. Thus, like a focus on opportunities for self-expression or a focus on access to other people's articulations of their ideas and sentiments, a focus on a societal desideratum such as the growth of knowledge cannot explain why selective restrictions on communications are often especially objectionable.

To come up with a germane explanation, we need to train our attention instead on the relationship between a system of governance and the society over which that system presides. When such a system imposes selective constraints on communications, the control which it exerts over central aspects of people's lives is particularly fine-grained. For reasons that will be broached fleetingly here and then expounded fully in Chapter 4, the minuteness of the fine-grained control is both overweening and degrading. It is overweening because it assigns to governmental officials a decisive role in channeling the specificities of communicative interaction qua communicative interaction,[8] and it is degrading because it makes the success of a system of governance partly dependent on the non-occurrence of modes of expression which an ethically more robust system of governance could tolerate. Toleration is of course not equivalent to condonation; as will be emphasized in Chapters 4 to 6, a key aspect of the ethical robustness of a system of governance is the extent to which its operations avert any untoward effects that might ensue from the modes of expression which it leaves legally unrestricted. Consequently, a prime measure of the ethical health of a system of governance is its ability to sustain the self-restraint that is constitutive of freedom of expression. We can recognize as much when we ruminate on the types of neutrality (in the domain of communicative interaction) that are required under the principle of freedom of expression. Chapter 4 will return to this matter at far greater length, and will thereby clarify and deepen the highly compressed remarks in this paragraph.

[8] Recall here that an utterance can legitimately be restricted if it constitutes serious misconduct whose wrongness is communication-independent.

2.3.2 Restrictions and Disadvantages

Under the principle of freedom of expression, no system of governance is ever morally permitted to treat the communicative character of any mode of conduct as a basis for the imposition of sanctions or other disadvantages on anyone who has carried out that mode of conduct. Having pondered what counts as communicative conduct, and having likewise pondered the kinds of neutrality (between any system of governance and the communicative activities of individuals or groups) that are morally obligatory under the principle of freedom of expression, we should now consider what will count as restrictions or disadvantages.

2.3.2.1 Legal Prohibitions and Restrictions

As Chapter 1 has remarked, the foremost entitlements conferred by the First Amendment in the United States and by homologous constitutional guarantees in various other countries are Hohfeldian immunities. Those legal immunities held by individuals and groups are correlated with legal disabilities borne by legislatures and other governmental bodies. In any system of governance where such disabilities do obtain, they preclude the imposition of legal restrictions that are at variance with the prevailing constitutional free-speech guarantee.

Now, although the specifics of the moral requirements established by the principle of freedom of expression do not coincide fully with the specifics of the legal requirements established by the First Amendment or by any other existent constitutional guarantee, the general feature just recounted is morally obligatory everywhere. That is, under the principle of freedom of expression, every system of governance is morally obligated to include constitutional limits or other legal limits on its own abilities to create laws that prohibit or restrict people's communicational activities. It is also morally obligated to include such limits on its own abilities to give effect to laws in ways that prohibit or restrict people's communicational activities. Legal prohibitions and restrictions are among the cardinal means by which a system of governance might endeavor to curtail the communicational interactions of individuals and groups. Consequently, the principle of freedom of expression is centrally concerned with such prohibitions and restrictions and also with the processes through which they are implemented.

As should be manifest, however, not all legal mandates that curb people's communicative activities are in contravention of the principle of freedom of expression. Mandates which do contravene that principle are directed against communicative endeavors qua communicative endeavors rather than qua misdeeds whose wrongness is communication-independent. Nevertheless, some mandates that violate the principle of freedom of expression will have impinged less severely on communicative activities than will some mandates which comply with that principle. What determines the consistency or inconsistency between any given legal norm and the principle of freedom of expression is not the extent of the norm's burdensomeness for communicative conduct, but is instead the orientation of its purposes—that is, the orientation of any ends pursued by that norm and the orientation of any means adopted for the attainment of those ends. Still, although the extent of the burdensomeness of a legal prohibition or restriction does not in itself determine whether such a measure is consistent with the principle of freedom of expression, legal prohibitions or restrictions are within the coverage of that principle because they are generally burdensome.

How, then, are legal prohibitions and restrictions generally burdensome or disadvantageous for the people to whose conduct they are applicable? Here we come back to some points made in Chapter 1. Most obvious among the effects of a legal ban is the removal of certain deontic liberties (legal liberties and perhaps also moral liberties) from those people. Plainly, someone who is legally forbidden to engage in some type or instance of conduct is not legally at liberty to engage therein. Moreover, if a person acts at odds with her legal duty to eschew the forbidden type or instance of conduct, she will have subjected herself to legal liabilities to incur further legal duties and liabilities; she will be legally liable to undergo arrest or other enforcement proceedings, and she will be legally duty-bound to submit to such proceedings if they are pursued against her.

Alongside the deontic and other normative effects of a legal mandate that forbids some type or instance of conduct are the effects on people's physical liberties. Though such a mandate in itself does not reduce the physical freedoms or the combinations of jointly exercisable physical freedoms that are available to anyone, the processes of enforcement that normally back up a legal requirement will indeed remove some such freedoms or combinations of freedoms. Insofar as those processes are preventative (with anticipatory steps taken to preclude any infractions of the mandate in question), they remove certain physical freedoms outright. Insofar as the mechanisms of enforcement are instead punitive or compensatory—with criminal-law sanctions or private-law sanctions that are administered post hoc in response to infractions that have taken place—certain combinations of physical freedoms available to each person are no longer such that the freedoms within each combination are jointly exercisable. This effect of curtailing the range of each person's combinations of jointly exercisable physical freedoms is occurrent even before the mechanisms of enforcement are activated on any particular occasion. The fact that those mechanisms would be activated in the event of any infractions is sufficient to bring about that freedom-curtailing effect.[9]

A legal prohibition and the sanctions appurtenant to it can produce further freedom-curtailing effects. Somebody who incurs a criminal conviction for

[9] Of course, the fact that the mechanisms of enforcement would be activated in the event of any infractions is probabilistic rather than certain. Strictly speaking, every ascription of any physical freedom (or of any combination of jointly exercisable physical freedoms) is probabilistic. On the role of probabilities in ascriptions of freedoms and unfreedoms, see Kramer 2003, 83–7, 174–8, 415–25, *et passim*.

violating such a prohibition can lose her legal liberties and powers to enter into certain professions—for example, to qualify as a practicing lawyer. Similarly, because of the stigma attached to lawbreaking, the incurring of criminal sanctions or tort-law sanctions can impair a person's opportunities for paid employment or for other lucrative ventures. These further freedom-diminishing effects do not always occur, of course, but they are always possible and are sometimes highly likely. Hence, the prospect of them has to be taken into account when we are gauging the extent of anyone's deontic liberties or physical liberties (or anyone's combinations of jointly exercisable physical liberties).

2.3.2.2 Physical Obstructions and Constraints

Unlike any measures of enforcement that give effect to a law which imposes a prohibition or restriction, that law itself does not directly reduce anyone's physical freedoms. However, other interventions by a system of governance (including measures of enforcement for legal restrictions, of course) do directly impinge on physical freedoms or on combinations of jointly exercisable physical freedoms. In a variety of ways, people who wish to communicate with others can be prevented from doing so—whether or not they are also prohibited from doing so.

The starkest form of prevention consists in the removal of someone's bodily ability to speak or write, at least for a certain period. For example, when the evildoer Aaron in Shakespeare's *Titus Andronicus* is captured by soldiers under the command of Lucius, he delightedly recounts his nefarious exploits. After Lucius has listened with horror to this recitation of villainy for a while, he issues a directive to some of his men: "Sirs, stop his mouth, and let him speak no more" (V.i.151). Earlier in that same play, the rapists of Lucius's sister Lavinia cut out her tongue and chop off her hands to prevent her from disclosing their identities through speech or writing.

Though a robustly liberal-democratic system of governance will never resort to the grisly tactics of Lavinia's rapists and will very seldom resort to the tactic ordered by Lucius against Aaron, there are many other ways of removing people's communicational abilities. For example, the transmitting equipment of a pirate radio station or of some other broadcaster can be shut down, and similarly the printing facilities or distributional network of a newspaper or publisher can be disrupted. Additionally, the bank account of a broadcaster or publisher or newspaper can be seized, so that the funds on which the operations of the company depend are no longer available. A foreign orator can be physically prevented (as well as legally prohibited) from entering a country, and a domestic orator can be jailed or otherwise prevented from delivering a speech. Even if an oration is intoned, the audience can be prevented from hearing it—because the words are drowned out through a cacophony created by governmental agents or by hecklers, or because the public-address system that would have rendered the oration audible is blocked. Furthermore the members of an audience, perhaps acting in cooperation with governmental officials, can close themselves off from the words of a speaker.

For example, when Stephen in the Acts of the Apostles has launched into a tirade against his addressees, "they cried out with a loud voice and stopped their ears and rushed together upon him" (Acts 7:57). In other cases, because of the actions of governmental agents or hostile third parties, people who keenly wish to hear certain speakers can be forcibly prevented from coming into proximity with them at all.

The examples broached in the preceding two paragraphs are only a small sampling of the ways in which the physical freedoms of people to interact communicatively with others can be expunged. Though some of the steps taken to remove such freedoms might be measures of law-enforcement or might be accompaniments to those measures, many of the other freedom-expunging steps are independent of any processes of law-administration. Hence, notwithstanding that the bestowal of legal immunities by constitutional guarantees such as the First Amendment is crucial for securing the legal liberties of people to engage in communicative conduct, the bestowal and implementation of those immunities will not be sufficient for the realization of freedom of expression. Also essential is the imposition of legal duties that require any system of governance not to undertake measures which eliminate the communicative abilities of people in contravention of the principle of freedom of expression. In any society where that principle is duly upheld, individuals and groups will be vested with legal claim-rights against the circumscription of their abilities through such measures.

Of course, not every law that curtails people's legal liberties to engage in communicative conduct is a contravention of the principle of freedom of expression, and so too not every governmental action or policy that curtails people's physical freedoms to engage in communicative conduct is a contravention of that principle. Only if such an action or policy is directed against the communicative character of the behavior which it stymies, does it run athwart the principle of freedom of expression. If instead the action or policy is directed against that behavior qua serious misconduct whose wrongness is communication-independent, the principle of freedom of expression will not have been violated. Thus, the legal claim-rights to which I have referred in the preceding paragraph are obviously not claim-rights against all measures through which a system of governance might eliminate various communicative abilities of people. Some such measures are neither in contravention of the principle of freedom of expression nor in contravention of any of the other moral requirements that are incumbent on every system of governance. Still, the point in this subsection has plainly not been to suggest that every physical obstruction or constraint imposed on people's communicative activities by a system of governance is morally illegitimate. Rather the point is to indicate that, because any such obstruction or constraint which has been so imposed is generally burdensome or disadvantageous for anyone affected by its freedom-removing impact, it has to be assessed for its consistency or inconsistency with the principle of freedom of expression.

2.3.2.3 Subsidies and Assistance

Subsidies and other forms of assistance are generally beneficial for people who receive them, of course. However, precisely because those supportive measures are generally advantageous for their recipients, they are generally disadvantageous for many of the people who are excluded from them. Hence, the lavishing of subsidies or rewards or privileges can breach the requirements of communication-neutrality and content-neutrality and speaker-neutrality just as much as can the imposition of legal or physical constraints.

In countless situations, indeed, the distinction between the lavishing of support and the imposition of restrictions will be imponderable. Let us think back, for example, to the scenario of the municipal buses with side panels and back panels that can be rented by individuals or organizations for the placing of notices and advertisements. As has been remarked, a local government is not morally obligated to make the sides and backs of its buses available to advertisers at all. Hence, if it does make those areas available (in return for the payment of fees) in a manner that is at variance with the requirement of subject-neutrality or viewpoint-neutrality or speaker-neutrality, its approach to the matter can equally well be characterized as the differential conferral of a benefit or as the differential imposition of a restriction. By providing access to the sides and backs of the buses for advertisers who wish to communicate on the favored topics or who wish to articulate the favored viewpoints, the local government is bestowing a privilege on those advertisers. Equally, by withholding such access from advertisers who wish to communicate on the disfavored topics or who wish to articulate the disfavored viewpoints, the local government is imposing a restriction on those advertisers. It is disadvantaging them in comparison with the advertisers to whom the access has been granted. Consequently, if the principle of freedom of expression attached any importance to the distinction between a policy that provides for the conferring of benefits and a policy that provides for the administering of detriments, we would face the hopeless task of trying to determine whether the local government's policy on advertising belongs to the former side or to the latter side of that distinction. Fortunately, the principle of freedom of expression does not in fact attach any significance to such a distinction. Forms of favorable treatment and forms of unfavorable treatment, dispensed by any system of governance, are alike in having to be assessed for their consistency or inconsistency with that principle.

Naturally, this point is applicable not only to contexts in which we have to appraise laws and policies for their content-neutrality or speaker-neutrality, but also to contexts in which the type of neutrality at issue is general communication-neutrality. Subsidies and other kinds of support furnished by a system of governance to communicative activities qua communicative activities—or to non-communicative activities qua non-communicative activities—are just as much in violation of the principle of freedom of expression as are prohibitions or other disadvantages imposed on communicative activities qua communicative activities.

Of course, not all subsidies and other kinds of support furnished by a system of governance to communicative activities are in violation of the principle of freedom of expression. If support is provided to activities not because of their communicative character but instead on communication-neutral grounds, it can be entirely consistent with that principle. However, the point here has not been to impugn the obvious fact that most subsidies or other forms of assistance dispensed by a system of governance to people who undertake communicative activities or non-communicative activities are in keeping with the principle of freedom of expression. Rather, the point has been to emphasize that policies of support as well as policies of restriction always have to be assessed for their conformity to that principle. In a wide range of circumstances the relevant assessments can be left implicit, because in a wide range of circumstances the consistency of policies with the principle of freedom of expression is so evident. As Dworkin observed in a comment quoted earlier, we do not need to pose questions overtly when the answers to them are already apparent to everyone. Nevertheless, even though multitudes of supportive or restrictive policies are uncontroversially congruent with the principle of freedom of expression, any such policies will have contravened that principle if they are pursued for purposes that are not neutral in all the ways which it requires. The scope of the principle of freedom of expression is not limited by any distinction between subsidies and restrictions, or between privileges and burdens.

2.3.3 How are Purposes Ascertained?

Under the principle of freedom of expression, the purposes of various laws and policies—the ends sought by them, and the means adopted for the attainment of those ends—have to be neutral in all the senses expounded in §2.3.1 above. How do we ascertain the purposes of laws and policies? Here we come to some issues which are not unique to debates over freedom of expression but which bear crucially on those debates.[10]

2.3.3.1 Not a Search for Mental States

A key point to be noted straightaway is that the purpose of any law or policy is not a mental state of anyone (though it might correspond in content to certain mental states of somebody responsible for the law or policy). A number of political philosophers have failed to grasp this point. Consider, for example, George Sher's worry

[10] For an admirable discussion, see Rubenfeld 2001, 793–7. I draw here intermittently upon my own much longer discussion in Kramer 2017, 75–87, where I cite many other relevant works. I hope that my account here will dispel the misconceptions about purpose-centered legal interpretation that are on display in Goldberg 2016, 714–15.

about the attribution of a purpose to any law that is a product of many people's efforts and ambitions:

> Because policy makers and legislators are not always candid, because individuals often lack insight into their own reasons, and because different persons can support the same laws or policies on very different grounds, there is often no way to discover whether, or to what degree, a proscribed sort of [purpose] has been operative. (Sher 1997, 117)

This pronouncement by Sher tallies with a concern which he articulates at an earlier juncture, when he declares that "we must reject the suggestion that the legitimacy of a well-entrenched law or political structure depends on the mental processes of long-dead persons" (1997, 24). To a large extent, Sher is here echoing the anxiety voiced by Robert Goodin and Andrew Reeve when they pose a question which they presumably regard as rhetorical: "Can we make any sense of the notion of collective intent when, for example, a large number of people back the same plan of action but for a number of different reasons?" Goodin and Reeve respond to their rhetorical question by declaring that "it is unclear that we can attribute to [governments] motives and intentions of the sort that individual moral agents certainly have" (1989, 199).

These worries by Sher and Goodin and Reeve are misdirected. They stem from the notion that anyone who appositely ascribes a purpose to some law L will have successfully peered into the mental states or processes of the people responsible for L. We should put that notion aside, for the task of imputing a purpose to L is not an exercise in mind-reading. Rather, anyone's performance of that task is an effort to make sense of L in its context and amidst the statements that have been uttered about it. Such an endeavor might of course lead to the conclusion that more than one purpose can germanely be attributed to L. (Like Sher and Goodin and Reeve, I will concentrate here on the ascription of purposes to laws. However, my remarks are equally applicable to governmental policies or measures that are not encapsulated in formally enacted laws.)

In the first instance, as is suggested in the quotation from Rubenfeld in §2.1.2 above, we need to look at the terms in which L is formulated. Examining those terms, we should seek to identify the values or objectives which L is apt to promote either as ends or as means. Alternatively put, we should seek to identify the problems which L is apt to avert or remedy and the means through which it will avert or remedy them (Fuller 1969, 83). Sometimes the answer to each of these questions will be quite apparent, at least in part. For example, a law which requires the recitation of a prayer at the outset of every professional baseball game is manifestly favoring certain religious modes of expression (even if those modes of expression are rendered mandatory only instrumentally for the furtherance of the objective of public order, and indeed even if they are rendered mandatory in order to discredit them by evoking impatience and disgruntlement among the spectators and players at baseball games). Such a law blatantly contravenes the requirement of content-neutrality that is incumbent on every system of governance under the principle of freedom of expression. However, the terms of numerous other laws do not yield such clear-cut answers to questions about their purposes.

When interpreting most laws, then, we need to move beyond the surfaces of their formulations. That is, we need to investigate the context in which any law L has been adopted (if it is of recent vintage) or in which it has been preserved (if it is of longer standing). We likewise need to explore the sundry statements that have been made specifically about L by people responsible for the introduction or preservation or administration of it. The sincerity of those statements can be gauged by reference to the settings in which they are articulated and by reference to the general views of the people who utter them. When we have enquired into all these matters, the initial judgments which we have reached on the basis of the terms of L might be partly or wholly confirmed or partly or wholly disconfirmed; or, particularly if those initial determinations are marked by substantial uncertainty, they might be clarified and amplified. Of course, in some cases, any initial puzzlement might remain or might even be deepened. There is no guarantee that any given law will lend itself to the imputation of a definite purpose. However, in a functional system of governance, officials and knowledgeable citizens will be able to ascribe purposes to most laws with high degrees of confidence.

2.3.3.2 Surfaces, Contexts, and Statements

To identify correctly a purpose of some law L, then, an ascription of that purpose has to be borne out (1) by the terms of L and (2) by L's context and (3) by the statements of people responsible for L. To be borne out by the terms of L, the ascription of a purpose must at the very least be credibly consistent with those terms. Thus, for example, the aforementioned law which requires the recitation of prayers at professional baseball games does not support the ascription of any purpose that calls for neutrality between religious modes of expression and non-religious modes of expression; the terms of that law are not credibly consistent with any such aim. Of course, while consistency is indispensable, it is not per se sufficient. The terms of L do not really support the ascription of some purpose thereto unless those terms are such that the implementation of L will tend to be promotive of the specified purpose rather than merely consistent with it.

If the attribution of some purpose to L is to be borne out by L's context, there must be no significant grounds in that context for thinking that the purpose in question has been invoked as a subterfuge to conceal some ulterior aim. To grasp the importance of the contexts in which various laws are introduced or sustained, we should first ponder briefly an example that does not pertain to freedom of expression. Suppose that a municipal government discontinues the operations of a public swimming pool after a court has issued a desegregation order that applies to the pool and to some other public facilities. The terms of the decision by the local government are credibly promotive of the aim of economizing on public expenditures, and the statements uttered by the people responsible for the pool's operations might all invoke that aim. Nonetheless, because of the context in which the decision has been reached, we are warranted in doubting that the objective of frugality in public expenditures is the purpose that chiefly accounts for what has been done. We should instead conclude that the dominant intention is to defy the desegregation order.

Contextual considerations often loom large when interpreters are coming to grips with laws that bear upon people's communicative activities. Suppose, for example, that the legislature in a country with a system of military conscription has enacted a statute that provides for the imposition of sanctions on anyone who has destroyed his or her draft card. Suppose that the statute presents itself as a measure designed to enhance the efficiency and fairness of the system of military conscription, and suppose that some of the public statements of the statute's supporters are likewise focused on considerations of efficiency and fairness. In fact, however, the statute has been enacted in a context in which the destruction of draft cards has come to be employed as a means of protesting against the continuation of an unpopular war. In some on-the-record statements and many off-the-record statements, the supporters of the statute have acknowledged that the prohibition on the destruction of draft cards is aimed at putting an end to this vividly effective practice of protest. Given this context, which quite closely resembles the context in which the U.S. Congress prohibited the destruction of draft cards by Americans in the 1960s (Alfange 1968, 3–6, 14–16; Rubenfeld 2001, 775), we can correctly conclude that the statutory ban on the destruction of draft cards is neither communication-neutral nor viewpoint-neutral. Assessed in its context, the ban is not a communication-neutral law that forbids some instances of communicative conduct as well as some instances of non-communicative conduct. Rather, a major purpose of the ban—its foremost purpose, indeed—is to minimize the incidence of the specified communicative conduct.

In addition to the formulations of laws and the contexts in which they have been enacted or preserved, the sundry relevant statements made by people responsible for introducing or sustaining any given law L are determinants of the purpose(s) with which L is endowed. Of course, some of those statements are themselves elements of the context in which L has emerged or in which it has been preserved, whereas other relevant statements are made directly in the processes whereby L is enacted or implemented. If the attribution of a certain purpose is to be borne out by the statements of people responsible for the introduction or sustainment or administration of L, then a significant proportion of those statements must invoke that purpose as something that warrants the adoption or retention or implementation of L. Among the medley of relevant statements, moreover, there must not be any significant proportion that would cast doubt on the ascription of the specified purpose to L.

2.3.3.3 Implementation and Purposes

When we have investigated the wording of a law L and the context of L's operativeness and the statements about L by officials who are responsible for it, we are in a solid position to draw some conclusions about the purpose(s) with which L is invested. That is, we are in a position to draw some conclusions about the value(s) which L is designed to advance, or the perceived problem(s) which L is designed to avert or remove. Of course, the most plausible conclusion might be that no clear-cut purpose is accurately attributable to L. In a functional system of law, however, that purely negative conclusion can often be avoided as interpreters converge in ascribing some purpose(s) to L.

One further element, which has been discussed in §2.1.2 and §2.3.1.4 above, is the implementation of L. Frequently, the administrative processes and judgments that bring L to bear on people's conduct over time can help to illuminate the purposes that are accurately imputable to L. In some other cases, however, the administrative processes and judgments themselves are what stand most in need of assessment. We have encountered just such a case in §2.1.2, when glancing at the facts of *Davis v Norman*. On the one hand, there were no grounds in that case for thinking that the terms or purposes of the municipal ordinance which forbade the unenclosed storage of ruined automobiles were inconsistent with the principle of freedom of expression. On the other hand, there were quite substantial grounds for suspecting that the enforcement of the ordinance against Mr Davis's display of the wrecked truck was at odds with that principle. To reach a firm conclusion on that latter point, we would need to enquire into the purpose of the act of law-application itself. An enquiry of that kind would look at the ways in which the ordinance had been given effect during the years that led up to its being enforced against Mr Davis. If it had seldom or never been invoked theretofore, or if it had been invoked only in cases of blatant transgressions involving multiple dilapidated vehicles, we would have quite ample grounds for inferring that the ordinance was brought to bear on Mr Davis in a manner that was neither communication-neutral nor viewpoint-neutral. In other words, we would have quite ample grounds for thinking that Mr Davis's display of a demolished truck was singled out by the police officers for removal because they objected to the message communicated by it (a message directed against them). One's suspicions on that point would of course be reinforced if an enquiry into the matter were to unearth some statements by the police officers in which they indicated that the communicative content of the display was a basis for their applying the ordinance to it. Even without such explicit statements, however, the context of the act of law-enforcement might itself be sufficient to establish that that act was in contravention of the principle of freedom of expression.

In short, when we are gauging whether the operations of a system of governance conform to the principle of freedom of expression, we have to probe not only the purpose(s) of any law or policy that is under consideration; in addition, we have to probe the purpose(s) of any process and judgment whereby that law or policy is given effect. Only thus will we have ascertained whether all facets of the system's workings—the adjudicative and administrative facets as well as the legislative facets—are in compliance with the constraints of neutrality that are imposed by the principle of freedom of expression. Transgressions of those constraints are some overweening efforts to control the patterns of public discourse.

2.3.4 Private Parties

Throughout this book, I address the topic of freedom of expression as a matter of the proper relationship between a system of governance and the citizenry over whose activities the system presides. The self-restraint denoted in the title of the book is that of a system of governance, as the moral responsibilities imposed by the principle of freedom of expression are incumbent on the officials and institutions of every such system. Nevertheless, although the role of those officials and institutions in directing or impeding people's communicative activities is the primary focus of this book, the role of private parties in directing or impeding such activities does have to be taken into account as well—not least because the role of private parties can activate the role of governmental officials. In later chapters, especially Chapters 5 and 6, the import of private parties as sources of restrictions on the communicative activities of their fellow citizens will surface at several junctures. Here we should glance at two main matters, each of which will arise again in those later chapters: the problem of hecklers and hostile audiences; and the responsibilities of large organizations, with regard to their control over certain areas or institutions that are correctly classifiable as public fora, and with regard to their treatment of potential or actual employees.

2.3.4.1 Hecklers and Hostile Audiences

Unlike governmental officials in their public capacities, private individuals are largely unbound by constraints of communication-neutrality and content-neutrality and speaker-neutrality. Private individuals are largely entitled to decide for themselves (and perhaps for some or all members of their families) whether to shun or to embrace certain types of communications and certain speakers. To be sure, in the next subsection we shall investigate some contexts in which the usual prerogatives of private individuals are not fully operative—because those individuals occupy positions that render them partly assimilable to governmental officials. All the same, when private individuals do not occupy such positions, they are generally at liberty to countenance or discountenance various modes of communication as they see fit. Under the principle of freedom of expression, such choices are left to them rather than to any system of governance.

However, what has just been said is applicable to situations in which private individuals are making choices for themselves (and perhaps for some or all members of their families). Quite different is any situation where private individuals are in effect making decisions not only for themselves but also for many others by disrupting the communicative activities of speakers or writers. Although the problem of heckling and of hostile audiences is of long standing,[11] it has become especially prominent in recent times as throngs of protesters in the United States and elsewhere have endeavored to interrupt or prevent the delivery of orations by controversial speakers who are mostly on the far right of the political spectrum. Municipalities and universities have borne the substantial expenses of arranging for the special police protection with which the speeches can go ahead and with which the incidence of clashes between the detractors and the supporters of the controversial orators can be minimized.

2.3.4.1.1 Straightforward Points

In connection with this problem, some points under the principle of freedom of expression are quite straightforward. First, the statutes or ordinances that can be invoked against disruptive heckling and against the violence of hostile audiences are general laws which prohibit serious breaches of the peace or public disturbances. Ordinarily, the purposes of those laws are consistent with the principle of freedom of expression. Moreover, those laws can be applied unproblematically to persistently disruptive hecklers or to unruly protesters, provided that the acts of law-enforcement are directed against the disruptiveness or unruliness rather than against any messages conveyed by the hecklers or protesters. At odds with the principle of freedom of expression would be any pattern of law-enforcement that proceeds with special severity or celerity against hecklers and protesters who articulate certain disfavored viewpoints, and likewise at odds with that principle would be any pattern of law-enforcement that proceeds with special severity or celerity against hecklers and protesters who articulate messages instead of simply making noise. Nonetheless, so long as the relevant law is given effect in a manner that is communication-neutral and content-neutral and speaker-neutral, its being brought to bear to protect speakers against obstreperousness is very much in keeping with the principle of freedom of expression (and indeed is obligatory under that principle, as will be argued presently). Of course, many acts of heckling and protesting are themselves instances of communicative conduct. Thus, when

[11] For an excellent overview of the problem, see Schauer 2019b. For another fine discussion, see Kagan 1996a, 461–4. See also Abrams 2012, 123–5; Alexander 2005, 111–13; Barnum 1981; Coenen 2017, 1555–7; Ely 1975, 1499–1500; Greene 2012, 95–6; Leanza 2007; McGaffey 1973; Nehushtan 2015, 45–6; Post and Molnar 2012, 28; Stone 1983, 214–16, 237–8; Welshon 2020; Wright 2017.

a legal prohibition on breaches of the peace is applied to excessively vociferous heckling and protesting, it will in effect be outlawing certain instances of communicative conduct. However, it will be outlawing them not because of their communicative character but instead because of their disruptiveness and violence. It will be outlawing them not qua acts of communication but instead qua acts of serious public disorder. Hence, legal constraints on such heckling and protesting can be fully in harmony with the principle of freedom of expression.

Second, some legal constraints on vehemently strepitous heckling and protesting are not only compatible with the principle of freedom of expression but in addition are morally obligatory under that principle. Were a system of governance to acquiesce in the disruption of speeches or theatrical productions by upheavals at the hands of people who are ferociously opposed to those speeches or productions, it would in effect be undertaking "an improper delegation of authority to the public to suppress messages [which the public] disfavors" (Kagan 1996a, 463). After all, a system of governance is both morally entitled and morally obligated to maintain the basic orderliness of a society. If it declines to carry out that responsibility in contexts where people are under siege as they try to engage in communicative activities, or if it responds to the prospect of a siege by requiring those people to forgo or discontinue the communications which they are seeking to perform, it is endowing the rioters with an inordinate measure of control over the patterns of public discourse. When a system of governance fails to protect communicative endeavors against the violent interference of other people, it is breaching not only its moral duty to preserve elementary civil peace but also its moral duty to uphold the principle of freedom of expression; it breaches that latter duty by allowing the perpetrators of the violent interference to determine what sorts of communications will take place in the society over which the system of governance presides. When the onset of violent interference is forestalled by such a system through the shutting down of speeches or theatrical productions or other communications, the system's officials are again contravening the principle of freedom of expression in the manner just specified—for they are enabling people to gain control of public discourse through threats or violence. Accordingly, the resistance of governmental officials to such threats or violence is not only morally legitimate but also morally obligatory.

Third, when acts of heckling or protesting are not significantly disruptive—and are not legitimately prohibitable on any other communication-neutral grounds—a system of governance is morally obligated to permit them to proceed. Indeed, since such non-disruptive acts will themselves usually be communicative, the obligation to permit them to proceed will usually be grounded partly in the principle of freedom of expression. Given the absence of significant disruptiveness and the absence of other communication-independent factors that could justify the proscribing of the conduct in question, governmental officials will contravene the principle of freedom of expression if they punish or disadvantage anyone for engaging in that conduct. No less than the communicative freedoms of the speaker or theatrical company or orchestra whom the hecklers or protesters are targeting, the communicative freedoms of the hecklers or protesters are covered by the principle of freedom of expression. Of course, the inclusion of one's communicative freedoms under the ambit of that principle is morally consistent with the elimination of those freedoms by a system of governance on communication-neutral grounds; however, it is not morally consistent with the elimination of those freedoms by a system of governance on grounds that are lacking in communication-neutrality or content-neutrality or speaker-neutrality.

2.3.4.1.2 A More Difficult Matter

As has just been maintained, a system of governance is morally required to protect speakers or other communicators against the unruliness of hecklers or protesters who aim to prevent some instance(s) of communicative conduct from going ahead. If violence is threatened or occurrent, the law-enforcement officials in the area are morally obligated to take steps against the people who threaten or perpetrate the violence. However, as has become apparent from some incidents in the United States in recent years,[12] a municipality or university can occasionally be faced with hordes of protesters and counter-protesters who are so numerous and truculent that the only way to keep them from perpetrating serious violence against each other is to disperse them. In such extreme circumstances, a political rally or some other communicative event may have to be aborted or suspended.

Let us presume throughout that a rally or any other communicative event aborted in circumstances like those envisaged here has not itself constituted a communication-independent mode of misconduct such as incitement to violent criminality. In that case, the discontinuation of the communicative event is a contravention of the principle of freedom of expression. In the extreme circumstances outlined, the municipality or university may have been confronted with a moral conflict in which its moral responsibility to preserve or restore basic public orderliness and its moral responsibility to abide by the principle of freedom of expression could not be jointly fulfilled. If the former obligation in the circumstances was more stringent than the latter obligation, then the municipality or university may have acted correctly by aborting or suspending the communicative event. Even so, its aborting or suspending of that event is a breach of a moral duty. That breach may have been correct in that it was the lesser of two wrongs between which the municipality or university had to decide; however, even if the breaching of the duty was correct by dint of being a less grave transgression than the sole feasible

[12] For a collection of essays—by scholars from various academic disciplines—on one of the worst such incidents, see Nelson and Harold 2018. The incident in question, during August 2017 in the city that is the home of the University of Virginia, is discussed saliently in Schauer 2019b. (Schauer is also one of the contributors to the collection of essays which I have cited here.)

alternative course of action, the lesser of two wrongs is still a wrong.[13] After all, in the situation hypothesized, a system of governance has terminated or prevented the occurrence of a communicative event because some people have objected vehemently to its content. However unwillingly, the system of governance in relation to those people has carried out an illiberal delegation of authority along the lines mentioned in §2.3.4.1.1 above. It has thereby infracted the principle of freedom of expression.

What should be the legal upshot of such a contravention of the principle of freedom of expression? If the officials in a system of governance have acted precipitately by shutting down a communicative event at a point when the presence of numerous protesters and counter-protesters has not yet generated any serious tumults or any clear and present danger of imminent serious tumults, the people who have organized the aborted event should be able to pursue legal proceedings successfully for damages against the relevant agency of the system of governance (most likely a police force). If contrariwise the officials have not been precipitate when putting an end to the communicative event, an award of damages might still be obtainable against the bureau or department in which they are employees; after all, however unwillingly, the officials have contravened the principle of freedom of expression. In most circumstances of this kind, however, a better course of action is instead to provide for legal proceedings against the demonstrators who have disrupted the communicative event (Schauer 2019b, 1694). Damages can be sought against the people whose recalcitrance has prevented the exercise of basic liberties. Whether or not such a remedy is currently available in the law of any jurisdiction, it should be available to give effect to the principle of freedom of expression—in response to any situation where the actual or imminent unruliness of protesters has resulted in the discontinuation of a communicative event that did not itself constitute any communication-independent misconduct.

2.3.4.2 Large Organizations

Especially because private parties include not only individuals but also large organizations, some private parties make decisions not solely for themselves when they favor or disfavor various modes of communication. Of course, that fact is not per se sufficient to establish that the obligations imposed by the principle of freedom of expression are incumbent on any private parties. For example, when a company that produces popular motion pictures or television programs has opted to fund the creation of certain films or programs rather than others, its decisions will significantly affect the array of options available to people for their leisure-time

[13] Of direct relevance here is my distinction between two senses of the adjective "right" in Kramer 2014, 8: "right" as a synonym of "morally correct" and "right" as an antonym of "morally wrong." The decision by the municipality or university may have been right in the former sense, but it was not right in the latter sense.

entertainment. All the same, the company has not violated the principle of freedom of expression by making those decisions. That principle obviously does not place the company under a moral obligation to fund the creation of every film or program that might be proposed. Still, although the absence of any obligation of that sort is quite evident, there are some special moral responsibilities borne by large private organizations. Notwithstanding that many aspects of this topic are beyond the scope of this book, we should briefly ponder two types of contexts in which such special responsibilities can be operative.

2.3.4.2.1 Public Fora

As has to some degree been recognized in American constitutional law under the First Amendment,[14] a corporation that controls a public forum—an area or institution that is generally open to members of the public for common use, such as a thoroughfare or a park or a shopping mall or a plaza—is under the same freedom-of-expression obligations as is any governmental body that controls such a forum. On that point, though with a considerably broader understanding of what counts as a public forum, the moral principle of freedom of expression is convergent with the First Amendment. Thus, for example, when people wish to distribute leaflets or brochures in an area that is open to members of the public for common use, they are morally entitled to do so without any prior approval from the corporation that owns and controls the area. They cannot permissibly be subjected to any sanctions for declining to seek or obtain such prior approval, and they cannot permissibly be prevented (by employees of the corporation or by governmental functionaries) from distributing their literature. Of course, they can permissibly be required to abide by limitations that are justifiable on communication-neutral grounds. For instance, they can permissibly be required to refrain from impeding the passage of pedestrians or automobiles; and, in public fora with circumscribed spaces such as airports or train stations or shopping malls, the people with the leaflets or brochures can permissibly be required to confine their endeavors to certain allotted areas. However, they cannot permissibly be required to abide by any limitations that are at odds with the types of neutrality integral to the principle of freedom of expression. For example, they cannot permissibly be required to refrain from distributing materials whose contents are disliked by the functionaries of the corporation that controls the public forum.

In addition to large edifices and stretches of land that are properly classified as public fora, certain institutions on the Internet are properly so classified. As will be discussed tersely in Chapter 6, social-media platforms such as Facebook and Twitter and YouTube have become public fora. Although the companies that create and run those platforms are not morally obligated to sustain them in existence at

[14] The degree to which this point has been recognized in the law of the First Amendment is far too limited. See BeVier 2004, 122–7; Schauer 2008, 915, 919.

all, the role of controlling a public forum morally obligates each such company to comply with the principle of freedom of expression while performing that role. No constraints that deviate from the kinds of neutrality required under that principle are morally legitimate. Of course, as in other settings, constraints that are justifiable on communication-neutral grounds can be morally legitimate. We shall contemplate a few such constraints (for instance, prohibitions on targeted harassment) in Chapter 6. Moreover, some of the legal restrictions to be discussed in Chapter 3—most notably the legal restrictions that can permissibly be imposed by a system of governance on the dissemination of defamatory assertions—are clearly legitimate and also obligatory in the public fora on the World Wide Web. Nevertheless, if any prohibition is not similarly justifiable on communication-neutral grounds, it cannot legitimately be operative in a public forum regardless of whether that forum is controlled by a governmental agency or by a private corporation.

In some cases, the applicability of the principle of freedom of expression to the operations of a privately controlled public forum is especially manifest because those operations directly involve some organ of a system of governance. For example, in the 1946 case of *Marsh v Alabama*, the issue brought before the U.S. Supreme Court was whether an Alabaman law that prohibited trespassing could be enforced by the Alabaman courts against the defendant for her distribution of religious literature on a sidewalk of a company-owned town without prior approval. However, even when the involvement of a system of governance is more tenuously indirect—as is the case, for example, in many of the arrangements for sanctions and exclusions in the public fora on the World Wide Web—a private company that manages a public forum is morally obligated to comply with the requirements of neutrality that are imposed by the principle of freedom of expression. Such a company is subject to those requirements because, in its role as a controller of a public forum, it is functioning as an extension of the prevailing system of governance. Like the officials in that system of governance, the employees of the company are presiding over a forum in which the patterns of public discourse emerge and evolve. No more than the governmental officials, are the employees of the company morally entitled to exert any fine-grained direction over those patterns of public discourse. What would be wrongfully overweening on the part of the officials is likewise wrongfully overweening on the part of the company's employees, given the functional affinities between their positions in relation to the public fora over which they respectively preside.

Of course, as has already been remarked, some of the public fora managed by private corporations were devised by those corporations in circumstances where the creation of each of the fora was non-obligatory. For example, Mark Zuckerberg and the other founders of Facebook were not morally obligated to introduce the social-media platform that bears the company's name. Nor are the executives of Facebook morally obligated to preserve that platform in existence indefinitely. Nonetheless, having created the Facebook platform as a public forum, and having taken on the role of operating it as such, the people who run Facebook are morally required to comply with the constraints of neutrality (communication-neutrality, content-neutrality, and speaker-neutrality) that are intrinsic to such a role. In this respect, the situation of Facebook is akin to that of the municipality whose buses we have contemplated in §§2.3.1.2.1 and 2.3.1.2.2 above. On the one hand, the municipality is not morally duty-bound under the principle of freedom of expression to make the sides and backs of its buses available to potential advertisers for their notices and blandishments. On the other hand, given that the municipality has indeed adopted a policy of making the sides and backs of its buses available in that manner, it is morally duty-bound to ensure that its conduct of the policy complies with the requirements of neutrality that are imposed by the principle of freedom of expression. Questions about the obligatoriness of abiding by those requirements of neutrality in an organization's running of a public forum are distinct from questions about the obligatoriness of an organization's creation of a public forum.

2.3.4.2.2 Hiring and Retention of Employees

Chapter 6 will include a short discussion of the role of various governmental bodies in making decisions about the hiring and retention of people as workers. What will be said there about the leeway of governmental agencies at the point of deciding whether to take on people as employees is obviously applicable as well to private companies.[15] If some of the statements made by Clarissa in the past are such that they reveal her unfitness for the position of employment which she is seeking—either because they point to her general discreditability as a person or because they indicate that she lacks some of the specific traits that are crucial for the position in question—a private company is acting in a perfectly legitimate fashion when it takes those statements into account as a basis for declining to hire Clarissa. Indeed, in many circumstances the company would be acting irresponsibly if it failed to take those statements into account (for example, if it remained unaware of the statements even though it could have learned of them without immoderate exertion).

Trickier situations can arise at later junctures, when a company has to decide whether to retain people who have already been hired and who may have been working for the company over long periods of time. Let us ponder here a variant of a scenario broached by Alexander (2005, 109). Suppose that Thaddeus who works as a waiter in a restaurant has made a number of statements—perhaps in social media or perhaps in other settings—wherein he condemns homosexuality as viciously immoral on a par with paedophilia. We should presume here that his statements do not constitute any communication-independent misconduct. Though repugnantly worded, his utterances are properly classifiable as advocacy rather

[15] My remarks here will focus mainly on profit-making companies, but will also be applicable to other organizations—such as charities—in the private sector.

than as incitement; they are designed to influence people's views rather than to provoke people into perpetrating imminent misdeeds. We should presume further that Thaddeus in the performance of his job has not allowed his strong sentiments on the matter of homosexuality to inflect his behavior at all. When he serves people in his capacity as a waiter, he treats same-sex couples and homosexual individuals with the same degree of courtesy with which he would treat any heterosexual couples or individuals. Now, at some point, his statements about homosexuality come to the attention of people in his community. Some of those people approach the manager of the restaurant and demand that Thaddeus be fired or that he at least be required to abstain from making any further statements on the topic. When the manager declines to accede to their angry expostulations, they organize a boycott of the restaurant that results in a substantial diminution of its profitability.

Were Thaddeus working for a governmental agency, he would clearly be morally protected against the imposition of any sanctions for the statements which he has made. Given that (*ex hypothesi*) his statements do not constitute any communication-independent wrongdoing, and given that the attitudes expressed by them have not led Thaddeus to behave objectionably in his performance of his job, there are no content-neutral grounds for his employer to penalize him. If he were to be subjected to dismissal or to other penalties, the adverse treatment of him would be due to his having expressed a repellent viewpoint. Any disciplinary measures undertaken for such a reason would be blatantly in contravention of the principle of freedom of expression.

On this point, a private employer such as the restaurant is morally indistinguishable from a public employer such as a governmental agency. If the restaurant were legally authorized to impose sanctions on Thaddeus for the statements which he has made, then the system of governance responsible for that authorization would thereby have assigned an inordinate degree of control over the tenor of public discourse to the restaurant and the protesters. Backed with such authorization, the manager of the restaurant would be legally empowered to subject Thaddeus to restrictions or disadvantages that are squarely inconsistent with the requirement of viewpoint-neutrality. Such neutrality would be transgressed because the expressions of a bigoted viewpoint by Thaddeus have not constituted any communication-independent misconduct and have not been paralleled by any invidious patterns of behavior in the work which he carries out for the restaurant as a waiter. A system of governance is not morally at liberty to assign viewpoint-suppressing legal authority to the restaurant, any more than to hecklers and hostile audiences.

Of course, the manager of the restaurant can permissibly take certain steps to alleviate the impact of Thaddeus's statements on the profitability of her business. She can permissibly emphasize to the protesters that she looks askance at the substance of those statements, and she can permissibly point out to them that the law of the jurisdiction—which, we can assume here, is in accordance with the principle of freedom of expression—does not entitle her to adopt the punitive or restrictive measures which they are imploring her to undertake. Moreover, harboring the reasonable suspicion that the attitudes expressed in Thaddeus's statements might skew his demeanor in his role as a waiter, she can permissibly monitor his workplace doings to ascertain whether anything therein is seriously amiss. Furthermore, provided that she makes clear to Thaddeus that she lacks any legal power to obligate him to desist from pronouncements on the topic of homosexuality that are not constitutive of any communication-independent misconduct, she can permissibly ask or encourage him to desist from such pronouncements.

If no permissible measure has led to a satisfactory resolution of the situation, the manager of the restaurant might choose in extremis to dismiss Thaddeus as an employee. Though such a step will be far from incomprehensible if the boycott has severely diminished the proceeds of the business, it is morally impermissible as a violation of the principle of freedom of expression. Consequently, if the law of the jurisdiction is in conformity to that moral principle (as I have been assuming), Thaddeus will be able to pursue legal proceedings successfully against the restaurant for his wrongful dismissal and will thus be able to gain compensation for the way in which he has been treated.

Some readers might initially feel that the implications of the principle of freedom of expression for situations like that of Thaddeus and the restaurant are extravagant. Why should private organizations have to go to such lengths to accommodate the communicative freedoms of their employees? Any reactions of this kind on the part of readers would probably be attributable (at least in part) to the specifics of the example which we have just been mulling over. After all, the sentiments expressed by Thaddeus are benighted. Although the protesters are themselves somewhat benighted in their blindness to the requirements of the principle of freedom of expression, they are right to take strong exception to the views which Thaddeus has articulated. Indeed, through some malign modifications of the scenario, the ugliness of his views could have been accentuated. Suppose for instance that, instead of making derogatory remarks about homosexuality, Thaddeus has several times proclaimed his admiration for the efforts of the Ku Klux Klan to restore the racial purity of the United States. Or suppose that he has made several statements in which he has deemed the historical accounts of the Holocaust to be fictions devised by Jews to gain special privileges for themselves and for the country of Israel. Had either of these two variants of my scenario been broached in lieu of the original version, the dissatisfaction of some readers with the perceivedly extravagant requirements imposed by the principle of freedom of expression may have been intensified.

However, the aspect of my thought-experiment that has just been accentuated can alternatively be reversed through some benign modifications. Suppose that, instead of giving voice to some morally backward pronouncements on homosexuality, Thaddeus has spoken repeatedly in rebuttal of such pronouncements by other people. Many morally obtuse members of his community feel that his enlightened stance on the issue is inimical to the ethos of their society, and they proceed to remonstrate with his employer in the manner of the protesters in the original version of my thought-experiment. Or suppose that Thaddeus has repeatedly and eloquently deplored the activities of the Ku Klux Klan, and that the morally obtuse people who predominate in his community are incensed over what they regard as his uppitiness. Or suppose that he has spoken out persistently against antisemitism and Holocaust-denial, and that the numerous bigots who reside in his community have urged his employer to fire him or silence him.

Or, to alter the scenario in a direction that assimilates it to a real-life controversy which took place during the writing of this chapter (Deb 2019; Greer 2020), let us suppose that Thaddeus is a player on a professional basketball team whose owners have been hoping to arrange some lucrative sporting tours in China. Thaddeus makes some public statements in which he denounces the ferocious governmental persecution of Muslims in the Xinjiang region of China, and he likewise speaks out against the Chinese government's devastation of the indigenous culture in Tibet. High-ranking officials from China furiously make contact with the owners of the basketball team to demand that Thaddeus be fired or that he be required to furnish a public apology to the people of China for his criticism of their system of governance. The officials warn the owners that their team will be permanently excluded from the Chinese market unless these demands are met.

In each of the benignly revised versions of my thought-experiment in the preceding two paragraphs, the communicative conduct of Thaddeus is admirable, and the outlooks of the people who aim to stifle that conduct are rebarbative. In application to those benignly revised versions, the requirements imposed by the principle of freedom of expression will doubtless strike far fewer readers as extravagant. A system of governance will have transgressed that principle if the system legally authorizes the employer of Thaddeus to silence him or to dismiss him or to discipline him in some other way for his statements. Given the responses by numerous enthusiasts of the game of basketball to the real-life controversy on which the scenario in the last paragraph above is based, there are good grounds for thinking that the implications of the principle of freedom of expression in any of the benignly revised versions of my tale of Thaddeus will strike many people as commendable rather than as extravagant. Yet the differences between those benignly revised vignettes and the original vignette are entirely matters of content. Neither in the original scenario nor in the benignly revised scenarios has Thaddeus perpetrated any communication-independent misconduct. Neither in the original scenario nor in the benignly revised scenarios have his public pronouncements revealed him to be unfit for the performance of his job; moreover, the attitudes expressed by those pronouncements have not negatively affected the ways in which he performs that job.

The key differences between the original version and the benignly revised versions of my thought-experiment are centered on the fact that the attitude toward homosexuality conveyed by Thaddeus's statements in the original version is repellent, whereas the attitudes conveyed by his statements in any of the benignly revised versions are praiseworthy. Such content-centered differences are of great moral importance, of course, but they do not have any bearing on the applicability of the principle of freedom of expression to the situations at issue in the various renderings of my thought-experiment. That principle requires strict content-neutrality on the part of any system of governance. It thus requires any such system to regulate the situation of Thaddeus's employer uniformly across the different versions of my thought-experiment. Thaddeus's pronouncements are protected by the principle of freedom of expression in the original version as much as in any of the subsequent versions, because no content-neutral grounds militate against such protection in the original version. Thus, if some readers are inclined toward the view that the moral responsibility incumbent on the restaurant in the original version of the tale of Thaddeus is extravagant, and if they are simultaneously inclined toward the view that the moral responsibility incumbent on the employer in any of the benignly revised versions of the tale is sensible and vital, they are exhibiting their readiness to deviate from the principle of freedom of expression. In the manner of the rain that falls on the just and the unjust, the neutrality-requiring principle of freedom of expression extends its protection to the enlightened and the benighted alike.

3
Legitimate Restrictions

As the preceding chapter has maintained, the principle of freedom of expression disallows any governmentally imposed restrictions on communicative conduct that are not in keeping with the constraints of communication-neutrality and content-neutrality and speaker-neutrality. Before this book proceeds (in Chapter 4) to elaborate the moral basis for that principle, the present chapter will anticipate and parry some objections that might be raised against any insistence on the aforementioned constraints. Quite apart from the fact that the burdensomeness of those constraints obviously stands in need of justification—as Chapter 2 has readily acknowledged—they might seem to carry implications that undermine the credibility of the principle of freedom of expression as a precept of political morality. Here the chief aim is to show that no outlandish implications follow from that principle and from the requirements of neutrality which it establishes.

More specifically, this chapter will maintain that the principle of freedom of expression is perfectly consistent with legal prohibitions on various types of misdeeds that can be perpetrated through communicative conduct. Of course, Chapter 2 has already broached some of those types of misdeeds. As has been observed, for example, a deliberate attempt to provoke a dangerous public disturbance—such as the attempt of a man who maliciously shouts "Fire" in a dark and crowded theater—can legitimately be subjected to sanctions even when the attempt occurs through communication. Provided that the sanctions are directed not against the communicative character of the attempt in question but instead against its communication-independent wrongfulness, they do not transgress the principle of freedom of expression at all. Likewise, we have pondered the distinction between advocacy and incitement (a distinction to which this book will return in Chapters 5 and 6). Though both advocacy and incitement are expressive modes of conduct, the latter can permissibly be forbidden under laws that are aimed at it as direct participation in the criminality which it impels. So aimed, those laws are bans on communication-independent misconduct rather than on the conveyance of messages or sentiments or other communicative contents. Similarly, Chapter 2 has touched upon the "fighting words" doctrine which will receive more sustained attention in Chapters 5 and 6. The utterances covered by that doctrine are rightly construed by it as efforts to trigger brawls through the delivery of individualized invective at close range. Although those efforts are of course communicative, they are liable to legal penalties not because of their communicativeness but because of the wrong-making properties which they have in common with non-communicative

Freedom of Expression as Self-Restraint. Matthew H. Kramer, Oxford University Press (2021). © Matthew H. Kramer.
DOI: 10.1093/oso/9780198868651.003.0003

efforts to trigger brawls. Hence, they too are prohibitable as communication-independent misconduct. Further examples have surfaced briefly in Chapter 2 and will emerge at greater length in subsequent portions of this book.

Though the present chapter will advert to some of the kinds of communication-independent misdeeds that are discussed elsewhere in this book, it will mainly be concerned with certain kinds that are not examined anywhere else herein. Some legal restrictions and some other governmentally imposed restrictions on misdeeds perpetrated through communicative behavior are morally unproblematic, and might nonetheless appear to be aimed squarely at the communicative character or content of that behavior. Were the appearances accurate, and were the specified restrictions therefore morally legitimate while also being at variance with the constraints of communication-neutrality and content-neutrality, the principle of freedom of expression would be untenable. Thus, by arguing that the appearances are not accurate and that those morally legitimate restrictions are consistent with the constraints of neutrality just mentioned, this chapter will be contributing crucially to my overall vindication of the principle of freedom of expression.

Before we scrutinize the sundry laws which might seem to contravene that principle, I should clarify the hyphenated adjective "communication-independent." That adjective has been employed several times already herein, and it has been used repeatedly in Chapter 2. Though its meaning is probably clear to most readers by now, a bit of elucidation here will avert any misconceptions that might otherwise arise. Given that the notion of communication-independence is central to this chapter's cogitations and indeed to this book as a whole, the dispelling or forestalling of such misconceptions is a vital preliminary to those cogitations.

3.1 What is Communication-Independence?

My references to communication-independent misconduct or to communication-independent wrongfulness might mislead some readers because those references might be taken to suggest that the classifiability of utterances as such misconduct (or as partaking of such wrongfulness) is not due to what the utterances have communicated. Let us have in mind here a couple of the examples of communication-independent misconduct from Chapter 2: the malicious shouting of "Fire" in a dark and crowded theater, and the incendiary urgings of an orator addressed to a mob outside the home of a corn-dealer. My discussion in this section will proceed with reference to those two examples—in order to make the discussion more concretely accessible—but its points are generalizable.

As is evident, the shout in the theater forcefully expresses a message to its addressees. It is designed to induce some immediate life-endangering actions on the part of those addressees, but that effect is deliberately achieved by way of the alterations in their beliefs and attitudes that are brought about through the transmission of the admonitory message. Consequently, the wrongfulness of the shout supervenes on what has been communicated in the circumstances wherein the shout has occurred. Any satisfactory account of that wrongfulness has to make reference to the content and context of the utterance. Those features of the utterance are what warrant its being classified as the inducement of a dangerous public disturbance (or as an attempt to induce a dangerous public disturbance). In other words, the classifiability of the malicious shout as an instance of communication-independent misconduct is due to the message which the shout has conveyed and to the circumstances in which the conveyance of that message has occurred.

Accordingly, if the adjective "communication-independent" were supposed to indicate that the wrongfulness of the act of shouting "Fire" is not due to the communicative import of such an utterance, then that adjective would be inapposite. However, when I characterize the wrongfulness of the utterance as communication-independent, or when I contend that the utterance can properly be subjected to sanctions as a communication-independent mode of misconduct, there is no suggestion that the wrongfulness is unattributable to the content and context of the message which the shout of "Fire" has expressed. Rather, the point is that that shout belongs to a category of misconduct—the category of inducement (or attempted inducement) of a perilous public disturbance—that is not inherently communicative. Any number of potential or actual instances of such misconduct are communicative, and any number of potential or actual instances of such misconduct are non-communicative. These heterogeneous instances are categorized together on the basis of the wrong-making properties which they have in common. Those properties are instantiated by any endeavor to initiate or exacerbate a situation of dangerous public disorder, whether the endeavor is communicative or non-communicative in its character. Precisely because the actions that instantiate those wrong-making properties can be either communicative or non-communicative, the instantiation of those properties is communication-independent. And because the wrongness of any such action does not hinge on whether the action is one of the communicative instances or one of the non-communicative instances in the category of misconduct to which it belongs, its wrongness is likewise communication-independent.

Let us now turn to the harangue by the firebrand orator who goads the mob into undertaking a lethal rampage of violence against a corn-dealer. Patently, the fulminations of the orator are communicative; through them he intentionally conveys both a clear-cut message and some malign sentiments to the members of the mob. Because of those communicative contents and because of the circumstances in which those contents are imparted, the speaker's tirade is constitutive of his direct participation in a lynching. Given the proximity of his utterances to the exertions of violence against the corn-dealer, and given the role of his utterances in deliberately spurring the mob to proceed with those exertions, his declamations are properly classified as some of the initial stages of the violence. Their classifiability as such stages—their classifiability as his direct participation in a lynching—is due to their communicative contents and context. Hence, when I claim that his diatribe constitutes a communication-independent mode of misconduct, there is no suggestion that the wrongness of the diatribe is somehow unattributable to what it has communicated. Its wrongness is communication-independent, but not in that ridiculous sense.

Instead, the communication-independence of the misconduct (or the communication-independence of the wrongness of the misconduct) consists in the fact that the direct participation of a person in a lynching can occur either through communicative actions or through non-communicative actions. An inflammatory tirade that stirs up a mob into a frenzy is one way in which somebody can directly contribute to the perpetration of a lynching, and the placing of a rope around the victim's neck is another such way. Those two modes of direct participation, along with countless other possible modes of such participation, are grouped together in a category of evildoing on the basis of the wrong-making properties which all of them share. Because the fiery tirade belongs to that category of evildoing, it is aptly classifiable as communication-independent misconduct. It belongs to a genus that cuts across the distinction between the communicative and the non-communicative, and its membership in that genus of wrongdoing is what accounts for its legitimate prohibitability. Proper sanctions will be directed against the orator's incitement not qua act of communication but instead qua act of direct participation in a murderous crime. Anyone who has participated directly in that crime in a non-communicative manner will be similarly liable to undergo such sanctions, for the range of the applicability of proper sanctions—like the category of wrongdoing to which they are punitive responses—cuts across the distinction between the communicative and the non-communicative.

In the respect that has just been summarized, rather than in the ludicrous respect that has been broached in the penultimate paragraph above, the misconduct constituted by the orator's harangue is communication-independent. That type of misconduct (participation in a deadly act of violence) comprises communicative instances and non-communicative instances alike, and any legitimate prohibition of such misconduct is aimed against what those instances have in common rather than against any features that appertain solely to the communicative instances. Like the type of wrongdoing itself, then, a legitimate prohibition of it is communication-independent. Extending to the type's communicative instances and non-communicative instances across the board, such a prohibition complies with all the constraints of neutrality that are integral to the principle of freedom of expression.

3.2 Prohibitable Misdeeds

With the relevant sense of "communication-independence" suitably clarified, we should now contemplate some kinds of communications which are constitutive of communication-independent wrongdoing and which are therefore morally susceptible to being forbidden or prevented or restricted by a system of governance. Their susceptibility to such measures is indeed obvious and is taken for granted in the United States and elsewhere, but what is less apparent is the status of each of these kinds of communications as a communication-independent mode of misconduct. Often the assumption has been that these sorts of expressive activities can legitimately be prohibited or prevented or restricted qua expressive activities. Were such an assumption correct, the principle of freedom of expression would not genuinely be a moral absolute. That principle would not be a precept of political morality that is binding always and everywhere, but would at most be a "rule of thumb." Fortunately, however, the assumption just broached is not correct. As this chapter will maintain, nearly every type of expressive activity surveyed herein is correctly classifiable as a communication-independent mode of misconduct. Consequently, nearly every such type can be prohibited or prevented or restricted by a system of governance in accordance with the principle of freedom of expression. Appropriate measures of prohibition or prevention or restriction will not encroach on the absolute sway of that principle.

3.2.1 Solicitation to Commit a Crime

Solicitation of another person to commit a crime is itself a crime in virtually every jurisdiction. Someone who engages in such solicitation intends to get the other person to perpetrate a felony (or some other offense), and, to that end, the party engaging in the solicitation endeavors to persuade or induce or entice the other person to carry out the specified offense.[1] Plainly, solicitation and incitement overlap; indeed, incitement can appositely be regarded as one major variety of solicitation. However, not every instance of solicitation is an instance of incitement (at least when incitement is understood in line with the U.S. Supreme Court's *Brandenburg* judgment, as it is in this book). Whereas incitement almost always involves febrile rhetoric that arouses passionate emotions such as fury and resentment, numerous instances of solicitation do not trade on such tempestuous stirrings. Solicitation can occur as effectively through calculated appeals to greed or

[1] This understanding of solicitation is encapsulated, for example, in the wording of the main federal law on the matter in the United States. See 18 U.S. Code §373. For some valuable ruminations on the crime of solicitation (with attention to freedom of expression), see Greenawalt 1989, 110–26; Kagan 1996a, 437 n70; Wechsler, Jones, and Korn 1961, 621–8.

through the issuance of orders—in a criminal gang, for example—as through the whipping up of vehement emotions.

Closely related, and even more important in the present context, is that many instances of solicitation to commit a crime do not involve the element of imminence that is a key ingredient of every instance of incitement. As has been recounted in Chapter 2, and as will be discussed further in Chapter 5, the matter of imminence is the chief factor that distinguishes incitement from advocacy. Whereas incitement is operative only when the crime which an orator seeks to bring about is likely to be perpetrated imminently because of the orator's utterances, the connections between advocacy and any hoped-for crimes are more distant and are often indefinite. Solicitation can be oriented toward criminality that is likely to be perpetrated imminently because of the inducements put forward by the solicitation, but frequently the envisaged criminality is more distant. To be sure, as Chapter 5 will observe with a germane example, the element of imminence that is integral to incitement does not always amount to virtual immediacy. Nonetheless, even when that point is taken into account, the requirement of imminence under the *Brandenburg* criterion for incitement is unsatisfied by many instances of solicitation to commit a crime. Sometimes, a person's course of conduct can be correctly classifiable as such solicitation even though the offense which the person seeks to initiate is weeks away in the future.

This dissimilarity between incitement and many instances of solicitation may seem to render those instances especially problematic under the principle of freedom of expression. After all, as has just been mentioned—and as will be underscored further in Chapter 5—the temporal proximity between an inciter's utterances and the criminality which the inciter aims to instigate is a key factor underlying the status of those utterances as some of the opening stages of the criminality. If there is no such proximity between some acts of solicitation and the offenses which those acts induce (or are meant to induce), then there might appear to be no basis for the subsumption of those acts into the offenses as some of the initial stages thereof. Yet, if the acts of solicitation would not be subsumed into the crimes which they induce or are meant to induce, then any measures whereby a system of governance prohibits or prevents such acts might appear to contravene the principle of freedom of expression. Those measures might appear to be morally on a par with endeavors by a system of governance to prohibit or prevent the advocacy of certain ideas. Mere advocacy is morally protected by the principle of freedom of expression against such governmental endeavors, as it is not subsumed into any crimes that might be inspired by it. Were mere advocacy to be prohibited or prevented by a system of governance, it would be prohibited or prevented qua act of communication rather than qua instance of communication-independent misconduct. Much the same might appear to be true of the type of solicitation that is under consideration here, which I shall henceforth designate as "extended-interval solicitation." Because the element of temporal proximity is missing from instances of extended-interval solicitation, any step by a system of governance to prohibit or prevent them might appear to be directed against them qua acts of communication.

Such appearances, however, would be unfounded. Though the element of temporal proximity is a crucial consideration that distinguishes incitement from advocacy, its absence from instances of extended-interval solicitation does not warrant the grouping together of those instances with advocacy as protected modes of expression rather than with incitement as unprotected modes of expression. Although those instances of solicitation differ from incitement in the respect just stated, they also differ importantly from advocacy—such that they are subsumed into the crimes which they bring about (or are aimed at bringing about).

Let us first ponder the dissimilarity between incitement and extended-interval solicitation. Incitement works by inflaming volatile passions in order to prod people into giving vent to those passions through headlong misdeeds. Because of this characteristic manner in which an utterance of incitement achieves its effects, the interval between the articulation of the utterance and the occurrence of the headlong misdeeds has to be short if the misdeeds are to be correctly ascribable to that utterance as some of its effects. As Shakespeare's Friar Laurence observes in one of his admonitions to Romeo, the efficacy of an explosive impetus is ephemeral: "These violent delights have violent ends/And in their triumph die, like fire and powder,/ Which as they kiss consume" (*Romeo and Juliet*, II.vi.9–11). Extended-interval solicitation works very differently. Instead of being designed to kindle a burst of vehemence, it characteristically operates through techniques such as persuasion or commands or the proffering of rewards. Such techniques do sometimes culminate swiftly in the perpetration of the criminality which they are aimed at delivering, but frequently the interval between the plying of such a technique and the perpetration of the intended criminality is significantly longer. In contrast with the unleashing of a surge of ardent emotion, an act of extended-interval solicitation is a medium-term project. Given that the intended effects of such an act unfold more coolly, the requirement of imminence for the classification of conduct as incitement is not appropriate as a requirement for the classification of conduct as solicitation to commit a crime.

However, precisely because the criminality prompted by extended-interval solicitation unfolds more gradually than the criminality prompted by an act of incitement, we confront the question whether such solicitation can be barred by a system of governance in accordance with the principle of freedom of expression. Here we turn to the key difference between such solicitation and advocacy. Whereas an act of advocacy is not oriented toward any particularized or highly specific course of criminality in which it will eventuate, an act of extended-interval solicitation is indeed oriented toward a highly specific criminal venture. This point was underlined by Herbert Wechsler and William Jones and Harold Korn in their influential studies on the contours of the crime of solicitation in the law of most jurisdictions in the United States. Pondering the tension between the outlawing of solicitation and the ideal of freedom of expression, they wrote that the legal standard for the classifiability of an utterance as solicitation requires that

> the criminal conduct allegedly solicited by the speaker be "specific." It is, of course, unnecessary for the actor to go into great detail as to the manner in which the crime solicited is to be committed. But it is necessary ... that, in the context of the knowledge and position of the intended recipient, the solicitation carry meaning in terms of some concrete course of conduct that it is the actor's object to [induce]. (Wechsler, Jones, and Korn 1961, 627)

Because an act of solicitation is so much more concretely focused than is an act of mere advocacy, the former—unlike the latter—is subsumed into the wrongdoing to which it designedly gives rise. Having arranged that wrongdoing and put it into motion with a fairly high degree of definiteness, the solicitation is one of the initial stages thereof. In that respect, extended-interval solicitation is like incitement even though the period of time between the opening stages and the concluding stages of the criminality is significantly longer than the corresponding period in a case of incitement. Mere advocacy, by contrast, is not subsumed into any wrongdoing that might be inspired by it. With an orientation that is far more diffuse than the orientation of an act of solicitation, mere advocacy does not prescribe or arrange any particularized course of misconduct. Accordingly, given its abstractness, it is not correctly classifiable as one of the opening stages in any instance of criminality that might emerge in response to it.

In sum, the definiteness of the connections between an act of extended-interval solicitation and an offense which that act arranges and induces is what underpins the status of the solicitation as an opening portion of the offense. It is what distinguishes such solicitation from mere advocacy and is what aligns such solicitation with incitement as a mode of communicative conduct that is constitutive of communication-independent wrongdoing. When properly proscribed by law, extended-interval solicitation is forbidden not qua act of communication but instead qua act of participation in a crime such as murder or robbery. Hence, the measures through which a system of governance prohibits or prevents such solicitation can be fully consistent with the principle of freedom of expression.

3.2.2 Perjury

Few if any champions of the ideal of freedom of expression have ever doubted that perjurious statements can properly be forbidden by law. A system of governance can permissibly impose legal sanctions on anyone who speaks deceitfully while under oath in a trial or in some other kind of legal proceeding. Rightly uncontroversial is the proposition that perjury can legitimately be prohibited by a system of governance, but that proposition—with which everyone aptly concurs—has been a source of some confusion in the literature on freedom of expression. It has led some eminent theorists to declare that perjurious statements are beyond the scope of the principle of freedom of expression.

In §2.1.4 of Chapter 2, I have discussed and rejected Frederick Schauer's trichotomous schema which distinguishes among communicative actions that are uncovered by the First Amendment, communicative actions that are covered but unprotected by the First Amendment, and communicative actions that are protected by the First Amendment. In light of that general schema propounded by Schauer, we should not be surprised that he regards perjurious testimony as uncovered—and not merely unprotected—by the principle of freedom of expression (1982, 13, 89, 92, 102–3). As he writes:

> An activity is not within the coverage of the Free Speech Principle merely because that activity is described as "speech" in ordinary language. Conspiracy, perjury, fraud and extortion, for example, are all "speech" in the ordinary sense, yet are not "speech" under *any* conception of freedom of speech . . . [S]uch acts are not within the scope of the Principle at all.[2]

More surprising is that Jed Rubenfeld, who generally eschews anything along the lines of Schauer's trichotomy, adopts a largely similar position on the matter of perjury:

> The domain of *speech* to which the [principle of freedom of expression] applies is not all-encompassing. There is a kind of orthodoxy that government can and does enforce every day, even in the sense of prescribing what people must and must not say. I refer to the orthodoxy of true and false facts. While it is true that "there is no such thing as a false *idea*" under the First Amendment, there is clearly such a thing as a false *fact*. The laws of libel, fraud, perjury, and so on, all [impose sanctions on] people for speaking falsely on matters of fact. (Rubenfeld 2001, 819, emphases in original; footnote omitted)

Given that facts are true propositions, the notion of false facts invoked by Rubenfeld is puzzling. He presumably is referring to false empirical propositions (or false empirical assertions). Also puzzling is the suggestion in this passage that falsity is what the legal proscription of perjury is directed against. A false empirical assertion made under oath during a legal proceeding is not perjurious unless it is mendacious. Laws that prohibit perjury are directed against deliberate deception

[2] Schauer 1982, 91–2, emphasis in original. For an endorsement of Schauer's position on the matter of perjury, see Greenawalt 1989, 7 n1. Greenawalt (1989, 3, 5, 7 n4) also endorses Schauer's general trichotomous schema.

rather than against falsity alone. Falsity is an aspect of such deception, of course, but insincerity also has to be involved.

At any rate, even more important than these other shortcomings in this passage from a generally excellent article by Rubenfeld is his contention—in line with Schauer's view—that perjurious testimony is not covered by the principle of freedom of expression. Any such contention, which is a denial of the absoluteness of that principle, is misconceived. Perjurious statements are like other modes of expression in that no system of governance can ever permissibly forbid or prevent them qua acts of communication. The imposition of sanctions on someone for making such statements is morally permissible only if the statements are being penalized qua acts of communication-independent misconduct.

Here my elucidation of the notion of communication-independence in §3.1 above is especially germane. As is manifest, the harm inflicted by perjurious statements is brought about through their expressive character and content. Someone who utters such statements is intentionally conveying some false message(s) in order to hoodwink other people and thereby prejudice the fairness of a trial or of some other legal proceeding. That effort by the perjurer to shirk his oath through cozenage is obviously a communicative effort, and any nefarious success that it achieves is due to the convincingness of the perjurious statements as communications. In all these respects, the vitiating of a legal process through the utterance of perjurious statements is not communication-independent.

However, in the sense that is dispositive under the principle of freedom of expression, the misconduct constituted by the utterance of such statements is communication-independent and is therefore susceptible to being prohibited by a system of governance in compliance with that principle. A law that forbids any acts of perjury can be morally legitimate if and only if it is directed against such acts qua endeavors to undermine the integrity of legal proceedings rather than qua instances of communicative conduct. Because perjurious testimony belongs to a broad category of wrongdoing that comprises communicative actions and non-communicative actions alike, someone who furnishes such testimony can permissibly be subjected to legal sanctions if the sanctions are aimed at the wrong-making properties which the perjurious conduct has in common with the non-communicative actions that belong to the same category of misdeeds. In the broad category just mentioned, of course, are all modes of conduct whereby somebody deliberately prejudices or seeks to prejudice the integrity of legal proceedings. Some of those modes of conduct, such as the utterance of perjurious statements in a trial or in some other legal setting, are communicative in character. Other modes of conduct in the category, such as the payment of bribes to adjudicators or the concealing of evidence, are non-communicative in character. If the communicative modes of conduct and the non-communicative modes of conduct are forbidden by a system of governance because they deliberately undermine the veracity of legal proceedings, the communicative instances and non-communicative instances are being treated relevantly alike—in which case the proscription of each of those sundry instances is in keeping with the requirements of neutrality that are established by the principle of freedom of expression. In the envisaged scheme of legal regulation, where perjury is subject to legal penalties because of the deceitfulness and damagingness that it has in common with the non-communicative modes of behavior through which the propriety of legal proceedings can be deliberately prejudiced, those requirements of neutrality are satisfied. The specified penalties are imposed on perjury not qua type or token of expressive conduct but instead qua type or token of communication-independent misconduct.

In the envisaged scheme of legal regulation, perjury might be treated in a separate statute such as the Perjury Act of 1911 in England and Wales, or it might be covered in a statute as one species of the general type of wrongdoing which it constitutes. Either approach can be consistent with the principle of freedom of expression. In a jurisdiction where perjury is handled in a statute devoted specifically to it, the overall scheme of legal regulation can nonetheless be in compliance with the principle of freedom of expression if other laws within the scheme address the non-communicative techniques by which the integrity and outcomes of legal proceedings can be vitiated. Sometimes the consistency or inconsistency between a particular law and the principle of freedom of expression can be satisfactorily gauged in isolation, but ofttimes a law is properly assessable only in combination with additional existent laws that pertain to the same general problem or the same area of life. If a statute like the Perjury Act of 1911 exists alongside some statutes that deal comparably with the non-communicative species of the general kind of wrongdoing to which the Perjury Act pertains, then those several statutes have to be appraised in combination when we seek to ascertain whether the system of governance responsible for them is abiding by the principle of freedom of expression. Were the Perjury Act to be considered on its own with no attention to the cognate laws that cover the non-communicative means of deliberately undermining the veracity of legal proceedings, we would be acquiring a distortively compartmentalized view of the operations of the prevailing system of governance. Of course, to insist as much is not per se to submit that the Perjury Act of 1911 or any other such statute is indeed consistent with the principle of freedom of expression. Each such statute has to be examined in conjunction with any other laws that apply to the same general type of misconduct. One's conclusion in any particular jurisdiction might be that the statute under scrutiny does indeed contravene the principle of freedom of expression by singling out a communicative species of that general type of misconduct for anomalously harsh treatment (or for anomalously lenient treatment). Nevertheless, my point in this paragraph has simply been that such a verdict does not ineluctably follow from the sheer fact that the crime of perjury is addressed in a separate statute.

In a different context, this point about the need for a synoptic view of the operations of a system of governance will arise afresh in Chapters 5 and 6. There we shall be mulling over the principle of freedom of expression in relation to pornography and hatefully bigoted utterances. As will be seen, some philosophers in favor of legal restrictions on those modes of expression have contended that a policy of legal tolerance abjectly acquiesces in practices which seriously impair the dignity and basic well-being of people who are peculiarly vulnerable to bigotry. Chapters 4 to 6 of this book will maintain that, in any system of governance which fulfills the chief moral responsibilities incumbent upon it (including its moral responsibility to uphold the principle of freedom of expression), the legal toleration extended to pornography and to hateful declamations is combined with numerous techniques for countering those modes of expression and their effects. Such countering measures, which will be explored in some detail in those later chapters and which do not prevent or legally restrict the objectionable modes of expression that are combated by the measures, enable a system of governance to cleave to the principle of freedom of expression while also satisfying its moral obligation to protect the dignity and basic well-being of highly vulnerable people. That latter moral obligation might appear to be neglected by a liberal-democratic system of governance, if we concentrate in a blinkered fashion on the fact that such a system legally tolerates the marketing of pornography and the advocacy of hateful doctrines. However, when the blinkers are lifted, and when we thus take account of the full range of laws and policies adopted by that system of governance, our conclusion about its fulfillment of its moral responsibilities—a conclusion no longer distortively inflected by the blinkers—will very likely have changed sharply.

Similarly, although a statute devoted specifically to perjury might appear to transgress the requirement of communication-neutrality established by the principle of freedom of expression, any conclusion to that effect is likely to change when we undertake a survey of the laws in the relevant jurisdiction that forbid other ploys through which the propriety of legal proceedings would be undermined. If our adoption of that synoptic view of the matter reveals that perjurious statements are being treated on a par with those other ploys (most of which are non-communicative), we can conclude that the statute focused specifically on perjury does not violate the requirement of communication-neutrality. Whereas Chapters 5 and 6 will be commending a synoptic view of the operations of a system of governance for anyone who seeks to ascertain whether the system's adherence to the principle of freedom of expression is compatible with its fulfillment of its other moral responsibilities, my present discussion is commending a synoptic view of the laws in this or that jurisdiction for anyone who seeks to ascertain whether the system of governance that presides over the jurisdiction is complying with the principle of freedom of expression or not.

3.2.3 Restrictions on Malicious or Reckless Pre-Trial Reporting

In an interview conducted in 1962 with the famous U.S. Supreme Court Justice Hugo Black, Professor Edmond Cahn broached the matter of pre-trial restrictions on the reporting of crimes:

> In order to preserve the guaranteed freedom of the press, are you willing to allow sensational newspaper reports about a crime and about police investigation of the crime to go so far that they prejudice and inflame a whole state and thus deprive the accused of his right to a fair jury? (Black and Cahn 1962, 555)

Perhaps because Black had not been apprised beforehand of the questions that would be posed to him by Cahn, his reply to this inquiry about pre-trial restrictions was ramblingly lengthy in his characteristically homespun style. However, a few pregnant portions of his reply should be noted here.

Black first impugned the socio-psychological assumption that underlay Cahn's query:

> The question assumes in the first place that a whole state [in the United States] can be inflamed so that a fair trial is not possible. On most of these assumptions that are made with reference to the dangers of the spread of information, I perhaps diverge at a point from many of those who disagree with my views. I have again a kind of an old-fashioned trust in human beings. (Black and Cahn 1962, 555)

He added that, in any event, judges could serve to rectify egregious verdicts handed down by juries whose members had read or heard some inflammatory reports before they were empaneled as jurors:

> I do not think myself that anyone can say that there can be enough publicity completely to destroy the ideas of fairness in the minds of people, including the judges ... [W]e should not forget that if the jury happens to go wrong, the judge has a solemn duty in a criminal case not to let an unfair verdict stand. Also, in this country, an appellate court can hear the case. (555–6)

Moreover, Black maintained, the susceptibility of jurors to tendentious reporting could be greatly alleviated through improvements in education. Such improvements would be far superior to censorship as a means of striving to ensure the fairness of criminal trials:

> I do not myself think that it is necessary to stifle the press in order to reach fair verdicts. Of course, we do not want juries to be influenced wrongfully. But with our system of education we should be in better condition than they were in those

> days in England, when they found that the jury was one of [the] greatest steps on their way to freedom. (556)

Black closed his answer to Cahn's question by warning that the imposition of pre-trial restrictions on reportage would augment the dominance of the sway exerted by a system of governance:

> I do not withdraw my loyalty to the First Amendment or say that the press should be censored on the theory that in order to preserve fair trials it is necessary to try the people of the press in summary contempt proceedings and send them to jail for what they have published. I want both fair trials and freedom of the press. I grant that you cannot get everything you want perfectly, and you never will. But you won't do any good in this country, which aspires to freedom, by saying just give the courts a little more power, just a little more power to suppress the people and the press, and things will be all right. (556)

Especially given that Black was speaking at a time before the full dismantling of the system of Jim Crow racial segregation in parts of the United States (and at a time when adverse pre-trial publicity could be especially damaging to the prospects of a fair trial for a black defendant accused of a serious crime), his faith in the sensibleness of potential jurors was startlingly complacent. Still, in other respects, his instincts on the matter of pre-trial restrictions were sound. He was correct in thinking that pre-trial restrictions on the reporting of information about suspects or about their alleged offenses are incompatible with the principle of freedom of expression—though, as will be readily accepted shortly, the imposition of sanctions on newspapers or broadcasters for maliciously false reporting is perfectly consistent with that principle.

Whereas Black recognized that the requirements of communication-neutrality and content-neutrality under the principle of freedom of expression are absolute constraints on the legitimacy of governmental regulations and prohibitions, many philosophers and legal theorists have presumed that the matter of pre-trial restrictions on reporting should be addressed in a consequentialist vein through cost/benefit analyses. Most notably, Schauer has embraced just such a consequentialist tack. He declares that "we must balance one special right against another special right," and he submits that either of the two factors in the balance can take priority over the competing factor:

> [W]here one distinct limitation on state power is set against another, we do not know from the existence of the free speech interest that the presumption should be in its favour. In some cases the Fair Trial Principle may be more important than the Free Speech Principle. The Free Speech Principle is important in all cases within its scope, but it is only necessarily more important in cases where no

identifiable individual right is present on the other side of the balance. (Schauer 1982, 134)

Although the U.S. Supreme Court for much of the past century has been enamored of the rhetoric of "balancing" employed by Schauer and numerous other legal theorists, it has fortunately aligned itself with Black against those theorists by disallowing the imposition of pre-trial restrictions on reporting. The landmark case on the issue, *Nebraska Press Association v Stuart* (427 U.S. 539), was decided in 1976. Notwithstanding that the Justices on the Court presented multiple opinions in support of their holding—with no single opinion endorsed by a majority of the Justices—they were unanimous in striking down some pre-trial restrictions that had been imposed on the reporting about a case of multiple murders in a small Nebraskan town. Three of the Justices affirmed unequivocally that pre-trial restrictions always contravene the First Amendment to the American Constitution (save in relation to malicious or reckless falsehoods), and two of the other Justices made clear their strong sympathy for that absolutist position. Moreover, even though the four remaining Justices left open the possibility of "balancing" in future circumstances, the very fact that they disallowed the restrictions in the case at hand was solidly indicative of the unlikelihood that pre-trial restrictions would ever be countenanced. In that 1976 case, the defendant in a Nebraskan town had been charged with murdering six members of a family. Some quite sweeping pre-trial restrictions on reportage were eventually narrowed down to restrictions on reports about confessions or other incriminating statements made by the defendant. Furthermore, the judicial order that forbade such reports was to be in force only until the empaneling of a jury. Even so, the U.S. Supreme Court held unanimously that that order was inconsistent with the First Amendment. As Anthony Lewis commented a few decades later: "If a bar on publishing a confession was [unconstitutional] in so aggravated a situation—a gruesome multiple murder in a small rural town—it was hard to see when one would be [constitutional]" (2007, 174–5).

Insofar as the *Nebraska Press Association* judgment absolutely disallows the imposition of pre-trial restrictions on accurate reports about crimes and their alleged perpetrators, the requirements of the First Amendment on that issue are in conformity with those of the principle of freedom of expression. Any such pre-trial restrictions would be violative of the communication-neutrality and content-neutrality which the principle of freedom of expression demands. Except in circumstances where the substance of a report is maliciously or recklessly inaccurate—circumstances that will be addressed at the end of this subsection—the dissemination of information by newspapers or broadcasters about criminality and alleged malefactors is a communicative activity that is not constitutive of any communication-independent misconduct. Thus, when the dissemination of such information is forbidden through pre-trial judicial orders, it is prohibited qua communicative activity rather than qua communication-independent wrongdoing. Accordingly, such orders are squarely at odds with the principle of freedom of expression.

Of course, we should not join Black in ingenuously presuming that people who might serve on juries are largely insusceptible to being swayed by reports about the lurid details of crimes in their localities. Precisely because there can be a real tension between upholding the principle of freedom of expression and ensuring that people accused of vile crimes are tried fairly, an array of measures to avert or minimize the damaging effects of pre-trial reportage—measures such as those recounted by Black himself and by the U.S. Supreme Court—will be essential in any context where that tension emerges and becomes acute. Such a crux is to be handled not by "balancing" away an absolute constraint on the types of legal restrictions that can permissibly be imposed, but by taking steps that can reconcile the satisfaction of that constraint with the provision of a fair trial.

As we have beheld, Black referred to education and to judicial oversight as two key techniques for such a reconciliation. Whereas the former is a wide-ranging program that can also yield many other benefits, the latter technique is brought to bear specifically in contexts where judicial interventions are needed to overcome the biases or blundering of juries. In addition, the Supreme Court in its *Nebraska Press Association* judgment adverted to a number of steps that can help to secure the fairness of a trial. Among them are the relocation of a trial to a venue where the publicity surrounding a case has been (or is likely to be) less extensive and sensational, the deferral of a date for a trial to a juncture when the furore engendered by the occurrence of a ghastly crime will have subsided, the meticulous probing of prospective jurors to ascertain whether they have been prejudicially affected by the coverage of a high-profile case in the media, and the issuance of repeated and emphatic instructions by the presiding judge about the duty of every juror to reach a verdict solely on the basis of the evidence presented during the trial. Furthermore, once a jury has been empaneled, it can be sequestered if necessary to avert any damaging effects of the renewed attention that will be devoted by the press and by members of the public to the flagitious crime(s) on which the trial is focused. If these and other methods enumerated by the Supreme Court are not employed by a presiding judge in a situation where some or all of them are vital for safeguarding the probity of a trial, an appellate court should be prepared to reverse any conviction that emerges from the trial. The moral responsibility of a system of governance to secure the fairness of criminal and civil trials is scarcely negated by the moral responsibility of such a system to comply with the principle of freedom of expression. Although pre-trial restrictions on newspapers and broadcasters are ruled out by the latter responsibility as means of fulfilling the former responsibility, the duty of a system of governance to ensure that trials unfold fairly is pressingly persistent. Measures like those outlined by the U.S. Supreme Court are therefore morally obligatory whenever someone accused of a high-profile crime is wending his or her way through a judicial proceeding conducted with a jury.

As has been remarked, the imposition of pre-trial restrictions on reportage is at variance with the principle of freedom of expression because the reportage that would be legally prohibited by such restrictions is not constitutive of any communication-independent misconduct. However, that rationale for disallowing those restrictions is not transferable to a context in which a newspaper or broadcaster has maliciously or recklessly published false allegations about someone who has been charged with a serious crime. Allegations of that kind can legitimately be subjected to tort-law sanctions for defamation (a topic that will be tackled presently in this chapter), and they can likewise properly be subjected to punitive sanctions as efforts to undermine the probity of legal proceedings. In other words, such allegations—advanced maliciously or recklessly—belong to the same general category of wrongdoing as perjurious statements. They are constitutive of communication-independent misconduct, for that general category of wrongdoing comprises various communicative actions and various non-communicative actions alike. Baseless allegations about a criminal defendant, advanced maliciously or recklessly, are legitimately punishable because of their wrong-making properties which they have in common with the non-communicative actions that have just been mentioned. They are legitimately punishable not qua acts of communication but qua efforts to prejudice the integrity of legal proceedings.

3.2.4 Defamation

As has just been noted, some statements that can properly be subjected to tort-law sanctions as instances of libel or slander are also classifiable as instances of other types of communication-independent misconduct. What must now be considered is whether defamation itself—libel or slander—is a communication-independent type of misconduct. Unless defamation is such a type of misconduct, the awarding of damages for instances of libel and slander is in contravention of the principle of freedom of expression.

Though Justice Black had successfully represented plaintiffs in lawsuits for libel during his career as a practicing attorney, he later came to the view that such legal proceedings are inconsistent with the First Amendment to the U.S. Constitution. As he declared in his interview with Cahn: "I have no doubt myself that the [First Amendment], as written and adopted, intended that there should be no libel or defamation law in the United States under the United States Government, just absolutely none so far as I am concerned" (Black and Cahn 1962, 557). Black believed that, through the Fourteenth Amendment, the First Amendment disallows any awards of damages for defamation in the state courts as well as in the federal courts:

> I do not hesitate, so far as my own view is concerned, as to what should be and what I hope will sometime be the constitutional doctrine that just as it was not

> intended to authorize damage suits for mere words as distinguished from conduct as far as the Federal Government is concerned, the same rule should apply to the states. (558)

Whereas Black was correct in his opposition to pre-trial restrictions on reporting by newspapers and broadcasters, he erred in thinking that awards of damages in tort law to individuals or private organizations for defamatory assertions made about them by others are always irreconcilable with the principle of freedom of expression (or with the First Amendment). He somewhat muddied the waters in his response to Cahn's question about defamation. Whereas the question was clearly about lawsuits pursued by individuals whose reputations have been sullied through defamatory allegations, Black devoted much of his response to inveighing against the idea of political or seditious libel. As he rightly contended: "Seditious libel, as it has been put into practice throughout the centuries, is nothing in the world except the prosecution of people who are on the wrong side politically; they have said something and their group has lost and they are prosecuted" (Black and Cahn 1962, 557). Black was justified in rejecting the notion that seditious or political libel can properly be criminalized, but the aptness of his stance on that point does not vindicate his broader rejection of the law of defamation.

On the one hand, the law of defamation in the United Kingdom has long been overweeningly restrictive, and it remains so despite some liberalization of the law during the past few decades. Even in the United States, where the law of defamation is much closer to being compliant with the constraints of neutrality that are morally incumbent on every system of governance under the principle of freedom of expression, some of the legal restrictions imposed on speakers and writers and broadcasters are excessive. On the other hand, notwithstanding that certain aspects of the law on this matter in most present-day jurisdictions are inconsistent with the principle of freedom of expression, some types of defamatory assertions can be met with legal sanctions which do not run athwart that principle—for defamatory assertions of those types are constitutive of communication-independent misconduct. Furthermore, not only are some legal curbs on defamatory allegations morally permissible, but in addition some such curbs are morally obligatory. Any system of governance that leaves the reputations of individuals and organizations entirely unprotected against malicious or reckless onslaughts is neglecting some of its moral responsibilities.

As has been seen in §3.2.2 above, Rubenfeld—very much at odds with the general tenor of his theorizing about freedom of expression—contends that defamation is to be grouped together with fraud and perjury as a kind of communication that is not covered by the principle of freedom of expression (or by the First Amendment).[3]

[3] For some slightly different versions of the view that defamatory statements fall outside the ambit of the principle of freedom of expression, see Altman 2004, 5; Frantz 1962, 1450; Meiklejohn 1948, 18; 1961, 259; Rawls 1993, 336; Schauer 1982, 32, 175. See also Bollinger 1986, 179–80, 185–6; Frantz 1962,

He thinks that libelous or slanderous statements can properly be treated as tortious qua acts of false communication. Presumably, he takes such a position because he believes both that some defamatory statements should be legally actionable and that those statements are not constitutive of any communication-independent misconduct. His belief on the former point is correct, but its correctness is due to the incorrectness of his belief on the latter point. Only because some defamatory statements do belong to a category of communication-independent misdeeds, are they legitimately susceptible to the imposition of tort-law sanctions.

To discern how some libelous or slanderous statements are constitutive of communication-independent misconduct that is legitimately prohibitable by a system of governance, we should note one major respect in which the current law of defamation in England is at variance with the principle of freedom of expression. In English law, the tort of libel or slander does not include any element of culpability. An empirical assertion about some person uttered to somebody else is legally defamatory if it is not provably true and is likely to cause serious damage to the reputation of the person about whom it has been made. Under the law of England, a successful litigant does not have to establish that a defamatory allegation was impelled by malice or recklessness or negligence. No showing of culpability is required. Under the moral principle of freedom of expression, by contrast, an element of culpability is indispensable. Even if an accusation is false and is significantly injurious to the reputation of the person about whom it has been made, it is morally exempt from legal penalties unless it has been undertaken maliciously or recklessly or negligently. A system of governance that does not include culpability as an element of the tort of defamation is *pro tanto* transgressing the principle of freedom of expression.

When a false empirical assertion is made to somebody and is very likely to be seriously harmful to the reputation of some other person in the estimation of upright members of his or her community, anyone who is maliciously or recklessly or negligently responsible for communicating that false allegation has engaged in a type of communication-independent misconduct. We should here again recall the discussion of communication-independence in §3.1 of this chapter. In one ordinary sense, as can be inferred from that discussion, a defamatory accusation and its effects are of course not communication-independent. Any significant injury which the accusation causes (or is very likely to cause) to the reputation of its target is brought about through the conveyance of the communicative content of the accusation to its addressees. However, the communication-independence at issue when we are enquiring into the protection conferred by the principle of freedom of expression is not the mundane variety of communication-independence that has just been broached. Instead, the bestowal of protection by that principle upon

1436; Rotunda 2004, 280 n40; Scanlon 1979, 523 n4; Waldron 2012, 146; Wellington 1979, 1115 n49. (Waldron does not ultimately endorse the position which he recounts.)

some mode of expressive activity hinges on whether or not that mode of activity is constitutive of misconduct that is generally perpetrated through non-expressive endeavors as well as through expressive endeavors. When a mode of expressive activity is constitutive of such misconduct, its wrongness is communication-independent in the sense that is decisive under the principle of freedom of expression. Any measure by a system of governance that prohibits or prevents the occurrence of that mode of activity is morally legitimate only if it is directed against the wrong-making properties that are shared by the communicative instances and the non-communicative instances of the misconduct. If such a measure is so directed, its orientation is communication-independent in the decisive sense. Its prohibitory or preventative impact is a communication-independent step taken against a communication-independent type of misconduct.

The key shortcoming in the remarks by Rubenfeld about the legal restrictions on defamation (and fraud and perjury) is that he elides the way in which those restrictions can be communication-independent in the manner that has just been outlined. His obfuscation of that matter is particularly evident in a sentence that has been quoted in §3.2.2 of this chapter: "The laws of libel, fraud, perjury, and so on, all [impose sanctions on] people for speaking falsely on matters of fact" (Rubenfeld 2001, 819). As has already been pointed out, Rubenfeld here omits altogether the factor of culpability. Admittedly, his omission of that factor is more understandable in relation to defamation than in relation to perjury—given that the law of England does not include any kind of culpability as an element of the tort of libel or slander. Still, any legal restrictions on defamation that are consistent with the principle of freedom of expression will be applicable only to utterances that are marked by malice or recklessness or negligence. At any rate, even more important and more bemusing is that Rubenfeld wholly fails to mention the chief purpose of the laws that proscribe defamation as a tort: namely, the purpose of protecting the reputations of individuals and private organizations against baseless incursions. Instead of being legally classified as tortfeasors simply for speaking falsely, people who utter defamatory statements are legally classified as tortfeasors because they have culpably engaged in instances of behavior that are apt to lower unfoundedly the reputations of the individuals or organizations about whom the statements have been made.

In light of the purpose that has just been imputed to laws which permissibly proscribe defamation as a tort, we should now ask whether the prohibitory force of such laws is communication-independent. Having identified the type of misconduct against which those laws are directed, should we conclude that that type of misconduct is communication-independent, or should we conclude instead that it is inherently communicative? Is the culpable and baseless tarnishing of people's reputations something that occurs only through communicative actions (that is, through defamatory assertions), or can it occur equally through non-communicative actions? As is manifest to anyone familiar with the multiplicity of ways in which people's reputations can be besmirched, the answer to these questions is that the general category of misconduct under consideration here is indeed communication-independent. Those reputations can be seriously impaired through sundry non-communicative ruses, as well as through the issuance of defamatory allegations. Consequently, insofar as such allegations are advanced from a culpable outlook, they are constitutive of communication-independent wrongdoing. Laws directed against that kind of wrongdoing—against its communicative instances and non-communicative instances alike—are consistent with the principle of freedom of expression.

One of the most insidious techniques for lowering the stature of a person in the estimation of others is the placement of some embarrassing or incriminating items in areas where they appear to have been stowed or possessed or used by that person. Many applications of that technique are depicted in Shakespeare's plays. For example, after Iago (in *Othello*) obtains a precious handkerchief that had been given by Othello to Desdemona as a seal of Othello's love for her, Iago leaves it in the lodging of Cassio. When Iago arranges to have Othello see Cassio clutching the handkerchief on the following day, he thereby blackens the reputations of Cassio and Desdemona in Othello's jealousy-infected mind. Another example occurs in *Titus Andronicus*, where the evildoer Aaron hides a bag of money amidst the roots of a tree in such a way that the money appears to have been stashed as a reward for two of Titus's sons to assassinate the brother of the Emperor of Rome. Similarly, in *Macbeth*, the bloody daggers with which Macbeth has murdered Duncan are placed by Lady Macbeth beside the sleeping grooms to trick onlookers into thinking that the grooms are the culprits. Numerous other applications of this technique are possible, of course, and have often been wielded by dictatorial regimes or nefarious individuals to discredit their opponents. For instance, inflatable life-size dolls or other sexual aids might be placed in someone's residence or office or car in circumstances where they are likely to be noticed by other people. Much the same can be done with any number of further embarrassing or incriminating items such as narcotics or skimpy lingerie. When this technique is plied deftly, it can be at least as effective in sullying the reputation of somebody as can any defamatory allegations.

Of course, most applications of the methods recounted in the preceding paragraph will be constitutive of communication-independent misconduct in more than one respect. Many of them are aimed at undermining the fairness and integrity of legal proceedings, for example. Still, one respect in which every such method partakes of communication-independent wrongness is that it aims to tarnish unfoundedly the reputation of the person who is its target. It thus belongs to the same general category of communication-independent misconduct to which the utterance of a defamatory accusation belongs. Like the utterance of such an accusation, the placement of incriminating or embarrassing items in a location craftily chosen to discredit another person is an endeavor to inflict reputational damage. That aspect of the harm wrought by such behavior is something for which the imposition of legal sanctions can warrantedly be undertaken, on top of any further legal sanctions that would be warranted for any additional aspects of the harm that has been wrought.

Other non-communicative stratagems designed to besmirch the reputations of people are also possible, of course. Suppose for example that Arthur is a skillful and influential orator who frequently delivers public lectures on the virtue of temperance. An envious rival manages to slip an intoxicant into the cup of tea which Arthur is drinking shortly before one of his major public appearances. As the rival has hoped and expected, the obvious inebriation of Arthur during the lecture is sufficient to disgrace him humiliatingly in the eyes of his audience. Although the rival's behavior is an instance of communication-independent misconduct in some other respects as well, of course, the damage which it maliciously inflicts on the reputation of Arthur is its central objective and is something for which the imposition of legal sanctions can permissibly be undertaken. A comparable example arises in a situation where an extremist who harbors animosity toward a certain corporation has managed to tamper with some of the products of the corporation and has thus undermined the confidence of consumers in those products. Again, although the behavior of the extremist is an instance of communication-independent misconduct in multiple respects, one such respect is the injury to the reputation of the corporation which the behavior maliciously inflicts. That reputational harm is something for which the imposition of legal sanctions can appropriately be undertaken by the prevailing system of governance.

In short, the culpable sullying of the reputation of an individual or organization is a communication-independent type of wrongdoing. That general type of misconduct comprises communicative actions and non-communicative actions alike. Accordingly, laws that protect the reputations of individuals and organizations by proscribing defamation as a tort can be morally legitimate. Such laws can be fully in accordance with the constraints of neutrality that are incumbent on every system of governance under the principle of freedom of expression, since they can be directed against defamatory assertions qua acts of culpably baseless injury to reputations. Of course, to submit that such laws can be fully compatible with the principle of freedom of expression is not per se to contend that the laws which forbid the utterance of defamatory allegations in this or that particular jurisdiction are indeed so compatible. Everything hinges on the purpose(s) that can correctly be ascribed to those laws. If they exist alongside various laws in the jurisdiction that protect individuals and organizations against the culpable infliction of reputational damage through actions that are non-communicative, then the legal prohibition on libel and slander is properly construable as communication-neutral. Though that prohibition focuses specifically on communicative actions, it operates in tandem with the laws that prohibit non-communicative actions which belong to the same general category of wrongdoing. Just as any law that forbids perjury is to be assessed from a synoptic perspective which takes account of laws that forbid non-communicative efforts to undermine the integrity of legal proceedings, so too any law that forbids defamatory allegations is to be assessed from a synoptic viewpoint. If from such a viewpoint we discover that there are laws in the jurisdiction which forbid non-communicative efforts to besmear the reputations of individuals and organizations, we can aptly conclude that those laws and the defamation-proscribing law are all in compliance with the principle of freedom of expression—since together they are directed against a communication-independent mode of misconduct.

By contrast, if the view from a synoptic perspective reveals that in some jurisdiction there are no legal protections against the staining of the reputations of individuals and organizations by non-communicative means, then a law which prohibits libel and slander in that jurisdiction contravenes the requirements of neutrality set forth by the principle of freedom of expression. Given the absence of legal safeguards against reputational damage that is culpably inflicted through non-communicative actions, the prevailing system of governance has singled out the communicative infliction of such damage for special treatment. In so doing, that system of governance has breached the aforementioned requirements of neutrality.

Here as elsewhere, then, the status of any specified legal restriction under the principle of freedom of expression—the compatibility or incompatibility between any such restriction and that principle—cannot be gauged in isolation. Still, the main point of this subsection is that the outlawing of defamation as a tort can indeed be consistent with the principle of freedom of expression. It can partake of all the varieties of neutrality that are required by that principle. Justice Black erred in thinking that there is an inherent inconsistency, and Rubenfeld goes astray in contending that laws which proscribe libel and slander are beyond the scope of the principle of freedom of expression. That absolute moral principle encompasses defamatory allegations as much as any other instances of communication, but it does not disallow the prohibition of them by any law that is directed against them qua acts of communication-independent wrongdoing rather than qua acts of communication. Such a law, in a jurisdiction where other laws address non-communicative instances of that same general type of wrongdoing, is consistent with the realization of the ideal of freedom of expression.

3.2.5 Fraudulent Statements

As has been observed, Rubenfeld declares that fraudulent statements are to be grouped together with perjurious statements and defamatory statements as modes of communication that fall outside the ambit of the principle of freedom of expression. He errs in contending as much, and he also stumbles by suggesting that fraudulent cajolery is legally restricted because of its falsity. Fraudulent assertions are indeed false or highly misleading, but not all false or highly misleading assertions are fraudulent. Even when the crucial ingredient of deceitfulness is added to falsity, those two properties are not jointly sufficient for the status of an assertion as an instance of fraud. Not all lies are correctly classifiable as fraudulent. What is further needed is that a deliberately false (or highly misleading) assertion be intended to bring about a dishonest benefit for the speaker or for someone favored by the speaker, or that it be intended to inflict a dishonest detriment on somebody else. A mendacious declaration is fraudulent only when it is aimed at bringing about such a benefit or at inflicting such a detriment. As an instance of fraud, a declaration so aimed can be subjected to legal sanctions in full consistency with the principle of freedom of expression.

Once we take into account all the properties of an utterance that are individually necessary and jointly sufficient for its fraudulence, we should readily fathom why the proscription of fraud by a system of governance can be entirely compatible with the principle of freedom of expression. Any proper legal prohibition on the wielding of fraudulent appeals and assertions is directed against them not qua acts of communication but instead qua instances of communication-independent misconduct. Those appeals or assertions are constitutive of such misconduct because their wrong-making properties are characteristic not only of communicative instances of fraud but also of all non-communicative instances. Precisely because fraudulent utterances have those properties in common with all the non-communicative instances of fraud, the outlawing of them—focused on those wrong-making properties—can be communication-neutral and can thus tally with the realization of the ideal of freedom of expression.

In the United Kingdom, the nature of fraud as a communication-independent type of misconduct is evident from the principal statute on the topic: the 2006 Fraud Act. That statute delineates four main categories of fraud along with a couple of ancillary categories. One of the main categories is fraudulent assertions ("fraud by false representation," which can be implicit as well as explicit), but the other three chief categories are the fraudulent non-disclosure of information, the fraudulent abuse of some position or office, and the dishonest obtention of non-complimentary services without paying for them. The two ancillary offenses specified in the statute are the possession of materials for use in frauds and the creating or supplying of materials for use in frauds. What unites these sundry kinds of behavior—the non-communicative and the communicative alike—is that each of them consists in acting dishonestly with the aim of benefiting oneself or some favored other(s) or with the aim of harming some disfavored other(s). Because that wrong-making feature of each of those kinds of behavior is communication-independent, a focus on it as the basis for legally prohibiting fraudulent misrepresentations (as well as other forms of fraudulent conduct) is unproblematically in keeping with the principle of freedom of expression.

Thus, on the one hand, contrary to what Rubenfeld has presumed, fraudulent assertions are indeed within the purview of the principle of freedom of expression.

Such assertions are like any other communications in this respect, and are therefore morally shielded under that principle against being prohibited or prevented by any system of governance in a manner that is not communication-neutral. On the other hand, the outlawing of fraudulent assertions (along with other modes of fraud) on the ground specified in the preceding paragraph is a communication-neutral measure. When such assertions are legally banned on that ground, the law that imposes the ban is directed against them not qua acts of expression but instead qua acts of communication-independent wrongdoing. It treats them in the same interdictory fashion in which it treats non-communicative modes of behavior that belong to the same general category of wrongdoing. The moral permissibility of such a law is not to be explained by the notion that fraudulent misrepresentations somehow reside beyond the scope of the absolute moral principle of freedom of expression; rather, it stems from the fact that the law in question does not transgress the constraints of neutrality which are established by that principle.

3.2.6 Advertising of Illegalities

Let us assume in this subsection that some morally noxious activity—such as an enterprise which hires out children as prostitutes or which sells migrants as slave-laborers—is properly subject to being forbidden or prevented by any system of governance. Let us assume further that the specified activity is indeed forbidden by law in some particular jurisdiction. Can advertisements that pertain to the products or services on offer through the illegal activity also properly be forbidden by law there? Are such advertisements morally protected by the principle of freedom of expression?

Though Rubenfeld comments only very briefly on the advertising of illegalities (2001, 830), his grasp of the matter is solid. He recognizes that advertisements of illegal products and services are indeed covered by the principle of freedom of expression, and he also recognizes that they are not protected by that principle against the legal prohibitions that are likely to be imposed on them. Such advertisements are covered by the principle of freedom of expression in that they cannot ever legitimately be proscribed or prevented by a system of governance qua instances of communication. In that very respect, advertisements of illegal products and services are on a par with political orations and with any other types of expression. Yet, notwithstanding that such advertisements are covered by the principle of freedom of expression in the manner just indicated, any typical legal restriction that will be imposed on them is countenanced by that principle—since any such typical restriction will be directed against the advertisements not qua instances of communication but instead qua instances of participation in serious criminality.

As has been maintained in Chapter 2, orations that amount to incitement can permissibly be outlawed as instances of participation in major wrongdoing. Such orations are subsumed into the major wrongdoing as some of the initial stages thereof. They are thus morally unprotected against laws that prohibit them as elements of such wrongdoing (though of course they remain morally protected against laws that would prohibit them as acts of communication). Much the same is true, *mutatis mutandis*, in connection with advertisements of illegal products and services. For example, when somebody advertises the availability of children as prostitutes for the gratification of paedophiles, he or she is deliberately bringing about—or is seeking to bring about—the imminent occurrence of heinous crimes. Any advertisement of that kind is one of the initial stages in the occurrence of those crimes, and as such it can legitimately be subjected to sanctions by the prevailing system of governance. Someone who undergoes those appropriate sanctions is punished not for expressing odious ideas but instead for participating directly in the perpetration of wicked abuse.

By contrast, if someone were to publish a newspaper article calling for the legalization of child prostitution and paedophilia (while rhapsodizing about the pleasures that could be derived from those activities), or if someone were to distribute copies of a leaflet with such a message, there would be no comparable basis for subjecting him or her to any legal sanctions. Though the ideas articulated in the article or leaflet might be just as reprehensible as the messages expressed in the forbidden advertisements, the propagation of those ideas through the article or leaflet does not constitute any direct participation in some communication-independent misconduct. As an instance of advocacy, the dissemination of those ideas is not subsumed into any acts of paedophilia or child prostitution as some of the initial stages thereof. Any causal connections between the advocacy and such acts are diffuse and remote, rather than highly focused and direct. In precisely that regard, the distribution of the article or leaflet differs crucially from the placing of an advertisement. Whereas an advertisement that notifies potential customers about the availability of slaves or child prostitutes is intended to initiate transactions that ensue directly from the notification, there is no such proximity between the publication of the aforementioned article or leaflet and any nefarious misdeeds that might ultimately be inspired by it. Consequently, the publication of the article or leaflet is not correctly classifiable as one of the initial stages in the perpetration of any of those misdeeds.

An interesting corollary of the discussion in this subsection is that some current legal restrictions on advertisements in the United States and in many other countries are at odds with the principle of freedom of expression. Throughout, this brief discussion has concentrated on the advertising of products and services which are legitimately subject to being prohibited by law and which are in fact so prohibited. Because advertisements of such products and services are the initial stages in transactions that can justly be forbidden on communication-independent grounds, the advertisements themselves can justly be forbidden on such grounds. By contrast, if the products or services to which some advertisements pertain are not forbidden by a system of governance—and especially if the products or services are not morally susceptible to being so forbidden—then any legal bans on those advertisements are inconsistent with the principle of freedom of expression. When a system of governance outlaws the advertisements even though it has not outlawed the products and services, it is directing its prohibitory powers against a type of communicative activity qua communicative activity. Although those advertisements constitute the initial stages of transactions involving the products and services which they commend, the transactions are not legally barred; ergo, the fact that the advertisements constitute those initial stages is not invocable as a basis for legally prohibiting them. Given that there is no other communication-independent basis for legally forbidding the advertisements, any legal bans on them are neither communication-neutral nor content-neutral. Such bans thus blatantly contravene the principle of freedom of expression.

Since 1971 (when a federal statute enacted in 1970 came into effect), the advertising of cigarettes on television and radio has been legally forbidden in the United States. During subsequent decades in that country, some further legal restrictions on the advertising of cigarettes have been imposed by the federal government and by most of the state legislatures. Throughout that period, however, the sale of cigarettes to adults and the smoking of cigarettes by adults have remained legally permissible activities. Though smoking in certain enclosed areas (especially in the presence of other people such as children) has been legally restricted in some states, there has never been any general legal prohibition on the purchase and use of cigarettes by adults. Accordingly, notwithstanding that advertisements which extol cigarettes are some of the initial stages of the transactions whereby such products are sold and bought, that feature of the advertisements is not invocable as a basis for the imposition of legal bans on them. Given that there is no other communication-independent basis for the imposition of those bans, the American policy on this matter for the past five decades has been in transgression of the principle of freedom of expression.

During those five decades, there have been sharp declines in the proportion of Americans who smoke. Along with health warnings and excise taxes, the legal curbs on advertisements of cigarettes have been chiefly responsible for those salutary declines. Nonetheless, immensely welcome though the decrease in the incidence of smoking is—particularly welcome for anyone like me with a visceral aversion to the stench of cigarettes—the legal restrictions on the advertising of tobacco that have helped to bring about the decrease are morally wrong as violations of the principle of freedom of expression. Notwithstanding that the banned advertisements would be the initial stages of transactions through which cigarettes are sold to adults, those transactions are legally permissible and should be legally permissible; hence, the fact that the advertisements would initiate those transactions is not a proper ground for any legal prohibitions. Nor is there any other communication-independent ground for such prohibitions. However effective the legal restrictions on advertisements of cigarettes may have been in helping to reduce the popularity of smoking, they have been directed against the advertisements qua acts of communication. Those restrictions have not been directed against the advertisements qua instances of communication-independent wrongdoing, since the advertisements are not constitutive of any such wrongdoing. Instead, the purpose of the legal bans is to avert the communicative effects—the conveyance of messages about the glamor and pleasurability of smoking—that would have been produced by the advertisements. Countering those effects (through measures such as health warnings) is a perfectly legitimate role for a system of governance, but preventing the effects by clamping legal curbs on the advertisements is thoroughly at variance with the principle of freedom of expression.

Even though the First Amendment to the U.S. Constitution is often convergent with the moral principle of freedom of expression, there are some important divergences. One respect in which the constitutional provision diverges from the moral principle is that it bestows a lower level of protection on commercial expression than on political expression. As has been recounted in §2.1.3 of Chapter 2, jurists and legal scholars who expound the First Amendment have commonly drawn upon a distinction between low-value speech and high-value speech. Whereas political discourse (even hateful political discourse) is almost always assigned to the latter category, commercial modes of expression—most notably commercial advertisements—are generally assigned to the low-value category or to some intermediate status. Excluded from the high-value tier, commercial advertisements are legally susceptible to some prohibitions and other measures that would be unconstitutional if brought to bear by the American government on political disputation (Bhagwat 2019, 94; Gerber 2004, 31–5; Post 2019, 109; Rotunda 2004, 274–88). Presumably for that reason, the legal curbs on the advertising of cigarettes in the United States have not been invalidated as unconstitutional during the five decades in which they have emerged and increased.

As has been emphasized in §2.1.3, the distinction between low-value speech and high-value speech cannot have any bearing on the applicability and implications of the principle of freedom of expression. With such a bearing, that distinction would ride roughshod over the requirements of subject-neutrality and viewpoint-neutrality that are integral to the ideal of freedom of expression. On this very point, then, the principle of freedom of expression is markedly different from the First Amendment. In contrast with that constitutional provision as it has been construed by the American courts, the principle of freedom of expression discountenances any legal restrictions like those that have been imposed on the advertising of cigarettes in the United States. Such restrictions are neither subject-neutral nor viewpoint-neutral, and the fact that they pertain to a low-value class of communications is inconsequential—since the principle of freedom of expression applies to low-value communications and high-value communications alike. Repellent though cigarettes are, the legal bans on advertisements for them in the

United States are deviations from the governmental self-restraint that is constitutive of freedom of expression.

3.2.7 Disclosure of Military or Governmental Secrets

As various commentators on the First Amendment have long recognized (Meiklejohn 1948, 18; Schauer 1982, 102), the disclosure of vital military or governmental secrets to the agents of a hostile nation or to the members of a terrorist network can legitimately be prohibited and prevented by a liberal-democratic system of governance. Under most circumstances, somebody who has carried out such a disclosure can properly be subjected to sanctions. Contrary to what Schauer contends (1982, 102-3), the permissibility of the imposition of sanctions in such cases is not due to the inapplicability of the principle of freedom of expression thereto. That absolute moral principle is applicable to the acts of communication through which people treasonously impart vital secrets to the functionaries of enemy nations, just as it is applicable to all other acts of communication. Nonetheless, as has been argued repeatedly in this book, the applicability of that principle to every type and instance of communication does not morally debar the clamping of legal restrictions on some types or instances of communication. Provided that a communicative activity has been outlawed qua type or instance of communication-independent misconduct rather than qua type or instance of communication, and provided that the implementation of the legal prohibition is likewise directed against the activity qua type or instance of communication-independent misconduct, the requirements laid down by the principle of freedom of expression have been satisfied.

Now, as is evident, an act of communication through which someone betrays vital military or governmental secrets to the operatives of a foreign adversary is an instance of communication-independent misconduct that can properly be forbidden by law in a liberal-democratic system of governance. Such a misdeed can suitably be classified as an act of treason or of espionage or of endangering national security, for example. In nearly all credible contexts, the statutes or other laws that prohibit such a misdeed will be directed against its communication-independent wrongness rather than against its communicative character. Sanctions prescribed by those laws will be levied not because the misdeed in question is an act of communication but because it is an act of treason or of espionage or of endangering national security. Hence, in nearly all credible contexts, the imposition of those sanctions is impeccably in keeping with the constraints that are incumbent on every system of governance under the principle of freedom of expression. Those sanctions have been levied in response to an act of communication, but only because that act is constitutive of serious misconduct that can be either communicative or non-communicative. (Note that the moral permissibility of the imposition of the sanctions by a liberal-democratic system of governance is unaffected by the motives that have impelled a person to furnish top-secret information to a foreign foe. Perhaps the traitor has been lured by the prospect of pecuniary gain, or perhaps she has instead acted on the basis of ideological convictions, or maybe she as a victim of blackmail has betrayed the secrets in order to avert some embarrassing disclosures about her own private life. Whatever the motives that have led to her perfidy, the subjection of her to legal sanctions is consistent with the principle of freedom of expression.)

3.2.7.1 Newspapers and Broadcasters

Some more complicated issues arise when disclosures of vital military or governmental secrets are undertaken not surreptitiously by spies or renegades but instead publicly by parties such as newspapers and broadcasters or whistleblowers (Edgar and Schmidt 1973; Henkin 1971; Kalven 1971, 25–36; Pozen 2013; Silverman 2003, 1107–13; Stone 2007a; 2007b; Strauss 2019; Weiss 2004, 1299–303). Let us here ponder briefly first the situation of newspapers and broadcasters and then the situation of whistleblowers. Neither through injunctions prior to publication nor through sanctions afterward, can a system of governance ever permissibly seek to suppress reportage that does not amount to communication-independent misconduct such as the deliberate or reckless endangerment of national security. The appropriate standard here is largely akin to the standard for the prohibitability of orations as incitement. That is, any report on governmental matters by a newspaper or broadcaster is morally protected under the principle of freedom of expression unless it deliberately or recklessly places the security of a society or the basic well-being of individuals in imminent and grave peril. In practice, as Geoffrey Stone has observed (2007b, 95), such a standard will confer moral protection on virtually all disclosures of information by journalists. The fact that a disclosure is highly embarrassing for a government, or the fact that it sets back the efforts of governmental officials to combat terrorism or other societal afflictions, is per se insufficient to overcome the moral shield erected by such a standard. Were a system of governance to impose sanctions on a newspaper or broadcaster in such circumstances, it would be penalizing a disclosure qua instance of communication rather than qua instance of communication-independent misconduct.

A few examples, tersely presented, will help to clarify the implications of this discussion.[4] Whereas each of the first two of these examples delineates a context in which some awkward reportage is morally shielded by the principle of freedom of expression against any legal restrictions, the third example outlines a context in which that principle allows the imposition of such restrictions.

[4] Versions of the first two of these examples appear in Stone 2007b, 94, 95. A version of the third example appears in Silverman 2003, 1108.

First, suppose that a newspaper or broadcaster reveals that the arrangements for preventing intrusions at several nuclear-power plants in some region of a country are seriously inadequate. Although the divulgence of that information will doubtless be highly embarrassing for any governmental agency whose responsibilities include the provision of such arrangements, and although the divulgence of the information might embolden some terrorists or other criminals to try ever more persistently to infiltrate the plants where the vulnerabilities have been exposed, it has not placed the security of the relevant society or the basic well-being of any individuals in imminent and grave peril. In any typical circumstances, moreover, the outlook most plausibly ascribable to the journalists at the newspaper or broadcaster is not that of malice or recklessness; rather, the outlook most plausibly imputable to them is an intention to stimulate improvements in the safeguards around the nuclear installations (as well as to inform the public of the current weaknesses in those safeguards). Consequently, despite the disconcertingness of the report, it does not constitute any communication-independent misconduct. In any typical circumstances, no system of governance can legitimately prevent a newspaper or broadcaster from publishing such a report, nor can any sanctions permissibly be imposed on the newspaper or broadcaster in the aftermath of the publication.

Second, suppose that a newspaper or broadcaster in the United States discloses that American intelligence officials have managed to penetrate the methods of encryption used by a major international terrorist network such as al-Qaeda. As a result of the dissemination of this report, the terrorists adopt new methods of encryption in order to restore the clandestinity of their transmissions. Quite plainly, the revelation by the newspaper or broadcaster has set back the endeavors of the American intelligence services to keep the United States safe from the machinations of terrorists. Furthermore, unlike the report about the need for greater precautions at the nuclear-power plants—a report likely to be a fillip that will prod governmental officials to remedy shortcomings in their operations—this disclosure of the success of the intelligence agents in deciphering the transmissions of the terrorists is not clearly apt to produce salutary effects beyond the dispensation of interesting information to members of the public. Given the considerable drawbacks involved in such a disclosure and the limitedness of any benefits that will predictably ensue from it, the newspaper or broadcaster has acted irresponsibly by going ahead with a report on the matter. Some editors there have exercised poor judgment. However, the key question is not whether that report should have been withheld by the editors. Rather, the decisive question is whether the American government will be acting in compliance with the principle of freedom of expression if it seeks to impose sanctions on the newspaper or broadcaster for the ill-judged disclosure. The answer to that latter question is negative. It is not the case that the publication of the report about the success of the Americans in penetrating the code of the terrorist network has placed the security of the United States or the basic well-being of individuals in imminent and grave peril. Accordingly, it is not the case that the publication of the report is constitutive of any communication-independent misconduct. Hence, under the principle of freedom of expression, officials in the American system of governance are morally obligated to refrain from preventing or legally penalizing the occurrence of that publication. Although the editors of the newspaper or broadcaster have acted unwisely in disseminating the news about the decryption of the terrorists' transmissions, the principle of freedom of expression bestows protection on any dismayingly inexpedient acts of communication that are not constitutive of communication-independent wrongdoing.

Third, suppose that a newspaper or broadcaster in the United States releases a report which divulges the identities of some Americans who are furtively working as spies in a hostile foreign nation ruled by a dictatorship (such as Iran or North Korea). Even if the editors responsible for the propagation of the report have not acted with malice, they have acted with extravagant recklessness. Because the report has exposed the identities of the Americans who are conducting undercover operations in the foreign country, it has placed them in grave and imminent peril. They will very likely be imprisoned and tortured and executed. That grievous danger posed to the spies by the unmasking of them must have been apparent to any editors who are at least minimally competent and careful. Thus, the report that has compromised the spies should be met with sanctions for its malicious or reckless endangerment of their lives and basic well-being. Although that report is of course communicative in character, it is constitutive of communication-independent misconduct—and any proper sanctions triggered by its publication will be directed against its communication-independent wrongness rather than against its communicative character. Such sanctions are therefore fully consistent with the principle of freedom of expression.

3.2.7.2 Whistleblowers

Disclosures of governmental or military secrets can also occur at the hands of public employees or contractors who seek to draw the attention of their fellow citizens to certain aspects of a government's functioning. Any such disclosures that are broadly comparable to the foolhardy report discussed in the last paragraph above—that is, any such disclosures that intentionally or recklessly place the security of a society or the basic well-being of individuals in grave and imminent peril—are constitutive of very serious communication-independent wrongdoing and are thus properly punishable by a system of governance without any encroachment on the principle of freedom of expression. Moreover, even when some revelations of governmental or military secrets would be protected by the principle of freedom of expression if they were carried out by newspapers or broadcasters, they can be unprotected by that principle if they are carried out by public employees or contractors. In other words, some disclosures that would not be constitutive of communication-independent wrongdoing if they were undertaken by journalists are constitutive of such wrongdoing when undertaken by public employees or contractors.

The reason for the discrepancy just mentioned is that public employees and contractors are very often under commitments to refrain from divulging various aspects of the governmental operations with which they are involved. Though whistleblowing that exposes the occurrence of serious criminality is always morally permissible and should always be legally permissible, other types of revelations can legitimately be restricted under the terms of contracts or similar agreements. When a governmental employee engages in one of those revelations after having entered into a nondisclosure commitment, his or her indiscretion—which breaches that commitment—is an instance of communication-independent misconduct. Under the principle of freedom of expression, the subjection of the employee to sanctions for that indiscretion can be entirely proper.

In this connection, disclosures akin to the first two examples recounted in §3.2.7.1 above will often be unprotected by the principle of freedom of expression when such disclosures are perpetrated by governmental employees. Suppose that a certain governmental agency has been entrusted with the task of keeping nuclear-power plants safe from terrorists and other intruders, and suppose that everyone who works for the agency has entered into a contractual commitment to refrain from discussing its operations with any outsiders. If an employee of the agency unauthorizedly releases information about the shortcomings in its endeavors, that employee has breached the terms of her contract. Though the breach of contract has of course occurred through an instance of communicative conduct, its moral and legal wrongness as a breach of contract is communication-independent. Deviations from the binding terms of contracts can ensue from non-communicative actions as well as from communicative actions; everything depends on the specifics of the terms. In any typical regime of private law, the availability of a remedy for a contractual breach will not hinge at all on the question whether the conduct constitutive of the breach is communicative or non-communicative. Consequently, within any such regime of private law, the imposition of sanctions in response to the unauthorized disclosure envisaged in this paragraph will be countenanced by the principle of freedom of expression.

In most modern-day systems of governance, there are also laws under which some unauthorized disclosures by employees in various governmental agencies can trigger the imposition of criminal sanctions. Those employees, especially in agencies that deal with matters directly affecting the safety of the public, are typically under legal obligations to avoid actions that are likely to impair seriously the functioning of their departments. Let us recall here the second example adumbrated in §3.2.7.1. If the intelligence services in some Western liberal democracy have succeeded in decrypting the transmissions of an international terrorist network,[5] and if that success has been revealed by an employee of those services, the

[5] I have declined here to identify the country concerned, because I want to prescind from the specifics of the statutory scheme in any particular liberal democracy. For a discussion of some of the

employee has almost certainly breached the terms of his contract—or the terms of an agreement ancillary to his contract—and he has almost certainly also contravened the requirements laid down by some general law(s) of the kind just mentioned. That is, we can safely assume that he has been under a general legal duty not to adopt courses of conduct that are likely to impair seriously the functioning of the governmental agency that employs him. Given as much, he has patently breached that duty through his unauthorized disclosure. Accordingly, he has rendered himself liable not only to dismissal or other disciplinary measures at the hands of his employer, but also to the sanctions that will be triggered by his having transgressed the general legal obligation which he has borne.

A general law that imposes such an obligation on governmental employees is consistent with the principle of freedom of expression, because the type of misconduct targeted by that law—the performance of actions by those employees that are likely to impair seriously the functioning of their governmental agencies—is communication-independent. Actions of the proscribed type can be either communicative or non-communicative. Indeed, even if a law imposes more specifically an obligation on governmental employees to refrain from unauthorized disclosures of information that are likely to impair seriously the functioning of the departments in which the employees work, it can be consistent with the principle of freedom of expression. Although a law of this latter kind is plainly not communication-neutral in isolation, it can be an element of a broader statutory scheme of regulation which proscribes *all* courses of conduct by governmental employees that are likely to impair seriously the functioning of their departments. Overall, a statutory scheme along those lines is in keeping with the constraints of neutrality that are imposed by the principle of freedom of expression, even though the law that prohibits unauthorized disclosures would on its own be at variance with those constraints. As has already been contended in my discussions of perjury and defamation, one's freedom-of-expression assessment of any law should be reached from a synoptic perspective which takes account of that law's place in an overarching array of legal norms. Such a perspective takes priority over a perspective that evaluates each law discretely, since the question always to be answered is whether a system of governance is operating in compliance with the principle of freedom of expression. That question can be answered affirmatively about a system of governance that enacts a law which prohibits public employees from engaging in unauthorized disclosures of information that are likely to damage seriously the functioning of their agencies—provided that the law in question is a component of a general regulatory framework that forbids public employees to engage in *any* actions that are likely to damage seriously the functioning of their agencies. As a

relevant statutes in the United States, see Stone 2007a, 186–97.

component of such a framework, the specified law is compatible with the principle of freedom of expression.

3.2.8 True Threats

Chapters 5 and 6 will include some ruminations on fighting words and true threats—two types of communications which are morally unprotected by the principle of freedom of expression and which are legally unprotected (in the United States) by the First Amendment to the American Constitution. However, whereas those chapters will devote quite a bit of attention to the category of fighting words, they will touch only cursorily on the category of true threats. Hence, although the present chapter will not include a separate discussion of fighting words, we should briefly ponder here whether the issuance of threats can be legally restricted by a system of governance in compliance with the principle of freedom of expression.

Like the phrase "fighting words," the phrase "true threats" derives from a decision of the U.S. Supreme Court.[6] In the 1969 case of *Watts v United States*, the Court (in a laconic *per curiam* judgment) held that the First Amendment leaves room for legal curbs on the issuance of true threats. Notwithstanding that the Court omitted to specify what constitutes a true threat, the judgment makes clear that the trueness of a threat consists in its genuineness or credibility—where genuineness or credibility is contrasted with evident idleness or playfulness.

At any rate, my focus here is on the principle of freedom of expression rather than on the First Amendment. Whatever might count as a true threat under that American constitutional provision, an utterance that can be classified as a true threat under the universal moral principle of freedom of expression must be construable by any reasonable addressee as a sincere indication that the addressor will imminently launch a serious attack on the body or property or liberty or reputation of the addressee or of somebody else. Of course a minatory indication of that kind very often carries a condition which, if fulfilled, will actually or purportedly avert the threatened attack. That attached condition can be either explicit or implicit. Suppose that a gun-brandishing hoodlum has confronted a mother walking with her young boy and has uttered menacingly: "If you don't hand over your wallet, I'll shoot both you and your son!" He then adds: "If you do hand over your wallet, I'll let you and your son escape unharmed." Whereas the first of these utterances is a true threat, the second is a statement of an explicit condition for averting the

[6] For some helpful reflections on the "true threats" doctrine, see Crane 2006; Fuller 2016; Gelber 2012a, 205 n46; Gey 2000; Price 2018, 823–4; Rothman 2001; Schauer 2003; Stanner 2006; Strossen 2018, 60–2; Weinstein 2019, 62–3; Weiss 2004. For some broader reflections on threats and freedom of expression, see Baker 1989, 60–5; Greenawalt 1989, 90–109.

threatened attack. Not all true threats are conditional either explicitly or implicitly, but most are.

As has already been stated, true threats are not morally protected by the principle of freedom of expression. A system of governance can permissibly impose sanctions on somebody for issuing such a threat. Schauer, in line with his trichotomous understanding of the First Amendment's coverage and protection, repeatedly asserts that the reason why true threats can legitimately be prohibited by law is that they fall outside the scope of the principle of freedom of expression (1982, 13, 89, 102). Such a position is misconceived, here as elsewhere. True threats are covered by the principle of freedom of expression, in that they cannot ever permissibly be forbidden by law qua acts of communication. However, although they are within the scope of that principle, they are not protected by it against laws that prohibit true threats qua acts of communication-independent wrongdoing.

True threats are very frequently components of serious communication-independent crimes such as robbery. In the example of the hoodlum in the penultimate paragraph above, his utterance of a true threat is partly constitutive of the crime of armed robbery. If the mother and her son manage to flee before the hoodlum has taken her wallet, the crime of armed robbery will not have occurred, but the crime of attempting to commit an armed robbery will have occurred; given the circumstances, the utterance of the true threat itself amounts to such an attempt.[7] Thus, either the issuance of the threat by the malefactor is an element of the crime of armed robbery, or else it stands on its own as the crime of attempting to commit an armed robbery. In either case, the issuance of the threat is constitutive of communication-independent misconduct that can aptly be prohibited by a system of governance in full conformity with the principle of freedom of expression.

Myriad other true threats, likewise, are partly constitutive of crimes such as robbery or are fully constitutive of attempts to commit crimes such as robbery. However, the category of true threats extends also to utterances that are voiced on the basis of sheer anger or hatred without ulterior motives. If Shawn snarls a threat at Cynthia wherein he credibly announces his intention to pummel and strangle her, and if he moves toward her in accordance with his announced intention, he has committed the crime of assault whether or not he reaches her and proceeds to treat her as he has threatened. If he does indeed pummel and throttle her, of course, he will have committed some further crimes that are much more serious than assault. However, even if Shawn does not manage to perpetrate those additional crimes—perhaps because Cynthia escapes, or perhaps because a third party intervenes, or perhaps because Cynthia pulls out a gun—his issuance of a true threat which he seeks to implement is constitutive of communication-independent wrongdoing. As an assault, it consists in an intentional and wrongful course of conduct that is

[7] In some jurisdictions the malefactor's unsuccessful effort would be classifiable as an instance of extortion, whereas in most jurisdictions it would be classifiable as an attempt to commit extortion.

highly likely to elicit a reasonable fear of imminent bodily harm on the part of any person toward whom it is directed. Even if Shawn does not succeed in thrashing and strangling Cynthia, and even if he is not endeavoring to achieve other objectives such as robbing her of her wallet, his articulation of a true threat constitutes an assault. As such, his course of conduct can properly be subjected to legal sanctions. (Note that true threats advanced on the basis of sheer anger or hatred, without ulterior objectives such as robbery, are especially common in contexts of bigotry such as racism or misogyny. Precisely for that reason, true threats of this kind will surface again in Chapters 5 and 6—which are focused on such contexts of bigotry.)

Like true threats as components of robberies or other crimes, true threats as freestanding instances of assault can legitimately be prohibited and punished by any system of governance. The moral permissibility of legal restrictions on them is due to the fact that such threats are constitutive of communication-independent wrongdoing. A law directed against them qua instances of such wrongdoing is fully consistent with the principle of freedom of expression. Assault as a general type of misconduct is communication-independent because it can be instantiated by non-communicative actions as well as by communicative actions. It can of course be instantiated by true threats, which are communicative; but it can likewise be instantiated by non-communicative actions such as pointing a gun at somebody, or moving toward somebody in a minatory fashion, or pulling one's arm back with a clenched fist in preparation for throwing a punch. On the one hand, each of the actions just mentioned can itself in some contexts be a way of communicating a true threat. On the other hand, each such action in many a context is a non-communicative initial stage of an endeavor to inflict serious harm on somebody else. In the latter contexts where the specified actions are non-communicative, as much as in the former contexts where they are communicative, they can be constitutive of assaults. Hence, when a system of governance forbids by law the perpetration of assaults—whether they occur through true threats or through non-communicative menacing behavior—it is operating in compliance with the principle of freedom of expression.

3.2.9 Negligent Misstatements

During the past several decades in England, plaintiffs have more and more often succeeded in their lawsuits against parties who have negligently and damagingly misled the plaintiffs through inaccurate statements about various matters.[8] (Some

[8] For a perceptive account of some of the relevant cases, see McBride and Bagshaw 2012, 172–90. For some interesting reflections on the bearings of negligent misstatements under the law of the First Amendment in the United States, see Weingarten 1984. See also Ballam 1989, 784–9; Lane 1988; Schauer 1992, 1346 n78; Spellman 1988.

lawyers and courts distinguish between "negligent misrepresentations" and "negligent misstatements." However, if such a distinction is tenable at all, it is understood in more than one way by the people who invoke it. Hence, I will use the phrases "negligent misstatement" and "negligent misrepresentation" interchangeably in this subsection.) In any typical situation that leads to such a lawsuit, the defendant has provided advice or assurances or information to the plaintiff in a context in which the defendant has explicitly or implicitly assumed responsibility for the veracity of the communicated content. Relying on the advice or assurances or information, the plaintiff has gone ahead with some transaction or project or activity and has been detrimentally affected when the content of the defendant's communication turns out to be unfounded. Had the defendant exercised reasonable care when interacting with the plaintiff, the baseless advice or assurances or information would not have been furnished and would have been supplanted by an accurate assessment of the matter(s) on which the defendant was pronouncing.

In contrast with a situation of fraud, a situation of this kind does not involve malice and an intention to swindle. It involves only negligence. Still, just as the falsity of fraudulent statements is not per se sufficient to render morally permissible the proscribing of them by law, so too the falsity of negligent misrepresentations is not per se sufficient to render morally permissible their actionability in tort-law proceedings. Without the element of negligence (or some other mode of culpability), the legal actionability of the misrepresentations would be morally impermissible.

Also crucial for the moral permissibility of any legal prohibition on such a misrepresentation is that there be a relationship of proximity between the plaintiff and the defendant—and between the defendant's negligently inaccurate communication and the plaintiff's incurring of some detriment. In the typical situation that has been recounted above, the proximity is given by the fact that the plaintiff has consulted the defendant who in some capacity has explicitly or implicitly accepted responsibility for the accuracy of the advice or assurances or information supplied to the plaintiff. In an atypical case, the requisite proximity between the plaintiff and the defendant (and between the defendant's negligence and the plaintiff's incurring of harm) is attributable to some other features of the situation. For example, in the prominent 1994 case of *Spring v Guardian Assurance*, the House of Lords held that the plaintiff could recover an award of damages for the negligence of a former employer whose managers had submitted a baselessly disparaging letter of reference about the plaintiff to a prospective employer. Because the letter of reference had been submitted at the request of the prospective employer rather than at the request of the plaintiff, there was no direct interaction between the plaintiff and the former employer that led to the production and transmission of the letter. Nonetheless, because the plaintiff was a former employee of the defendant, and because the request for a letter of reference was specifically about the plaintiff, the requirement of proximity between the parties to the proceeding was satisfied.

Also clearly satisfied was the requirement of proximity between the defendant's negligence and the plaintiff's incurring of harm, as the strongly derogatory content of the letter of reference thwarted the plaintiff's efforts to find a new position of employment.

Although a relationship of proximity between a plaintiff and a defendant and between the defendant's negligence and the plaintiff's detriment is central to any successful lawsuit for negligence in the jurisdiction of England, it is specifically vital for any lawsuit arising from a negligent misstatement. As we have seen in Chapter 2 with regard to the distinction between advocacy and incitement, and as we shall see further in Chapters 5 and 6 with regard to pornography and fighting words and hatefully bigoted declamations, a relationship of proximity between somebody's culpable course of communicative conduct and the occurrence of harm to somebody else is essential if the proscribing of that course of communicative conduct by law is to be in compliance with the principle of freedom of expression. In a case involving a negligent misstatement, the element of proximity is essential because it assimilates such a case to multifarious other types of cases in the law of negligence. Given the presence of that element—that is, given the proximity between the parties and the proximity between one party's negligence and the other party's incurring of some detriment—a negligent misstatement that is deemed by a court to be tortious is thereby treated on a par with non-communicative instances of negligent conduct. The general law that forbids such a misstatement is directed against it qua act of negligence rather than qua act of communication. In the sense that is decisive under the principle of freedom of expression, the wrong constituted by such a misstatement is communication-independent. Hence, the outlawing of such a misstatement is compatible with that moral principle.

By contrast, when there is no sufficient proximity between the parties or between one party's negligence and the other party's injury, the awarding of damages for a negligent misrepresentation would be neither in keeping with the requirements of the English law of negligence nor in keeping with the moral principle of freedom of expression. Suppose for example that a meteorological institute has set up a Web site on which it regularly posts an array of detailed seven-day forecasts of the weather in towns and cities throughout the United Kingdom. As a result of negligent miscalculations by technicians at the institute, the forecasts for some particular period are markedly inaccurate. Perhaps, for instance, the forecasts altogether overlook the arrival of a major storm on some day. Relying on the veracity of the forecasts, numerous people from diverse walks of life schedule activities that are ruined or precluded by the occurrence of the storm. Now, although there has been negligence on the part of some employees of the institute, and although many people have suffered losses as a result of being misled by the negligently inaccurate forecasts, the requisite element of proximity between the parties is missing. There has been no direct contact between the meteorological institute and the diffuse individuals who look at the forecasts on its Web site. Neither explicitly nor implicitly has there been any assumption of responsibility by the institute for the accuracy of its forecasts. Hence, there has not obtained the sort of relationship between the parties that can justify the imposition of legal accountability on the institute of meteorology. In other words, there has not obtained any relationship between the parties that has given rise to a duty of care owed by the institute to each of the aforementioned diffuse individuals, with regard to the communication of meteorological information. Were legal accountability to be affixed in these circumstances, the institute's posting of an inaccurate forecast would be legally penalized qua act of communication rather than qua breach of a duty of care.

Quite a few judges and tort-law scholars in England have opined that the absence of a duty of care in any situation like that envisaged in the preceding paragraph is attributable chiefly to consequentialist considerations. That is, they suggest that the concerns which principally underpin the limits on the operativeness of duties of care are focused on the deleterious consequences that would ensue from the proliferation of such duties. For example, one worry in this vein would be that any organization which performs socially valuable functions—such as the posting of weather forecasts free of charge by the institute of meteorology—might become disinclined to perform those functions if the continuation of them will leave the organization vulnerable to open-endedly profuse lawsuits brought by members of the public at large. Another typical worry in this vein is that the courts will be overwhelmed with litigation if they do not tightly circumscribe the range of situations in which duties of care are owed. With consequentialist worries of these sorts in mind, Edwin Peel and James Goudkamp have declared that

> general liability for carelessly causing harm to others would, at least as things are perceived by the courts, be too onerous for a practical system of law ... Duty is the primary 'control device' which allows the courts to keep liability for negligence within what they regard as acceptable limits. (Peel and Goudkamp 2014, 81, footnote omitted)

Like all consequentialist reasoning, the foregoing concerns are based partly on conjectures about empirical matters. Still, at least in their general outlines, the conjectures that inform those concerns are plausible. At any rate, for my present purposes, I do not need to assess the solidity of those conjectures; nor do I need to gauge how frequently the courts in England have adverted to consequentialist considerations in support of their duty-of-care decisions. Similarly beside the point here is the extent to which those considerations can—as an objective matter—morally vindicate the doctrines that have been developed by the courts of England to avert a proliferation of duties of care.

Such consequentialist concerns should be put aside here not because they are dubious or feeble, but because they are never sufficient to undergird the absoluteness of the principle of freedom of expression. That principle disallows all legal restrictions that violate any of the constraints of communication-neutrality and content-neutrality and speaker-neutrality. Thus, given that that principle and its requirements of neutrality are central to everything in this book, the contentions advanced in the current subsection—my contention about the presence of a duty of care in any typical situation where consultation is accompanied by an assumption of responsibility or in any situation which is relevantly similar to that of *Spring v Guardian Assurance*, and my contention about the absence of a duty of care owed by the institute of meteorology to the sundry users of its Web site—will have to be vindicated by reference to those requirements of neutrality. Why would the principle of freedom of expression be transgressed if judges or administrators were to hold that each person who looks at the weather forecasts on the Web site of the institute of meteorology is owed a duty of care by the institute? What is the crucial difference between the position of the institute and the position of a financial expert who dispenses some complimentary advice or information or assurances to a person who has asked for the expert's appraisal of the financial robustness of a certain company? What is the crucial difference between the position of the institute and the position of the erstwhile employer in *Spring v Guardian Assurance*?

In a typical situation where one person (Person A) directly consults another person (Person B) who explicitly or implicitly accepts responsibility for the veracity of the information or assurances or advice furnished in response to the request from Person A, a relationship has been established prior to the communication of the advice or information or assurances. Although that relationship is not contractual,[9] Person B knows that her actual or perceived expertise is being relied upon by Person A who has consulted her directly about some matter. Aware of that aspect of the situation, Person B goes ahead with her communication of advice or information or assurances to Person A. Likewise, in a situation akin to that of *Spring v Guardian Assurance*, the relationship between the quondam employer and the quondam employee has obviously pre-existed the transmission of the letter of reference, and that letter is written specifically about the former employee. In any of these situations, the existence of a relationship which generates a duty of care is distinguishable from the occurrence of an act of communication to which that duty pertains.

In a situation like that of the meteorological institute, by contrast, any relationship between the institute and each of the far-flung users of its Web site on the

[9] Of course, a lawsuit to recover for the losses suffered as a result of a negligent misrepresentation can also occur when the relationship between the parties is contractual. Indeed, given the existence of a contractual relationship, the task of showing that a duty of care has been owed by one party to the other is straightforward. However, if there is such a relationship, a plaintiff will usually opt to pursue remedies available in contract law. Hence, since I am focusing in this subsection on tort-law proceedings, I assume away any case in which a contract has existed between the parties. (In the other direction, I am also assuming away any case in which a defendant's negligent misstatement has been accompanied by an explicit disclaimer of responsibility. Such a disclaimer will generally shield a defendant against lawsuits.)

occasion of its posting of a negligently inaccurate forecast is established through that very act of posting the forecast. There has been no direct and particularized contact between the institute and each of those users; the only contact has been diffuse and remote, in the form of each user's perusal of the forecast on the institute's Web site. Doubtless, quite a few of the users will have looked at the institute's forecasts in the past as well as on the occasion when the negligent misstep occurs. However, those diffuse and remote contacts in the past did not constitute any duties of care owed by the institute then, and *a fortiori* they do not constitute any such duties of care now. Moreover, just as there has been no direct and particularized contact between the institute and each user of the Web site on the occasion of the negligently mistaken forecast by the institute (or on any previous occasion), so too nobody at the institute has possessed any direct and particularized awareness of each user's reliance on the accuracy of that forecast. Undoubtedly, the employees of the institute know at a general level that many members of the public at large have recourse to the forecasts on the institute's Web site from time to time. Nevertheless, that generalized knowledge about a far-flung welter of people does not make the employees familiar with the reliance of any particular user on a specified forecast, and it does not furnish any basis for the proposition that the institute in relation to each such user has somehow assumed responsibility for the accuracy of this or that forecast. Furthermore, there is no physical propinquity between the scattered viewers of the Web site and the employees of the institute on the occasion when the negligently inaccurate forecast is posted. In that respect, the situation differs sharply from the countless situations in which various parties (such as the drivers of vehicles on a road) owe duties of care to one another in large part because of their physical propinquity.

In the absence of any factors that constitute an independent relationship of proximity between the institute of meteorology and each viewer of the institute's Web site, the existence of a duty of care owed by the institute to each viewer on the occasion of the negligently mistaken forecast would have to be grounded in the publication of that forecast itself. In other words, the factor that would constitute the existence of such a duty of care is not distinguishable from the occurrence of the act of communication to which the duty would pertain. Thus, instead of being analogous to a case in which a party responsible for some negligent misstatement is properly held legally accountable for the misstatement—that is, a case where the legal accountability is a means of giving effect to a duty of care which is justificatorily underpinned by considerations that are independent of the act of communication through which the duty has been breached—a ruling that holds the institute of meteorology to owe a duty of care to each user of its Web site would legally disadvantage the institute for having engaged in an act of communication. Such a ruling, which treats that act of communication itself as a basis for imposing a legal disadvantage in the form of a duty of care, would indispensably be an element in any overall judgment requiring the institute to compensate each detrimentally affected user for the damage wrought by the breach of that duty of care. Hence, although the overall judgment would superficially resemble an ordinary judgment in the law of negligence (in which a defendant is ordered to pay damages to a plaintiff who has been adversely affected by the defendant's breach of a duty of care), the fact that the overall judgment would comprise the ruling which saddles the institute with a duty of care is sufficient to render the judgment inconsistent with the principle of freedom of expression. Such a judgment with such a ruling would violate the constraint of communication-neutrality which that principle ordains.

Thus, quite apart from any consequentialist reasons for delimiting the range of circumstances in which someone responsible for a negligent misstatement will be held to have owed and breached a duty of care, the principle of freedom of expression delimits the range of circumstances in which any such outcome is morally tenable. As it happens, the limits imposed by that principle generally correspond to the limits that have been set by the law of negligence in England in response to other considerations. Still, whatever the contours of the law of negligence in any particular jurisdiction, the principle of freedom of expression lays down some boundaries that are morally obligatory always and everywhere. Beyond those boundaries, an award of damages against a defendant for a negligent misstatement will contravene the requirement of communication-neutrality which is incumbent on every system of governance. Of course, like the other limits and distinctions established by the principle of freedom of expression, the boundaries just mentioned will be flanked by a gray area of borderline cases in which the applicability or inapplicability of the relevant concepts is not fully determinate. Every distinction drawn in the domain of political philosophy is accompanied by such a gray area. Nonetheless, although the potential for borderline cases is ineliminable, most cases do not fall within the gray area. In countless situations, including that of the institute of meteorology, the implications of the principle of freedom of expression are fully determinate.

3.2.10 Child Pornography

Chapter 5 will focus sustainedly on the topic of pornography, and it will touch upon the matter of child pornography at a few junctures. Hence, my treatment of that matter here will be very brief. Whereas Chapter 5 will argue at length that the distribution of most types of pornography is morally protected by the principle of freedom of expression, it will readily allow that the distribution of child pornography is not morally protected by that principle against laws which proscribe such pornography on content-neutral (and communication-neutral) grounds. That conclusion about moral unprotectedness is also applicable to any pornography in which the adults pictured have not been consensual participants in the processes of creating the pornography. While fraud and violent coercion are the most common techniques for inducing adults to appear nonconsensually in pornographic poses, every instance of the involvement of children in such poses is nonconsensual—since children are not capable of providing any genuine consent in such matters. Of course, in the vast majority of cases where children are displayed in pornographic poses, they have been subjected to severely violent abuse; however, even when violence is not wielded, the filming or photographing of the children for the creation of pornographic materials is itself grossly abusive. It is something which any system of governance can legitimately prevent and prohibit, and indeed it is something which any system of governance is morally obligated to prohibit and to strive to prevent.

Not only is the *production* of child pornography a type of wrongdoing that can properly be banned and thwarted by any system of governance, but so too is the *distribution* of such pornography. In part, the legitimate prohibitability of the latter as well as of the former is due to the fact that each of them is a stage in an overall enterprise that gravely mistreats children. In addition, the distribution of materials that depict children in pornographic poses is a fresh wrong to the children, as is the viewing of those materials by people who find them titillating or arousing. When children are grievously exploited by being splayed and photographed or filmed for the production of pornographic images, they are further exploited on every occasion when someone views those images lasciviously. On each such occasion, the nonconsensual use of the children as objects for the sexual gratification of others is repeated. Thus, the production and distribution and possession of such images can all properly be forbidden by law.

Legal prohibitions on the production and distribution and possession of child pornography can straightforwardly conform with the requirements of neutrality set forth by the principle of freedom of expression, because such prohibitions can very credibly be directed not against the content of the pornography but instead against the processes through which it has been created—and against the lasting wrongs inflicted on the victims of those processes. When legal prohibitions are so oriented, they are content-neutral and communication-neutral. With such an orientation, a legal ban disallows the production and distribution and possession of child pornography not qua acts of communication but instead qua acts of exploitation and abuse. That ban is focused not on what the pornography communicates but on how it is created.

Although the principle of freedom of expression does not always converge with the First Amendment to the American Constitution in its corollaries about specific issues, there is quite a striking convergence on the matter of child pornography. In the following passage, Elena Kagan deftly summarizes the bearing of the First Amendment on the prohibitability of such pornography:

> [T]he Constitution may well permit direct regulation of speech, if phrased in a viewpoint-neutral manner, when the regulation responds to a non-speech related

> interest in controlling conduct involved in the materials' manufacture. Assume here, as discussed above, that the government has a strong interest in regulating the violence and coercion that often occurs in the making of pornography. Does it then follow that the government may punish the distribution of materials made in this way as well as the underlying unlawful conduct? The Supreme Court's decision in *New York v Ferber* suggests an affirmative answer. In *Ferber*, the Court sustained a statute prohibiting the distribution of any material depicting a sexual performance by a child, primarily on the ground that the law arose from the government's interest in preventing the conduct (sexual exploitation of children) necessarily involved in making the expression. Similarly, it would appear, the government may prohibit directly the dissemination of any materials whose manufacture involved coercion of, or violence against, participants. (Kagan 1993, 891, footnotes omitted)

Of course, even though laws which prohibit the distribution of child pornography can be morally legitimate, any particular law of that kind might not be morally legitimate. Everything depends on the purposes that are correctly ascribable to such a law. On the one hand, the aim of putting an end to the inherently exploitative use of children in the creation of pornography for paedophiles will very often be the purpose that animates the imposition of a legal ban on the manufacturing and marketing of child pornography. On the other hand, given that the materials produced by the child-pornography industry are such as to elicit a sense of revulsion in any decent person who encounters them, an aim that is not content-neutral—an aim directed against the vileness of the depictions in the aforementioned materials—might alternatively or additionally underlie the imposition of such a legal ban. If an aim of the latter kind is indeed the dominant purpose that has led to some law which proscribes the creation and distribution and possession of child pornography, then that law contravenes the principle of freedom of expression. The fact that such a law could very plausibly have been underlain by a dominant content-neutral purpose is not sufficient to redeem it and its actual content-focused purpose.

Identifying the dominant purpose that lies behind a legal curb on the manufacturing and marketing of child pornography, then, can be quite a challenge. One way of gauging the frankness of a system of governance whose officials invoke solely a content-neutral purpose is to adduce the following thought-experiment. Suppose that some company produces child pornography in the form of comic books or animated cartoons or computer-generated imagery. No children are involved in the manufacturing of the pornographic materials, and the images in those materials are not based on the appearances of any individual children. Even so, the images are strikingly life-like, and the repulsiveness of their contents is sickeningly apparent to anyone who is not a hard-core paedophile. In these circumstances, a law that forbids the creation and distribution of the company's materials will violate the principle of freedom of expression—since the only rationales that can credibly be imputed to that law are not content-neutral. Given the circumstances envisaged here, the concerns about the grotesque abuse of youngsters in the production of child pornography are not applicable. Nor is the marketing of the company's products credibly prohibitable on the ground that the children involved in the creation of those products will continue to be used as objects for sexual titillation and gratification if the marketing is legally permitted to go ahead; after all, *ex hypothesi*, no children have been involved in the creation of the company's products. Consequently, because the company's materials are not vulnerable to the usual objections to child pornography which are focused on the processes through which the pornography has been made, a law that bans the production and distribution of those very materials will run athwart the principle of freedom of expression.[10]

Either such a law will be directed against the rebarbativeness of the contents of the company's materials and against the turpitude of the outlooks of people who can derive enjoyment from such filth, or else in a consequentialist fashion it will be directed against the criminogenic effects that might ensue from the dissemination of those materials. Aimed against the depravity of the contents of the company's films and publications, a legal prohibition will patently transgress the requirement of content-neutrality which the principle of freedom of expression imposes. Aimed against the possibility that those films and publications will increase the incidence of very serious crimes such as paedophilia, a legal prohibition will transgress the constraint of communication-neutrality—because any such criminogenic effects, if they were to materialize, would be diffuse and remote products of the imparting of certain communicative contents by the films and publications. Although the imparting of those contents might indeed debase the outlooks of some of the people who view the imagery in the films and publications, any such debasement (if it occurs) is a remote communicative effect and is thus not something that can permissibly be forestalled through a legal ban. A system of governance is both morally permitted and morally obligated to counter the occurrence of such debasement—through measures that will be discussed in Chapters 4 to 6—but it is not morally permitted to avert a remote communicative effect by legally proscribing the type of communication through which that effect might be engendered.

In sum, the pornographic films and magazines broached in the preceding two paragraphs are morally protected by the principle of freedom of expression. Thus, when we need to gauge the propriety of the purposes ascribable to a law which forbids the manufacturing and marketing of child pornography, a germane test lies in asking whether the interdiction imposed by the relevant law would extend to

[10] Thus, the law in South Africa on this matter is violative of the principle of freedom of expression. See Sachs 2019, 184.

the aforementioned films and magazines. Of course, the answer to that question might be unascertainable in any particular setting; however, insofar as an answer can be discerned, it indicates whether the purposes behind the relevant law are consistent with the principle of freedom of expression or not. If the answer to the question is negative in some jurisdiction, then we can be confident that the purposes behind the relevant law there are indeed consistent with the principle of freedom of expression. By contrast, an affirmative answer in any particular jurisdiction reveals that at least one main purpose sufficient there to account for the adoption or sustainment of the relevant law is incompatible with that moral principle. Of course, even though a content-focused purpose has itself been sufficient to impel the sustainment and implementation of the relevant law by a certain system of governance, we cannot automatically infer that the officials in that system are insincere when they also invoke content-neutral considerations. However, whether the officials are sincere or insincere, they are disposed to implement the relevant law in situations to which the content-neutral considerations are inapplicable. Accordingly, not only with regard to those situations but also more generally, a content-focused purpose has been sufficient to impel the sustainment and activation of the relevant law in the jurisdiction involved—which means that the orientation of the relevant law in that jurisdiction is at variance with the principle of freedom of expression.

3.2.11 Hate-Crime Laws versus Hate-Speech Laws

Although this chapter could profitably treat of several further topics—some of which will be handled in Chapters 5 and 6—it will conclude by tersely exploring the differences between hate-crime laws and hate-speech laws. Hate-speech laws are the main topic of Chapter 6, and they will also receive attention in Chapter 5. Such laws proscribe certain types of utterances on content-focused grounds, and therefore flagrantly contravene the principle of freedom of expression. Properly drafted hate-crime statutes, which will also surface in Chapter 5, are quite different. A statute of the latter type does not itself proscribe any mode of conduct, either as a matter of criminal law or as a matter of tort law. Rather, a hate-crime statute provides that a misdeed independently classified as a crime is more serious if it is motivated by hostility toward the victim's race or religion or ethnicity or sexual orientation. Such hostility, which can be evinced in various ways (including, of course, the use of bigoted epithets), is an aggravating feature that intensifies the gravity of any legal and moral wrong which someone has perpetrated. A person convicted of a crime that is motivated by such hostility will generally be subjected to a harsher punishment than will a person convicted of an otherwise similar crime that is not so motivated.

Whereas a hate-speech statute criminalizes certain modes of expression qua modes of expression, a hate-crime statute does not criminalize anything.[11] Someone's harboring of bigoted hostility is not outlawed under a hate-crime statute (or under any other morally legitimate statute), and even someone's acting on the basis of such hostility is not outlawed under a hate-crime statute. Unless an action motivated by such hostility is independently proscribed as a crime, a hate-crime statute is inapplicable to it. For example, if someone delivers a speech in which he advocates the banishment of all Muslims to foreign shores, his oration is motivated by religious hatred but is not a crime in any jurisdiction where the prevailing system of governance complies with the principle of freedom of expression. Accurately classifiable as advocacy rather than as incitement, the oration is morally protected by that principle and is legally protected by any applicable constitutional guarantee such as the First Amendment. Hence, given that the hate-fueled speech is not independently punishable as a crime, a hate-crime statute does not have any purchase on it.

Still, although a hate-crime statute does not outlaw any modes of expression or indeed anything else, it does place at a disadvantage everybody whose perpetration of a crime is motivated by bigoted animosity (in comparison with anyone whose perpetration of an otherwise similar crime is not so motivated). As has been observed in Chapter 2, legal prohibitions are not the only sorts of measures that can contravene the principle of freedom of expression. Any governmentally imposed burdens or governmentally bestowed benefits can run afoul of that principle in some circumstances. Thus, we need to ask whether the pattern of disadvantages brought about by the implementation of hate-crime laws is at variance with the principle of freedom of expression.

The answer to that question is negative, for the pattern of disadvantages to which the question refers is communication-neutral. Hate-crime statutes are not directed against any acts of communication qua acts of communication. Indeed, they are not really directed against acts of communication at all. Though some utterances spoken during the perpetration of certain crimes (or shortly before or after the perpetration of them) can serve to evidence the bigoted antipathy that has impelled the commission of those crimes, the stiffening of the punishments for those felonies or misdemeanors under the terms of a hate-crime statute is directed not against the utterances but against the bigoted antipathy which the utterances help to reveal. Moreover such antipathy can be manifested in any number of ways, rather than only through speech or writing. It is especially often manifested through the targeting of certain types of people as the victims of violent attacks, or through the targeting of certain types of buildings or tombstones or artefacts for vandalism. Hence, in addition to the fact that the role of utterances under a

[11] This point is missed in Malik and Molnar 2012, 88–9. See also Gellman 1992. For a fine corrective, see Weinstein 1992.

hate-crime statute is never more than evidentiary,[12] that evidentiary role can be performed by communicative conduct and non-communicative conduct alike. In multiple respects, then, the punishment-intensifying import of a hate-crime statute is communication-neutral. Under such a statute, communicative conduct is not singled out for disadvantageous treatment qua communicative conduct.

3.3 A Pithy Conclusion

Although this chapter has obviously not attempted to address all the morally legitimate ways in which any system of governance can restrict or preclude various types of communicative activities, the many topics which it does cover—in combination with topics covered in Chapter 2 and in the remaining chapters of this book—are sufficient to indicate how the absolute sway of the principle of freedom of expression is consistent with sundry governmental measures that can impinge on the expressive interaction of people. In regard to every such measure that is morally permissible, the appropriate conclusion is not that the modes of communication affected by that measure are somehow beyond the ambit of the principle of freedom of expression. No mode of communication lies outside that ambit. Instead, the correct conclusion is that each morally permissible governmental imposition conforms to the requirements of neutrality that are established by the principle of freedom of expression. Those requirements are satisfied because each such imposition that restricts communicative actions is directed against the actions only qua instances of communication-independent misconduct and not qua instances of communication. This chapter has sought to demonstrate that point in diverse contexts. Precisely because the topics covered by this chapter have indeed been diverse, my approaches to them have likewise varied. There is no algorithmic formula that can be applied mechanically across the multifarious contexts. Still, the basic objective of the chapter has been uniform across those contexts, as I have endeavored to show that the absoluteness of the principle of freedom of expression is reconcilable with a number of familiar curbs on what people are able or legally permitted to communicate (even while it is irreconcilable with some other such curbs). A grasp of this point is essential for a solid understanding of the principle of freedom of expression, and such an understanding in turn is essential for a fruitful engagement with the moral justification on which that principle rests. To that moral justification, elaborated in Chapter 4, we now turn.

[12] Hateful utterances are also adducible for evidentiary purposes in legal proceedings against people who are accused of racially discriminatory behavior. See Shaw and Molnar 2012, 399–400.

4

Governmental Self-Restraint and Individual Self-Respect

In the preceding three chapters we have explored the substance and some of the implications of the principle of freedom of expression, and we shall investigate those implications further in the subsequent chapters of this book. The present chapter, which is central to the book not only in its location but also in its importance, will delineate the justificatory foundations of that principle. Salient though versions of the principle of freedom of expression have been in the theories and institutions of liberal democracy for the past three or four centuries, that principle (in the version propounded by this book) is derivative of an even deeper moral responsibility that is incumbent on every system of governance. Any such system, presiding over a society, is morally obligated to bring about the political and economic and social conditions under which every member of that society can be warranted in harboring an ample sense of self-respect. As will be argued in this chapter, that fundamental responsibility of every system of governance—which I shall henceforth designate as the "paramount responsibility"—is what undergirds the principle of freedom of expression. As a moral duty that obtains always and everywhere, it can underlie a moral principle that is binding always and everywhere.

While the paramount responsibility of every system of governance is itself complex and in need of elucidation, the relationship between it and the principle of freedom of expression is likewise complicated. Hence, the present chapter will have to tackle both some matters of general political philosophy and some matters of justification specifically in the philosophy of free expression. Because my ruminations on those matters will depart quite markedly from the traditional efforts to justify versions of the principle of freedom of expression, we can best enter into my own rationale for that principle by first contemplating briefly a handful of the previous justificatory efforts that have attained prominence. My aim in so doing is not really to disparage or rebut those previous efforts, some of which are possessed of considerable moral force. Although I will indeed raise a few queries about those alternative justifications—and although I have already adumbrated a query about them in §2.3.1.4 of Chapter 2—the main objective in the first section of this chapter is to set the stage for my grounding of the principle of freedom of expression on the paramount responsibility of every system of governance. In that connection, the past attempts to justify versions of the ideal of freedom of expression will indeed be treated here partly as targets for demurrals but also (and even more so) as points of

Freedom of Expression as Self-Restraint. Matthew H. Kramer, Oxford University Press (2021). © Matthew H. Kramer.
DOI: 10.1093/oso/9780198868651.003.0004

contrast. Because those past attempts differ so significantly from the rationale for the principle of freedom of expression that will be unfolded in this chapter, a quick overview of them will serve to highlight the distinctiveness of that rationale.

4.1 A Conspectus of Some Previous Justifications

During the past four hundred years, and especially during the past century in the United States, philosophers and legal theorists and jurists have crafted numerous lines of reasoning in their endeavors to explain why the communicative freedoms of people should receive special protection against encroachments by governmental institutions and policies.[1] Those abundant and heterogeneous rationales have generally fallen into several chief clusters with characteristic foci.

4.1.1 A Focus on Potential Addressors

Some philosophers have particularly shown concern for the potential addressors of communications—speakers, writers, composers, artists, singers, dancers, and so forth—who may wish to convey their thoughts or sentiments to other people or to themselves. Theorists who adopt such a focus have submitted that abundant communicative liberties are essential for the self-determination or self-expression or autonomy or self-disclosure or dignity or individuality or self-fulfillment of the potential addressors. Some such theories have been developed in predominantly consequentialist directions, and other such theories have been predominantly deontological. Relatedly, some have focused largely or exclusively on the promotion of salutary psychological traits, whereas others have focused largely or exclusively on ethical issues concerning the latitude and standing that befit anyone who is endowed with the faculties of a rationally deliberative agent. Although these efforts to justify versions of the principle of freedom of expression have been profuse and diverse, they are united by their attentiveness to the interests or autonomy of addressors. Of course, philosophers who exhibit such attentiveness are not thereby precluded from discerning other respects in which the communicative freedoms of people are morally precious. Indeed, this general line of justification can be combined with one or more of the other lines that will be summarized below. Nevertheless, theories that ground their versions of the principle of freedom of

[1] For a classic survey of the rationales that have been invoked in favor of such special protection, see Emerson 1970, 6–20. See also Alexander 2005, 127–46; Badamchi 2015, 911–20; Barendt 2005, 6–36; Greenawalt 1989, 9–39; 2016, 356–86; Heyman 2009, 159–64; Oster 2015, 13–23; Raz 1994, 147–8; Rosenfeld 2012, 250–3; Sadurski 1999, 7–35; Smolla 1992, 3–17; Tribe 1978, 576–9. For some valuable up-dating of those earlier catalogues of justifications, with a plethora of citations, see Schauer 2017, 233–7.

expression on the interests or rational agency of addressors have embraced a distinctive focus that is attractive not only to many philosophers but also to countless ordinary people who reside in societies where communicative liberties are treasured. At a pre-theoretical level, the endeavors to underscore the invaluableness of such liberties by reference to the interests or autonomy of speakers and writers and other addressors are manifestly appealing.

Still, in a number of ways, the endeavors just mentioned are inadequate to serve the purposes of this book. Most obviously objectionable are the consequentialist varieties of such a line of justification, for (as has been emphasized since my opening chapter) consequentialist considerations are never sufficient to sustain the absoluteness of the principle of freedom of expression. Those considerations, whose applicability is always dependent on empirical contingencies, cannot ever account for a moral principle that is binding always and everywhere. Furthermore, even the deontological approaches within this category—which extol communicative freedoms not as vehicles for fostering commendable traits of character but instead as entitlements that are essential for respecting the dignity or individuality of each person as a potential addressor of communications—are inadequate.

In §2.3.1.4 of Chapter 2, we have beheld one of the weaknesses in any addressor-centered efforts to justify versions of the principle of freedom of expression (whether the tenor of such efforts be deontological or consequentialist). That is, an approach of that kind falls short because it is not able to explain why in some contexts a relatively fine-grained policy of excluding the occurrence of communications is morally wrongful whereas in those same contexts a blanket policy of excluding the occurrence of communications can be morally permissible. Let us recall here the municipality that owns and operates some buses as a public service. Although the officials of the municipality can permissibly exclude all advertisements from the sides and backs of the buses, they cannot permissibly exclude advertisements in ways that are at variance with the constraint of subject-neutrality or viewpoint-neutrality or speaker-neutrality. In other words, in certain contexts the principle of freedom of expression countenances some sweeping restrictions on opportunities for communications by addressors even while in those same contexts it flatly disallows sundry narrower restrictions on such opportunities. A deontological addressor-focused rationale might try to handle these cases by insisting that contraventions of any of the aforementioned constraints of neutrality are always morally wrong as violations of the equality of persons. However, that rationale will thereby have ceased to concentrate distinctively on the interests or autonomy of addressors, since an appeal to the equality of persons would be no less pertinent under a deontological address*ee*-centered approach. Such an appeal to equality moves away from the interests or autonomy of addressors, and directs attention instead to the fundamental parity of human agents—a relationship of fundamental parity that is neither distinctively addressor-focused nor distinctively addressee-focused. (As will be seen hereafter, a non-Kantian premise about the fundamental equality of human beings is an element in this chapter's justification of the principle of freedom of expression.)

An addressor-centered justification will founder in some other respects as well. For example, it cannot explain why any governmental measure to cut off the access of members of the public to the writings of long-dead authors is morally impermissible (Rubenfeld 2002a, 33–5). If the officials in a system of governance were to prohibit people from acquiring and reading copies of the plays of Sophocles, they would be blatantly contravening the principle of freedom of expression. However, the wrongfulness of such a contravention is not to be explained by reference to the self-expression or autonomy of Sophocles. Although the interests or autonomy of a person can continue for a time to possess moral force that generates some moral obligations even after the person has died,[2] the interests or autonomy of someone who has been dead for many centuries will not continue to possess such force. To explain why a system of governance would be acting impermissibly by barring people from purchasing or reading the works of Sophocles, we should not be seeking to pin down the wrong which such a policy would commit against Sophocles. Rather, we should recognize that the wrong committed is against the potential readers and spectators and performers of the plays, and indeed against the whole citizenry over whom the system of governance presides. Of course, the proponents of addressor-centered rationales for versions of the principle of freedom of expression can venture to combine their rationales with additional foci through which they can accommodate the example of Sophocles and other relevantly similar examples. Nonetheless, the very need for such supplementation of the addressor-focused approach is indicative of the shortcomings in that approach.

Those shortcomings are further exposed in §2.1.1.1 of Chapter 2, where—drawing on the work of Larry Alexander—I recount certain instances of communication which occur without any addressors of the messages or sentiments that are presumed to be conveyed by those instances of communication. Let us think again, for instance, of the people who congregate to watch sunsets in order to glean therefrom the messages which they believe to be transmitted by gods or angels. Were a system of governance to forbid those people to search for messages in the skies (perhaps because the system's officials fear that the messages are seditious), it would be arrantly violating the principle of freedom of expression. However, the wrongness of such a violation of that principle would patently not be explainable by reference to the interests or autonomy of the non-existent heavenly authorities. Once again, then, the champions of addressor-centered rationales for versions of the principle of freedom of expression will have to conjoin their rationales with some other justifications if they are to account for the wrongness of certain governmental measures which flagrantly breach any credible version of that principle.

[2] For a related though distinct point, see Kramer 2001, 49–52.

These terse remarks on a few of the failings in the addressor-centered theories of communicative liberties are scarcely meant to be a comprehensive critique of those theories. Given the variegatedness of the justifications that concentrate on the interests or autonomy of addressors, any comprehensive critique would be lengthy indeed. Instead, as this chapter has suggested at its outset, my laconic summary of those justifications is intended to underscore the ways in which they contrast with the Stoical rationale for the principle of freedom of expression that will be elaborated hereafter. Those alternative justifications serve valuably as a foil for the exposition of that rationale, since the types of scenarios that confound them are handled straightforwardly by my reflections on the principle of freedom of expression. Within my reflections, the glaring contraventions of that principle broached in the last few paragraphs above are rightly and unproblematically classifiable as contraventions. In the very areas where theorists falter when they attempt to vindicate versions of the principle of freedom of expression by reference to the interests or autonomy of the addressors of communications, the Stoical vindication of that principle can proceed without difficulty.

4.1.2 A Focus on Potential Addressees

Usually as an alternative to the addressor-centered approaches, though sometimes as a complement to them, a focus on the addressees of communications has won the favor of numerous philosophers. Concentrating on the potential recipients of communications—that is, on listeners, readers, spectators, interlocutors—these philosophers contend that the access of the recipients to the expressed ideas or sentiments or outlooks or information of addressors is the precious desideratum that should be protected by constitutional guarantees.

4.1.2.1 Communicative Freedoms and Democratic Self-Governance

In the eyes of some of the philosophers who adopt addressee-focused approaches, the pivotal importance of the access of addressees is a corollary of the moral requirement of respect for the dignity of reasons-responsive agents. Members of the public should be allowed to reach decisions for themselves about the communications to which they will devote their attention. Those decisions should not be made for them by censors or by other governmental officials. When officials do interpose their own judgments by taking steps designed to curtail the range of communications to which the citizens of a society can gain access, they thereby treat the citizens like children.

In the eyes of some other philosophers who espouse addressee-focused understandings of the import of communicative freedoms, the moral significance of access to the expressed views and sentiments of one's fellows is centered on the requirements of democratic deliberation. In this version of the addressee-focused approach, as in that approach more generally, there is a division between consequentialist lines of reasoning and deontological lines of reasoning. Indeed, such a division surfaces within the work of Alexander Meiklejohn, the foremost pioneer in the development of that general approach. He emphatically gave voice to an addressee-focused orientation in his account of the grounds and implications of the First Amendment to the American Constitution, as he declared that "the point of ultimate interest is not the words of the speakers, but the minds of the hearers." He regarded such an orientation as uniquely pertinent for the challenges of realizing the ideal of democratic self-governance:

> The final aim of [a democratic community] is the voting of wise decisions. The voters, therefore, must be made as wise as possible.... As the self-governing community seeks, by the method of voting, to gain wisdom in action, it can find it only in the minds of its individual citizens. If they fail, it fails. That is why freedom of discussion for those minds may not be abridged. (Meiklejohn 1948, 25)

As he added: "When men govern themselves, it is they—and no one else—who must pass judgment upon unwisdom and unfairness and danger. And that means that unwise ideas must have a hearing as well as wise ones, unfair as well as fair, dangerous as well as safe, un-American as well as American" (26).

In the writings of Meiklejohn himself, and in the broader tradition of thinking which he founded, there is—as has just been mentioned—a divide between a consequentialist way and a deontological way of connecting the requirements of a democratic polity to an addressee-centered perspective on communicative freedoms. Both of those paths for the elaboration of his position appear in the portion of his *Free Speech and Its Relation to Self-Government* from which I have already quoted, and they are especially salient in a later portion of that book (Meiklejohn 1948, 61–70). On the one hand, Meiklejohn can be construed as arguing that the decisions reached and debates undertaken by the members of a democratic polity will be uninformed and frequently misguided if those members have been denied access to certain viewpoints and ideas. In this vein, he was concerned more with the outcomes of the procedures of democratic decision-making than with those procedures themselves. As he asserted: "The welfare of the community requires that those who decide issues shall understand them. They must know what they are voting about" (25). On the other hand, Meiklejohn can be construed as concerning himself predominantly with the integrity of the procedures through which the institutions of a democratic polity arrive at determinations on matters of public affairs. Understood along such lines, he was maintaining that the deliberations of those institutions will not truly constitute self-government if the members of the polity have been prohibited or prevented from gaining access to certain perspectives or doctrines or information. In the presence of governmental measures that curb such access, the members of a community are not genuinely ruling themselves. Rather, they are being ruled by the legal-governmental officials who presume to judge for those members the breadth of the range of ideas on which they are permitted or able to draw.

These two main strands in Meiklejohn's ruminations, the consequentialist strand and the deontological strand, are not incompatible but are likewise patently not equivalent. Neither of them is capable of underpinning the absoluteness of the moral principle of freedom of expression (as will be observed presently), though the deontological rendering of his position is less frequently at variance with that principle than is the consequentialist rendering. Those distinct seams in his thought have been developed further, in diverse and sophisticated forms, by the many other philosophers who have invoked the ideal of democratic self-governance as a ground for protecting communicative freedoms.[3] A number of those philosophers have dwelt on some related concerns—about the role of constitutional free-speech guarantees in checking the tendency of governmental institutions to expand their powers at the expense of popular sovereignty, or about the role of the guarantees in fostering the sway of democratic outlooks and virtues among citizens. Theorists who pursue some of those additional concerns have at times moved away from the addressee-centered orientation in this wide-ranging school of thought, but such an orientation remains dominant therein.

4.1.2.2 A Few Queries about the Addressee-Centered Justifications

Whether a focus on the potential addressees of communications is linked to the ideal of democratic self-governance or to other ideals such as that of individual autonomy—or to sundry consequentialist objectives—it cannot serve as the justificatory basis for the principle of freedom of expression. Consequentialist versions of the addressee-centered approach, like the consequentialist versions of the addressor-centered approach, fall especially far short of vindicating the absoluteness of the principle of freedom of expression. Moreover, even when the addressee-focused justifications are at least partly deontological, they do not suffice to uphold the absoluteness of that principle. Let us briefly ponder here a few points that tell against the adequacy of such justifications.

First, we should remember afresh the example of the municipality that operates some buses for the transportation of residents and visitors. As has been remarked already in this chapter and in Chapter 2, the local government can permissibly decline to allow any advertisements and notices to be placed on the sides and backs of its buses. However, if it does allow advertisements and notices to be placed, it cannot permissibly impose any exclusions that are inconsistent with the constraints

[3] For one of the multitudinous examples of such an approach, see Dworkin 2000, ch. 4. In note 6 in §2.1.3 of Chapter 2, I have listed quite a few other philosophers who are in this general school of thought. For a powerful collection of essays that includes many contributions which are sympathetic to that school of thought (as well as some contributions that are wary of it), see Hare and Weinstein 2009.

of content-neutrality and speaker-neutrality. (Given that the local government will very likely receive more applications for the placing of advertisements and notices than it can accommodate, it can of course permissibly resort to some standard for selection that is compatible with the aforementioned constraints: perhaps an aleatory procedure, for example, or a criterion of first-come-first-served.) Hence, a policy of excluding every advertisement that pertains to the legally permissible activity of gambling or a policy of excluding every advertisement that is submitted by the local branch of the Ku Klux Klan will transgress the principle of freedom of expression, whereas a policy of excluding *all* advertisements can be fully consistent with that principle. Such a combination of verdicts will be inexplicably perverse when assessed from any distinctively addressee-centered perspective. After all, a blanket policy of declining to carry advertisements will impair the access of addressees to ideas and proposals far more than will either of the much more limited exclusions broached here. Because the proponents of addressee-centered theories who write within the Meiklejohnian tradition are inclined to regard commercial communications as low-value modes of expression that are open to extensive legal curbs, they will particularly balk at the notion that the blanket policy in this scenario is favored by the principle of freedom of expression over a policy of disallowing advertisements that pertain to gambling. Even the votaries of distinctively addressee-centered theories who write within other traditions (such as the Kantian tradition) will be at a loss to explain or countenance the combination of verdicts outlined here. Without going beyond their purely addressee-centered orientation, they are not in a position to fathom why a very modest diminution in the range of subjects or viewpoints to which members of the public have access within a certain context is somehow morally worse than the wholesale elimination of that range. They are not in a position to fathom why the wholesale elimination can be consistent with the principle of freedom of expression whereas the modest diminution is inconsistent therewith. (As has been suggested in §4.1.1 above, the deontologists in the addressee-focused camp might appeal here to the fundamental equality of persons in an effort to account for the special wrongness of exclusions that are selective. In so doing, however, they would be abandoning any distinctive orientation toward the interests or autonomy of addressees—for, as has been observed, the fundamental equality of persons is something that cuts across the divide between addressee-focused concerns and addressor-focused concerns.)

Another problem for the addressee-focused approach has surfaced in §2.1.1.2 of Chapter 2, where we have seen that some communications lack any genuine addressees. If a person engages in a séance by herself during which she believes that she is conversing with the spirits of several dead people whom she formerly knew, her colloquies with them lack any genuine addressees yet are straightforwardly covered by the principle of freedom of expression. Similarly, if somebody prays to a deity, his impetrations lack any genuine addressees but are patently covered by the principle of freedom of expression (and also, of course, by a principle of freedom of religion). As much as any political orations, the séance and the prayers are morally protected against laws or other governmental measures that clash with the requirements of communication-neutrality and content-neutrality and speaker-neutrality. That moral protection is not explicable by reference to addressee-focused considerations. Such considerations, that is, do not extend to various utterances that fall squarely within the scope of the principle of freedom of expression.

4.1.3 A Focus on the Good of Society

Another common point of reference for the justificatory endeavors of free-speech philosophers—indeed, the most common point of reference for the philosophers who seek to provide consequentialist justifications—is the welfare of a society as a whole. In the eyes of most of the philosophers who write in this vein, the attainment of knowledge has been especially prominent as a desideratum to be pursued. John Milton in *Areopagitica* and John Stuart Mill in the great second chapter of *On Liberty* famously gave pride of place to that desideratum in their classic cogitations on the preciousness of communicative freedoms, and numerous other thinkers have followed along broadly the same path. These consequentialist justifications commend expressive liberties as instrumentally valuable for the discovery of truths and the rebuttal of falsehoods in sundry areas of life. (Though the discovery of truths and the rebuttal of falsehoods are regarded by some consequentialists as intrinsically valuable, they are regarded by most consequentialists as instrumentally valuable for the realization of other desiderata such as economic prosperity.)

Of course, the advancement of knowledge is not the only societal good to which scholars and jurists have adverted in their efforts to highlight the import of communicative liberties. For example, most of the consequentialist accounts of the connections between such liberties and the ideal of democratic self-governance are not only addressee-focused but also society-focused; the achievement of the ideal of democratic self-governance is commended as a societal desideratum that will be fostered by the securing of ample expressive freedoms. Similarly, the achievement of the ideal of cultural diversity is quite often extolled as an objective that calls for an abundance of such freedoms. Still, the societal desideratum most frequently lauded by the consequentialist free-speech theorists is the goal of promoting the acquisition of knowledge.

To an even greater extent than the addressor-focused and addressee-focused theories of communicative freedoms, the society-focused theories—with their strongly consequentialist bent—fall markedly short of vindicating the principle of freedom of expression. Let us start here by reflecting again on the example of the local government that operates a bus service. As has been remarked in §2.3.1.4 of Chapter 2, philosophers who concentrate on the amassing of knowledge or on some other societal desideratum will be nonplused by the combination of the following two facts: (1) a decision by the municipality to exclude all advertisements and notices from the sides and backs of its buses can be in keeping with the principle of freedom of expression; and (2) a decision by the municipality to impose a modest subject-specific or viewpoint-specific or speaker-specific exclusion is always at variance with that principle. By the reckoning of the consequentialists who propound society-focused accounts of the value of communicative liberties, these two corollaries of the principle of freedom of expression are perverse in combination. Whereas a blanket policy of declining to allow the placement of any advertisements or notices on the buses is likely to retard somewhat the spread of knowledge in the locality, a deftly circumscribed policy at odds with the constraint of subject-neutrality or viewpoint-neutrality or speaker-neutrality would be likely to enhance rather than impede the spread of knowledge. Consider for instance a policy of declining to carry any advertisements by anti-vaccination extremists that are replete with superstitious falsehoods, or a policy of declining to carry any advertisements by Louis Farrakhan's Nation of Islam that teem with poisonously false allegations about Jews. Accordingly, philosophers who seek to defend their versions of the principle of freedom of expression by reference to the goal of expanding the attainment of knowledge will not be in a position to grasp why an adroitly fine-grained governmental curb on expressive activities can sometimes be morally worse than a blanket curb. (Of course, those philosophers might doubt that any governmental restrictions on expressive activities will in fact be adroitly fine-grained. However, my scenario of the municipality with the buses is meant to prescind from such doubts. The point which the scenario makes is not reliant at all on the notion that the officials in the local government are incompetent to design adeptly any restriction that is narrower than the wholesale exclusion of advertisements from the sides and backs of the buses.)

What is more, as will be noted again in §5.3.4.2.1 of Chapter 5, the empirical conjectures that underlie the truth-seeking rationale for the bestowal of stringent protection on communicative freedoms—the empirical conjectures that bestrew the eloquent remonstrations of Milton and Mill—are decidedly shaky. Of course, the empirical surmises that inform any of the consequentialist rationales for such stringent protection are inadequate to support the absoluteness of the principle of freedom of expression, since any such surmises are hostages to the vicissitudes of circumstances. However, the empirical premises that inform the truth-seeking rationale are especially dubious. As Frederick Schauer comments in his recent discussion of the matter, "[t]he search for truth/marketplace of ideas justification for a distinct principle of freedom of speech has for decades been subject to harsh criticism."[4] In an extreme form, some of the worries about the truth-seeking justification have been articulated by Brian Leiter in another recent discussion:

[4] Schauer 2017, 232. For a sample of the multitudinous writings that have impugned the truth-seeking justification, see Alexander 2005, 128–30; Baker 1978; 1989, 6–24; Bambauer 2006; Blasi 2004, 1–13; Brietzke 1997; DuVal 1972, 188–94; Dworkin 2009, vii; Goldman and Cox 1996; Ho and Schauer

> Non-mundane speech—speech about matters of political and moral urgency, speech that purports to be of aesthetic value, speech that purports to help us understand the truth about matters of societal importance, speech that is thought central to self-formation and the good life—is what is really at issue in debates about the regulation of speech. My claim is that most speech of this kind in fact has little or no net positive epistemic value (that is, value for helping us discover the truth) and not enough non-epistemic value (either for the speaker or listeners) to justify its expression, regardless of the costs to social welfare. In a slogan: most non-mundane speech people engage in is largely worthless, and the world would be better off were it not expressed. (Leiter 2016, 408–9, footnote omitted)

In a tone less caustic and sweepingly dismissive than that of Leiter, Schauer sounds a theme that has come to be widely accepted among the philosophers and legal scholars who have mulled over the knowledge-promoting rationale for versions of the principle of freedom of expression:

> Whether this or that method for identification of independently defined truth [such as the method that consists in the implementation of any expansive version of the principle of freedom of expression] will locate more truths, or expose more falsehoods, when compared to some other method having the same goal is not nearly as much a philosophical (or legal) question as it is a testable, empirical one. And as a testable, empirical proposition, it turns out that there are good reasons to doubt the soundness of the empirical claim [about the tendency of expansive versions of the principle of freedom of expression to foster the attainment of knowledge]. (Schauer 2017, 237, footnotes omitted)

Naturally, any contestation of the empirical surmises that undergird the truth-seeking rationale is conducted through contrary empirical claims. Those latter claims are well supported by arguments and by some data, but as empirical propositions they are of course subject to the ebb and flow of contingencies. My purposes here do not oblige me to recount and defend those arguments and data; instead, my aim at this juncture is simply to submit that the ordinary vulnerabilities of consequentialist theories to the vagaries of circumstances are particularly acute for theories which adduce the promotion of knowledge as an objective that is furthered by the robust protection of communicative liberties. There are quite solid grounds for thinking that the empirical premises of such theories are usually false or simplistic, and there are thus quite solid grounds for thinking that the inability of any consequentialist rationale to vindicate the absoluteness of a deontological principle will be especially severe when the rationale in question is focused on the

2015, 1161–75; Horwitz 2012; Ingber 1984; Kenyon 2014, 382; Piety 2007; Post 2000, 2364–6; Schauer 1982, 15–34; 2008, 922–5; 2010; 2012; 2017; Tsesis 2016, 8–11; Weinstein 2011, 502.

search for truth as a goal that can serve to underpin the principle of freedom of expression.

4.1.4 A Focus on Governmental Power

In the philosophical and legal literature on communicative freedoms, a focus on the dangers posed by the dominance and concentration of governmental power is often combined with some of the other foci that have been delineated above. A distrust of the mighty sway exerted by the officials in any system of governance has led numerous scholars and jurists to hold that the protection of ample leeway for the communicative activities of citizens is vital as a means of bridling that sway.[5] In one major respect, this fourth set of positions on the matter of communicative liberties is convergent with the Stoical justification for the principle of freedom of expression that will be expounded in this chapter. That is, rather than training its focus directly on potential addressors or potential addressees or the overall good of a society, a position of this fourth kind trains its focus directly on the system of governance that prevails in any given jurisdiction.

Theories in this fourth category are permeated by the concern that, even when the officials of a system of governance are well-intentioned and highly knowledgeable, their amassing of legal and physical powers is in grave tension with the ideals of liberal democracy. In part, the tension is acute because officials currently harboring good intentions might alter their objectives subsequently or might be replaced by officials with more sinister designs. A still more important reason for the acuteness of the tension is that even the actions impelled by good designs can go badly awry. Counterproductiveness and outright oppressiveness are particularly likely when the actions in question are undertaken by officials whose accumulating of inordinate powers has released them from many of the checks and balances that would otherwise have helped to rein them in. Such untoward consequences can emerge in many domains, but they loom especially large in the endeavors of governmental officials to regulate the communicative interaction of people. As Schauer declares, "official discretion to determine the value of speech content has long been understood to be incompatible with the principle of free speech itself, one of whose central themes is distrust of government" (1998, 111). Schauer elsewhere expands on that theme of distrust:

> Freedom of speech is based in large part on a distrust of the ability of government to make the necessary distinctions, a distrust of governmental determinations of truth and falsity, an appreciation of the fallibility of political leaders,

[5] Leiter (2016) adopts a version of this rationale. For some other versions, see Blasi 1977; Epstein 1992; Krotoszynski 2015; Lee 2009, 1733–5; Schauer 1982, 80–6; Stone 1993.

> and a somewhat deeper distrust of governmental power in a more general sense. (Schauer 1982, 86)

When the institutions of a system of governance confer wide-ranging protection on expressive freedoms, these dangers of governmental overreaching and blundering are thereby significantly reduced. Operating to provide such protection, those institutions will not authorize officials to reach determinations on matters—pertaining to people's communicative interactions—which the officials are peculiarly prone to mishandle. Moreover, because the officials are not authorized to reach such determinations, the consolidation of their ascendance over the citizenry will *pro tanto* be inhibited. As members of the public enjoy security against governmental interference in some crucial aspects of their lives, the lopsidedness of the relationship between them and the governmental officials is somewhat lessened.

Although this wariness-of-government rationale for the conferral of expansive protection upon communicative freedoms does devote its attention preponderantly to the position of a system of governance vis-à-vis the populace over whom the system presides, it otherwise differs markedly from this book's Stoical justification for the principle of freedom of expression. In the first place, it is thoroughly consequentialist in its orientation even though it is far removed from utilitarianism. Its advocacy of extensive constitutional or statutory protection against interventions by the agencies of government into the communicative activities of people is premised on claims about the seriously untoward consequences (particularly in the form of governmental overreaching or blundering) that will ensue causally from the absence of such protection. While the specifics of those claims vary substantially among the sundry incarnations of the distrust-of-government rationale, every such incarnation adverts to the prospect of deleterious causal consequences as the factor that tells decisively against most governmental restrictions on communications. Hence, with a consequentialist orientation, the distrust-of-government approach is unable to vindicate the absoluteness of the principle of freedom of expression—since the applicability of a rationale with such an orientation is always dependent on the contingencies of circumstances.

A very closely related consideration is that, like any other consequentialist line of reasoning, the distrust-of-government justification relies on certain empirical suppositions. To be sure, those suppositions are highly plausible. They are far more plausible than the empirical surmises that underpin some of the other lines of reasoning (such as the truth-seeking rationale) that have been propounded by consequentialists to vindicate constitutional free-speech guarantees. There are indeed strong reasons for doubting that the officials in any system of governance will be capable of avoiding numerous bad missteps if they are legally authorized to regulate people's communicative activities in ways that are at odds with the constraints of communication-neutrality and content-neutrality and speaker-neutrality. Similarly, there are strong reasons for suspecting that the augmentation of the powers of the officials through their being so authorized will worsen the lopsidedness of the relationship between them and ordinary citizens. Any inclinations of the officials to act domineeringly will be intensified in a situation where they have ample opportunities to give effect to those inclinations. Nevertheless, despite the cogency of the misgivings that are voiced by the proponents of the distrust-of-government rationale, those misgivings rest on empirical theses that are vulnerable to being disconfirmed in some credible contexts.

A third dissimilarity is directly connected to what has just been said. Unlike the distrust-of-government account, this chapter's justification of the principle of freedom of expression does not presume that the officials in any system of governance are likely to blunder frequently in their judgments if they are vested with legal powers to regulate the communicative activities of citizens extensively. Nor does this chapter's justification presume that any tendencies of officials toward high-handedness will be significantly magnified if the officials are vested with legal powers of the sort just mentioned. Notwithstanding the persuasiveness of the empirical contentions that inform the distrust-of-government rationale, this chapter can suppose *arguendo* that those contentions are largely baseless. I can suppose as much here for the sake of argument, since my meditations on the moral import of the principle of freedom of expression would retain their pertinence even in application to a fanciful system of governance where officials vested with wide-ranging legal powers to regulate people's communicative activities are not likely to reach inapposite judgments about those activities and are not disposed toward arrogance when interacting with citizens. Even in relation to such a far-fetched system of governance, this chapter's Stoical justification of the principle of freedom of expression would call for the system's strict adherence to that principle. Although the Stoical justification will recount a certain outlook (the quidnunc mentality) that is to be avoided by legal-governmental officials, this chapter will emphasize that the outlook in question is not an array of empirical traits of character such as domineeringness. Similarly, the Stoical justification is not concerned with the matter of lowering the likelihood of mistaken judgments by the officials in a system of governance, and it would therefore not be rendered any less germane by the prospect of a system in which that likelihood is somehow already very low. This chapter's concerns are thoroughly ethical rather than empirical and operational.

A final dissimilarity to be noted here is again closely linked to the foregoing remarks. Although the Stoical rationale and the distrust-of-government rationale initially converge in focusing on the relationship between a system of governance and the citizenry over whom the system presides, they thereafter diverge. For the Stoical justification, that initial focus is embedded in a much larger account of the paramount moral responsibility borne by every system of governance; the self-restraint exercised by such a system through its adherence to the principle of freedom of expression is among the conditions under which every member of a society can be warranted in harboring an ample sense of self-respect. That account of the deeper moral significance of the principle of freedom of expression is entirely consistent with the distrust-of-government line of reasoning, but neither of them entails the other, and they have never in fact been conjoined. Nor will they be conjoined here. Notwithstanding my sympathy with the attitudes and assumptions encapsulated in the distrust-of-government approach, any embrace of that approach here would be a distraction from the very different line of reasoning that will be advanced in this chapter.

4.2 The Moral Foundation of the Principle of Freedom of Expression

Given that I have been referring to this chapter's justification of the principle of freedom of expression as "Stoical," a preliminary comment is advisable here. Although the inspiration for that justification is indeed Stoical, and although any readers familiar with the main ideas of Hellenistic Stoicism will detect certain echoes of some of those ideas in this chapter,[6] the echoes will be quite tenuous. There are no attempts in this chapter to ground its arguments in any specific Stoical doctrines, and some of the ideas most prominently championed by the ancient Stoics are altogether ignored (and implicitly eschewed). This chapter's endeavor to vindicate the principle of freedom of expression will stand or fall on its own merits, rather than on the extent of its affinities with the outlooks and preoccupations of the Hellenistic Stoics.

Indeed, the intellectual backdrop for this chapter's ruminations on the moral import of the principle of freedom of expression derives at least as much from the work of John Rawls as from any of the ideas generally attributed to the philosophers in the ancient tradition of Stoicism. Though Rawls's musings on communicative freedoms are neither lengthy nor very profound, his reflections on the nature and ethical significance of self-respect—some reflections which I have elsewhere expounded at length and defended with a number of modifications and refinements (Kramer 2017, 299–340)—are integral to the justification for the principle of freedom of expression which this chapter will elaborate. That justification blends a largely Rawlsian understanding of warranted self-respect with a Stoical grasp of the interrelation between self-restraint and ethical strength. With a grounding in Rawlsianism as much as in Stoicism, this chapter's justification of the principle of freedom of expression is thoroughly liberal in its tenor. Its emphasis on the centrality of warranted self-respect as a desideratum for everyone is a point of departure that is indispensable within liberalism, as Rawls recognized.

[6] For some excellent overviews of Stoicism, see Brennan 2005; Inwood 1985; 2003; Nussbaum 1994; Sorabji 2000.

4.2.1 The Paramount Moral Responsibility

Paramount among the moral obligations incumbent on the system of governance that presides over any society is the duty to bring about the political and economic and social conditions under which every member of that society can be warranted in harboring an ample sense of self-respect. Before we contemplate how this fundamental moral responsibility pertains to matters of freedom of expression, we should consider some aspects of it that could easily be misunderstood if they were left unelucidated. Let us begin by exploring briefly the nature of self-respect.

4.2.1.1 Warranted Self-Respect

Although my lengthy discussion elsewhere of the nature of self-respect obviously cannot be reproduced in this chapter, a few strands from that discussion—in highly condensed forms—should be clarified and underscored here. A key paragraph from Rawls's cogitations on the topic can serve as an illuminating point of reference:

> We may define self-respect (or self-esteem) as having two aspects. First of all . . . it includes a person's sense of his own value, his secure conviction that his conception of his good, his plan of life, is worth carrying out. And second, self-respect implies a confidence in one's ability, so far as it is within one's power, to fulfill one's intentions. When we feel that our plans are of little value, we cannot pursue them with pleasure or take delight in their execution. Nor plagued by failure and self-doubt can we continue in our endeavors. It is clear then why self-respect is a primary good. Without it nothing may seem worth doing, or if some things have value for us, we lack the will to strive for them. (Rawls 1999, 386)

Although this passage is in need of some modifications, it elegantly distills several of the chief elements in my own account of warranted self-respect. Rawls was correct in declaring that self-respect is best understood as self-esteem which comprises both self-worth (a sense that one's projects and objectives are valuable) and self-confidence (a sense that one will be able to do many of the things which one sets out to do).

Rawls has been criticized by some commentators for running together the notion of self-respect with the putatively distinct notion of self-esteem. Such commentators usually hold that self-respect consists in a sense of oneself as an agent who should always be treated as an end and never solely as a means, whereas self-esteem consists in a favorable appraisal of one's own accomplishments or talents or projects or attractiveness or personality or relationships. Those critics maintain that the pivotal primary good that should have been identified by Rawls as such is self-respect in the Kantian sense just indicated, rather than self-esteem.[7] However,

[7] Critics of Rawls who invoke such a dichotomy are usually building upon the apt distinction drawn by Stephen Darwall (1977) between recognition respect and appraisal respect.

as I have sustainedly argued elsewhere (Kramer 2017, 300–22), any objections to Rawls along these lines are inapposite—partly because self-respect in the Kantian sense is always a component of self-esteem, and partly because self-esteem is what fully partakes of the features that led Rawls to classify it as a primary good.

Of course, although self-respect as self-esteem (or, rather, warranted self-respect as warranted self-esteem) is a primary good, it is a primary natural good rather than a primary social good.[8] In other words, it is never a distribuendum directly apportioned by any system of governance. Instead, it is like health or intelligence as a desideratum which should be fostered by a system of governance but which in its distribution cannot be directly controlled by any such system. Governmental functionaries cannot ever ensure that each person in a society will harbor an ample sense of self-respect, nor can they ensure that each person would be warranted in harboring such a sense. The level of self-respect actually experienced by any person *P* is principally dependent on *P*'s own conduct and talents and temperament, and the level of self-respect that is warranted for *P* is principally dependent on *P*'s own conduct and talents. Sundry additional contingencies beyond the control of any liberal-democratic system of governance, including most notably the actions and decisions of many other people, also bear significantly on the magnitude of *P*'s actual self-respect and on the magnitude of the self-respect which *P* is warranted in harboring. Consequently, although the social and economic and political factors that can be suitably influenced by a system of governance are crucial in affecting *P*'s situation, numerous other factors are vital as well.

One way in which the quoted remarks from Rawls stand in need of amplification is signaled by my parenthetical wording in the first sentence of the preceding paragraph. Rawls focused on self-respect as a primary good—indeed as the most important of the primary goods—but he should instead have focused on *warranted* self-respect. Whereas self-respect is fundamentally a psychological property, warranted self-respect is fundamentally ethical as well as psychological. It is the level of self-esteem that is appropriate in response to one's successes and failures and abilities and aspirations and relationships. Although the level of self-respect actually felt by anyone is a subjective property, the warrantedness or unwarrantedness of that level of self-respect is an objective ethical matter. (Note that the unwarrantedness of someone's sense of self-respect can be in the direction either of excess or of deficiency. A person can deludedly overestimate her achievements or other admirable qualities, but alternatively she can assess those achievements and qualities too negatively.)

[8] On the distinction between primary social goods and primary natural goods, see Rawls 1999, 54. See also Kramer 2017, 325–8.

4.2.1.2 A Government's Responsibility to Promote Warranted Self-Respect

Although the foregoing subsection furnishes only the barest synopsis of a much longer exposition of warranted self-respect in my 2017 book *Liberalism with Excellence*, it is sufficient for the purposes of this chapter. We should now ponder the role of a government in promoting the incidence of warrantedly high levels of self-respect among the people in the society over which the government presides. As has already been indicated, that role does not involve any direct distribution of levels of warranted self-respect. Warranted self-respect is a primary natural good rather than a primary social good. Instead of treating it as a distribuendum, a system of governance is morally obligated to bring about the political and socioeconomic conditions under which every member of a society can be warranted in feeling an ample sense of self-respect.

Of course, as has been stated, no system of governance can ensure that every member of a society will indeed harbor an ample sense of self-respect; nor can any such system ensure that every member will be warranted in harboring such a sense. Like the level of health enjoyed by any particular individual, the level of self-respect experienced by her is determined by numerous contingencies of her biography and temperament. Similarly, the level of self-respect that would be *warranted* for any particular individual is determined by numerous contingencies of her biography and abilities as well as by socioeconomic and political conditions. (My references here to a person's biography naturally encompass her relationships with other people.) Because the quantum of actual self-respect and the quantum of warranted self-respect for each person are so heavily dependent on the peculiarities of her attainments and circumstances, no system of governance is morally obligated to bring about a situation where everyone is warranted in harboring an ample degree of self-respect which he or she actually harbors. Such a situation can fail to obtain—indeed, it will scarcely ever obtain—even if a system of governance has fulfilled all its responsibilities.

What a system of governance is morally obligated to do, however, is to bring about the socioeconomic and political conditions under which every member of a society can be warranted in feeling a solid sense of self-respect. Dependent though levels of warranted self-respect are on the particularities of individuals' lives, they are also determined crucially by the general socioeconomic and political arrangements over which a government can exert substantial influence. Appropriate socioeconomic and political institutions are not a sufficient condition for every person to be warranted in sustaining a high level of self-respect, but they are a necessary condition for the warrantedness of such a level on the part of any ordinary person. Thus, every system of governance is morally obligated to develop and uphold such institutions. (As has been indicated at the outset of the present chapter, I shall be using the phrase "paramount responsibility" to refer to this moral obligation which is incumbent on every system of governance.)

4.2.1.2.1 Edificatory Perfectionism Rejected

Although the influence of socioeconomic and political arrangements on people's warranted levels of self-respect is multifaceted, my book *Liberalism with Excellence* has chiefly probed two main channels of that influence. A laconic account of each of those channels can help to illuminate the present chapter's justification of the principle of freedom of expression. Let us, then, first briefly consider my rejection of edificatory perfectionism in that 2017 book. Edificatory perfectionism comprises a motley array of theories whose proponents maintain that—at least in principle—governments are sometimes morally permitted and morally obligated to steer people toward ways of life that are more flourishing or upright or wholesome or successful or robustly autonomous. According to such philosophers, governments are morally permitted and morally obligated to undertake arrangements that will induce people to edify themselves by developing and exerting their capacities. I have argued at length that, insofar as a society's political institutions act for the purpose of edifying the citizenry rather than for the purpose of addressing injustices or fostering prosperity and public order and other public goods, those institutions will not be supportive of warrantedly high levels of self-respect (Kramer 2017, 251–96). Such counterproductiveness will be especially pronounced if the governmental actions involve coercion or manipulation, but it will occur even if those actions consist solely in positive enticements such as subsidies or tax exemptions. For two principal reasons, the endeavors to edify the citizenry are contrary to a government's paramount responsibility. Such endeavors tarnish the relationship between citizens and governmental functionaries, for they are based on officiously derogatory judgments akin to those that animate the meddlesomeness of a busybody; and they demean the system of governance by tying the success of its operations partly to matters that would be beneath its notice if it concerned itself not with citizens' harmless foibles but with its own paramount responsibility. In my defense of the principle of freedom of expression, we shall return shortly to this dynamic of overweening intrusiveness and degrading dependence.

4.2.1.2.2 Aspirational Perfectionism Championed

The effects of edificatory policies are scarcely the only nexus between socioeconomic or political conditions and the warranted levels of self-respect of individuals. In addition, my alternative variety of perfectionism—aspirational perfectionism—is centered on the ways in which the excellence of a society bolsters the levels of self-respect that can warrantedly be experienced by individuals. People very often do take pride in the accomplishments of their contemporaries and predecessors as well as in their own accomplishments, and they are frequently warranted in doing so. Vicarious pride is frequently warranted because the life of virtually every individual unfolds in networks of relationships that bear importantly on how well that life has gone.[9] Given that such pride is frequently warranted, the paramount

[9] As should be evident, the notion of how well a life goes is understood here in what Derek Parfit labeled as an "objective-list" sense (1984, 499). Such an understanding of the quality of a

responsibility of a government includes a responsibility to foster the occurrence of outstanding achievements. Those outstanding achievements help to endow with excellence the society over which a government presides, and they thereby contribute to the government's fulfilling of its paramount responsibility—since the members of the society can warrantedly feel better about themselves by dint of warrantedly feeling better about their status as such members. Conversely, the members of a meanly unaccomplished society can be warranted in feeling worse about themselves inasmuch as they are warranted in feeling abashed about their status as such members.

Although the cultivation of sterling accomplishments in areas such as art and literature and science and athletics can be crucial for the satisfaction of a government's paramount responsibility, the securing of people's basic rights and liberties is even more important for the satisfaction of that responsibility. If the securing of people's basic rights and liberties is itself understood as a mode of excellence—as Rawls took it to be in *A Theory of Justice*, and as I take it to be in *Liberalism with Excellence*—it is the foremost aspirational-perfectionist objective which any system of governance is morally obligated to realize. If aspirational perfectionism is instead construed more narrowly to comprehend all modes of excellence except for the securing of people's basic rights and liberties, then aspirational-perfectionist policies are lexically subordinate to the policies whereby those rights and liberties are protected. Whatever position anybody adopts on that matter of taxonomy,[10] the key point is that the upholding of basic rights and liberties and the fostering of other modes of excellence are the means by which a system of governance discharges its paramount responsibility. Albeit the nurturance of outstanding feats in areas such as art and literature and science and athletics is always lexically subordinate to the effectuation of the basic rights and liberties of individuals, it too is partly constitutive of the conditions under which each individual can be warranted in sustaining an ample quantum of self-respect.

This terse summary should close by highlighting one of the affinities between my Stoical aspirational-perfectionist liberalism and Rawlsian liberalism. Those two theories share an egalitarian insistence that the primary natural goods are to be promoted—not guaranteed or distributed, but promoted—for everyone alike.

life is singularly appropriate in ruminations on the objective warrantedness of levels of self-respect.

[10] It is a taxonomical matter rather than a substantive matter because it does not concern any of the following questions, each of which is to be answered affirmatively: (1) whether the effectuation of individuals' basic rights and liberties is a morally obligatory and vital endeavor for every system of governance; (2) whether the fostering of excellent accomplishments in areas such as the arts and sciences is typically a morally obligatory endeavor for a system of governance; and (3) whether the principle of justice that makes the former endeavor obligatory is lexically superior to the principle of justice that makes the latter endeavor obligatory. Instead, the sole matter at issue—a taxonomical matter—is whether aspirational perfectionism encompasses only the latter endeavor or also the former.

By the reckoning of aspirational-perfectionist liberalism, as has been repeatedly affirmed herein, the paramount responsibility incumbent on any system of governance is to bring about the political and social and economic conditions under which *every* member of a society can be warranted in feeling a hearty sense of self-respect. Now, among the members of a society, the level of self-respect that is warranted for anyone will be influenced most heavily by what he or she has done. In a typical situation, some of the members of the society will be much more accomplished than others, and most members will be at intermediate degrees of accomplishment. For the people toward the top end of the scale of personal achievements, the fostering of excellence by a system of governance beyond the sustainment of liberal-democratic institutions and values will generally not be necessary to enable those people to be warranted in harboring strong levels of self-respect. Significantly further down the scale of personal achievements, however, the level of self-respect that is warranted for each person will require more and more bolstering from the overall excellence of the society if that level is to remain ample (Kramer 2017, 366). Of course, almost inevitably, the levels warranted for some citizens will not be ample—perhaps because those citizens have devoted their lives to wrongdoing or perhaps because their projects have been blighted by dismal failures. An aspirational-perfectionist system of governance does not and cannot provide any guarantees against such outcomes. What it can and should do, however, is to supply the political and economic and social conditions under which the prospect of being warranted in enjoying a hearty sense of self-respect is meaningfully available to every citizen. For that purpose, such a system of governance has to take into account the likely spread of personal achievements.

4.2.2 The Paramount Responsibility and the Principle of Freedom of Expression

Of course, the foregoing paragraphs provide no more than a skimpy adumbration of the Stoical aspirational-perfectionist liberalism that imbues this book. The assertions in those paragraphs have not been buttressed here by any sustained argumentation. However, because I have presented the relevant argumentation at length in my earlier book *Liberalism with Excellence*, and because my purpose in this chapter is simply to show that the paramount responsibility of any system of governance is connected to the principle of freedom of expression, the remarks in the foregoing paragraphs are sufficient. What must now be explored in this chapter, therefore, is exactly how the compliance of a system of governance with the principle of freedom of expression is integral to the system's fulfilling of its paramount responsibility.

4.2.2.1 Shakespeare on Self-Restraint and Strength

As a point of departure for investigating the matter just broached, we should glance at a couple of passages from Shakespeare's plays (each of which I have quoted, along with several other Shakespearean passages, in *Liberalism with Excellence*). Whereas the first of these passages is from one of his lesser tragedies, the second is from one of his most popular comedies.[11]

4.2.2.1.1 The Eagle and the Little Birds

Let us begin with a few lines spoken by one of Shakespeare's most villainous characters, Tamora the former Queen of the Goths in *Titus Andronicus*. Expostulating with the Roman Emperor Saturninus in order to dissuade him from retaliating blatantly against his enemies and in order to assuage his fears that the hearts of his people have abandoned him and gone over to those enemies, she reassures him as follows:

> King, be thy thoughts imperious, like thy name.
> Is the sun dimm'd, that gnats do fly in it?
> The eagle suffers little birds to sing,
> And is not careful what they mean thereby,
> Knowing that with the shadow of his wings
> He can at pleasure stint their melody:
> Even so mayst thou the giddy men of Rome.
> (IV.iv.81–7)

As is to be expected from a repulsive evildoer such as Tamora, the sentiments expressed in this passage emanate from a haughtily elitist vision of Roman society and of her place within it—a vision that tallies with the Emperor's autocratic power, of course. Nevertheless, as will become evident, the insight articulated by Tamora is disseverable from the ugliness of her bloodthirsty lust for power and revenge. More generally, some of the valuable observations that can be gleaned from a number of Shakespeare's plays have to be detached from the ancient and medieval settings of the plays. Those settings skew the observations by embedding them in the hierarchical codes of human interaction that prevailed in bygone ages. My distillation of an ethic of self-restraint in this chapter is aimed at salvaging and modernizing a pair of Shakespearean aperçus by relocating their substance in the egalitarianism of liberal democracy.

4.2.2.1.2 Bird-Bolts and Cannon-Bullets

In an early scene of *Twelfth Night*, the countess Olivia reprimands her steward Malvolio for his scathing disparagement of the jester Feste. Malvolio in his

[11] I have used Shakespeare 1974 for all quotations from the Bard.

sanctimoniousness has taken exception to Feste's penchant for poking fun at the people in Olivia's household—not least at Malvolio himself, of course. Olivia chides the steward for his humorlessness and prickliness:

> Oh, you are sick of self-love, Malvolio, and taste with a distempered appetite. To be generous, guiltless and of free disposition, is to take those things for bird-bolts that you deem cannon-bullets: there is no slander in an allowed fool, though he do nothing but rail. (I.v.85–9)

Shakespeare may have been casting some gentle ridicule on Puritanism in the person of Malvolio, but the gist of Olivia's reproach to her servant is obviously generalizable well beyond any contexts of religious or political disputation during the reign of Elizabeth I. Similarly, the instructiveness of the reproach is not limited to the aristocratic society in which it is uttered. Although Olivia is a countess who may well have in mind an ethic of nobility in which she has been reared, and although her upbraiding of Malvolio proceeds somewhat *de haut en bas*, she does not commend forbearance as a virtue appurtenant to a high social rank. Rather, she commends it as the hallmark of an upright character (a virtue that belongs to somebody who is "generous, guiltless, and of free disposition"). Her conception of self-restraint can thus be aligned with the egalitarianism of liberal democracy.

Moreover, Olivia makes clear that self-restraint is a virtue not only because it can be a mode of excellence but also and even more importantly because it fulfills certain moral obligations. When somebody displays a paucity of forbearance—in circumstances which pose no dangers or injustices or other factors that might warrant such a dearth of forbearance—he not only lacks an admirable trait but furthermore exhibits a degrading trait that vitiates his interaction with other people. In the quoted passage, Olivia expresses this point by suggesting that Malvolio in his petulance is sick with self-love and that his sickness causes him to assess other people and their conduct distortively; he "taste[s] with a distempered appetite." His self-infatuation is a vice that leaves him unable to brook the witticisms and repartee that would amuse someone whose interaction with other people is not similarly warped. It also leaves him vulnerable to cozenage that trades upon his egocentricity. His disinclination to abide by his obligations of elementary civility in his dealings with the people around him—as he proclaims to them that they are "idle, shallow things" and that he is "not of your element" (*Twelfth Night*, III.iv.122–3)—is a manifestation of weakness in more than one sense.

4.2.2.2 The Dynamic of Self-Aggrandizement and Self-Abasement

With these Shakespearean passages in mind, we should now consider how the non-compliance of a system of governance with the principle of freedom of expression will have landed that system in a dynamic of self-aggrandizement and self-abasement akin to that which I have sketched in §4.2.1.2.1 above.

4.2.2.2.1 A Government-Focused Justification

Like the distrust-of-government rationale for versions of the principle of freedom of expression, this chapter's Stoical justification of that principle is focused directly on the relationship between a system of governance and the citizens over whom the system presides. This book is predominantly a work of political philosophy, and the self-restraint denoted in its title is predominantly a characteristic of some systems of governance. Hence, although the excerpt from *Twelfth Night* focuses on personal traits of temperament, both it and the excerpt from *Titus Andronicus* are to be construed here as shedding light on attributes of governmental institutions. Self-restraint as such an attribute, attained through the compliance of a system of governance with the principle of freedom of expression, is a virtue that is also a condition for the moral legitimacy of each law or policy adopted by the system. Any law or policy that stems from a lack of such compliance is morally illegitimate.

Still, although this book's commendation of self-restraint as a hallmark or constituent of strength of character is concerned with features of systems of governance and with the laws or policies for which those systems are responsible, every system of governance is of course run by human beings who reach and effectuate decisions within it. Hence, my delineation of the self-restraint that is achieved through compliance with the principle of freedom of expression will proceed partly by reference to the outlooks of legal-governmental officials. Two caveats are in need of emphasis from the outset, then.

First, the officials are appraised solely in their capacities as public functionaries who act on behalf of the system of governance in which they hold their positions as officials. They are not under appraisal as private individuals at all. Thus, my imputation of certain outlooks to them is *pari passu* an ascription of certain properties to their system of governance—which is indeed the point of the enterprise in this chapter.

Second, my attribution of certain outlooks to legal-governmental officials is not a hypothesis to be confirmed or disconfirmed through the introspection of the officials or through their being subjected to psychological testing. This chapter is not a venture in social science that advances an array of empirical claims—empirical conjectures—about the self-understandings of the officials. Rather, at a high level of generality, it is attributing to the officials the attitudes that would most credibly account for their decisions and behavior. Whether the officials would recognize those attitudes as their own is a matter that depends on the acuity of their self-knowledge; it is not a matter which affects the correctness of my contention that their actions bespeak those attitudes. Just as Chapter 2 of this book has emphasized that the ascription of intentions to legislative or administrative enactments is not an exercise in reading the minds of the legislators and administrators responsible for those enactments, so this chapter should stress that it will not embark on any exercise in reporting how legal-governmental officials perceive themselves and their doings. Instead, its project is interpretive and ethical. Its effort to make sense of the decisions and behavior of officials is undertaken for the purpose of ethically evaluating the systems of governance within which their decisions and behavior occur. Ethical properties of such a system supervene on the outlooks that are encapsulated in the public conduct of its officials.

4.2.2.2.2 Overweeningness and Demeaningness: Lessons from Olivia and Tamora

What the passage from *Titus Andronicus* and the passage from *Twelfth Night* have in common is their acceptance of the proposition that unaccommodatingness or intolerance in the absence of any adequate justification is a failing that amounts to a manifestation of weakness. Tamora in *Titus Andronicus* articulates that proposition predominantly in terms of sheer physical might, but Olivia in *Twelfth Night* articulates it straightforwardly as an ethical matter. Moreover, as has already been emphasized, Olivia indicates that self-restraint (in situations which do not involve any communication-independent wrongs that might warrant a dearth of forbearance) is not only a virtue but also a pattern of behavior that fulfills certain moral duties.

Indeed, the moral integrity of a system of governance is tarnished when the system's laws or policies restrict people's communicational activities in circumstances where those activities do not constitute any communication-independent wrongdoing. In the absence of such wrongdoing, the imposition of trammels on people's communications is a form of overreaching by a system of governance—where the overreaching both signals and reinforces the moral weakness of the system. In her own distortively evil way, Tamora in *Titus Andronicus* suggests why gratuitous curbs on the communicational freedoms of individuals are symptomatic and promotive of weakness. Although she formulates this point as an observation about the institutional or military potency of a Roman emperor, her insight can readily be extended to the ethical status of any system of governance.

On the one hand, quite important in itself is Tamora's claim that a ruler betrays his weakness when he demeaningly stoops to silencing the gnats and little birds that chirp in his society. A ruler secure in his power can blithely disregard the chirping, which poses no threat to him that is serious enough to be worth his attending to it. A mighty eagle should not lower himself to the level of a lesser bird by worrying about dissidents whose strength in comparison with his own is feeble; he would thereby evince a low estimation of himself and would provide grounds for others likewise to form a low estimation of him. Now, although this observation by Tamora is relatively superficial and is only contingently applicable to any given situation, it is perceptive as far as it goes. For example, a striking fact about the despotic kleptocracy which has governed China for the past several decades is that the tyrants at the top of that kleptocracy are so repressively insecure as to ban various computing facilities that are available to people in most of the rest of the world. In so doing, the Chinese dictators not only subject the citizens of China to humiliating infantilization but also demean themselves by conveying the impression that their sway over those citizens is shuddersomely precarious. Their restrictions on the communicative freedoms of people in China are a manifestation of weakness, however tenaciously the despots preserve their hold on power.

On the other hand, my primary concern in this chapter is with the ethical bearings of any system of governance rather than with the dynamics of power. Tamora's insight has to be reconstrued if it is to be brought to bear on that ethical concern. In what respects are inordinate fetters on the communicative activities of people both indicative and promotive of ethical weakness in a system of governance? The wrongness of such fetters is of course often due partly to their negative effects on the interests of addressors and addressees (and on the interests of a society) that have been examined in §4.1 above. However, of unique importance in some contexts and of great importance in all contexts is that the inordinate fetters bespeak the self-aggrandizement of the officials responsible for them—and, consequently, the self-aggrandizement of the system of governance on whose behalf those officials act.

By characterizing the restrictions on the communicative interaction of people as "inordinate," I am indicating that they are not necessary for the fulfillment of the moral responsibilities that are incumbent on any system of governance. Some curbs on communications can of course be morally permissible as means of carrying out those responsibilities, if the communications in question are constitutive of communication-independent misdeeds. Curbs so imposed can be perfectly in compliance with the principle of freedom of expression. Thus, for example, as Chapters 2 and 3 have recounted, legal prohibitions on fraud and on defamation and on incitement and on solicitation to commit crimes and on the disclosure of vital military information (especially in times of warfare) can be morally legitimate. Though the moral soundness of those prohibitions is dependent on their being reasonably formulated and oriented and interpreted, they can be unproblematic by any liberal-democratic reckoning. Here, however, we are pondering some restrictions on people's communicative interaction that are not similarly consistent with the principle of freedom of expression.

4.2.2.2.3 Overweeningness and Demeaningness: The Quidnunc Mentality

In some contexts, governmental restrictions that comply with the principle of freedom of expression will impinge more severely on the opportunities of potential addressors or potential addressees than will governmental restrictions that do not so comply. One such context is that of the municipal bus service which we have contemplated repeatedly in this chapter and in previous chapters. We shall return hereafter to the example of the buses and the advertisements. Let us for the moment concentrate instead on some other contexts, where the opportunities of potential addressors and potential addressees are affected only minimally by certain governmental restrictions that do not conform with the principle of freedom of expression. Some type of communicative activity, such as the flow of utterances in an especially puerile game, might be degrading and even dispiriting for the people who participate in it as addressors or addressees. Why would a legal prohibition on that mode of communication be an instance of governmental overreaching rather than an instance of governmental solicitude for the goodness of the lives of citizens?

As should be clear from what has been stated already, the dichotomy posed in this question is a false dichotomy. Wrongfully officious policies can be solicitously well-intentioned while nonetheless being wrongfully officious. We can see as much clear-sightedly when we turn our attention directly to the system of governance that adopts a legal prohibition on the flow of utterances in an asinine game. Whereas Rawlsians and other Kantians will doubtless explain the wrongfulness of such a prohibition by contending that it manifests disrespect for the deliberative agency of sane adults who will not be permitted to determine for themselves whether to participate in the communications that have been banned, this chapter is concentrating instead on the ignominious weakness that is displayed by the system of governance which imposes the ban. Specifically, the functionaries who run that system are interacting with their fellow citizens in broadly the same fashion in which a busybody of a village interacts with her fellow villagers. Her sense of how well her life goes is partly dependent on the patterns of conduct adopted by those other villagers, notwithstanding that the relevant patterns of conduct affect her only through her own sentiments of offendedness and gratification. She feels better about her life when the inhabitants of her village behave in accordance with her standards of propriety, and she feels worse about her life when they deviate from those standards. She gauges the success of her doings partly by the extent to which she secures the conformity of those inhabitants to her standards. Accordingly, she keeps track of how her fellow villagers behave, and she hectors or ostracizes or importunately cajoles anyone whom she believes to be falling significantly short—even though the falling short is not adversely affecting other people to any discernible degree. She possesses the mentality of a quidnunc, which far-reachingly informs and taints her relationships with her contemporaries.

At the level of an individual, the quidnunc mentality is quite evidently a failure of self-restraint. It is both a form of self-aggrandizement and a form of self-abasement. It is a meddlesome form of self-aggrandizement because it takes for granted that one's fellows can permissibly be prevailed upon—through outright force or coercive vehemence or bribe-like inducements—to modify patterns of communicative behavior that are not harmful to anybody except perhaps the individuals themselves who engage in those patterns of behavior. Yet the quidnunc mentality also consists in self-abasement, since it makes one's own sense of satisfaction partly dependent on the responsiveness of one's fellows to one's officious badgering about their private pursuits. Instead of abiding by a live-and-let-live ethos, a busybody partly ties the success of her own life to her effectiveness in not letting other people lead their lives as they see fit. That is, the success of her own life partly hinges on the willingness of other people to desist from conduct which she regards with distaste (even though the conduct does not otherwise harm her or anybody else). In precisely that respect, one's possession of a quidnunc mentality is a manifestation of weakness.

At the level of a system of governance, a quidnunc mentality that underlies various laws or policies is even more egregiously a failure of self-restraint. Again, it is both a form of self-aggrandizement and a form of self-abasement. It is a meddlesome form of self-aggrandizement because—*ex hypothesi*—the laws or policies that emanate from it are not aimed at prohibiting or preventing the occurrence of any communication-independent misconduct. Rather, those laws or policies are aimed at prohibiting or preventing the occurrence of communications that are not constitutive of any such misconduct. Furthermore, the overweeningness of the quidnunc mentality in that regard is integrally linked to the way in which such a mentality is also a self-abasing manifestation of weakness. It is an outlook of self-abasingness because it makes the success of a system of governance partly dependent on the decisions of citizens to alter their jejune communicative pursuits in response to directives from the system's officials. Instead of confining the system's efforts to the dispensation of information and the maintenance of fair conditions for informed decisions by citizens about the aforementioned pursuits, the officials responsible for the laws or policies that stem from a quidnunc mentality have tied the success of the system's endeavors partly to its effectiveness in not letting citizens arrive at disfavored decisions about the types of communications in which they will engage (where certain modes of communication are disfavored not because they are constitutive of communication-independent wrongdoing but because they are insufficiently wholesome). Given that the officials have rested the fortunes of their system of governance partly on the responsiveness of citizens to the directives of the officials about communicative activities that do not transgress any obligations of justice, the officials have manifested the system's ethical weakness. A scheme of governance should not be dependent for its success on its prodding of citizens about their patterns of communications when no requirements of justice are at stake; a government should not resemble a busybody whose equanimity hinges on the effectiveness of the similarly obtrusive prodding in which she engages.

In short, were a system of governance to take steps to prohibit or prevent the flow of utterances in the puerile game which we have been envisaging here, its operations would *pro tanto* be redolent of the quidnunc mentality. No matter how the officials who undertake those steps might consciously perceive themselves and their endeavors, we can best account for their adoption and implementation of such laws and policies if we attribute to them the attitudes of a busybody. To the extent that their system of governance does conduct itself in this fashion, it partakes of the moral failings that have been recounted in the preceding paragraph. Those failings morally vitiate the system's interaction with citizens, both because the system is intrusively self-aggrandizing and because it ignominiously depends for its success on the responsiveness of the citizens to its meddlesome ministrations. Well-intentioned though the ministrations might be, the outlook associated with them—the quidnunc mentality—deprives them of moral legitimacy. Insofar as a system of governance encounters its citizens in the manner of a busybody, it sullies its moral integrity by operating on the basis of attitudes that render it both grandiosely presumptuous and demeaningly vulnerable.

4.2.2.2.4 Overweeningness and Demeaningness: Harmful Communications

An obvious objection may have arisen in the minds of some readers at this stage. In my discussion of the ways in which some governmental restrictions on the communicative interaction of people are besmirched by the quidnunc mentality that impels those restrictions, the focus has lain on communications that are not harmful (save perhaps to the addressors of those communications). However, many of the current controversies over the regulation of people's communicative activities pertain to modes of expression that are harmful in sundry respects. We shall investigate some of those controversies in Chapters 5 and 6, as we examine the sophisticated efforts of philosophers—especially Rae Langton and Jeremy Waldron—to diagnose the various subtle and unsubtle harms that are inflicted by the dissemination of pornography and by the utterance of hatefully bigoted sentiments. Though the empirical assumptions that underlie the arguments of these philosophers are acknowledged by them to be contestable, this book will grant some of those assumptions and will therefore accept that the repellent types of communications covered by Chapters 5 and 6 can be significantly harmful in a number of contexts. Instead of being confined to the addressors of those communications, the harms inflicted by them are undergone chiefly and nonconsensually by addressees and by other parties. Accordingly, my critique of the dynamic that is intrinsic to the quidnunc mentality—that is, my critique of the dynamic of self-aggrandizement and self-abasingness—might seem to have no purchase on laws and policies that restrict the marketing of pornographic materials or the venting of hateful bigotry. After all, the quidnunc mentality is the outlook ascribable to a system of governance which officiously intrudes into matters that are not properly any of its business. Yet the damage inflicted on the lives of women by the prevalence of pornography and the damage inflicted on the dignity of members of vulnerable minority groups by the propagation of venomous screeds are hardly matters that are not properly any of the business of a system of governance. On the contrary, those injurious effects are harms which the functionaries in any such system are both morally permitted and morally obligated to strive to avert. Their striving for that purpose does not bespeak any quidnunc mentality. Such is the objection that may have occurred to some readers.

The gist of my rejoinder to such an objection is that, even when some prohibitions imposed by a system of governance on the distribution of pornography or on the voicing of rancorous prejudices are not attributable to a quidnunc mentality, those prohibitions are fraught with the same basic dynamic of overweeningness and degradingness that is associated with such a mentality. To discern this point, we should begin by recalling briefly what the principle of freedom of expression allows and what it disallows. As has been observed repeatedly in this book, legal bans or other measures wielded by a system of governance against certain modes of communication qua serious communication-independent misdeeds can be fully consistent with the aforementioned principle. If the purpose of a ban or of some other measure is to avert such misdeeds (rather than to stifle communicative activities qua communicative activities), then the governmental measure does not detract from the realization of the ideal of freedom of expression. Thus, for example, if a tirade of racist bile by a bigot is properly classifiable in its context as "fighting words"—in that it constitutes an effort to provoke a violent scuffle—it can be subjected to sanctions without any encroachment on the principle of freedom of expression. Similarly, if such a tirade is properly classifiable as a "true threat" in the sense expounded in §3.2.8 of Chapter 3, it can be subjected to sanctions without any encroachment on that principle. Likewise (as has been argued in §3.2.10 of Chapter 3), insofar as legal bans on child pornography are aimed at preventing the exploitation of children as nonconsensual objects for the derivation of sexual gratification by paedophiles, the bans are not at variance with the principle of freedom of expression.

These governmentally imposed restrictions on the manufacturing and marketing of pornography and on the utterance of poisonous hatred, as well as some other such restrictions, are not discountenanced by the principle of freedom of expression. Where such restrictions are directed against communication-independent wrongdoing, they tally with that principle even in circumstances where the wrongdoing is perpetrated through communicative actions. This point will be emphasized further in Chapters 5 and 6. Still, as will also become apparent in those chapters, the principle of freedom of expression does morally disallow the hate-speech statutes that are championed by Waldron and most of the legal restrictions on pornography that are advocated by feminists such as Catharine MacKinnon. Those laws clash with the principle of freedom of expression because the curbs which they impose are directed against the distribution of pornography and the utterance of hateful sentiments not qua modes of communication-independent misconduct but instead qua modes of communication. Targeted by such curbs are the distinctively communicative effects of the pornography and the hateful utterances.

Still, although the restrictions imposed by the laws in question are violative of the principle of freedom of expression because they are directed against the distinctively communicative effects of pornography and bigoted ranting, those communicative effects are significantly harmful (or so this book is granting *arguendo*). Such laws are therefore not symptomatic of a quidnunc mentality on the part of a system of governance that enacts them. They address problems that are legitimately of great concern to that system. Consequently, we return to inquiring why such laws are morally impermissible and why the enactment of them by a system of governance is both self-aggrandizing and self-abasing. In a clear sense, we are asking why the principle of freedom of expression distinguishes between the morally permissible and the morally impermissible as it does. Why does that principle hold that the difference between communication-independent wrongdoing and distinctively communicative wrongdoing is of decisive importance? Why can laws directed against the former type of wrongdoing be morally legitimate, whereas laws directed against the latter type of wrongdoing are always and everywhere morally illegitimate?

Although the answer to such a query will become more perspicuous and detailed in Chapters 5 and 6, the query has to be addressed here. As will become evident in those later chapters, the key to such an answer lies in the moral obligations that are incumbent on every system of governance. All of those obligations are grounded in the paramount responsibility of any such system to bring about the political and social and economic conditions wherein a hearty sense of self-respect can be warranted for every member of the society over which the system presides. Among the moral obligations which flow from that paramount responsibility is the duty of a system of governance to affirm and uphold the fundamental equality of every citizen. Of particular concern in this regard is the upholding of that fundamental equality in the face of any bigotry or other invidious treatment directed against certain people (such as women or homosexuals or the members of racial or religious or ethnic minorities). If a system of governance fails to take ample steps to counter such bigotry or invidious treatment, it is *pro tanto* failing to fulfill its paramount responsibility. And here, as elsewhere, the nature of the misconduct to be countered is crucial in determining the permissibility or impermissibility of various measures that might be plied in anticipation or in response.

When communications are constitutive of serious communication-independent misdeeds, measures of outright prevention or prohibition by a system of governance can be morally legitimate. Misdeeds that can properly be met with punishment when perpetrated through non-communicative conduct are no less properly met with punishment when they are perpetrated instead through communicative conduct. For example, if Joe is a member of a criminal gang who participates in an abduction solely by luring the victim with friendly words and by writing the ransom notes, he can just as fittingly be punished for the crime of kidnapping as can the members of the gang who have grabbed the victim and tied her up. A system of governance that subjects Joe to criminal sanctions is clearly operating permissibly in so doing.

When communications are not constitutive of serious communication-independent wrongdoing, however, things stand quite differently. Suppose that Ken is a bigot who delivers an oration replete with racist invective, or suppose that he distributes some copies of a pamphlet filled with similar invective. Suppose further that his oration or distribution does not amount to "fighting words" or to a "true threat" or to incitement or to any other type of communication-independent misconduct. Although the sentiments which Ken expresses might be just as hideous as the sentiments expressed by some other bigot whose utterances do fall into one of those categories of communication-independent misconduct, the context and nature of Ken's communicative endeavor are such that the endeavor is not included in any of those categories. As is manifest, then, the subjection of Ken to legal sanctions for his oration or distribution would be at variance with the principle of freedom of expression that has been expounded in this book. Any such subjection of him to sanctions would be morally impermissible not because the countering of his propagation of hatefulness is no business of any system of governance, but instead precisely because every such system is morally obligated to undertake numerous measures to counteract the ranting of bigots (and to counteract the noxious effects of the marketing of pornography). Many of the techniques that can and should be employed for that purpose by any system of governance will be recounted in Chapters 5 and 6. Some of those techniques are anticipatory, whereas others are responsive to what has already occurred. Some are wide-ranging, whereas others are more narrowly focused. Diverse though those techniques are, however, they are alike in that they neither prohibit nor prevent any communicative activities that are not constitutive of communication-independent misconduct. Any system of governance is morally obligated to make use of a large number of those sundry non-prohibitory and non-preventative methods. In so doing, it will not only be striving to fulfill its responsibility to foster a robust ethos of liberal democracy in its society; in addition, it will be acting in furtherance of the ideal of freedom of expression. That ideal is furthered by those methods partly because they are fully consistent with the principle of freedom of expression, but also (and even more) because they obviate the need for any governmentally imposed restrictions which are inconsistent with that principle.

On the one hand, even in a society with a robust liberal-democratic ethos—fostered by the techniques that have just been mentioned—some hatefully bigoted declamations will occur, and pornographic films and magazines will continue to be marketed. Such a society is not a fanciful utopia where the ugliness of those declamations and the dreariness of pornography have been altogether left behind.[12] On the other hand, the sway of a robust liberal-democratic ethos in a society will have defused the effects of those noisome modes of communication. As will be argued at some length in Chapter 6, the dominant effect of racist tirades in the presence of such an ethos is the discrediting of the people who deliver the tirades.

[12] The absence of fancifulness in my invocations of an ethos is one major difference between those invocations and the appeals to an ethos in Cohen 2008. In my view, the ethos envisaged in Cohen's book is both fanciful and sinister.

Likewise, as will be argued in Chapter 5, the distribution of pornographic materials in the presence of such an ethos will leave the political and economic and social standing of women unimpaired.

An ethos of the requisite kind, with its ability to defuse the noxiousness of these rebarbative modes of communication, is not something that can be taken for granted by any system of governance. On the contrary, it is something that has to be actively nurtured and sustained through governmental measures like those that will be elaborated in Chapters 5 and 6. When it is so nurtured and sustained, however, it endows a society with the ethical strength whereby a policy of legal toleration toward pornography and bigoted ranting—provided that the pornography or ranting does not amount to any communication-independent misconduct—is a way of reaffirming and reinforcing the reign of liberal-democratic values in the society. Like the eagle in Tamora's speech that underscores its own pre-eminence and lofty assurance through its preparedness to let the little birds chirp, a system of governance through the aforementioned policy of legal toleration can underscore and strengthen its success in endowing its society with an ethos of liberal-democratic values that is sturdy enough to turn pornography and racist vitriol into chirping.

Hence, when a system of governance seeks to outlaw pornographic materials or hateful diatribes that are not constitutive of any communication-independent wrongdoing, such an endeavor presupposes the failure of the system to bring about a robust ethos of the type just outlined. For that system of governance, an endeavor along those lines is simultaneously overweening and demeaning. Its demeaningness is flagrantly apparent from what has already been said here. A system of governance that has failed to cultivate and sustain a robust societal ethos of liberal-democratic values is thereby in contravention of one of its chief moral responsibilities. At least partly as a result of that contravention, the officials who run the system are inclined to control and stifle modes of expression that would be legally tolerated—as chirping—in a society with a proper level of ethical strength. Like an eagle that degradingly has to squelch the noises of little birds which it should be in a position to abide disdainfully, a system of governance degrades itself when its legal powers of prohibition and physical powers of prevention are wielded against modes of expression which it should be in a position to tolerate. Pornographic materials and racist fulminations that do not constitute any communication-independent misconduct are such modes of expression. Having to attend to such baseness through legal restrictions, a system of governance thereby implicitly avows the tenuousness of its achievements in its efforts (if any) to gain currency for the values of liberal democracy within its society.

Even while a system of governance demeans itself through the imposition of legal curbs on those modes of communication, it likewise aggrandizes itself. Its position in that respect is akin to the position of a public-health agency which fails to prepare adequately for a foreseeable outbreak of some disease and which then arrogates to itself various legal and physical powers to control the details of people's lives in order to stanch the outbreak. The overweening directiveness of a system of governance as it outlaws communicative activities qua communicative activities is integrally connected to the weakness of the system that stems from its failures to carry out the moral responsibilities which are incumbent on it—most notably its moral obligation to foster and entrench an ethos of liberal-democratic values in the society over which it presides. When a system of governance fulfills that ethos-producing obligation satisfactorily, the officials of the system are comfortably in a position to comply with the cognate moral obligation imposed by the principle of freedom of expression. Securely in a position of ethical strength to uphold that principle, they can treat the wares of pornographers and the maunderings of bigots as execrable chirps that are to be endured with contempt (again, provided that those wares and maunderings are not rightly classifiable as communication-independent misconduct).

In short, although the quidnunc mentality is not operative when a system of governance exercises its legal powers of prohibition or its physical powers of prevention to avert the distinctively communicative effects that might be caused by the marketing of pornography or by hatemongering, the pattern of overweeningness and demeaningness associated with that mentality is paralleled in this context. Those exertions of powers by that system of governance are degrading—for the system itself and for the society over which it presides—because they presuppose the failure of the system to bring about the societal ethos that would effectively counter the noxiousness of any pornographic materials and hateful utterances that are not constitutive of communication-independent misconduct. That is, such exertions of powers presuppose the failure of the system to discharge its moral duty to nurture such an ethos, and they presuppose the failure of the citizenry to embrace such an ethos. Those exertions by the system of governance are likewise overweening because with them the system's officials take control of communications that should have been defused (through the system's fulfillment of its moral obligations) without prohibitory or preventative impositions. The inordinate controllingness of the system ensues from its weakness, in ways that can be inferred from the Shakespearean passages quoted in §§4.2.2.1.1 and 4.2.2.1.2 above. That is, because the system of governance has left itself and its society needlessly vulnerable to the baneful effects that can ultimately flow from certain types of communications where the effects have not been adequately warded off, the officials in the system feel obliged to offset their remissness with illiberality. Here as elsewhere, self-condemnation and self-aggrandizement go hand in hand.

4.2.2.3 The Connection to Warranted Self-Respect

Contraventions of the principle of freedom of expression by a system of governance detract from the moral integrity of the system in the ways that have been outlined here, and they therefore also detract from the levels of self-respect that are warranted for the members of the society over which the system presides. Such contraventions tarnish the moral integrity of a system of governance precisely because—as we have just been exploring—they always involve overreaching and self-degradation. When legal-governmental officials transgress the constraints established by the principle of freedom of expression, the position of their system of governance vis-à-vis the citizenry has become overbearing. They are prohibiting or preventing the occurrence of certain communications, even though the communications do not amount to any communication-independent misdeeds. Instead of being aimed at the communications qua such misdeeds, the prohibitory laws or preventative actions of the officials are aimed at the objectionableness of the communications qua communications. Those laws or actions thus presumptuously supplant the judgments of individuals about the ideas and sentiments conveyed by communications that are not constitutive of any communication-independent wrongdoing, and they implicitly or explicitly rest on the premise that the society governed by the officials is not ethically strong enough to fend off any untoward effects that could ultimately be caused by those communications. Given that the officials collectively are always morally obligated to cultivate and preserve in their society a hardy ethos of liberal-democratic ideals—an ethos that would endow the society with sufficient ethical strength to defuse and parry the untoward effects that have just been mentioned—the presumptuous measures undertaken by the officials presuppose the failure of their system of governance to fulfill a major moral obligation that is always incumbent upon it. Thus, when a system of governance introduces any laws or policies that violate the principle of freedom of expression, its posture is at once overweening and self-condemning. Such laws and policies are blemishes on the moral integrity of the system.

In more than one way, those blemishes impair the levels of self-respect that can warrantedly be harbored by the members of the relevant society. Some aspects of the impairment would readily be recognized by Rawlsians and other Kantians. That is, when legal-governmental officials close off the access of citizens to various ideas or sentiments conveyed by others—where the conveyance of the ideas or sentiments is not correctly classifiable as communication-independent misconduct—they evince their distrust of the citizens' deliberative faculties. Instead of allowing sane adults among the citizens to reach their own judgments about the ideas or sentiments in question, the officials lump those adults together with infants and lunatics as people from whom such judgments are to be taken away. Being treated in such a disrespectful fashion, each sane adult among the citizens is warranted in lowering his or her sense of self-respect. His or her life has been worsened through the subjection of him or her to such treatment.

Rawlsians and other Kantians are quite correct to complain about this aspect of the officials' actions. Laws that prohibit communicative activities qua communicative activities—on the ground that the occurrence of those communications would insidiously poison the outlooks of various people who are frequently exposed to them—are indeed disrespectful toward adults of sound mind, whom the laws assimilate to gullible and irresponsible children. Sane adults treated in such a fashion are warranted in feeling aggrieved and are unwarranted in taking any more favorable views of the matter.

Still, important though the addressee-centered concerns of Rawlsians and other Kantians are, the focus of this chapter lies predominantly on the relationship between any system of governance and the citizens over whom the system presides. When such a system both aggrandizes itself and demeans itself through the adoption of laws or policies that bar the occurrence of communicative endeavors qua communicative endeavors, its sullying of its moral integrity in that manner negatively affects the level of self-respect that is warranted for each person in the relevant society. That negative impact occurs not only in the relatively straightforward way highlighted by the Rawlsians, but also in a somewhat more subtle and elaborate fashion highlighted by the aspirational liberalism that informs this chapter. As has been tersely summarized in §4.2.1.2.2 above, the doings of nearly every human individual are embedded in matrices of social and political and economic relationships that bear crucially on the quality of his or her life. Those relationships will of course heavily influence the successes achieved and the failures incurred by any particular person. However, in addition to the many direct influences exerted by the political and social and economic conditions in which the life of someone unfolds, an indirect influence is of distinctive importance in aspirational perfectionism.

Each person is warranted in gauging the quality of her life not only by reference to her own successes and failures but also by reference to the society (or societies) in which the trajectory of her life is located. As I have noted in §4.2.1.2.2 above, and as I have argued at length in *Liberalism with Excellence* (Kramer 2017, 341–74), the members of any given society can be warranted in experiencing vicarious pride about its excellences and vicarious dismay over its shortcomings. Associated as those members are with their society, they can be warranted in thinking that their own fortunes are to some degree bound up with its fortunes. At least insofar as its thriving does not conflict significantly with their own, they can warrantedly feel that its thriving enhances their respective lives. Its thriving elevates them. Because their identities have been formed in their society, and because they are identified with it by other people, its flourishing can make their own lives better—not only because that flourishing may improve their material prosperity but also because it can itself be a source of warranted pride for them as the society's members.

Now, as I have emphasized in *Liberalism with Excellence* (Kramer 2017, 367–73), the premier form of flourishing for any society is the sustainment of a liberal-democratic system of governance along with a corresponding ethos which pervades the society and which bolsters such a system. As has been contended in that earlier book, the operations of the institutions which implement the requirements of justice in a liberal democracy are an outstanding collective accomplishment. Both on the part of legal-governmental officials and on the part of ordinary citizens, the patterns of self-restraint involved in the workings of just institutions are prodigious. Every generally law-abiding person who belongs to a society governed by a liberal-democratic regime can warrantedly take pride in those workings. Of course, in any actual liberal democracy—as opposed to a well-ordered Rawlsian society—the operations of the prevailing institutions are imperfectly just, and the compliance of citizens with the just requirements of those institutions is likewise imperfect. Nevertheless, in any society whose system of governance is liberal-democratic to a high degree and whose citizens are largely faithful to the values of liberal democracy, the widespread embrace of those values is a mode of excellence in which every generally law-abiding citizen can warrantedly take pride. It is a mode of excellence that enhances the life of every generally law-abiding person who belongs to the society. In any actual liberal democracy, where citizens naturally tend to concentrate on the shortcomings of the regnant institutions, many of them sometimes lose sight of the magnitude and preciousness of the achievement that consists in the sustainment of those institutions. All the same, they can warrantedly derive satisfaction from that achievement—as the overall trajectory of the life of each generally law-abiding person P is made better by it. Because the course of P's life is inevitably affected (for better or for worse) by the tenor of the system of governance that presides over the society with which P is associated, the conformity of that system to the values of liberal democracy is something that heightens the level of self-respect which P can warrantedly feel.

My claim here about the heightening of each person's warranted self-respect is not an empirical conjecture about the likelihood that each person will be materially better off as a result of the sway of a liberal-democratic system of governance in his or her society. On the one hand, there are quite strong and familiar correlations between liberal-democratic systems of governance and material prosperity. On the other hand, such correlations—important though they are—are not directly to the point here. My claim about the shoring up of each person's warranted self-respect is focused on the inherent moral quality of liberal-democratic governance rather than on the beneficial consequences that are likely to ensue causally therefrom.

Rawls well captured two of the ways in which the inherent moral quality of liberal-democratic governance raises the level of self-respect which each generally law-abiding person in a society can warrantedly feel. Throughout the long final chapter of *A Theory of Justice*, he frequently declared that a liberal-democratic system of governance enables its citizens to realize their nature as free and equal persons. His contentions to that effect should be construed as making two main points. First, each person under a liberal-democratic system of governance is treated with the respect that befits a rationally deliberative agent who possesses a sense of justice and a conception of what is valuable in life. Second, each person under such a system of governance is morally and legally required to exercise the self-restraint that exhibits due respect for other rationally deliberative agents. Being required to exercise such self-restraint is a hallmark of one's status as a free and equal person, as is being treated with commensurate forbearance by everybody else. Patterns of reciprocal forbearance among citizens, and patterns of forbearance in a government's interaction with citizens, encapsulate the status of every sane adult as a free and equal person. Rawls grasped and indeed emphasized that those patterns of forbearance increase the level of self-esteem which a generally law-abiding person is warranted in experiencing. Having reminded his readers that his "account of self-respect as perhaps the main primary good has stressed the great significance of how we think others value us," he proclaimed that a key "basis for [warranted] self-esteem in a just society is ... the publicly affirmed distribution of fundamental rights and liberties" (Rawls 1999, 477). He elaborated: "In a well-ordered society then [warranted] self-respect is secured [partly] by the public affirmation of the status of equal citizenship for all" (478). Of course, in addition to referring to the fundamental rights and liberties of citizenship, Rawls should have referred here to the fundamental responsibilities thereof. Each citizen's status as a free and equal person—along with the quantum of warranted self-respect that is appurtenant to that status—is upheld not only through her being endowed with the fundamental rights and liberties, but also through her being expected and required to accept that each of her fellow citizens is endowed with those rights and liberties.

For a further crucial regard in which the sway of a liberal-democratic system of governance elevates the level of self-respect that can warrantedly be harbored by each person who lives under the jurisdiction of the system, we again need to go beyond Rawls and be guided by this chapter's aspirational-perfectionist liberalism. As has already been remarked, the sustainment of a liberal democracy in any country—even with some imperfections—is a sterling collective achievement that should elicit feelings of pride in every generally law-abiding person who belongs to that country. Because the trajectory of the life of each such person includes her association with a country in which that great achievement has occurred, each such person can warrantedly conclude that her life has gone better by dint of the achievement (quite apart from any material benefits that have causally accrued to her as a result of it). *Pro tanto*, she can warrantedly feel better about herself and her projects than she otherwise could.

Conversely, of course, somebody who is a member of a society governed by a repressively illiberal regime can warrantedly conclude that her life has gone worse by dint of her links to that society (quite apart from any material hardships that have beset her as a result of the regime's grim oppression). Because the overall course of her life includes her connection to the country ruled by that system of governance, it is marred by the collective failure of the citizens of that country—among them, most notably, the system's officials—to uphold the values of a liberal democracy. This point about the ethical worsening of a person's life is independent of her approval or disapproval of the tyrannical rulers. On the one hand, the trajectory of her life will be substantially worse ethically if she has been complicit in maintaining the grip of the despots on power. On the other hand, my point here has not been about her personal responsibility for the persistence of the tyranny or for any of its iniquities; rather, this paragraph is about the collective responsibility of her fellow citizens with whom she is associated as a member of their community. Even if she has struggled gamely against the repressiveness of the system of governance in her country, her life that has been ennobled by her struggling is worsened ethically by the need for it—because the need for that struggling is a product of a collective failure on the part of a community to which she belongs.

Hence, contraventions of the principle of freedom of expression—which, as deviations from self-restraint, are both presumptuous and ignominious for any system of governance that engages in them—derogate from the level of self-respect that is warranted for each person in the society where the contraventions occur. Beyond any effect of reducing the opportunities for people to communicate their thoughts or sentiments, and beyond any effect of reducing the opportunities for people to gain acquaintance with the thoughts and sentiments of others, the violations of the principle of freedom of expression debase the moral integrity of any system of governance that perpetrates them. Because the moral tenor of such a system in any society should elicit pride (if benign) or consternation (if malign) among the members of the society, the degradation of that tenor through the aforementioned violations directly lowers the level of self-respect that is warranted for each of those members. It directly diminishes the extent to which each of them can warrantedly take pride in the prevailing system of governance as something with which each of them is associated. It diminishes the extent to which that system reflects well upon them. Consequently, the transgressions of the principle of freedom of expression by the system's officials are breaches of the system's paramount responsibility.

Of course, in a country where such transgressions occur, it is very likely that many of the inhabitants can still be warranted in harboring ample levels of self-respect. Indeed, if the transgressions are very few and modest, and if the prevailing system of governance is otherwise fulfilling the sundry moral responsibilities that are incumbent on it, then everyone there can still be warranted in sustaining a hearty sense of self-respect.[13] As will be discussed at greater length in Chapter 7, the compliance of any system of governance with the principle of freedom of expression is a scalar property. Although the principle itself is absolute, the extent to which any government adheres to it is obviously variable. A system of governance that falls short of full conformity with that principle might nonetheless achieve a very high degree of conformity therewith. In a society where such a degree of conformity has been attained, the minor deviations from the principle of freedom

[13] As has already been noted in this chapter, the fact that everyone can still be warranted in experiencing a high level of self-respect does not entail that everyone will actually be warranted in experiencing such a level. Nor does it entail that everyone will actually experience such a level.

of expression will not appreciably lower the level of self-respect that is warranted for any member of the society. Still, a system of governance fully complies with its paramount responsibility—its moral obligation to bring about the political and social and economic conditions under which everyone within the jurisdiction of the system can be warranted in experiencing a strong sense of self-respect—only when it abides fully by the principle of freedom of expression. Even a few modest infractions of that principle go against the fulfillment of the paramount responsibility, as they bespeak and partly constitute the ethical weakness of the system of governance that commits the infractions.

4.2.2.4 Return to a Troubling Thought-Experiment

This chapter will conclude by returning to the thought-experiment that is so troublesome for the standard justifications which have been advanced by other philosophers to support versions of the principle of freedom of expression. Let us recall the municipality whose officials are pondering whether the backs and sides of the local public buses should be made available to advertisers for the posting of notices and displays. Although the municipality is of course morally at liberty to use an aleatory procedure or a first-come-first-served criterion (or some comparable standard) to apportion the spaces on the buses among the advertisers, it is not morally at liberty to employ any criterion that is at variance with the constraint of communication-neutrality or content-neutrality or speaker-neutrality.

Now, as has been observed in Chapter 2 and in earlier portions of this chapter, the orthodox rationales for versions of the principle of freedom of expression are unable to explain the following combination of facts: (1) the fact that the municipality is morally at liberty to exclude advertisements and notices from its buses altogether; and (2) the fact that the municipality is not morally at liberty to exclude advertisements and notices from its buses in ways that are inconsistent with any of the constraints of neutrality that have just been mentioned. For every one of those orthodox rationales, a sweeping restriction on communications in a given context is always more problematic morally than is any sensible narrower restriction in that same context. For example, a sensible narrow restriction will leave more room for people to communicate their ideas and sentiments than will any blanket restriction, and it will similarly leave people with greater access to the thoughts and sentiments of others. Likewise, a sensibly cabined limitation on communications in a given context can be highly conducive to the expansion of knowledge, whereas an across-the-board limitation in that same context will typically retard the growth of knowledge. Even the proponents of the distrust-of-government rationale for versions of the principle of freedom of expression, who doubt that systems of governance will make sensible choices in designing any narrow curbs on communications, are at least as wary of any wholesale curbs. Those proponents scarcely become enamored of the wisdom of governmental officials when the officials clamp down on communications wide-rangingly rather than fine-grainedly.

Like the other orthodox justifications, then, the distrust-of-government line of thought lacks the resources to explain the combination of the two enumerated facts broached in the opening sentence of this paragraph.

By contrast, this chapter's Stoical approach to the principle of freedom of expression can account for that combination of facts quite straightforwardly. Let us start with the first of those facts. As has been remarked in §2.3.4.2.1 of Chapter 2, a system of governance is not morally obligated to allow its sizeable chattels (such as buses) to be used as fora for communications by individuals or organizations—provided that there are enough alternative public fora for such communications. On the one hand, a decision by the system's officials against making its buses available as public fora can sometimes amount to a violation of the constraints of neutrality established by the principle of freedom of expression. For example, the officials may have reached their decision because they are worried that certain unsavory organizations or individuals will apply to have advertisements displayed on the buses. If an intention to keep such advertisements off the buses is correctly ascribable to the policy of excluding advertisements altogether, then that policy contravenes the principle of freedom of expression. On the other hand, the operativeness of such an intention behind a policy of that kind is very much a contingent matter. Instead of acting on the basis of considerations that run athwart the constraint of content-neutrality or speaker-neutrality, the officials in any given municipality might simply be acting with the aim of promoting clarity for potential passengers. Those officials might reasonably believe that such an aim will best be furthered if the sides and backs of the municipality's buses are reserved for the name and emblem of the public bus service and for information such as the place(s) where each bus stops. A purpose of this sort is compatible with all the requirements of neutrality that are set forth by the principle of freedom of expression. Hence, if such a purpose is correctly ascribable to the municipality's policy of declining to allow advertisements on the sides and backs of its buses, and if there are adequate locations elsewhere (including the World Wide Web) for the posting of the advertisements, the specified policy is perfectly in keeping with the principle of freedom of expression.

Let us move to the second of the enumerated facts: namely, the fact that a municipality is never morally at liberty to exclude advertisements and notices from its buses in ways that are inconsistent with communication-neutrality or content-neutrality or speaker-neutrality. As has just been observed, the moral obligation distilled in this second fact is applicable to a policy of declining to allow the posting of any advertisements and notices on the buses at all. Although such a policy can be morally legitimate, it is not morally legitimate if the adoption of it rests on any purposes that clash with the constraints of neutrality which have just been listed. Of even greater interest in the present discussion, however, is that those constraints of neutrality disallow nearly every selective policy of excluding advertisements and notices from the buses. Whereas a policy of wholesale exclusion can be morally legitimate in highly credible circumstances, virtually any policy of selective exclusion would run afoul of the constraints of neutrality—because any such policy that is likely to be contemplated by a system of governance would be either content-focused or speaker-focused. Now, the two facts enumerated above are together inexplicable under any of the standard justifications for versions of the principle of freedom of expression. How does this chapter's justification explain the second of those facts? That is, given that every policy of selectively excluding advertisements and notices from the buses will transgress the constraint of content-neutrality or speaker-neutrality, why should we conclude that every such policy is morally wrong? Why is the principle of freedom of expression endowed with morally interdictory force in application to every such policy?

To discern the answer to each of these questions, we need to return to a distinction that has been broached fleetingly at several junctures in Chapter 2: the distinction between the extent of a restriction and the fine-grainedness of a restriction. That distinction and its moral significance can now be fully comprehended in the light of this chapter's Stoical rationale for the principle of freedom of expression. What the Stoical rationale highlights are the ways in which any contraventions of that principle are both self-aggrandizing and self-abasing for the system of governance which undertakes those contraventions. In numerous contexts—including the scenario of the municipality and its bus service—that dynamic of overweeningness and demeaningness is particularly acute in relation to fine-grained curbs on communications. In those contexts, the efforts by a system of governance to exert the minute control involved in fine-grained curbs are peculiarly presumptuous and peculiarly ignominious.[14]

When the officials in the local government decide not to make the municipal buses available for the placing of advertisements and notices, and when their decision has been reached in the morally legitimate fashion outlined in the antepenultimate paragraph above, they are not acting with the purpose of directing the flow of public or private discourse at all. Their decision will have a coarse-grained impact on the flow of public discourse, but that impact is not what they are seeking, and it is offset by the fact that there are ample public fora elsewhere for the placing of the materials that might have been placed on the buses. By contrast, when the officials make the sides and backs of the buses available for advertisements while imposing a subject-specific or viewpoint-specific limit on the range of advertisements that can be placed, they are acting with the purpose of directing the flow of public discourse. Their fine-grained impact on that flow is precisely what they are seeking. They are providing an additional forum for advertisements which address the favored topics or which proceed from the favored viewpoints, and they

[14] I have made a parallel point elsewhere in explaining why the use of interrogational torture is always and everywhere morally impermissible even while some instances of deliberate killing are morally permissible. See Kramer 2014, 197–201; 2017, 259–60.

are deliberately denying that additional forum to advertisements which address the disfavored topics or which proceed from the disfavored viewpoints. The officials are designedly exerting minute control over an area of public discourse.

When a system of governance seeks minute control over an area of public discourse, and when the system exerts the control not for the purpose of restricting some communicative activities qua communication-independent misdeeds but instead for the purpose of restricting some communicative activities qua communicative activities, the presumptuousness of the laws or policies that confer the control is egregious. Those laws or policies assign to the system of governance the authority to choose for citizens the range of topics or viewpoints to which they will be exposed in a setting that is otherwise a public forum. *Pari passu* assigned by those laws or policies to the system of governance is the authority to choose the range of topics which people are permitted to address in that setting or the range of viewpoints which people are permitted to articulate therein. Such authority is bestowed because the system's officials presume to be uniquely entitled to make such choices—even though the communicative endeavors which they disfavor are not constitutive of any communication-independent wrongdoing.

The presumptuousness of the laws or policies in question is directly linked to their ignominiousness. In a society with a system of governance that has fulfilled the major moral obligations incumbent upon it—including its obligation to generate a robust ethos of liberal-democratic values among the citizenry—the contemptibleness of any subject-specific or viewpoint-specific curtailment of the range of communications that are eligible for posting on the public buses would be starkly apparent. Any such curtailment is a mark and a source of ethical weakness, as a system of governance that introduces it is thereby attending to some matters which should have been addressed without the curtailment through the fulfilling of the system's moral responsibilities. For example, if the officials in the municipality are worried that some nefarious organizations or individuals will apply to have advertisements placed on the city's buses, and if the officials consequently adopt a viewpoint-specific or speaker-specific exception to a general policy of allowing the display of advertisements and notices, their actions presuppose the failure of their system of governance to fulfill its moral obligations. If the officials are concerned that the messages conveyed by the nefarious organizations are likely to be efficacious in enticing many members of the public to espouse the views peddled by those organizations, then the officials are assuming that their system of governance has failed to inculcate and sustain a hardy ethos of liberal-democratic values among its citizens. In a society where such an ethos has been successfully fostered, advertisements posted by the nasty organizations will appeal to hardly anyone and will instead bring additional contumely upon those organizations. Thus, in a society where the operative system of governance has complied with its moral duty to bring about such an ethos, any advertisements conveying the messages of those organizations can rightly be perceived by the system's officials as the chirping of odious little birds—not because the messages are unharmful, but because their harmful effects are solidly kept in check. In a locality where the officials who run the bus service have excluded such advertisements in a viewpoint-specific or speaker-specific manner, the exclusion presupposes the non-fulfillment of the ethos-producing moral duty and is thus a condemnation of the overall system of governance. (Note that the breach of the system's moral duty does not consist in the fact that there are some vile people on the margins of the society who adhere to poisonously bigoted views. The moral obligations pondered throughout this book are realistically fulfillable rather than outlandishly utopian. Hence, given that the outright elimination of stupidity and narrow-mindedness from a society is obviously not realistically attainable, the moral duty discussed here does not require any system of governance to achieve such a state of affairs. Rather, what is required is the engendering of a regnant societal ethos—imbued with the values of liberal democracy—which is strong enough to ensure that the people on the margins of the society with their poisonously bigoted views are indeed very firmly on the margins. In the presence of such an ethos, those people and their ugly blandishments are kept on the periphery not by legal mandates but by the disdain of the vast majority of their fellow citizens.)

If the concern underlying the adoption of a viewpoint-specific or speaker-specific exclusion of certain hateful advertisements from the buses is instead that people who are enraged by such advertisements are likely to perpetrate violence or serious vandalism, the exclusion again bespeaks and exacerbates the ethical weakness of the prevailing system of governance. In my discussion of hecklers and hostile audiences in §2.3.4.1 of Chapter 2, I have emphasized that the prospect of violence or serious vandalism by opponents of certain types of communications—where the types in question are not constitutive of any communication-independent misconduct—is never sufficient to render morally legitimate the prohibition or prevention of those communications. When a system of governance adverts to the prospect of violence or serious vandalism as a factor that justifies the barring of some disfavored type of communication, it is thereby abjectly conferring upon the would-be perpetrators of the violence or vandalism a position of decisive control over an area of public discourse. In a system of governance which instead fulfills the moral responsibilities that are binding upon it, the prospect of violence or serious vandalism is addressed in alternative ways that comply with the principle of freedom of expression. Any such system is morally obligated to preserve basic public orderliness and to furnish the policing that is necessary to safeguard people against assailants. If there are reasons for anticipating that violence or serious vandalism is likely to occur in a certain location, the system of governance with authority over that location is morally obligated to increase the level of policing commensurately. Moreover, given that (in the scenario envisaged here) the threat of violence or vandalism arises out of hostility toward advertisements placed on the buses by hateful organizations, the prevailing system of governance in its overall operations can help to defuse the threat by undertaking the sundry measures that serve to counter or avert any noxious effects of the advertisements. Those measures have been broached already in this chapter, and will be recounted in much greater detail in my next two chapters. One small step to be taken in the scenario under consideration here is that the municipal agency which runs the buses should make emphatically clear that the views expressed in the postings on the sides and backs of the buses are those of the advertisers rather than of the agency itself. Finally, in extreme circumstances like those contemplated in §2.3.4.1.2 of Chapter 2, where the threat of violence is on a scale far greater than can be handled by the police forces available to the municipal authorities—and where the display of an advertisement therefore has to be disallowed or removed—the overall system of governance should make available some legal avenues for redress such as those which have been suggested in Chapter 2's discussion.

Let us in conclusion ponder briefly a subject-specific restriction that might be imposed on the range of advertisements which the municipality accepts for displays on the sides and backs of its buses. Suppose for example that advertisements concerning some politically sensitive topics are excluded, and suppose that the purpose of the exclusion is to avert altercations that would be likely to occur among members of the public if advertisements on the sensitive topics were permitted. While such an endeavor to exert fine-grained control over the flow of public discourse is blatantly self-aggrandizing for the system of governance which carries out the endeavor, it is also self-condemning for that system. It is so partly because the considerations adduced in the preceding paragraph are (*mutatis mutandis*) fully applicable here as well. In addition, in a society where a strong ethos of liberal-democratic values has been sown and sustained, the likelihood of violent altercations in response to advertisements on politically delicate topics will be unworrisomely low. No such robust ethos exists in a society where the officials who run a municipal transportation service can sincerely advert to the likelihood of brawls as a reason for disallowing the placement of political advertisements on the sides and backs of the public buses. In a society where the political sentiments of large numbers of people are so explosive, the prevailing system of governance has miserably failed to fulfill its moral duty to instill widespread respect for the values of liberal democracy.

In short, unlike the standard justifications for versions of the principle of freedom of expression, this chapter's Stoical aspirational-perfectionist rationale can handle smoothly the scenario of the municipality and the buses. Any content-specific or speaker-specific curbs on the types of advertisements that will be accepted by the officials who manage the buses are both overweening and demeaning for the system of governance that imposes those curbs. As a consequence, such restrictions detract from the extent to which the members of the relevant society can warrantedly take pride in that system. Accordingly, those restrictions diminish the level of self-respect that is warranted for each person in the society. Although the diminution in that level may be slight if the content-specific or speaker-specific limitations that have been imposed are minor, every such limitation is a failing that takes a system of governance away from the execution of its paramount responsibility—which is why every content-specific or speaker-specific exclusion of advertisements from the public buses is morally impermissible even while the blanket exclusion of advertisements therefrom can be morally permissible.

5

Pornography, Subordination, and Silencing

In the efflorescence of sophisticated writings by feminist philosophers during the past few decades on the nature and effects of pornography, the work of Rae Langton—especially her 2009 book *Sexual Solipsism*—has stood out. Influenced by the pioneering ideas of Catharine MacKinnon, Langton has in turn influenced a large array of philosophers who have explored (and sometimes modified or rejected) her reflections on the perniciousness of pornography. Her approach to the issue, which analyzes the effects of pornography through the lens of speech-act philosophy, is by no means the only significant contribution of *Sexual Solipsism* to contemporary philosophical debates. Written with admirable lucidity and brio and occasional wittiness, the book illuminatingly and rigorously addresses a host of topics. It is a top-notch work of analytic philosophy generally. Here, however, my focus will lie on Langton's treatment of pornography and specifically on her contention that pornography subordinates and silences women. Her claims about the subordinating and silencing effects of pornography are at the heart of her book, and they bear directly on controversies over freedom of expression. Pornography has for decades been an especially vexed matter within those controversies. Langton along with other feminist philosophers has greatly enriched the discussions of that matter over the past thirty years, and her treatment of it will enable me to expand on why most types of pornography should not be subject to legal proscription.[1]

Much more than MacKinnon, Langton is circumspect about drawing any illiberal conclusions from her meditations on the noisome role of pornography in contemporary societies. Even in her review of Jeremy Waldron's 2012 tome *The Harm in Hate Speech*—a tome that will be examined closely in my next chapter—she ultimately recoils from endorsing any illiberal conclusions outright, notwithstanding that the review contains a few chillingly illiberal pronouncements (Langton 2016). In her other writings, Langton is even more cautious as she refrains from countenancing unequivocally any legal bans on the vile pornographic materials which she is discussing. Nevertheless, she repeatedly edges toward illiberal recommendations even though she stops short of them, and the factors that incline her away from legal prohibitions appear to be concerns about the potential inefficacy and counterproductiveness of such measures rather than concerns about their inherent

[1] As has been recounted in Chapter 3, child pornography and any pornography produced through violent coercion can properly be outlawed. Morally permissible legal restrictions are aimed not at the content of such pornography but instead at the processes through which it has been made.

Freedom of Expression as Self-Restraint. Matthew H. Kramer, Oxford University Press (2021). © Matthew H. Kramer.
DOI: 10.1093/oso/9780198868651.003.0005

illegitimacy.[2] Hence, the chief aim of my present chapter is to maintain that legal prohibitions on most types of pornography would indeed be inherently illegitimate. Repellent though the pornographic magazines and films discussed by Langton are, the imposition of legal bans on them would be both overweening and degrading for any system of governance that undertakes such an imposition. In contending as much, this chapter will of course draw upon some of the arguments and considerations that have been marshaled in my earlier chapters.

Langton has long relied heavily on the theory of speech-acts developed by J.L. Austin in the mid-twentieth century, and more recently she has also made valuable use of the work undertaken separately by David Lewis and Robert Stalnaker on the pragmatics of conversations and other discourses. Hence, before expounding and challenging her ideas about the noxious effects of pornography on women, this chapter will recount a few of the principal tenets of Austin's theory. (In due course, it will also recount a few of the elements of Lewis's philosophizing upon which Langton has drawn.) I will then synopsize and impugn the lines of reasoning which underlie Langton's conclusion that pornography subordinates and silences women. Thereafter, the chapter will move on to its main task of explaining sustainedly why Langton's arguments do not militate at all in favor of legal restrictions on pornography.

5.1 Preliminary Clarifications

At this preliminary juncture, a handful of observations will help to avert some potential misapprehensions about my critique of Langton's piquant writings on pornography. First, as Langton makes abundantly clear from the outset of *Sexual Solipsism* (2009, 3–4), she does not purport to be offering an analysis that is applicable to every kind of pornography. As she indicates in a footnote, she generally confines her attention to pornographic materials that have been "made for consumption by heterosexual men [in Western cultures]" (3 n6). More specifically, she confines her analysis to materials that consist in "the graphic sexually explicit subordination of women in pictures or words that also includes women dehumanized as sexual objects, things, or commodities."[3] This circumscription of the scope of her enquiry is of course entirely apt, and I shall not be contesting it at any point—though I will ponder the ambiguity of the formulation that has just been quoted.

Second, like Langton herself most of the time, I readily accept that pornographic materials are appropriately classified as "speech" even though quite a few of those

[2] In much the same vein is Jenkins 2017, 108 n16.

[3] Langton 2009, 4. Langton is quoting, in an abridged form, a definition presented in MacKinnon 1987, 176. See also MacKinnon 1993, 15–16. For a definition similar to Langton's and MacKinnon's, see McGowan 2017, 40–1.

materials are composed of images with few or no words. As has been explained in Chapter 2, the classifiability of anything as an instance of "speech" is not dependent on its containing or using any elements of a natural language such as English. Instead, the classification hinges on whether something is an instance of expression (or communication) in the sense specified by Chapter 2. What is expressed or communicated can be a propositional message, but it can alternatively be non-propositional such as a sentiment or an outlook. As my earlier chapters have maintained, this expansive understanding of the category of "speech" is uniquely germane in ruminations on the limits and foundations of the principle of freedom of expression. The appropriate breadth of that category is determined by the values that underpin the principle of freedom of expression as self-restraint, and those values are sweepingly wide-ranging in their application.

By and large, Langton concurs with me in taking as given that pornography is to be classified as "speech." Her stance on that point stems partly from her awareness that pornography has long been so classified in litigation pursued under the First Amendment to the U.S. Constitution, and partly from her inclination to dissect the workings of pornography with the apparatus of speech-act philosophy. As she remarks: "On this way of thinking, pornography is something to which speech act theory could apply" (Langton 2012, 78). However, Langton is also aware that a number of other philosophers have queried the classification of hard-core pornography as "speech,"[4] and she has fleetingly expressed some sympathy with such doubts (Langton 2009, 100–2). Still, generally resisting the temptation to go down that path, she is wise not to succumb to it. After all, as is evident from my earlier chapters, she is not thereby committing herself to the proposition that—under the principle of freedom of expression—pornography is protected against legal restrictions. Although the classifiability of pornography as expressive or communicative is a necessary condition for the conferral of protection upon it by the principle of freedom of expression, it is hardly a sufficient condition. As Waldron rightly declares, "calling something speech is perfectly compatible with also calling it an action that may be harmful in itself or that may have harmful consequences" (2012, 38). Thus, although this chapter will contend that most types of pornography are indeed protected by the moral principle of freedom of expression, my verdict along those lines is grounded on far more than the fact that pornography is properly subsumed under the heading of "speech."

Third, Langton is quite right to insist—in opposition to Ronald Dworkin—that the concerns of contemporary feminists about pornography are very different from the moralistic concerns of social conservatives. Early in his career, Dworkin powerfully resisted the efforts of social conservatives to justify legal bans on

[4] See, for example, Antony 2011, 388–90; 2017, 67–8, 72; Hornsby 2011, 380, 382–4; Maitra and McGowan 2007; Schauer 1979; 1982, 181–4. See also Jenkins 2017, 94–5; Maitra and McGowan 2010; McGowan 2012.

pornography (Dworkin 1978, 256–8; 1985, 335–72). In his retorts to those efforts, he affirmed that the cultural pollution and the feelings of disgust and offense occasioned by many varieties of pornographic materials are not social harms of a kind that can ever vindicate the outlawing of those materials. When he later sought to come to grips with arguments propounded by MacKinnon, he never really succeeded in engaging with those arguments on their own terms. Instead, he clung to the notion that she was obfuscatorily repackaging the conservative objections which he had parried years earlier:

> The continued popularity of bad arguments such as those in [MacKinnon's] *Only Words* testifies to the strength of the real but hidden reason why so many people despise pornography and want to ban it. The sado-masochistic genre of pornography, particularly, is so ... degrading that we are appalled and shamed by its existence. Contrary to MacKinnon's view, almost all men, I think, are as disgusted by it as almost all women. Because those who want to forbid pornography know that offensiveness alone does not justify censorship, however, they disguise their repulsion as concern that pornography will cause rape, or silence women, or harm the women who make it. (Dworkin 1996, 233–4)

Langton justifiably rejects Dworkin's conflation of the complaints voiced by feminists and the complaints voiced by social conservatives, as she expounds the feminist view that "we have reason to be concerned about pornography, not because it is [moralistically] suspect, but because we care about equality and the rights of women."[5] Indeed, some of the most subtle and incisive pages of *Sexual Solipsism* are devoted to oppugning Dworkin's attempted rebuttals of the worries of feminists about pornography, and to showing that his ripostes tell only against moralistic positions. (Langton also ingeniously brings together several strands of Dworkin's writings to reveal that his equality-centered liberalism is in fact supportive of feminist objections to pornography.) My own rejoinders to Langton will concentrate on her distinctive lines of reasoning—which combine feminist political philosophy with the philosophy of language—and will not suppose that those lines of reasoning rest on any moralistic feelings of prudishness.

Fourth, although there have been conflicting results in the myriad of empirical studies that have endeavored to ascertain whether the prevalence of pornography exacerbates the incidence of various social evils such as gender-based inequality and sexual violence, the findings in a number of those studies have pointed to the conclusion that the widespread availability of pornography does tend to breed such evils. Langton adverts to some of those latter studies at several junctures in her book. Moreover, cumulatively equivocal though the empirical investigations

[5] Langton 2009, 117. For a similar view, see Brison 1998, 324–5.

of the effects of pornography have been, the investigations that largely tally with the complaints of feminists about those effects are—in the words of Judge Frank Easterbrook of the U.S. Seventh Circuit Court of Appeals—"consistent with much human experience."[6] Thus, although evidence on the matter is mixed, I will not be challenging the proposition that the lawful availability of hard-core pornographic materials is likely to increase the incidence of certain gender-related misconduct. That proposition is plausible, and its truth is consistent with everything in my critique of Langton's approach to pornography.

Fifth, Langton occasionally insinuates that liberals who deem pornography to be protected by the principle of freedom of expression are inclined to perceive pornographers as mavericks whose activities constitute challenges to the prevailing sexual mores of their societies. Perceived in that way, pornographers would be comparable to orators who iconoclastically articulate views on socio-political matters concerning the respective roles of men and women.[7] Now, although this allegation by Langton is largely accurate in application to a few remarks by Dworkin, and although some pornographers might indeed be mavericks who strive to lessen what they disdain as the priggishness of their societies, my ripostes to Langton in this chapter do not ascribe any such ambitions to pornographers. While insisting that the principle of freedom of expression protects most pornographic materials against the legal restrictions that have been imposed on them, I can allow *arguendo* that every pornographer is motivated solely by pecuniary considerations. That is, I can allow *arguendo* that the lone aspiration of every pornographer is to pander lucratively to the desires for his products among the men in his society. Worth adding here is that—like Dworkin himself—I believe that pornography, especially hard-core pornography, is entirely devoid of any admirable qualities. Pornographic materials, even at the milder end of the spectrum, elicit in me a visceral sense of revulsion. Were the principle of freedom of expression applicable only to utterances or actions or materials that possess some worthy features, all the hard-core pornography on which Langton trains her sights would fall outside the scope of that principle. However, as this chapter has already suggested and as some of my earlier chapters have explained, the protective ambit of the principle of freedom of expression is not confined to modes of communication that are commendable to any degree. Consequently, this chapter's defense of most types of pornography against the imposition of legal constraints does not presuppose that pornography or the pornographic industry is commendable in any respect.

[6] The quoted phrase appears in *American Booksellers Association v Hudnut* 1985, 329 n2. Dworkin (1996, 240–1) was correct in remarking that Easterbrook accepted the conclusions of certain empirical studies only *arguendo* as a way of deferring to the views of the Indianapolis lawmakers on a disputed empirical matter. See also Koppelman 1996, 233 n51. However, the wording in the note by Easterbrook—and in the main text of his opinion—makes clear that he regarded the conclusions of those studies as quite plausible.

[7] Langton 2009, 19, 44, 45, 173–4. Langton especially has in mind Dworkin 1994, where Dworkin assimilated pornographers to people who participate in debates over socio-political matters.

5.2 An Elementary Précis of Speech-Act Philosophy

While Langton's approach to pornography has built fruitfully on ideas from more than one tradition in the philosophy of language, the ideas that figure most saliently in her approach are derived from Austin's account of speech-acts. No large-scale exposition of Austin's philosophizing is requisite here, but an acquaintance with a few of his key distinctions is essential for one's understanding of Langton's claims about the pernicious effects of pornography. Hence, this section will provide a terse précis of the relevant distinctions.

Austin was particularly keen to highlight the ways in which any number of instances of speech and writing constitute actions that bring about effects beyond saying and describing. That aim of his is evident from the title of his immensely influential book *How to Do Things with Words*. He there differentiated among three broad categories of acts that can be instantiated by utterances. (Though I would normally treat an utterance not as multiple actions but as a single action with multiple aspects or dimensions,[8] this chapter will follow Austin and his interpreters by analyzing any relevant utterance into acts of multiple kinds.)

Most obviously, a meaningful spoken or written utterance is a *locutionary* act. That is, in order to communicate something, it employs certain words that are endowed with some discernible semantic content. One of Austin's homely examples was "You can't do that" (1975, 102). The second-person pronoun in this locution refers to an addressee; the pronoun "that" refers to some mode of conduct in which the addressee is engaging or attempting to engage; and the verb phrase "can't do" refers either (as a modal locution) to the impossibility of the aforementioned mode of conduct or (as a deontic locution) to the impermissibility of the conduct.

In addition to saying something, the utterance "You can't do that" performs a communicative action of some kind. That performance is what Austin designated as an *illocutionary* act. The kind of action performed is fixed by the context of the utterance, which includes any applicable background conventions. "You can't do that" could be a warning or a protest or a taunt or a remonstration or an information-imparting assertion, for example. Whatever the specific illocutionary act may be, it is constituted rather than caused by the locutionary act. As I have recounted in §1.6 of this book's opening chapter, a constitutive relationship is to be understood as follows. X is constituted by Y if and only if (1) Y, in combination with all the prevailing circumstances other than any causal laws, logically entails X; and (2) without Y, the prevailing circumstances other than any causal laws would not logically entail X. In a constitutive relationship between a locutionary act and an

[8] I have made clear elsewhere that I side with the unifiers in the unifier/multiplier controversy within the philosophy of action. See Kramer 2003, 281 n6. For a fine overview of the unifier/multiplier controversy, see Carter 1999, 175–83.

illocutionary act, the prevailing circumstances of course include the background conventions that govern the performance of actions through words.

In addition to constituting an illocutionary act, an utterance such as "You can't do that" typically causes various communicative effects (most notably in the outlook and behavior of any addressee of the utterance). Its causing of such effects is what Austin designated as a *perlocutionary* act. Thus, the perlocutionary upshot of "You can't do that" might consist in dissuading the addressee(s) from attempting to engage in some mode of conduct, or in persuading the addressee(s) to abandon some current course of conduct, or—especially if "You can't do that" is construable as a taunt—in stiffening the resolve of the addressee(s) to carry out some course of conduct. If there are multiple addressees of the utterance, these and other perlocutionary effects can occur in tandem.

Austin introduced many subtleties and complexities and reservations into his exposition of the distinctions among locutionary and illocutionary and perlocutionary acts, and he elaborately catalogued sundry species of illocutionary acts. However, most of the elements of his theory that are needed for the purposes of this chapter's engagement with Langton's work are contained in the bare summary above. Some additional elements requisite for those purposes will be added later.

5.3 Langton on the Subordination of Women by Pornography

Langton endeavors to vindicate the wording in MacKinnon's definition of pornography that has been quoted in §5.1 above. Specifically, she endeavors to vindicate the claim that pornography consists in "the graphic sexually explicit subordination of women in pictures or words." Now, one quite natural way of construing the phrase "subordination of women" in MacKinnon's formulation is to equate it with "depiction of women as subordinate." So construed, MacKinnon's wording would not suggest that pornographic materials *constitute* any degradation of the status of women in the world outside the pictures and maunderings of those materials—though they might of course contribute to *causing* such a degradation. When pornography is understood along these lines, any complaints about its role in lowering the status of women would be empirical claims about the diffuse causal impact of denigratory representations. This understanding of pornography is exactly what Judge Easterbrook adopted when he held in the mid-1980s that an Indianapolis anti-pornography ordinance devised by MacKinnon was inconsistent with the First Amendment to the American Constitution (Langton 2009, 25–6).

Like MacKinnon herself, Langton contends that the definition of pornography is not to be construed in the way just broached—or that it is not to be construed exclusively in such a fashion. She insists that the role of pornographic materials in diminishing the status of women is not solely perlocutionary. Instead, the subordination to which MacKinnon's definition refers is an illocutionary act (or a medley of illocutionary acts) through which the lowering of the status of women is constituted rather than merely caused. Langton maintains that the subordination comprises three main aspects. Pornographic materials authoritatively rank women as beings of inferior worth; they legitimize the discriminatory treatment of women; and they deprive women of certain liberties and normative powers. Pornography constitutes these changes directly in the normative standing of women.

To clarify and bolster her contention that pornographers perform illocutionary acts of subordination, Langton adduces a striking analogy (2009, 34–6, 42–3; 2011, 426). She asks her readers to envisage a legislator in South Africa during the era of apartheid. Suppose that the legislator is in a position to determine the outcome of parliamentary balloting on a proposed statute that will disenfranchise all black adults, and suppose that he officially indicates his approval of the statute by declaring that "black adults are henceforth not entitled to vote in any elections or referenda." In that event, his locutionary act of uttering those words will constitute an illocutionary act of subordination. Given the prevailing system of governance in the legislator's society, his endorsement of the statute is an act that authoritatively ranks black people as inferior; moreover, it deprives them of certain legal liberties and legal powers; and it renders legally permissible the discriminatory treatment of black people. In combination with the prevailing system of governance—and with the ballots that have been cast by the other members of the law-making body—the legislator's act of endorsement logically entails these effects of subordination. Those effects follow not causally but constitutively. They are illocutionary rather than perlocutionary.

5.3.1 The Felicity Condition of Authority

Attempts to perform illocutionary acts can go awry in various ways, and can thus fail to produce the illocutionary acts which they aim to produce. Austin applied the term "infelicities" to the sundry routes by which any attempts to perform illocutionary acts can misfire (1975, Lectures II and III). Hence, when an attempt to perform an illocutionary act of some kind has succeeded in so doing, it has satisfied all the felicity conditions for the performance of an act of that kind. Now, as Langton readily observes (2009, 36–7), the felicity conditions for the performance of an illocutionary act of subordination include the authoritativeness of the person who performs the act. As she writes: "Subordinating speech acts are authoritative speech acts, so if we are ever to count some class of speech acts as subordinating speech, the speakers in question must have authority" (37). In the scenario of the disenfranchisement of South African blacks, for example, the legislator succeeds in performing an illocutionary act of subordination only because he is vested with the legal authority to perform such an act in the circumstances.

We have now reached a major crux that stymies Langton's efforts to bring to bear Austinian speech-act philosophy in support of MacKinnon's definition of pornography. If the scenario of the South African legislator is to be illuminatingly analogous to the situation of pornographers as they manufacture and purvey their products, then the pornographers must be possessed of authority that is at least roughly comparable to the authority of the legislator. Though Langton acknowledges that "[p]ornography falls short of this devastating paradigm [of subordination in the form of apartheid legislation] in a number of important respects," she unflinchingly accepts that the possession of authority by pornographers is "a crucial felicity condition" for the feats of illocutionary subordination which she attributes to them (2009, 43, 44). Yet, at least at first glance, any ascriptions of authority to pornographers are outlandish. It is not surprising, then, that previous commentators on Langton's analysis of the baneful effects of pornography have raised this problem of authority more frequently than any other difficulty. I too will be exploring this problem, though I will seek to avoid the misunderstandings that have plagued some of the past critiques of Langton's work. To steer clear of those misunderstandings, we should attend to some vital distinctions that have been accentuated by Langton herself (especially in essays written after the publication of *Sexual Solipsism*).

5.3.2 Starkly De Facto Authority versus Morally Binding Authority

One of the distinctions just mentioned should have been apparent to everybody from the outset. Given that Langton is ascribing authority to pornographers, and given that her foremost analogy in support of her ascription is the scenario of the South African legislator, she plainly has in mind starkly de facto authority rather than morally binding authority. Whereas the norms that endow somebody with morally binding authority are correct principles of morality, the norms that endow somebody with starkly de facto authority are those of some institution or practice or activity or system of governance that is lacking in moral legitimacy.

At least on any matters pertaining to the distinctive treatment of black people, the South African system of governance during the era of apartheid was endowed with starkly de facto authority rather than with morally binding authority. Thus, Ishani Maitra uncharacteristically goes astray when she writes as follows:

> It's plausible to suppose that the South African legislator [envisaged by Langton] can subordinate in saying what he does only because he has the right kind of authority. A legislator in a democratic society has the authority to give or take away

rights and powers from members of that society by enacting legislation. (Maitra 2012, 95)

During the era of apartheid, the South African system of governance was not democratic—as most adult inhabitants were disenfranchised because of their race. Thus, whatever authority the South African system of governance possessed, it was not the morally binding authority that is properly imputable to the legislature in a genuinely democratic society. It was instead the starkly de facto authority of a repressive regime which promulgated an array of legal norms and which gave effect to those norms through administrative and adjudicative processes. The legislator in Langton's scenario was endowed with his authority under that array of norms; his authority was starkly de facto rather than morally binding.

Similarly, of course, if pornographers were to possess any authority, it would be starkly de facto. The messages conveyed by the rebarbative materials that fit MacKinnon's definition are not morally binding on anyone, and the processes of manufacturing and distributing those materials are not conducted with authority bestowed by any correct principles of morality. Hence, we should recognize that—in regard to the distinction between the starkly de facto and the morally binding—Langton's imputations of authority to pornographers are aligned with her imputations of authority to people who engage in hatefully bigoted utterances. As Langton has emphasized in a recent essay (2018a, 135–8), the authority which she attributes to the people who engage in those hateful utterances is starkly de facto. Much the same is true of the authority which she attributes to pornographers.[9]

Even when any confusion on this point has been dispelled, naturally, the difficulties that afflict Langton's account of pornography as subordination are formidable. After all, whereas the nature of the starkly de facto authority wielded by the apartheid-era system of governance in South Africa can quite readily be discerned, the nature of any starkly de facto authority wielded by the manufacturers and purveyors of pornography is not readily discernible. Through its legislative and administrative and adjudicative organs, the South African system of governance promulgated legal norms that were implemented through the system's mechanisms of enforcement. Albeit some of those norms (such as ordinary legal prohibitions on murder and arson) were morally benign, many of them (such as any laws that provided for racial segregation and discrimination) were morally odious. Frequently in the operations of that system of governance, then, the authority exercised by it was starkly de facto rather than morally binding. Nonetheless, because

[9] The interesting discussion of Langton in Antony 2017, 80–5 is weakened by its somewhat simplistic dichotomy between authority and power. Requisite instead is a trichotomy that differentiates among morally binding practical authority, starkly de facto practical authority, and raw power. For some very brief but perceptive remarks on starkly de facto practical authority, see McGowan 2012, 127–8.

those operations involved the promulgation and effectuation of norms by legal-governmental officials, and because the effectuation of the norms was carried out not only against the people who were enfranchised but also against the more numerous people who were disenfranchised, the system's workings affected people's normative statuses (the statuses which people occupied under a prevailing matrix of norms) in far-reaching ways. Hence, although the system's workings were often without any moral bindingness, they were possessed of authority over the whole population. With their starkly de facto authority, the operations of the system of governance produced countless major normative effects such as the sweeping disenfranchisement of black people.

When we turn our attention to pornographers, we do not behold anything that is even remotely comparable. As Langton concedes, "[t]he authority of hate speech [or pornography] is unlike the [authority of] law in kind and degree, and it would be grotesque to suggest otherwise" (2018a, 137). Although each company that manufactures or distributes pornography is doubtless run internally as an institution to some degree, and although many such companies might form a trade association that is also institutionalized, those companies do not operate in relation to the public at large through mechanisms of enforcement with officials who give effect to misogynous norms that have been promulgated to members of the citizenry. Even vis-à-vis the readers and viewers of pornographic materials, no such operations of giving effect to misogynous norms are undertaken. *A fortiori*, no such operations are conducted vis-à-vis people who shun pornographic materials. There are no pornographic "officials" who implement a prevailing network of misogynous norms and who thereby authoritatively determine the normative statuses of people at large.

Thus, although Langton has certainly been on solid ground in invoking the distinction between starkly de facto authority and morally binding authority, her invocation of that distinction does not take her very far toward clinching the proposition that pornographers carry out illocutionary acts of subordination. In itself, the distinction between the starkly de facto and the morally binding does not help her to show that pornographic materials constitutively deprive women of liberties and normative powers, nor does it help her to show that such materials constitutively render legitimate the discriminatory treatment of women under any prevailing set of norms. Moreover, although the pornographic materials targeted by Langton do undoubtedly rank women as inferior, her distinction between starkly de facto authority and morally binding authority falls far short of establishing that the pornographic rankings are authoritative; those rankings imparted by pornographers do not saddle anyone with obligations of any kind to accept what the pornographers have determined. Consequently, Langton still faces some daunting hurdles in her efforts to uphold MacKinnon's definition of pornography. To try to overcome those hurdles, she avails herself of some further distinctions.

5.3.3 Practical Authority versus Epistemic Authority

Especially salient in Langton's recent writings is the distinction between practical authority and epistemic authority (Langton 2011, 430; 2016, 872; 2017, 33; 2018a, 125–6, 141–3). Practical authority, in its morally binding incarnations and in its starkly de facto incarnations, is what I have been discussing heretofore in this chapter. It consists in permissions and normative powers to alter the normative statuses of other people, especially through the imposition of obligations on other people to act as they are directed to act by anybody endowed with such authority. If the authority is morally binding, then the obligations imposed by the exercise of it are moral obligations. If instead the authority is starkly de facto, the obligations imposed by the exercise of it are austerely legal or institutional or activity-relative.

Epistemic authority is quite different. Instead of understanding it with reference to the distinction between the starkly de facto and the morally binding, we should understand it with reference to the distinction between the putative and the genuine. Genuine epistemic authority consists in expertise on the matter(s) to which the authority is applicable. When someone possessed of such authority provides information to somebody else about a matter within the purview of the authority, the person to whom the information has been communicated will have a solid reason for believing what he or she has been told. Likewise, if somebody possessed of such authority supplies advice to someone else about the best way of dealing with a problem to which the authority pertains, the addressee of the advice will have a solid reason for adopting the recommended course of action. When someone with genuine epistemic authority has furnished some information or advice to an addressee, the information or advice is credible in that it ought to be regarded as correct by its recipient.

Putative epistemic authority consists not in any genuine expertise but instead in supposititious expertise. Although somebody endowed with putative epistemic authority is not a source of reliable information or advice about the matter(s) to which that ersatz authority pertains, he or she is unfoundedly thought to be such a source by other people. Putative epistemic authority obviously varies in its extent, both in relation to the range of topics which it covers and in relation to the number of people who are hoodwinked by it. An assertion or a piece of advice from someone endowed with such authority might be correct on a particular occasion, but its correctness is wholly fortuitous; in general, the assertions and advice dispensed by such a person do not track the truth. Nonetheless, among some gullible people, the assertions and advice so dispensed are credited as trustworthy.

Now, of course, Langton does not believe that pornographers are possessed of genuine epistemic authority any more than she believes that they are possessed of morally binding practical authority. Through their production and vending of materials that convey benighted views about the appropriate treatment of women, pornographers fall grotesquely short of being reliable sources of information about sexuality and human interaction. Nevertheless, Langton contends, pornographers are perceived as such sources by many of the people—especially male adolescents—who read or view their materials. Devoid though pornographers are of any genuine epistemic authority, they are vested with putative epistemic authority by many of the consumers of their products.

On the one hand, Langton's ascriptions of putative epistemic authority to pornographers are occasionally somewhat overconfident. For example, when Langton recounts the findings of a 2013 survey of attitudes among teenagers toward sexuality and pornography, she remarks that the male respondents were "frank about pornography" as they confessed to using pornographic materials not only as vehicles for entertainment but also as sources of information (Langton 2017, 30). Very likely, quite a few of those respondents were in fact being less than frank by omitting to acknowledge that they availed themselves of pornographic materials predominantly as vehicles for sexual arousal that would enhance their masturbatory experiences.[10] Still, on the other hand, Langton's claims about the putative epistemic authority of pornographers among male adolescents are generally persuasive. There is little doubt that, in the eyes of numerous such adolescents, pornographers are to varying degrees perceived as fruitful sources of information.

5.3.3.1 Starkly De Facto Practical Authority from Putative Epistemic Authority?

Convincing though Langton generally is in her attributions of putative epistemic authority to pornographers, her stance on that matter does not confirm that pornographers carry out illocutionary acts of subordination through the production and marketing of their materials. Their possession of putative epistemic authority (in the eyes of some male adolescents) does not endow them with any starkly de facto practical authority. Pornographers do not possess any such practical authority over male adolescents, and even more clearly they do not possess such authority over members of the public at large. Their actions of manufacturing and distributing their repellent materials do not constitutively deprive women of any liberties or normative powers, nor do those actions constitutively render legitimate the discriminatory treatment of women under any prevailing norms. Likewise, the pornographers' actions do not constitutively rank women in ways that are binding on women or on anyone else. In other words, the actions of the pornographers do not illocutionarily subordinate women in any of the dimensions envisaged by Langton.

Langton apparently thinks that the putative epistemic authority of pornographers does somehow invest them with starkly de facto practical authority. She adopts such a view partly because she has embraced too much of Joseph Raz's

[10] Another ground for caution is that it is unclear whether the pornography read and watched by the respondents in the 2013 survey was some of the hard-core pornography that would fit MacKinnon's definition.

highly paternalistic conception of practical authority. Having paid insufficient heed to the sundry critiques of his conception of authority that have emerged during the past couple of decades,[11] she approvingly quotes the following pronouncement from Raz: "[A]n analysis maximizing the similarities between authority for action [namely, practical authority] and authority for belief [namely, epistemic authority] is, other things being equal, preferable" (Raz 2009a, 8, quoted in Langton 2018a, 126). Later in the same recent essay, Langton writes as follows:

> *Authority for belief may be practical*, as Raz observes. A doctor has an ability to prescribe, based on his [genuine] epistemic authority, which includes expertise and credibility. We can add that a *quack* doctor's ability to prescribe is likewise based on his [putative] epistemic authority. (Langton 2018a, 131, emphases in original, footnote omitted)

She returns to the example of the doctor at a subsequent juncture, when she again lauds Raz's insistence on the intimate connection between practical and epistemic authority: "Practical and epistemic authority interact, as Raz pointed out. Your doctor's orders have their status as directives, in part because of what your doctor knows, or is taken to know ... The doctor is able, as we say, to *prescribe*" (141–2, emphasis in original). She adds:

> [W]hat Raz says about [genuine] epistemic authority, construed as expertise, applies also to [putative] epistemic authority, construed as [baselessly perceived trustworthiness]. It applies to the quack doctor, as well as to the [capable] doctor ... The [mistakenly credited] quack doctor is an authority, for his gullible patients, not only on the causes of illness but also on their cures. (142)

Langton has here aligned herself far too closely with Raz. Let us ponder in turn the capable doctor and the inept doctor in her example.

5.3.3.1.1 The Capable Doctor

One thing to be noted straightaway about the capable doctor is that he is not relevantly analogous to pornographers. His epistemic authority concerning medical matters is genuine, whereas the epistemic authority of the pornographers concerning matters of sexuality and the treatment of women is putative rather than genuine; the epistemic authority of the pornographers exists only in the eyes of the credulous adolescents (and perhaps older men) who are beguiled by their

[11] Among the main critiques of Raz's conception of authority are Darwall 2009; 2010; Hershovitz 2003; 2011; Himma 2007; Perry 2013; Quong 2011, 110–20. For some of Raz's principal elaborations of his theory of authority, see Raz 1986, chs 2–4; 2009a, chs 1–2; 2009b, chs 5, 13. For criticism of several aspects of Raz's paternalism, see Kramer 2017, 227–49.

products. However, even if we leave that point aside, there are ample grounds for doubting that the capable doctor is endowed with any practical authority over his patients. On the one hand, his prescriptions are indeed prescriptive in that they supply his patients with reasons for adopting certain therapeutic courses of action. On the other hand, those reasons are not duty-imposing. For each patient, the adoption of the therapeutic course of action prescribed by the doctor is advisable—perhaps strongly advisable—rather than obligatory. Not every reason for action is deontic. If a patient decides against following the recommended therapy, she might be acting foolishly but will not be committing a wrong against the doctor.

To be sure, as is indicated by the quotidian phrase "doctor's orders," physicians often presume to be vested with the authority to impose obligations on their patients. Langton endorses the presumptuousness of those physicians:

> The interaction of epistemic and practical authority is reflected in the speech acts available to the doctor, or indeed the quack doctor. Suppose your doctor says, looking sadly at your file, "Sorry, cigarettes are *out*." That would exemplify, perhaps, a mix of speech act types, drawing on his epistemic *and* practical authority: a verdictive, ranking cigarettes as unhealthy; an exercitive, making it count as an inferior option, in this context; and a directive, ordering you not to smoke. (Langton 2018a, 142, emphases in original)

Albeit somewhat tentatively, Langton here takes at face value the self-understanding of many a doctor. That paternalistic understanding of the doctor–patient relationship is suitable for paediatricians whose patients are not yet sufficiently mature to reach decisions competently about their own health and lifestyles, but it is inapposite for doctors whose patients are adults of sound mind. Such patients are morally entitled to reach decisions about their own health and lifestyles, with the aid of expert recommendations—rather than binding directives—from their physicians. Though the recommendations might often be framed in the imperative mood, they are properly construable as advisory rather than as obligation-imposing.

Three caveats or qualifications should be attached to what has just been said. First, the ethical bearings of the interaction between a capable physician and an adult patient are not entirely clear-cut. Many of the recent critiques of Raz's conception of practical authority have adduced examples that involve experts such as stockbrokers and travel agents. In each of those examples, the fact that an expert's advice does not impose any obligations on the addressee of the advice is straightforward. By contrast, in some scenarios where capable physicians prescribe certain courses of treatment to their patients, the absence of any obligations incumbent on the patients is considerably less clear. In some such scenarios, the patients might be under duties of courtesy to carry out the therapeutic courses of action that have been prescribed to them. Such an upshot does not always occur in cases where capable doctors instruct patients to undertake some steps that will cure or avert maladies, but there are no compelling reasons for insisting that it never occurs. Given the centrality of good health to a satisfactory human life, there can be situations where somebody who omits to follow prescribed therapeutic measures is thereby exhibiting disrespect for the medical experts who have gone to the trouble of diagnosing her ailments and counseling in favor of those measures.

Second, some patients owe general moral duties of support to dependents such as their children or elderly parents. If compliance with a doctor's prescription is crucial for the continuation of a patient's ability to fulfill those general duties, the prescription itself is obligation-imposing. Issued in the presence of those general background duties, a prescription from a knowledgeable physician can generate an obligation to comply with its terms.

Third, even if we leave aside the possibility of circumstances in which patients incur moral duties to follow the recommendations dispensed to them by their doctors, some legal or institutional or practice-specific obligations might be incurred in particular circumstances. Suppose that, because of legal requirements or because of policies introduced by the medical profession in some country, patients there who fail to abide by prescribed regimens will undergo certain penalties. Perhaps they will be fined, or perhaps certain modes of treatment will thereafter be unavailable to them. Now, the question here is not whether any such penalties would ever be morally justified. Whether or not any of the patients have been placed under moral duties by the doctors' prescriptions in the envisioned circumstances, they have been placed under legal or institutional duties. Legal norms or institutional norms can vest physicians with practical authority which the physicians exercise when they prescribe treatments to their patients. Insofar as expert recommendations are backed up in this manner by the prospect of the levying of penalties for noncompliance with the recommendations, the genuine epistemic authority of the experts is combined with practical authority.

As should be evident, none of these caveats or qualifications will be of any avail to Langton. Patients might sometimes be under duties of courtesy to follow the counsel supplied to them by their capable doctors, but such duties are not owed to pornographers either by the readers and viewers of pornographic materials or by the countless people (including most women) who eschew those materials. Likewise, quite ludicrous is the notion that the products of pornographers trigger any background moral duties owed by people to their dependents. Similarly, notwithstanding that the genuine epistemic authority of capable doctors can be conjoined with practical authority through the arrangements recounted in the preceding paragraph, there are no similar arrangements that conjoin the putative epistemic authority of pornographers with starkly de facto practical authority. No system of governance in any liberal democracy has ever introduced the prospect of penalties for readers and viewers of pornographic materials who do not adjust their behavior to conform to the messages conveyed by such materials about the ways in which women can appropriately be treated. No legal system endows pornographers with legal authority—which in this case would be a species of starkly de facto practical authority—in that fashion. Nor do the manufacturers and vendors of pornographic materials themselves operate any system of monitoring and enforcement that would give effect to institutional norms under which the consumers of the materials face penalties if they do not treat women abusively. There is no such system of monitoring and enforcement, and there are no such institutional norms that would be sustained by that system.

5.3.3.1.2 The Inept Doctor

Whereas a capable doctor endowed with genuine epistemic authority is not relevantly similar to pornographers, a medical charlatan endowed only with putative epistemic authority is relevantly similar to them. However, precisely because the inept doctor is not possessed of any genuine epistemic authority, the points which I have made about the capable doctor are applicable even more strongly here. Whereas the recommendations articulated by a capable physician furnish her patients with reasons for following her instructions, the recommendations articulated by a mountebank do not supply his patients with any corresponding reasons. Of course, the hapless people who are cozened by the mountebank's posturing will doubtless believe that his prescriptions supply them with reasons for heeding his advice, but they err in so believing. Hence, because the patients of an inept doctor do not have any reasons for attending to his unreliable diagnoses and prescriptions, we have no occasion to ponder whether the reasons are obligation-imposing or not. Similarly, the readers and viewers of pornographic materials do not have any reasons for attending to the messages about the treatment of women that are conveyed by such materials. Some of those readers and viewers might think that they have such reasons, but they err in so thinking. Thus, we have no occasion to ponder whether the reasons presented to those readers and viewers are obligation-imposing or not.

No duties of courtesy are engendered when an inept doctor dispenses advice to his patients. Even if the inept doctor is merely inept and not also fraudulent, his patients do not show him any discourtesy by seeking alternative advice or by simply not following his prescriptions. In that regard, again, an incompetent doctor is relevantly analogous to the purveyors of pornography. As I have already maintained, no duties of courtesy are owed to those purveyors by the viewers and readers of pornographic filth. It would be ridiculous for pornographers to complain that they are being treated discourteously if the consumers of their products adopt patterns of behavior toward women that are far more enlightened than the patterns of behavior on display in pornographic films and magazines.

Unlike some prescriptions issued by knowledgeable physicians, the recommendations articulated by quacks do not trigger any background duties owed by patients to dependents. Save by pure fortuity—which, in this context, cannot be the basis of an obligation—compliance with a recommendation issued by a quack will not help to secure a patient's ability to fulfill any of those background duties. Consequently, no such recommendation carries any obligation-imposing force with which it might have been endowed if it had been reliably conducive to the maintenance of that ability.

Like a capable doctor, a woefully maladroit doctor might back up his prescriptions with the prospect of sanctions for patients who disregard what they have been told to do. Indeed, if the maladroit doctor is formally qualified to practice medicine, his attaching of the prospect of sanctions to his prescriptions might be in fulfillment of legal requirements—since those requirements in any particular country might call for such an approach and might not include any way of differentiating between formally qualified physicians who are capable and formally qualified physicians who are incompetent. In these circumstances, the issuance of ostensibly therapeutic instructions by the maladroit doctor to his patients will in effect place the patients under legal duties or other institutional duties to abide by those instructions. Legal norms or other institutional norms will have endowed the inept physician with starkly de facto practical authority, which is thus conjoined with his putative epistemic authority. He exercises his starkly de facto practical authority whenever he prescribes a course of treatment to a patient. Such a state of affairs is plainly possible, but what is equally plain is that its possibility offers no succor to Langton in her efforts to show that pornographers are endowed with starkly de facto practical authority. As has been remarked in my discussion of the capable doctor, no legal system has vested the manufacturers and distributors of pornography with starkly de facto practical authority along the lines envisaged in this paragraph. No legal system calls for those manufacturers and distributors to introduce penalties that will be imposed on viewers or readers whose conduct toward women is better than the conduct depicted in pornographic materials. Nor do the manufacturers and distributors introduce such penalties on their own initiative. They do not employ officials who monitor the doings of viewers and readers in order to discipline anyone whose behavior toward women is far less benighted than the behavior that is celebrated in pornographic films and magazines. Because there never has been such a system of monitoring and enforcement in operation—indeed, because the very specter of such a dystopian system is quite preposterous—Langton's analysis does not have any purchase on the actualities of the pornographic industry.

5.3.3.2 The Catholic Church as a Point of Contrast

Langton in *Sexual Solipsism* does not distinguish between epistemic authority and practical authority as clearly and explicitly as she does in her later work, but an example plumbed in her book can help to underscore the conclusions which I have reached in the foregoing discussions of capable doctors and incompetent doctors. Her example will reinforce those conclusions by supplying a germane point of contrast with the pornography industry. That is, we should here briefly contemplate an organization that does maintain a system of monitoring and enforcement to give effect to the norms that are promulgated by the organization's officials.

In response to an early critique of her work by Leslie Green, Langton mulls over the role of the Catholic Church in the subordination of homosexuals.[12] The Church clearly possesses epistemic authority in the eyes of devout Catholics, not only on the esoterica of faith but also on matters of sexuality. Moreover, the putative epistemic authority of the Church is conjoined with starkly de facto practical authority over Catholic believers and over anyone else who comes within the jurisdiction of the Church. As Langton observes, the Church has promulgated some norms which condemn homosexuality as sinful and which forbid anyone to engage in homosexual intercourse. The speech-acts through which those norms came into existence have authoritatively ranked homosexuals as inferior, and have deprived them of certain liberties and normative powers. In addition, those speech-acts have institutionally authorized certain patterns of discrimination against homosexuals. Thus, the norms of the Catholic Church as an institution have subordinated homosexuals in ways that parallel the ways in which many South African laws during the era of apartheid subordinated blacks.

Why does the Catholic Church (even in a predominantly non-Catholic country) possess starkly de facto practical authority over adherents of the Catholic faith and over some other people, whereas the manufacturers and distributors of pornographic materials do not possess any such authority except over their own employees? One quite obvious difference is that the Catholic Church is much more explicit and systematic in its promulgation of norms of conduct. Typically, the manufacturers and distributors of pornography do not explicitly formulate any norms of conduct at all; the misogynous norms of conduct inferable from their materials are implicitly conveyed rather than expressly stated and codified. Even more important is that the Catholic Church gives effect to its promulgated norms by operating a system of institutionalized control. That system exercises the control through techniques of monitoring (such as confessionals) and through the prospect of institutional sanctions (such as excommunication) and through the prospect of otherworldly sanctions. In these very respects, the relationship between the Catholic Church and its members is markedly in contrast with the relationship between pornographers and their customers. Companies that make and peddle pornographic materials do not monitor the behavior of their customers and do not hold out the prospect of sanctions for customers whose conduct has been insufficiently misogynous. Exactly the features of the institutional workings of the Catholic faith that warrant one's ascription of starkly de facto practical authority to the Church are not features of the pornographic industry.

[12] Langton 2009, 92–100. Despite my criticism of Langton in my next subsection, I concur with some of her ripostes to Green. In particular, her rejoinders to Green's excessively Razian understanding of authority are quite similar to points which I have made in Kramer 1999, 78–112.

The disanalogy between the Catholic Church and the pornographic industry is particularly important because the norms promulgated and administered by the Church constitutively subordinate some people who are not adherents of Catholicism. Suppose that Carlos and Martin are a homosexual couple who wish to be married, and suppose that Carlos is a practicing Catholic—albeit with a rather relaxed attitude toward some of the doctrines of the faith—whereas Martin is not an adherent of any religion. Carlos and Martin in a number of Western countries will be legally empowered to enter into a civil marriage, but the norms of Catholicism do not institutionally empower them to enter into a marriage that would be recognized as such by the Church. Not only has Carlos been deprived of the normative power to form a Church-recognized marriage with another man, but so too has the non-believer Martin. What decisively underlies their having been deprived of such a power is not the fact that only one of them is a Catholic; a heterosexual Catholic and a non-Christian partner of the opposite sex, with a dispensation from a local bishop, can enter into a non-sacramental marriage that is recognized as valid by the Church. Rather, what underlies the fact that Carlos and Martin lack the power to enter into a marriage recognized by the Church is that they are a same-sex couple. In that respect, *mutatis mutandis*, all homosexuals even in a predominantly non-Catholic country have been constitutively subordinated by the illocutions that enact and sustain the norms of the Church.

Because the norms of the Roman Catholic Church constitutively subordinate homosexuals beyond the membership of the Catholic faith (albeit in very limited ways), a tenable analogy between the practical authority of the Church and the practical authority of pornographers would to some degree be serviceable for Langton's analysis of the subordinating impact of pornography on women. However, as has been argued, there is no such tenable analogy. The very features of the operations of the Church that endow it with starkly de facto practical authority are not paralleled by any corresponding features of the pornography industry. Ergo, the example of the Church weakens rather than bolsters Langton's analysis.

5.3.3.3 Conflations of Epistemic Authority and Practical Authority

In her response to Green—some aspects of which I endorse—Langton tends to conflate practical authority and epistemic authority, and she likewise (and relatedly) tends to conflate illocutionarily constituted subordination and perlocutionarily caused subordination. She does so initially with reference to the Catholic Church and subsequently with reference to the pornographic industry. When these conflations are remedied, the response by Langton to Green turns out to underscore the fact that the manufacturers and purveyors of pornography lack the practical authority which she imputes to them. Thus, although their wares might contribute causally through perlocutionary effects to certain types of wrongs and hardships suffered by women, those wares do not constitute the illocutionary subordination which Langton recounts.

While ruminating on Green's scenario of a homosexual named "Max" who is a non-Catholic in a predominantly non-Catholic country, Langton ponders whether Max could be subordinated by the Catholic Church despite his rejection of the Church's authority. She limns a situation in which the position of the Church resembles that of pornographers in some contemporary countries:

> [S]uppose that ... the Church is a powerful minority, whose members accept its voice as authoritative, while non-members are substantially in the power of the members ... The minority, being powerful, have the power to hire and fire Max, control his civil rights, and sometimes exercise that power. In these conditions, I suggest, Max would indeed be subordinated. (Langton 2009, 97–8)

Langton is correct in asserting that Max would be subordinated in circumstances where practicing Catholics possess and exercise normative powers (in their lives outside the Church) to deprive him of various liberties and other entitlements. However, the subordination of him in those circumstances is not constituted by the norms of the Church or by any illocutions of the Church's officials. Instead, it is constituted by the illocutions through which the practicing Catholics exercise the aforementioned normative powers. Of course, in exercising those powers, the practicing Catholics might be acting partly on the basis of bigoted attitudes which they have formed through their absorption of the Church's teachings and norms on homosexuality. If so, then there are remote causal connections between the subordination of Max and certain speech-acts by officials of the Church. However, those causal connections—which operate through some perlocutionary effects of the officials' speech-acts—are not the constitutive connections which Langton professes to be unearthing. The role of the Church's pronouncements in bringing about the subordination of Max is remote and perlocutionary-causal rather than direct and illocutionary-constitutive.

In other words, Langton's scenario does not involve the possession or wielding of any practical authority by the Church over Max. Instead, it involves the Church's possession and wielding of putative epistemic authority over its members (on the matter of homosexuality). Because those members perceive the Church as a reliable source of information about the ethical bearings of homosexuality, the Church's pronouncements on the matter lead some of those members to form hostile attitudes toward people like Max. Such attitudes, which are perlocutionary effects of the pronouncements, then incline certain Catholics to subordinate Max by firing him or demoting him or abridging his entitlements in other ways. Though the role of the Church's pronouncements in bringing about his subordination is despicable, that role is due to the persuasiveness of the pronouncements (among practicing Catholics) rather than to their constituting of any changes in his normative positions. It is due to the putative epistemic authority of the clerics who issue the pronouncements, rather than to their being endowed with any practical authority over Max.

When Langton again trains her focus on the role of pornography in bringing about the subordination of women, she similarly conflates epistemic authority and practical authority. She aims to maintain that pornographers are relevantly similar to South African legislators in wielding starkly de facto practical authority through which they constitutively subordinate a group of people. To try to sustain that thesis, she suggests that the influence of the activities of pornographers on the place of women in contemporary societies is comparable to the influence of the Catholic Church on the place of homosexuals in Max's society:

> Suppose that the norms prescribed by pornography are ... accepted as setting standards of behaviour in the community of which a woman is a member, although she does not accept them ... Suppose there is significant contact between the woman and those in her community who accept the norms of pornography, so that locally they have the power to hire or fire her, control her education, affect her civil rights, and they sometimes exercise that power ... [S]uch a woman, where she is, in that context, is *subordinated*. (Langton 2009, 100, emphasis in original)

What Langton recounts here is indeed a situation in which the unnamed woman—whom I will designate as "Alice"—is subordinated. However, the subordination of Alice is constituted not by the illocutions of pornographers but instead by certain illocutions of the users of pornography in her community. When the users do engage in illocutions that subordinate Alice, they might be acting on the basis of outlooks and sentiments which they have formed partly through their viewing and reading of pornographic materials. If so, those perlocutionary effects of the materials are causal links between the manufacturing or marketing of pornography and the subordination of Alice. However, such causal perlocutionary connections are not the constitutive illocutionary connections which Langton has postulated between the peddling of pornography and the subordination of women.

When Langton postulates those constitutive illocutionary connections, she presupposes that pornographers wield practical authority (starkly de facto practical authority) over women. However, the only authority ascribable to the pornographers in her brief discussion of Alice is the putative epistemic authority which they possess in the estimation of some of their customers. Because the pornographers possess such epistemic authority in the eyes of some customers, those hoodwinked customers form attitudes toward women that are aligned with the attitudes which pornographic materials encourage and embody. Harboring such attitudes which have been cultivated or intensified by the pornographic materials, some of the consumers of those materials then exercise the starkly de facto practical authority which they possess over Alice and over any other women who are under their control. The practical authority over women in Langton's scenario is correctly ascribable to the consumers rather than to the pornographers; likewise, the illocutions that constitutively subordinate Alice and other women are uttered by the consumers rather than by the pornographers. (Obviously, the starkly de facto practical authority over women exercised by some of the consumers of pornography is possessed by them not in their status as such consumers but instead in their statuses as employers or governmental officials.) Lamentable though the role of pornography is in bringing about the subordination of women within Alice's society, that role is causal and perlocutionary rather than constitutive and illocutionary.

This chapter will later highlight the significance of the fact that the role of pornography in subordinating women is remotely causal rather than constitutive. Even at this stage, however, that significance is perhaps becoming apparent—especially in the light of my earlier chapters and the remarks near the outset of the present chapter. Langton has developed her account of the subordinating upshot of pornography in part because of her desire to move away from the old debates about the adequacy and reliability of the social-scientific evidence pertaining to the harmful effects that are allegedly caused by the availability and use of pornographic materials. She has drawn on the philosophy of language to support MacKinnon's contention that pornography is directly constitutive of the subordination of women as well as causative of sundry types of harm to them. My arguments in this chapter are suggesting—and will continue to suggest—that Langton has not succeeded in vindicating MacKinnon's contention. She has not succeeded in moving beyond the foci of the longstanding controversies over pornography, because she has failed to establish that the subordination of women by pornographic materials is constitutive rather than causal.

Many of the participants in those longstanding controversies have concentrated on questions about the robustness and tenor of the social-scientific studies that have investigated the causal consequences of pornography. Such questions concern, for example, the apparent inconsistencies between sets of findings or the appropriateness of various statistical techniques for interpreting the findings. Now, although I am doubtful about the resolvability of the empirical disputation over the effects of pornography,[13] I have already indicated that this chapter will not dwell on any such disputation. Instead, it will concern itself with the freedom-of-expression implications of the failure by Langton to show that some of the injurious effects of pornography on women are constitutive rather than remotely causal. As will be

[13] Despite the far-reaching differences between the issue of capital punishment and the issue of pornography, the intractability of the empirical wrangling over the latter issue is strongly reminiscent of the intractability of the wrangling over the empirical soundness of some of the rationales for the death penalty. In each case, the contestation centers on inconsistencies between sets of findings and on the heavy model-dependence of interpretations of the findings. For a discussion of the empirical difficulties that plague the deterrence-oriented rationale for capital punishment, see Kramer 2011, 30–8.

argued later, the conclusion properly inferable from her failure is that most types of pornography cannot legitimately be proscribed by any system of governance.

5.3.4 Authority from the Pragmatics of Discourse

Especially in her essays that are subsequent to *Sexual Solipsism*, but also in one of the trailblazing chapters of that book—a chapter originally published as an article co-written with Caroline West (Langton and West 1999)—Langton has supplemented her speech-act approach to pornography with the insights of Lewis and Stalnaker into the pragmatics of conversations and other discourses. She has also drawn on valuably astute writings by contemporary feminist philosophers such as Ishani Maitra and Mary Kate McGowan. In so doing, Langton has not abandoned her original Austinian approach. Rather, she has sought to bolster that approach by parlaying some of the ideas of these diverse philosophers into an account of the provenance of the authority with which pornographers are endowed (or with which they are presumed by Langton to be endowed). She has striven to equip herself with a satisfactory explanation of the source and properties of that authority, so that she can sustain her original thesis that the materials manufactured and distributed by pornographers illocutionarily subordinate women.

5.3.4.1 Presuppositions and Accommodation

Langton has concentrated above all on the import of presuppositions and accommodation in the unfolding of any discourse. Her understanding of presuppositions is aptly expansive and is similar to Stalnaker's understanding:

> A person's presuppositions are the propositions whose truth he takes for granted, often unconsciously, in a conversation, an inquiry, or a deliberation. They are the background assumptions that may be used without being spoken—sometimes without being noticed—for example as suppressed premisses in an enthymematic argument, or as implicit directions about how a request should be fulfilled or a piece of advice taken. (Stalnaker 1973, 447)

Accommodation is a process whereby a presupposition introduced into a discussion and not contested by any of the participants therein is thus incorporated into the taken-for-granted background or register of the discussion. At subsequent stages of the conversation, an accommodated presupposition will implicitly or explicitly be treated as if it is true. To illustrate the phenomenon of accommodation, Langton adduces an example that was originally offered by Lewis:

> Someone says "Even George could win," presupposing that George is an unpromising candidate. No-one interrupts with a "Whadda ya mean, 'even'?" and the

> presupposition is taken on board ... [A]cting as if something is correct play in a conversation tends to make it correct play, if nobody stops you. Hearers routinely accommodate what speakers presuppose, and the hearer's omission is a quiet engine of the speaker's success.[14]

Worth noting here, as an aside, is that Langton repeatedly errs by endorsing Lewis's untenable view that the sport of baseball differs from a conversation in that no rules of accommodation are operative among the rules of a baseball game. She writes, for example, as follows:

> A game of baseball does not tend to evolve in whatever way is required to make the play that occurs count as correct. If a player walks to first base after three balls rather than four, his behavior does not make it the case that there *are* four balls and his behavior is correct.

She adds: "Conversational score, however, *is* governed by a rule of accommodation. Conversational score, unlike baseball score, does tend to evolve in whatever way is required to make the play that occurs count as correct play."[15] Contrary to what is asserted here by Langton (in agreement with Lewis), baseball is like conversational interaction or any other norm-structured activity in comprising some rules of accommodation to deal with uncorrected errors. On the one hand, if a batter walks to first base after only three balls rather than four, he is of course making a mistake—or else he is trying to cheat. On the other hand, in the unlikely event that nobody notices and corrects the batter's misstep, the misstep will be incorporated into the flow of the game as if it were an instance of correct play. It will *count* as correct within the game, even though it was mistaken and is mistaken. In that respect, it is exactly like an erroneous presupposition that is introduced into a conversation by one of the participants therein. If nobody takes exception to the unfoundedness of the presupposition, it will count within the conversation as a correct contribution even though it was mistaken and is mistaken. Though the details of the rules of accommodation in conversations might differ from the details of the homologous rules in baseball games—for example, the periods of time for the remedying of mistakes might be lengthier in one of those domains than in the other—the dynamics of baseball games and the dynamics of conversations are alike in including some rules of accommodation. Much the same is true of any other norm-structured activities such as the operations of legal systems (Kramer 2004, 115–40; 2007, 8–12, 196–201; 2011, 46–7; 2018, 125–30).

[14] Langton 2018a, 126–7. For the same example, sometimes with slight variations in the details, see Langton 2009, 179, 181, 182–3; 2012, 83; 2018a, 143–4; 2018b, 148.

[15] Langton 2009, 181, emphases in original. For other instances of this error, see Langton 2018a, 126, 143; McGowan 2003, 171.

5.3.4.2 The Accommodation of Presuppositions of Authority

Langton's enquiries into the dynamics of conversations and other discourses bear on the matter of authority because presuppositions about the authority of some speakers or writers are among the presuppositions that can get accommodated in those dynamics. As Langton writes: "Sometimes a speaker will presuppose their authority, and get what they presuppose. Perhaps they start bossing people around, and no-one objects . . . Sometimes you get the authority you presuppose, if nobody blocks you" (2018a, 127, 143). Langton draws here on some piquant examples propounded by Maitra. Let us glance at each of those examples.

5.3.4.2.1 The Racist Diatribe

In Maitra's opening scenario (2012, 100–1), an Arab woman is riding in a crowded subway car in some American city. A white man walks up to her and launches into a tirade of racist expletives against her. Neither the Arab woman herself nor anyone else in the subway car says anything in reply to the man's harangue, even though it is loud enough to be heard clearly by everybody else in the car. All other conversations cease, and many people turn to stare at the bigot and his victim, but nobody intervenes to try to halt his verbal abuse of the woman.

Now, the first thing to be said about this scenario is that the communicative conduct depicted in it can be legally prohibited in consistency with the moral principle of freedom of expression and in consistency with the First Amendment to the American Constitution. This point about the First Amendment is in need of emphasis, because some estimable philosophers appear to be unattuned to it. McGowan, for instance, begins one of her essays with a vignette that is closely similar to Maitra's scenario of the racist diatribe. (In McGowan's version, an African-American man boards a public bus where he is subjected to an outburst of racist invective by an elderly white man.) Somewhat startlingly, McGowan asserts: "Although virtually everyone would deeply disapprove of what this elderly white man said, most would nevertheless defend his right to say it. After all, the First Amendment guarantees the right to free speech." Elaborating on what she takes to be "the all too familiar liberal defense of racist hate speech," McGowan attributes to liberals the view that "we cannot really trust the government to decide what should and should not be said . . . Consequently, our commitment to free speech seems to require granting the elderly white man (and others like him) the right to utter even such hateful racist speech" (2012, 121). She apparently believes that "the government [in the United States] protects his right to say what he said" (131).

McGowan is mistaken in suggesting that either the First Amendment or the liberal principle of freedom of expression serves to exclude the proscription of individually targeted vituperation that is delivered at close range. Under the First Amendment such vituperation can legitimately be forbidden by law, for it will typically be comprehended by either or both of the following two doctrines that have been developed in First Amendment jurisprudence: "fighting words" and "true threats." McGowan does not evince any awareness of the "true threats" doctrine which I have summarized in §3.2.8 of Chapter 3, but in a footnote she does go some way toward acknowledging the applicability of the "fighting words" doctrine: "Of course, some racist hate speech is already regulated, but such 'fighting words' (*Chaplinsky v. New Hampshire*) are identified in terms of their *causal* effects. I am interested, by contrast, in racist hate speech that *constitutes* discrimination" (McGowan 2012, 121 n2, emphases in original). This comment by McGowan is puzzling, for—despite the many shortcomings of the reasoning in the 1943 *Chaplinsky v New Hampshire* judgment by the U.S. Supreme Court—the "fighting words" doctrine has come to be construed in a way that reconciles it with the liberal principle of freedom of expression.[16] Moreover, the reconciliation is pertinently describable with reference to the constitutive/causal distinction. An instance of communicative activity falls within the "fighting words" category only if it consists in severe and individually targeted abuse that constitutes an attempt to provoke a violent scuffle. Such an instance of activity constitutes serious misconduct whose wrongness is communication-independent in the sense delineated by Chapter 3. Misconduct of the specified kind can be undertaken through actions that are not communicative; the fact that somebody perpetrates the misconduct instead through communicative actions does not exempt it from legal prohibition.

In one major respect, then, Maitra's scenario of the racist harangue does not shed light on the problem of pornography. (In the essay where Maitra adduces the scenario, she is principally addressing the problem of hateful speech rather than the problem of pornography.) Whereas the invective by the man in the scenario constitutes serious communication-independent misconduct, the wrongness of the production or distribution of most pornographic materials is not communication-independent. Thus, whereas the individually targeted tirade of racism delivered at close range in Maitra's vignette is susceptible to legal proscription, most types of pornography are not similarly susceptible.

Let us briefly ponder a closely related divergence between the racist abuse in Maitra's scenario and the production of pornographic materials. Whereas the racist abuse occurs in the immediate proximity of its victim—indeed, the immediate presence of the victim is what triggers the outburst, which would not otherwise have occurred—the women who might suffer harm as a result of the production of pornographic materials are very seldom if ever in the immediate proximity of the activities of production. (Recall that I am assuming throughout this chapter that the women pictured in pornographic materials have not been subjected to fraud

[16] See Barry 2007, 257–8 n23; Bodney 2009, 605; Cohen 1996, 135; DeCew 2004, 85; Ely 1980, 114; Goldberg 2016, 713; Greenawalt 1995, 50–3; Heinze 2009, 282–3; 2016, 28; Jacobson and Schlink 2012, 217–18; Lakier 2015, 2190–2; Post 1997, 1518 n6; Price 2018, 823; Rubenfeld 2001, 830; Strossen 2018, 64; Weinstein 2009, 53. See also Stone 1994, 80–1. For a misunderstanding of the "fighting words" doctrine, see Baer 2019, 43.

or violent coercion for the purpose of inducing them to participate. Whenever that assumption is false, the materials in question are susceptible to legal proscription.) Any harmful effects of the making of pornography are diffuse and remote rather than focused and proximate. The ethical import of this diffuse/focused distinction in the context of freedom of expression has been highlighted in Chapters 2 and 3, and it will be highlighted afresh later in this chapter.

Having touched on a couple of contrasts between the situation portrayed in Maitra's opening example and the situation of the pornography industry, I should now anticipate some discussions in my next chapter by underscoring a point of convergence between Maitra's reflections on her example and my own reflections on the matter of pornography. Maitra rightly lays stress on the role of the bystanders in the dismal situation which she recounts. Their acquiescence in the torrent of bigotry directed against the Arab woman by the white man is not responsible for the original vile torrent itself, of course, but it is partly responsible for prolonging the abuse and for sustaining the sway which the man exerts with impunity. Maitra is not suggesting that the acquiescence amounts to approbation. Much more likely, the failure of the subway passengers to intervene is due to timorousness and is accompanied by their strong disapproval of the fulminations that are left uncontested by them (Maitra 2012, 116). Nonetheless, whatever may be the motivations behind their passivity, their reluctance to intervene has endowed the man with a rudimentary and transient form of starkly de facto practical authority. If he is disposed to retaliate against anyone who might try to counteract his screed, his reprisal would be his means of enforcing the ghastly norms—pertaining to the treatment of Arabs—which he is imposing for a limited time on a limited group of people.[17] Maitra recognizes of course that the norm-imposing dominion of the man is indeed extremely limited both in time and in the range of people over whom it is exerted. However, she maintains that the nastiness of a society in which similar incidents become commonplace "will be such as to reinforce the subordination that each instance separately contributes, and to thus pervade the lives of people of color" (117–18). She concludes that anybody who is present during such an incident of racist invective is morally obligated to speak up in order to disrupt the starkly de facto practical authority of the perpetrator.

Maitra accepts that the moral obligation of resistance may be limited by considerations of personal safety. Otherwise, however, the fulfillment of that obligation is essential for one's avoidance of some degree of complicity in an act of racist abuse. Maitra's conclusion here is sound and is very much in accordance with Langton's recent ruminations on "blocking as counter-speech," where the aim is to ward off the entrenchment of invidious presuppositions and assertions that have been

[17] This point becomes even more palpable if we envisage a situation that involves several racists rather than only one man.

introduced by hateful utterances. In an essay which bears that quoted phrase as its title, Langton writes as follows:

> What it takes for evil to succeed is for others to "look on and do nothing," said J.S. Mill. This applies quite literally to evil speech, if it can acquire authority and force from the omissions of others. Hearers and bystanders who do not block will sometimes, through that omission, make a speech act more evil, whether they mean to or no. (Langton 2018b, 161, footnote omitted)

Despite the major divergences between the challenges posed by racist diatribes and the challenges posed by the marketing of pornography, the importance of countering the miasma of noxious messages is common to the two sets of problems. This topic—the countering of odious messages—has been prominent in Chapter 4 and will be especially salient in Chapter 6's dissection of Waldron's approach to hateful utterances. However, it is also a topic that should be central to any cogitations on the matter of pornography, and it will indeed surface intermittently throughout the present chapter. At this juncture, then, a few remarks in amplification of Maitra's and Langton's analyses are appropriate.

First, this book is primarily a work of political philosophy, for the principle of freedom of expression is primarily about the proper relationship between a system of governance and the populace over whom the system presides. Hence, although the focus of Maitra and Langton on the resistance of *individuals* to the poisonousness of bigoted utterances in small-scale settings is illuminating and salutary, a focus on the resistance of *systems of governance* to such poisonousness is even more pressing here. That latter focus is particularly germane in a chapter on the evils of pornography, for many of the operations of producing and marketing pornographic materials are large-scale enterprises that reach far beyond the small-scale settings on which Maitra tends to concentrate. Countering the malign effects of the pornography industry is an endeavor in which discrete individuals have vital roles to play, but it is also an endeavor for a system of governance. For example, education on matters of sexuality is a key component of any efforts to avert the ensconcement of the presuppositions and values propagated by pornographers. Education on such matters within families and among friends is crucial, but education in schools and in other public settings is at least as important for the project of dispelling the fetor of pornographers on a broad scale.

Second, unlike the imposition of legal restrictions on most types of pornography, the governmental efforts mentioned in the preceding paragraph are fully in accordance with the principles of liberal democracy. Such efforts, aimed at offsetting the values and assumptions that are encouraged by the pornographic industry, are squarely within the range of responsibilities which any system of governance is morally entitled and morally obligated to fulfill. As Chapter 4 has contended, any such system is morally duty-bound to strive to foster an ethos of justice in which respect for the institutions and values of liberal democracy is secured. Among those values is the fundamental equality of human beings—a value that is wholly irreconcilable with the notion that women can properly be treated as sexual playthings or as objects of violence for the satisfaction of the concupiscence or sadism of men. Consequently, any system of governance is morally entitled and morally duty-bound to strive to counter the messages conveyed by the hard-core materials of the pornography industry. That duty is an element of the paramount responsibility of every such system to bring about the social and political and economic conditions under which everyone can be warranted in harboring an ample sense of self-respect.

Third, this emphasis on the blocking of presuppositions and the contesting of assertions is very much in keeping with the traditional liberal insistence on more speech as the appropriate antidote to repellent speech. Most famously associated with the great American jurist Louis Brandeis, the recommendation of "more speech" is viewed quite disparagingly by Langton. She applauds the magnanimity of the recommendation, but discountenances what she regards as its naiveté: "That hope is inspiring but implausible, given limits on capacities to fight bad speech with good. 'Truth will out' is an empirical hypothesis disguised as a principle, and it deserves a skeptical eye."[18] If the "more speech" prescription were based on the "Truth will out" hypothesis, it would of course be facile. Langton herself adduces many reasons for doubting the breezy optimism of the "Truth will out" nostrum, and—as I have recounted in Chapter 4—the grounds for doubt have long been familiar in the legal and philosophical literature on freedom of expression. Nevertheless, we are well advised not to read Brandeis so ungenerously. Although Brandeis undoubtedly did have chiefly in mind the efficacy of reasoned argumentation as a means of rebutting the doctrines of hatred and extremism which he held to be immune from legal prohibition, his "more speech" recommendation is scarcely confined to that one technique.[19] It encompasses also the blocking of presuppositions which Langton explores and commends, and it likewise encompasses the use of mockery and comedy to deride the preposterousness of the aforementioned

[18] Langton 2018b, 144. Langton muddies the water in her rejoinder to Brandeis when she queries his specific mention of "falsehood and fallacies" as the evils that would be remedied by more speech. She invokes the example of a sign on a bus in the American South during the Jim Crow era of racial segregation: "Colored passengers are required to sit here." Langton is correct in maintaining that the sign stated a truth rather than a falsehood, but she is incorrect in thinking that the example is relevant to an assessment of Brandeis's position. The example is in fact irrelevant because, whether the sign was displayed on a publicly owned bus or on a privately owned bus, it partly constituted a scheme of racial discrimination whose serious wrongness was communication-independent (Lawrence 1990, 443–4). Accordingly, the display of the sign could be legally forbidden in line with the principle of freedom of expression; it would not be among the modes of expression which a supporter of Brandeis could aptly seek to shield against legal prohibition.

[19] Albeit without reference to Brandeis, Katharine Gelber approaches this matter largely in line with what is being advocated here. See Gelber 2012a, 214–16; 2012b. See also Brettschneider 2012; Lepoutre 2017; 2019; Post and Molnar 2012, 21–2; Strossen 2018, 8–9, 128–32, 157–82.

doctrines of extremism and hatred. Quite a few additional bigotry-counteracting methods will be touched upon in Chapter 6. Even when "more speech" does take the form of reasoned argumentation, its principal audience will often not be the bigots or pornographers or fanatics whose pernicious ideas and values are impugned by the argumentation; often instead the principal audience comprises the countless members of the public whose minds have not fallen wholly under the sway of those ideas and values. Whereas the bigots and fanatics and pornographers themselves are frequently insusceptible to persuasion through reasoning, most of the myriad members of the public at large are open to persuasion and education through the provision of arguments and counter-evidence. It is they who are typically the primary addressees of Brandeis's "more words." (Having said as much, I should underline the significance and laudableness of programs that marshal arguments and counter-evidence for the purpose of redeeming individuals who have fallen prey to loathsome ideologies. The people who work in such programs are admirable practitioners of Brandeis's injunction to combat bad speech with "more speech.")

Fourth, when a system of governance legally tolerates the production and distribution of most types of pornography while it also employs multifaceted techniques to counter the assumptions and outlooks that are associated with pornography, it *pro tanto* fulfills the responsibilities incumbent on it under the principles of liberal democracy. It abides by the principle of freedom of expression while additionally complying with the obligation to promote an ethos of justice and mutual respect. When we take account of the multiplicity of functions carried out by a wide-ranging system of governance, and when we therefore do not make the mistake of assessing some of those functions distortively in isolation, we can discern the tendentiousness and illiberality of the notion that a system of governance which legally tolerates the marketing of most types of pornography is thereby condoning the ways in which pornographic materials depict women. That perception of toleration as condonation has gained some traction, in one form or another, among a number of philosophers who write about pornography or hateful speech. It is conspicuous in a pioneering article by Mari Matsuda (1989) on racist utterances, for example, and—as we shall see in my next chapter—it is similarly prominent in the quite recent book by Waldron (2012) on such utterances, as he repeatedly asserts that liberals who uphold the principle of freedom of expression are fecklessly proposing that nothing be done in response to the advocacy of bigoted doctrines by racists. Langton herself has tentatively moved toward Waldron's position, though she stops short of any outright endorsement of it. She asks: "Does a law that merely tolerates hate speech nonetheless confer 'derived' authority on it?" She replies to her own inquiry: "We postpone these hard questions. But if the answers are affirmative, the harm in hate speech may be the doing, not only of the low types [of hateful speakers] we have considered, but also of an innocent law, and of innocent others who merely stand by" (Langton 2018a, 147–8). In the debates over pornography, likewise, the equation of toleration with connivance has gained some currency. In these debates, as in her work on hateful utterances, Langton has edged disconcertingly toward that highly illiberal equation:

> Furthermore, pornography's authority could be "derived" from the omissions of another authoritative party, including perhaps the tolerance of the state itself ... This is a striking thought, which requires more defense than I can give it here. But on this suggestion, the state's blind eye toward pornography ... contribute[s] to the dynamics of pornography's authority. (Langton 2017, 34)

McGowan broaches the same view, though with even greater tentativeness: "[O]ne might argue that since the U.S. government protects pornography under the rubric of free speech, it [pornography] thereby has the authority of the government behind it."[20]

Some of the pronouncements quoted in the preceding paragraph are cautiously phrased, but they all bespeak a tendency to gauge certain operations of a system of governance in isolation rather than in combination with other governmental policies and undertakings. If such a system is fulfilling the moral duties that are incumbent on it, a synoptic view of its operations will reveal that its robust tolerance in the domain of freedom of expression is oft combined with disdainful abhorrence. Its robust tolerance is not a "blind eye." A suitably synoptic perspective on a system of governance is all too easily neglected when philosophers begin their meditations on matters of political philosophy by contemplating the ethical responsibilities of individuals in very small-scale situations. (Another possible source of the temptation to equate tolerance with indolence or complicity is the failure of some philosophers to keep in mind the point which I have made already about hateful utterances that consist in individually targeted ranting at close range. Many such utterances are classifiable as "fighting words" or "true threats," and are thus legitimately proscribable under the principle of freedom of expression—and under the First Amendment. Some of the utterances recounted by Matsuda do belong to the category of fighting words or of true threats, or to other categories of serious communication-independent wrongdoing. Not only can the outlawing of those utterances be morally legitimate, but in addition it is morally obligatory. Were a system of governance to impose no legal restrictions on such thuggery, it would indeed be fecklessly in dereliction of its responsibilities. However, the unconscionability of legal toleration in response to individually targeted onslaughts is no basis whatsoever for concluding that legal toleration

[20] McGowan 2017, 53. See also McGowan 2012, 131.

in response to the marketing of pornography—or in response to the advocacy of hateful doctrines—is unconscionable. Far from being insupportable, the toleration of pornography and of hateful doctrines is both morally permissible and morally obligatory under the principle of freedom of expression.)

5.3.4.2.2 The Political Poster

In Maitra's second vignette, a rally is being held in an American city to protest against some governmental policies (2012, 101). Quite a few of the demonstrators carry aloft signs that bear political messages. On the sign held up by one activist is the following slogan: "Don't forget to pay your taxes! Twenty-one million illegal aliens are depending on you!" Above the slogan is a photograph of four Hispanic men who are depicted as saying "*Muchas gracias*!" The poster is clearly visible to other participants in the demonstration and also to the television cameras that are recording the event. Nobody objects to the brandishing of the poster by the activist.

Unlike the racist diatribe in the subway car, the display of the sign by the demonstrator is clearly protected—under the principle of freedom of expression—against any legal prohibition. Repugnantly bigoted though the display is, it does not constitute any misconduct that is communication-independent. In being morally exempt from legal curbs, the activist's flourishing of the poster is relevantly similar to the marketing of most types of pornography.

Though Maitra says far less about this second scenario than about her first and third scenarios, she appears to present it as an illustration of "licensed" authority. She explains: "When speaker authority depends on (relevant) others refraining from challenging the speech, I shall say that the speaker [or the speech] is 'licensed' by those others" (Maitra 2012, 107). Because nobody at the political rally has taken exception to the brandishing of the sign by the protester, the display of the sign has been undertaken with impunity. The protester has established that, within the spatial and temporal confines of the rally, his conveyance of a viciously anti-Hispanic message is socially acceptable. He has been "licensed" to establish that point by the acquiescence of his fellow demonstrators.

However, nothing in this second vignette goes any way toward shoring up Langton's thesis about the subordination of women by the pornography industry. Even within the spatial and temporal confines of the political rally, the participant who holds aloft the anti-Hispanic placard has not thereby deprived Hispanics or other immigrants of any liberties and normative powers. Although he might induce some of his fellow demonstrators to harden their negative attitudes toward Hispanics or other immigrants, any such developments would be perlocutionary effects of his communication rather than illocutionary aspects thereof. When we shift our scrutiny outside the temporal and spatial confines of the political demonstration, the absence of any illocutionary subordination is even more evident. Outside those confines, the activist's display of his bigoted poster will not have constituted any norms at all.

In short, Maitra's second scenario—to which Maitra herself devotes scant attention—will not be of any avail to Langton in her efforts to maintain that pornographers possess starkly de facto practical authority through which their products illocutionarily subordinate women. Even if we grant that the acquiescence of the other participants at the political rally has conferred upon the protester a form of licensed authority to establish that the display of his placard during the rally is acceptable among those participants, we cannot draw any further conclusions about the authority or upshot of the protester's conduct. Even within the boundaries of the political gathering, his conduct does not constitute the subordination of Hispanics in the illocutionary manner in which pornography supposedly constitutes the subordination of women. Outside the ambit of the gathering, his having displayed his placard there does not illocutionarily constitute any normative effects whatsoever.

5.3.4.2.3 The Burning of the Cross

Maitra presents her next scenario in a basic version and an amplified version (2012, 101, 109–10). In the initial delineation, a black working-class family have recently moved into a predominantly white and affluent community in the United States. Through a number of subtle gestures, the neighbors convey to the family the impression that they are not welcome in their new setting. One morning, the members of the family awaken early to discover that a cross has been left burning on their front lawn. The malefactors responsible for placing and igniting the cross on the lawn have fled, and the family have no inkling of their identities.

In the expanded version of this vignette, the following facts are added to those which have just been recounted. In the community to which the black family have moved, certain residents are the makers of manners. That is, those residents play key roles in shaping the mores of the community by differentiating between acceptable and unacceptable behavior. Perhaps those residents are members of an official body such as a town council, or perhaps they are simply longstanding and widely esteemed members of the community. When they learn of the cross-burning on the lawn of the black family, those leaders of the community do not say anything in condemnation of the action or of its perpetrators. Nor do they issue any words of consolation to the family who have been victimized by the incident.

In most relevant respects, Maitra's third vignette is similar to her first. For one thing, the communicative conduct that has occurred in it is not morally immunized by the principle of freedom of expression against being legally proscribed, nor is that conduct legally immunized by the First Amendment against being so proscribed. Sanctions in tort law or in criminal law can legitimately be imposed in response to the cross-burning as an act of trespass or arson or malicious damage to property. To be sure, in the 1992 U.S. Supreme Court case whose facts are the basis for Maitra's third scenario—*R.A.V. v St Paul*—the Court invalidated a hate-speech ordinance under which a miscreant had been prosecuted for setting alight a cross on the lawn of a black family in the Minnesota city of St Paul. However, the ordinance was invalidated not because the burning of the cross was exempt from every legal prohibition, but instead because the ordinance (on its surface and in its underlying purpose) forbade the burning of the cross as an act of communication rather than as an instance of communication-independent misconduct. Had the person who burned the cross been prosecuted instead under a law banning trespass or arson or malicious damage to property, the prosecution could have been consistent with the First Amendment and with the principle of freedom of expression.[21] After all, the purpose of such a law is to prohibit serious communication-independent misconduct. Provided that that law is not being applied selectively to deal only with certain communicative instances of the misconduct while serious non-communicative instances are pretermitted, the application of such an ordinance to an act of burning a cross on someone else's lawn will be unproblematically in keeping with the principle of freedom of expression and with the First Amendment. (Indeed, as §3.2.11 in my third chapter has explained, the sanction imposed on the perpetrator of the act of cross-burning can legitimately be intensified under an applicable hate-crime statute. Although the hateful communicative content of such an action cannot legitimately be invoked as a basis for subjecting the action to legal restrictions, the hateful content can legitimately be taken into account for evidentiary purposes during the process of sentencing as a court seeks to gauge the gravity of the wrong that has been committed.)

Of course, in Maitra's third vignette, the culprits have successfully fled and will therefore not undergo any prosecutions. Of particular importance, then, are the reactions of the community's leading citizens (Strossen and Molnar 2012, 380). Their stony silence in the aftermath of the cross-burning is even worse than the passivity of the passengers on the subway car during the torrent of racist invective in Maitra's first scenario—partly because the leading citizens would not be endangering themselves by offering some expressions of support and solace to the black family, and partly because as leading citizens they carry special responsibilities for upholding the decency of the community. Shirking those responsibilities, the leaders of the community have adopted a posture of callous taciturnity that is straightforwardly construable as a posture of approbation or indifference. Hence, particularly pertinent here are my earlier remarks (in §5.3.4.2.1) about the need for a system of governance to counter the noxious effects of various speech-acts. Any such system of local governance that takes no steps to reassure the black family in reaction to the cross-burning has grossly abdicated its responsibilities. Such steps

[21] Kagan 1996a, 491. Similarly, when Stanford University's code of speech was struck down as unconstitutional in the mid-1990s, the invalidation occurred not because the conduct covered by the code was exempt from prohibition but instead because the code itself was neither communication-neutral nor content-neutral. See Kagan 1996b, 958 n3.

are particularly pressing because no legal proceedings can be undertaken against the perpetrators of the racist incident, who have successfully absconded.

Still, Maitra's third scenario does not lend any support to arguments in favor of legal restrictions on the production and distribution of pornography.[22] The situation depicted in it is markedly different from the situation of pornographers. Although the harm inflicted on the black family is caused rather than constituted by the burning of the cross, the causal links are direct and particularized and clearly intended. By contrast, as has already been remarked, any causal connections between the marketing of pornography and certain harms inflicted on women are diffuse and remote. Thus, whereas the act of burning the cross constitutes a course of misconduct whose wrongness is communication-independent, the wrongness of the marketing of pornography is not similarly communication-independent.

5.3.4.2.4 The Teacher's Helper

Maitra's remaining four anecdotes do not depict instances of hateful speech. Instead, they are adduced to illustrate how the people who engage in such speech could come to be vested with authority. Most of these remaining scenarios involve the acquisition of morally binding practical authority, but the point of each of them can be extended to circumstances in which the practical authority acquired is instead starkly de facto.

In the fourth scenario, a teacher in an elementary school directs her students to embark on a project in which each of them will perform a distinctive task (Maitra 2012, 105). Just when the teacher is about to specify the task for each student, she is summoned out of the classroom. She quickly instructs one of the students, Frederick, to assign the tasks while she deals with the matter that is calling her outside. Frederick proceeds to do so.

Maitra is plainly correct in declaring that Frederick has acquired practical authority over the other students through the instructions of the teacher. His derived authority is morally binding, but the point of the example is extrapolable to contexts in which the derived practical authority is instead starkly de facto. Even so, the example has virtually no bearing on the activities of pornographers (nor does Maitra suggest otherwise). It illustrates one way in which practical authority can be acquired by somebody who initially has none, but that way of deriving authority is patently inapplicable to the endeavors of pornographers. In relation to the producers and distributors of pornographic materials, there is no counterpart of the schoolteacher. Nobody who already possesses practical authority has instructed those producers and distributors to propagate their degrading portrayals

22 Maitra does not suggest otherwise. She does submit that her various examples can rebut a couple of the objections that have been leveled against Langton's account of the ways in which pornography subordinates women (Maitra 2012, 102–4), but she does not purport to be mounting a comprehensive defense of that account. Rather, she concentrates chiefly on the problem of hatefully bigoted speech.

of women. Even more obviously, nobody who already possesses practical authority has instructed women to bring their behavior into conformity with those degrading portrayals.

5.3.4.2.5 The Presumptuous Student

Maitra's fifth scenario is a variant of her fourth (2012, 105–6). Again a teacher in an elementary school directs her pupils to carry out a project in which each student is to perform a distinctive task. On this occasion, however, the teacher is not summoned out of the room. Instead, while the teacher is present, an impatient and bossy student begins to assign the various tasks to his classmates. Some of those classmates take umbrage at the bossy student's characteristic officiousness, and they look expectantly at the teacher in the hope that she will intervene to countermand his directives. After briefly contemplating the situation, she dashes their hopes by forbearing from any intervention as she silently busies herself with some paperwork.

In this example, there has not occurred any explicit grant of authority by the schoolteacher to the bossy student. Nevertheless, the student has acquired practical authority from the teacher through her acquiescence in his issuance of instructions to the other children. His derivation of authority from her has proceeded through his presuming to have such authority and through her declining to undo his presumptuous assignments of tasks. Consequently, notwithstanding the differences between this scenario and the preceding one, the upshot in the form of derived practical authority is essentially the same between the two of them. The practical authority is probably morally binding, but again the point of the example can be extended to situations in which any derived practical authority is instead starkly de facto.

Successful though Maitra's vignette is in highlighting the fact that practical authority can be derived from the acquiescence of someone who is already endowed with such authority, it does not furnish any basis for legal restrictions on most types of pornography. Here we should recall what has already been argued in §5.3.4.2.1 above. When a system of governance complies with the principle of freedom of expression by leaving most types of pornography legally unprohibited, it does not thereby confer any practical authority upon pornographers. As has been emphasized, the policy of strict legal tolerance required by the principle of freedom of expression is not properly assessable in isolation from the other policies and functions undertaken by a system of governance. If such a system is abiding by the sundry responsibilities incumbent on it under the principles of liberal democracy, its legal toleration of most types of pornography is combined with its persistent striving against the messages that are conveyed by the products of the pornographic industry. Through educational programs and numerous other workings (including, of course, the institutions of criminal law that operate to punish violence or harassment directed against women), such a system of governance pits itself firmly against the outlook on the world that is conveyed in pornographic materials. In that respect, its workings are decidedly not akin to the passivity of the teacher as she connives at the bossy student's arrogation of the prerogative to assign tasks to his classmates.

Also worth noting here is that the reasons which justificatorily underlie the lawfulness of most types of pornography in a liberal democracy are markedly different from the reasons that explanatorily underlie the decision of the schoolteacher against countermanding the directives of the officious student. Maitra's framing of her fifth anecdote suggests that the teacher acquiesces in the bossy student's presumptuousness largely because any intervention would be somewhat burdensome. Moreover, even if the teacher is instead motivated chiefly by a concern not to humiliate the impertinent pupil, she could have accomplished that aim through a suitably gentle reprimand that would not have left the other children subject to his sway. By contrast, a policy of legal toleration in response to most types of pornography is indispensable as an element of a full-blown liberal democracy, for any more restrictive policy would contravene the principle of freedom of expression. Far from being an easy way out, legal toleration in application to hard-core pornography is quite a demanding mode of self-restraint. That self-restraint is unforgoable in a liberal democracy—since it is constitutive of freedom of expression—but it is a strenuous and precious achievement rather than a product of lassitude or evasiveness.

5.3.4.2.6 The Organizer of a Hike

In Maitra's penultimate scenario, several friends have agreed to participate in a hike on the following weekend (2012, 106–8). When they meet to settle upon the logistics, the discussion continues protractedly without agreement on any of the main matters. One member of the group, Jeffrey, begins to worry that the discussion will peter out with no resolution. He fears that the hike will therefore never occur. He accordingly takes control of the flow of discourse and assigns a distinct logistical responsibility to each member of the group (including himself). Nobody dissents from Jeffrey's pattern of assignments, and everybody in fact performs the task with which he or she has been entrusted. As a result, the hike goes ahead successfully.

Like the overbearing schoolboy in Maitra's fifth scenario, Jeffrey has acquired practical authority (morally binding practical authority, indeed) through the acquiescence of somebody else. However, here the acquiescence is not on the part of anyone who is already invested with practical authority over the addressees of Jeffrey's utterances; rather, it is on the part of the addressees themselves. The acquisition of practical authority by Jeffrey could have been partly or wholly blocked if any of his friends had objected either to his specific assignments or to the general fact of his having taken charge of their planning. However, given that nobody takes exception to what Jeffrey has done, he has vested himself with practical authority by presuming to have it. His presumption, in combination with the preparedness of his friends to countenance his presumption, can endow him with practical authority over the group even though no one has theretofore possessed such authority over them. His authority is morally binding, but—once again—the point of Maitra's tale can be generalized to contexts in which the practical authority acquired through the acquiescence of addressees is starkly de facto rather than morally binding. After all, problems of coordination and collective action have to be overcome by the participants in evil enterprises as much as by the participants in morally worthy enterprises.

Though this sixth scenario does show that practical authority over people can be acquired in circumstances where no such authority over them has previously existed, it does not shed any light on the activities of pornographers. On the one hand, the viewers and readers of pornographic wares do acquiesce in the propagation of certain messages and sentiments by those wares; indeed, through their purchases, the viewers and readers provide outright consent rather than mere acquiescence. On the other hand, the viewers and readers do not thereby incur any obligations to one another or to the manufacturers and vendors of the pornographic materials. In Maitra's sixth scenario, Jeffrey acquires practical authority over his friends because they have all come to rely on one another to fulfill the responsibilities that have been respectively assigned to them by Jeffrey—and because each of them knows that everyone else is relying on him or her. There is no comparable interlocking of expectations and responsibilities among the consumers of pornography. None of them relies on the other consumers to play roles assigned to them in some collective project, nor does anyone among them suppose that the others are relying on him.

Even more obviously, the women who would have to play subservient roles in actualizing the fantasies portrayed by pornographic materials are not engaged in any collective endeavor aimed at realizing those fantasies. As women ignore or disdain the hard-core materials, they are not acquiescing in any assignments of responsibilities to them by pornographers. They are not depending on one another or on men to carry out any such assignments, nor does anyone among them suppose that everybody else is depending on her.

Now, the language in the preceding two paragraphs has deliberately been emphatic—brimming with universally quantified negative propositions and with negations of existentially quantified propositions—in order to underscore the stark differences between the dividing up of responsibilities by Jeffrey among his friends and the marketing of films or magazines by pornographers. Still, the strength of that language is not integral to my assessment of Maitra's sixth scenario. I can allow that there might be a scattering of extravagantly deluded consumers of pornographic materials who do somehow believe that they are participating in a collective project (presumably aimed at the domination of women) through their purchases and perusal of those materials. If such deluded individuals exist, they take themselves to be relying on other consumers of pornography to play their parts in that collective project, and they believe that the other consumers are similarly relying upon them. They think that they themselves along with the other consumers have respectively been assigned their roles in the collective project by the manufacturers of pornographic materials. The existence of people who harbor such daft misconceptions is clearly possible, as is the existence of people who harbor other bizarre misconceptions about pornography or about anything else. There is no need for me to rule out the existence of people who are so asinine. Instead, the point here is that such people are anomalous and that—despite the weird misunderstandings to which those people might cleave—the marketing of pornography is not an effort to surmount problems of collective action by dividing up responsibilities among the far-flung consumers of pornographic products.

5.3.4.2.7 The Director of Traffic

In Maitra's final vignette, a bad accident involving several cars has occurred on a highway (2012, 106–8). Some of the vehicles and heavy debris are strewn across the road, such that only one lane is still open to any traffic. Though police teams and road-safety personnel are on the way, some action is needed in the meantime to alleviate the severe congestion of traffic that has ensued from the collision and its aftermath. A driver, Agnes, gets out of her car and begins to direct the flow of vehicles with appropriate gestures. After letting through approximately a dozen cars from one direction, she then signals for the drivers from that direction to halt, and she lets through approximately a dozen vehicles from the other direction. She continues to alternate in this fashion for several minutes, until the emergency personnel arrive.

This final scenario resembles some examples in the critiques of Raz's conception of authority to which I have referred near the outset of §5.3.3.1 above.[23] In it, Agnes acquires morally binding practical authority over the motorists in both directions. She does so partly because of the exigencies of the situation and partly because of the other drivers' acceptance of her reaction to those exigencies. Through her temporary resolution of an urgent problem of coordination, Agnes—like Jeffrey in Maitra's sixth vignette—has acquired practical authority by presuming to have it. Just as the friends of Jeffrey have conferred practical authority upon him by going along with his decision to take control of the organizing of their hike, so too the motorists on the highway have conferred practical authority upon Agnes by going along with her decision to take control of the flow of vehicles.

Even more patently than the scenario of Jeffrey and his friends, this scenario of Agnes and the other drivers does not portray a situation that is similar to the

[23] Indeed, there is a discernible connection. Maitra credits the scenario to Waldron, from whom she heard it at a workshop in Princeton in 2010 (Maitra 2012, 106 n30). At a conference in London in May 2009, Waldron encountered a version of the scenario in a paper that would later be published as Hershovitz 2011.

marketing of pornography. Pornographers do not set out to resolve any problems of coordination when they produce and peddle their materials. To be sure, because of the putative epistemic authority that might be attached to such materials in the estimation of some of the male adolescents who view or read them, the sexual behavior of each of those adolescents might come to resemble the sexual behavior of his fellow teenagers in certain respects—as each of them separately strives to imitate the modes of conduct that are on display in pornographic films and magazines. However, even if such resemblances do emerge as perlocutionary effects of the films and magazines, they do not arise from efforts among the teenagers to coordinate their behavior in compliance with responsibilities assigned to them by pornographers. Apart from any severely deluded people like those discussed at the end of the preceding subsection, no adolescent takes himself to be relying on his fellow teenagers to align their behavior with his by emulating some of the sexual feats depicted in pornographic materials, nor does any adolescent believe that his far-flung fellow teenagers are in turn relying on him to emulate those feats.

Of course, there can occur local exceptions to what has just been said. For example, a notorious instance of gang rape perpetrated in Massachusetts in 1983 was quite closely akin to a simulated instance of gang rape portrayed in the magazine *Hustler* a few months earlier (Merrill 1998, 99). Although there was no evidence that the men who committed the gang rape in Massachusetts had seen the relevant issue of *Hustler*, the situation could plausibly have been different in that very regard. That is—as a thought-experiment—we can here suppose counterfactually that the men were seeking to imitate the pattern of conduct that had been depicted in *Hustler*. In that event, each of the culprits would have been relying on his fellows to play their parts in their evil collective project of imitating that pattern of conduct, and each of them would have known that the other perpetrators were in turn relying upon him.

Now, although the participants in the actual gang rape in 1983 were probably not inspired by *Hustler*, the counterfactual scenario that has just been broached here—in which they were so inspired—is not at all fanciful. The rebarbative event could very credibly have unfolded in the counterfactual manner envisaged, even though it did not do so. Still, credible though a situation would be in which some rapists collectively orient themselves toward what they have seen or read in pornographic materials, their being so oriented is a perlocutionary effect of the dissemination of those materials rather than an illocutionary aspect thereof. It is a nefarious effect of exactly the kind that has been attributed to the pornography industry by some of the older feminist indictments of that industry. Unless the rapists are severely deluded, they will not suppose that they are complying with mandates issued to them by pornographers. They will not suppose that the relationship between pornographers and themselves is relevantly similar to the relationship between Agnes and the motorists on the highway. They might ascribe epistemic authority to the pornographers, and they might take guidance from certain pornographic materials precisely because of such ascriptions of epistemic authority, but (unless they are severely deluded) they will not believe that their taking of guidance is in fulfillment of duties imposed on them by pornographers. Putative epistemic authority is not starkly de facto practical authority.

Thus, although Maitra's closing anecdote is similar to each of her other vignettes in elegantly making the point for which it has been propounded, it is also similar to them in being unsupportive of Langton's claim that the subordination of women by pornographers is illocutionary and constitutive rather than solely perlocutionary and causal. Maitra adumbrates a number of distinct routes by which people can acquire practical authority, but none of those routes has a bearing on the relationship between pornographers and the consumers of pornography (much less on the relationship between pornographers and women). Her scenarios leave in place my contention that pornographers lack the starkly de facto practical authority that would enable them to subordinate women in the illocutionary-constitutive ways recounted by Langton.

5.3.5 Subordination without Special Authority through the Pragmatics of Discourse?

The pioneering work by Langton and West on the pragmatics of discourse in application to pornography has helped to inspire some other feminist philosophers to develop further analyses in broadly the same vein. Among those philosophers, McGowan has received particular attention from Langton for exploring how the norms of situations can be altered by people who are not possessed of any special authority. Drawing on many of the same philosophical traditions that have figured saliently in Langton's theorizing, McGowan has percipiently analyzed the intricacies of conversational norms and the intricacies of the conversational dynamics in which the operativeness and applications of those norms are sustained or modified. Not only are her meditations on these matters fascinating in themselves, but in addition they may seem to offer a path through which Langton can escape from the impasse of trying to demonstrate that pornographers are endowed with practical authority over the consumers of pornography and over women. As Langton remarks, McGowan's attentiveness to the pragmatics of conversations "has promise, as a way to show how informal speech by ordinary speakers may change beliefs and alter norms, without needing to meet the strong felicity conditions typically required by traditional Austinian speech acts" (Langton 2012, 84). Among the strong felicity conditions to which Langton refers is the authority condition required for illocutionary acts of subordination.[24] If McGowan's analyses of the pragmatics of

[24] In the terms of Austin's speech-act philosophy, these illocutionary acts fall into two main categories: *verdictives* which authoritatively rank certain people as inferior; and *exercitives* which

conversations could help Langton to explain how the activities of pornographers amount to illocutionary acts of subordination even though the pornographers do not wield any special practical authority, the foremost obstacle to the success of Langton's defense of MacKinnon would be removed. Thus, to conclude my investigation of Langton's claims about the subordination of women by pornographers, this chapter will briefly ponder whether McGowan's charting of the dynamics of conversations can help to vindicate those claims.

For the purposes of this chapter, no detailed exposition of the involutions of McGowan's analyses is necessary. A laconic one-paragraph summary will suffice. Availing herself of Lewis's insights into the adjustments that occur through rules of accommodation during any ordinary conversation, McGowan highlights the effects of conversational exercitives. Such an exercitive is a conversational move whereby an interlocutor alters what can permissibly be said in the conversation thereafter. Normative powers to effect such alterations are conferred upon the participants in a conversation by the rules of accommodation that are operative therein. McGowan contends that numerous mundane contributions to conversations are exercitives of this kind, as she declares that "any conversational contribution that invokes a rule of accommodation is an exercitive speech act in virtue of changing what is permissible in that conversation" (2003, 172). She emphasizes that interlocutors in ordinary conversations are endowed with normative powers to bring about changes along these lines, in spite of their not being possessed of any special practical authority over their fellow interlocutors.

Subtle and insightful though McGowan's enquiries into the pragmatics of conversations are, they are not serviceable for Langton's project. They do not furnish any support for the proposition that the manufacturing or marketing of pornography illocutionarily constitutes the subordination of women. Let us consider here three queries in an ascending order of importance.

5.3.5.1 Impermissibility versus Inappropriateness

Although all deontic facts are normative facts, not all normative facts are deontic facts. The complex normative structure which McGowan attributes to any conversation is concerned with differentiating between contributions that would be appropriate and contributions that would be inappropriate. Sometimes the distinction between the appropriate and the inappropriate coincides with the distinction between the permissible and the impermissible, but often a conversational move can be inappropriate without being impermissible. McGowan goes somewhat astray by frequently moving back and forth between references to what is inappropriate and references to what is impermissible, as if the two were equivalent. (The conflation of the inappropriate and the impermissible is fostered by the

deprive the perceivedly inferior people of certain liberties and normative powers, and which legitimize the subjection of those people to various forms of discriminatory treatment.

fact that "wrong" is both a synonym of "incorrect" and a synonym of "impermissible." Although the extensional intersection between those two senses of "wrong" is very wide-ranging, the two senses are not equivalent either intensionally or extensionally.)

In non-conversational activities, inappropriateness and impermissibility are plainly not equivalent. For example, the manager of a baseball team can make an inappropriate tactical decision that results in a loss for his side, yet the decision can be entirely within the rules of the sport, and—provided that it has been made in good faith—it can be consistent with the manager's general duty to do his best to bring about victories for his team. Inappropriate though his choice of tactics may have been, it was a permissible choice. In conversational contexts, likewise, contributions can be inappropriate without being impermissible. The conversational norms which McGowan distills are aimed at promoting the smoothness or liveliness or limpidity or capaciousness of a conversation. In other words, they call for contributions that are conducive to good exchanges in which the parties do not have to struggle to understand each other and in which the parties are not likely to form serious misapprehensions about the views or sentiments imparted to them by their interlocutors. In addition the norms expand the range of purposes which a conversation can fulfill, by prescribing various devices through which some contributions to a conversation can play roles (such as the telling of jokes or the expression of sarcasm) that go beyond straightforward assertions. Now, certain departures from the conversation-structuring norms are undoubtedly impermissible—especially, though not exclusively, any departures that quite clearly bespeak disrespect or self-indulgence in relation to one's interlocutors—but many departures from those norms are not credibly classified as wrongs. Contributions to a conversation that impair its smoothness can nonetheless be well within the bounds of permissibility. Conversations are considerably more flexible, and the participants in conversations are considerably more resilient, than might be inferred from many portions of McGowan's foremost article on conversational exercitives.

McGowan herself acknowledges as much near the end of that article (2003, 185–8), when she allows that the rules of accommodation in a conversation are sufficiently expansive to absorb numerous departures from the other conversational norms which she delineates. She accepts that "obvious violations of conversational permissibility facts [or conversational appropriateness facts] trigger a principle of charity rule of accommodation which, in turn, changes the score [of a conversation] so that no such violation actually occurs" (186). She goes on to maintain correctly that not all deviations from her conversational norms will be accommodated in this fashion. I have readily granted that point; as has been stated above, many inappropriate moves in a conversation are indeed impermissible moves. Still, much of the normative structure of a conversation is concerned with differentiating between the appropriate and the inappropriate—that is, with differentiating between contributions that are conducive and contributions that are inconducive to conversational desiderata such as smoothness—quite beyond any differentiation between the permissible and the impermissible.

Even in the closing portion of her article, McGowan overestimates the constrainingness of the norms which she recounts. She there refers back to an example which she had propounded at an earlier juncture. In that example, Donal and Seamus are in a group of several interlocutors who are looking at a map of the world. Everyone in the group happily concurs with Donal when he states that Ireland is shaped like a sideways teddy bear. Somewhat later in the conversation, Seamus denies that Italy is shaped like a boot. He points out that the coastline of Italy is squiggly, whereas the sides of a boot typically are not. "Seamus's denial that Italy is boot-shaped requires higher standards of accuracy than were operative in the conversation at the time of Donal's utterance. The standards [which govern the conversation] immediately and automatically adjust, though, so that what Seamus said is [counted as] true enough" (McGowan 2003, 171–2). At the close of her article, when McGowan reflects afresh on Seamus's raising of the standards of accuracy, she declares that "it is easier to raise such standards than it is to lower them. Consequently, it is difficult for Seamus's interlocutors to subsequently change the standards to what they were" (187–8). Such a contention markedly overstates the degree to which Seamus has limited the leeway of his conversational companions. Either at the time of his utterance about Italy or at any point thereafter, any of the interlocutors can easily block or undo his raising of the standards of accuracy. By brusquely admonishing Seamus not to be such a pedantic bore, or by employing a dismissive grimace or a contemptuous backward wave of the hand, or even by ignoring Seamus's contribution to the conversation, anyone among the interlocutors can preserve or reinstate the standards of accuracy that were presupposed by Donal's utterance about Ireland.

My opening query about McGowan's analysis of the pragmatics of conversations can, indeed, be summed up with reference to the following two sentences from her discussion of Seamus's captious observation about the shape of Italy: "Notice that, by raising the standards, Seamus's utterance limits what it is appropriate for his interlocutors to say. Thus, by saying what he said, Seamus managed, without any special authority, to enact difficult-to-reverse permissibility conditions" (McGowan 2003, 188). One reason for balking at these sentences is that, here as well as at many other junctures in her article, McGowan moves too quickly from talking about conditions for appropriateness to talking about conditions for permissibility. In addition, as I have suggested, she is greatly overstating the entrenchedness of the elevated standards of accuracy which Seamus introduces through his tiresome remark. A key reason for the susceptibility of those standards to being lowered by the other interlocutors is precisely that Seamus has made his remark "without any special authority." Had he possessed some special practical authority over the other conversationalists with regard to the standards of accuracy for their discourse, his raising of those standards would doubtless have limited the latitude of his conversational partners in line with what McGowan maintains. However, because Seamus in fact has no such special authority, the normative change which he effects through his quibbling about the shape of Italy is a readily reversible alteration in the standards for appropriateness rather than an abiding alteration in the standards for permissibility. Though McGowan adduces the scenario of Seamus and Donal for the purpose of showing how people without any special authority can significantly transform the deontic norms of social settings, my subjection of the scenario to wary scrutiny reveals that the normative transformations brought about by such people are far short of what McGowan supposes.

5.3.5.2 A Conversation without Interlocutors

McGowan's whole analysis is centered on the pragmatics of ordinary conversations, yet the analysis is supposed to be applicable to the marketing of pornography. After all, McGowan propounds her account of conversational pragmatics as a vehicle for circumventing the problems that have bedeviled the efforts by Langton to uphold MacKinnon's critique of pornography. McGowan aims to demonstrate that the manufacturers and distributors of pornography do constitutively subordinate women even though they do not possess any special practical authority over women. If she is to make progress in demonstrating that point, the insights from her exposition of conversational pragmatics will have to be transferred to the domain of pornography.

Any such transfer, however, will be deeply problematic. Let us temporarily leave aside the fact that women as non-consumers of pornography are not parties to any "conversation" with pornographers; we will return to that fact in my next subsection. Let us here notice instead that even the men who view or read pornographic materials are not parties to any "conversations" with the manufacturers and distributors of those materials. Even in the age of the World Wide Web, when pornographic sites provide opportunities for interactive viewing and reading, the flow of "conversation" is predominantly in one direction from the producers to the consumers. *A fortiori*, the flow of "conversation" is in one direction when the materials viewed or read by consumers are the traditional pornographic films and magazines. (Web sites devoted to the sharing of homemade pornography efface the distinction between producers and consumers. The applicability of McGowan's theorizing to such sites is not impugned by what is said in my next two paragraphs—though her theorizing, even in application to such sites, will remain vulnerable to my arguments that follow those two paragraphs.)

McGowan does not seek to address this problem until the final main section of her article, and her approach to it is curious and unsatisfactory. She begins as follows: "The proposal offered here is that pornography functions like a conversational exercitive. Since I am not suggesting that pornography actually *is* a conversational exercitive, there is no need to establish that pornography is involved in what can properly be called a conversation" (McGowan 2003, 181, emphasis in original). Having opened her discussion of the matter in this rather puzzling fashion, McGowan then explains how her enquiry into the dynamics of conversations can shed light on the role of pornography in the subordination of women:

> In order for pornography to be *akin* to a conversational exercitive, however, rules of accommodation need to be operative in the domain over which pornography allegedly enacts permissibility facts. Since pornography is alleged to enact permissibility facts in the sociosexual arena, the proposal that pornography is akin to a conversational exercitive requires that there are rules of accommodation operative in that arena. (McGowan 2003, 181, emphasis in original)

Because the phrase "socio-sexual arena" is quite nebulous, its referent is not clear from these quoted sentences. However, the subsequent remarks by McGowan make clear that she is referring to the sundry sexual encounters between men and women. Those remarks are dubious in two main respects.

First, notwithstanding the disavowal by McGowan of the notion that pornographic materials actually are conversational exercitives, she—with her continued insistence that "pornography functions like a conversational exercitive"—still has to explain how the interaction between the producers and the consumers of pornographic materials is similar to conversational interaction. Her analysis of the pragmatics of conversations will not be applicable to the pernicious influence of pornography unless she can establish that the relationship between the aforementioned producers and consumers is quite closely akin to the relationship between the participants in a conversation. Yet McGowan does not even begin to establish that point. Rather, she shifts her attention away from the relationship between the manufacturers and the consumers of pornography, and she trains her focus instead on the countless relationships between men and women in sexual encounters. Those encounters do very often involve conversations, but they differ in that very respect from the interaction between the manufacturers and the consumers of pornography.

Second, McGowan does not go any way toward explaining how pornography exerts its influence on the socio-sexual arena. Instead, she repeatedly instructs her readers to suppose that that influence is exerted:

> Suppose that pornography, via the rules of accommodation operative in the sociosexual arena, renders certain speech acts unspeakable for women... Suppose that pornographic speech enacts, via the rules of accommodation [that are operative in the socio-sexual arena], permissibility facts such that it is permissible to force a woman to have sex under certain circumstances ... Suppose that pornographic speech enacts, via the rules of accommodation, permissibility facts such that it is normal and appropriate for a man to be sexually excited by the degradation of, and violence towards, women ... Suppose finally that pornographic

> speech enacts, via the rules of accommodation, permissibility facts such that it is permissible for men to operate on the assumption that the nature of women is to serve man (sexually or otherwise). (McGowan 2003, 182)

One major problem for McGowan is that all these suppositions are indeed suppositions rather than explanations. What she needs to explain, if her analyses are to be serviceable for Langton's defense of MacKinnon, is how pornographic materials could constitute normative changes in the socio-sexual arena. When McGowan simply supposes repeatedly that pornographic materials do indeed constitute such normative changes, she has not yet explained how those changes are so constituted.

Even more important, despite the repeated use of the verb "enacts" in the suppositions just quoted, McGowan appears to ascribe to pornographic materials an influence that is causal rather than constitutive. As is true in a much more recent essay of hers (McGowan 2017, 54–6), her references to the "enactment" of norms by pornographic materials are in fact references to the shaping of normative beliefs by those materials. The idea is that the viewing or reading of pornographic materials induces men to form beliefs about the moral permissibility of the mistreatment of women in sexual contexts. As those beliefs become widespread and longstanding among the men who consume pornography in a given society,[25] there emerge within that society some norms of conventional morality which deem the mistreatment of women in sexual contexts to be legitimate. Pornographic materials debase the conventional morality of the society in this manner, by inducing the formation of odious beliefs which collectively constitute some odious norms within that conventional morality. Pornographic materials "enact" certain norms of conventional morality in this fashion.

Now, whether or not pornographic materials do bring about the alterations in conventional morality which McGowan envisions, the role attributed to those materials in bringing about the alterations is patently causal rather than constitutive. Any noisome beliefs formed by the men who view or read pornographic materials are perlocutionary effects of those materials rather than illocutionary corollaries thereof. They are caused rather than constituted by the materials. Hence, the norms of conventional morality that are constituted by the noisome beliefs are themselves linked to the pornographic materials causally rather than constitutively. With her many uses of the verb "enacts," McGowan tends to obscure the causal character of the relevant links. That verb baselessly conveys the impression that the changes brought about in a society's conventional morality by the marketing of pornography are akin to the changes brought about in the legal entitlements of blacks by

[25] Though I use the term "society" here, I am not suggesting that the effects envisaged by McGowan have to occur at a country-wide level. The society in question could be a locality within a much broader territory. For a related point, see Langton 2009, 98, 100. For an account of the influence of pornography that quite closely resembles the account which I am ascribing here to McGowan, see Jenkins 2017.

the votes of South African legislators. However, whereas the latter changes are illocutionary and constitutive, the former are perlocutionary and causal.

Note, moreover, that any effort by McGowan to transmute her suppositions into assertions will commit her to various empirical claims that will have to be substantiated empirically. That is, if she seeks to maintain that the marketing of pornography actually does coarsen the conventional morality of some society in the way which she envisages, she will be advancing a complex empirical thesis. Such a thesis cannot be vindicated through suppositional musings or through abstract philosophical reasoning; any pertinent attempt to vindicate it will have to consist in social-scientific investigations. Yet McGowan herself begins her principal article on conversational exercitives by adverting to the pitfalls of trying to demonstrate the truth of complicated empirical claims about the causing of harms through the marketing of pornography: "Many [theorists] argue . . . that [pornography] ought to be prohibited because of the harm it *causes*. These arguments rely on the truth of complex causal claims and such claims are notoriously difficult to establish" (McGowan 2003, 155, emphasis in original). Of course, as McGowan rightly observes on the next page of her article,[26] any full defense of MacKinnon's assertions about the *constituting* of women's subordination through the marketing of pornography would also ultimately have to involve difficult empirical studies. Still, McGowan at the outset of her article indicates that she is aiming to defend those assertions by MacKinnon about the constitution of women's subordination. She is aiming to improve upon Langton's defense of those assertions. Thus, the fact that she ends up instead with some claims about the role of pornography in perlocutionarily *causing* the subordination of women—claims whose causal character is obfuscated by her repeated use of the verb "enacts"—is decidedly peculiar.

5.3.5.3 Beyond the Conversation

Let us assume *arguendo* that the interaction between pornographers and the consumers of pornography can somehow appositely be modeled as a conversation. We can therefore likewise assume for now that McGowan's analysis of the pragmatics of conversations is somehow applicable to the interaction between pornographers and the consumers of pornography. Even so, the theses which McGowan is striving to defend are about the subordination of women—yet the vast majority of women do not consume pornography of the kind which MacKinnon and Langton are targeting. Thus, even if McGowan has correctly analyzed the ways in which the parties to a conversation can affect the normative positions of one another through their contributions, and even if her analysis of the dynamics of conversations can be extended to the marketing and consumption of pornography, she will not

[26] McGowan 2003, 156. Langton fully recognizes this point as well. See Langton 2009, 91–2.

thereby have explained how the normative positions of women are affected. She addresses this matter in a footnote near the end of her article:

> Presumably, it is most often the case that only one party to real heterosexual sexual interaction is part of the "conversation" of (i.e., consumes) pornography. Since mostly men do so, it seems that pornography, as akin to a conversational exercitive, changes the permissibility facts for men in the heterosexual sociosexual arena and, because of male dominance, men are able (consciously or not) to enforce or impose these permissibility facts on women. (McGowan 2003, 185 n49)

This passage reinforces the queries which I have raised in the preceding subsection. In the first place, given the nature of the "conversation" between pornographers and consumers of pornography, the changes in permissibility facts to which McGowan adverts are brought about not through the workings of anything akin to a conversational exercitive but instead through the influence of pornographic materials on the deontic beliefs of the men who consume those materials. Cumulatively, the pornography-debased beliefs of those men constitute a conventional morality under which the sexual mistreatment of women is classified as permissible. Acting in accordance with that conventional morality, the male consumers of pornography exert their superior strength to inflict the mistreatment which they believe to be permissible. Such is the picture of the socio-sexual arena that can be gathered from McGowan's remarks above.

That picture returns us to the two difficulties that have been highlighted in my preceding subsection. Because of the nature of the "conversation" between pornographers and consumers of pornography, the role of pornographic materials in altering certain aspects of a society's conventional morality—if such alterations do indeed occur—is causal-perlocutionary rather than constitutive-illocutionary. Those materials cause some dismaying changes in the outlooks of men who view or read the materials, and the transmogrified outlooks constitute a conventional code of morality that is in line with the values promoted by the pornography industry. Men then impose those values on women in the socio-sexual arena. Now, even if this account of the nefarious role of pornography in causing the degradation of a conventional code of ethics is fully accurate in application to some specified society, that causal influence is very different from the role which Langton imputes to pornography in her defense of MacKinnon. Her defense of MacKinnon rests on the attribution of a constitutive-illocutionary role to pornography—rather than a causal-perlocutionary role—in the subordination of women.

Furthermore, when we ask whether the changes in conventional morality outlined by McGowan do occur in any given society, we are pondering a vexed empirical matter. Similarly complex as an empirical matter is the question whether such changes lead to an increased incidence of violence (and other abuse) in the socio-sexual arena. Those knotty empirical questions about complicated chains of causation are what McGowan professes to be leaving aside at the outset of her article. Since her article turns out to bring us back to such questions, it is not serviceable for Langton's purposes. We are left to conclude that Langton's claims about the role of pornography in constituting the subordination of women are not bolstered through an analysis of the pragmatics of conversations.

5.4 Langton on the Silencing of Women by Pornography

In addition to contending that women are subordinated by the marketing of pornography, Langton contends that they are silenced thereby. Whereas she maintains that the subordination of women by pornographic materials is illocutionary and constitutive, she submits that the silencing of women by those materials is perlocutionary and causal. However, although the silencing of women (as portrayed by Langton) is caused rather than constituted by the production and distribution of pornography, there is an illocutionary dimension to it—for the silencing consists in the inability of women to perform certain speech-acts.

According to Langton, pornographic materials warp the outlooks of the consumers of those materials, who consequently become disposed to silence women in various ways. She differentiates among three main types of silencing, two of which will be summarized only briefly here. These three broad types of silencing correspond to the threefold categories of Austin's speech-act philosophy: locution, illocution, and perlocution (Langton 2009, 48–9). We shall mull over these types of silencing—as Langton does—by concentrating on the efforts of women to refuse sexual advances from men.

In the first place, a woman can be prevented from engaging in any locution through which she would refuse such advances, or she can be intimidatorily deterred from undertaking such a locution. That is, she can be prevented or deterred from saying anything that might constitute a refusal. For example, suppose that an assailant clamps a hand or a gag over the mouth of a woman whom he has pinned against a wall, so that she is not able to say anything. She has been locutionarily stifled, in that she is not able to articulate any words at all during her terrible ordeal. Or suppose that a domineering husband has so thoroughly intimidated his wife that she is disinclined to demur whenever he approaches her for sexual intercourse. She too is locutionarily stifled, not by being strictly prevented from uttering any words of refusal but instead by having been browbeaten into declining to utter such words.

Instead of being locutionarily stifled, a woman might undergo perlocutionary frustration. That is, she can articulate the words which she wishes to articulate, and her utterance of those words constitutes the illocutionary act which she has aimed to perform; yet her illocutionary act does not bring about the perlocutionary effects which she has been seeking to induce. Perlocutionary frustration is common in countless areas of life—as Langton observes—but it is especially troubling in contexts where women are endeavoring to rebuff the sexual advances of men. Sometimes the refusal of a woman to consent to the sexual overtures of a man might be disregarded by him because he attaches far more importance to the gratification of his concupiscence than to the autonomy of the woman whose body he desires. He recognizes that she does not wish to engage in sexual intercourse with him, but her wishes about the matter are of very little weight in his estimation. In some other cases, the refusal of a woman to consent to the sexual advances of a man is a factor that greatly strengthens his determination to follow through on those advances. He derives a feeling of sexual elation from his awareness that he is overpowering her against her will. Here too the rapist recognizes that the woman on whom he forces himself has refused to gratify him; by his sadistic reckoning, however, her refusal is a stimulus rather than an impediment.

Locutionary stifling is obviously a type of silencing, but so too is perlocutionary frustration (at least in the contexts just sketched). When the refusal of a woman to engage in sexual intercourse is wantonly disregarded or wantonly relished, she has *pro tanto* been deprived of her ability to be heard meaningfully. She can speak and be understood, but she cannot get her interlocutor to heed her wishes on a matter of vital concern to her. If the interlocutor's unreceptiveness to her entreaties is due to the corrupting of his outlook through his continual exposure to hard-core pornography, the pornographic materials can aptly be said to have silenced the woman who voices those entreaties.

Important though locutionary stifling and perlocutionary frustration are as types of silencing in the socio-sexual arena, the type to which Langton devotes most of her attention is illocutionary disablement. That is, she maintains that the marketing of pornographic materials can affect the outlooks of men in ways that prevent women from performing certain illocutionary acts which they attempt to perform. In particular, it can prevent them from performing acts of refusal in the socio-sexual arena. Let us now attend to this third mode of silencing.

5.4.1 Illocutionary Disablement

To introduce and clarify the notion of illocutionary disablement, Langton draws upon a striking passage from an essay by Donald Davidson:

> Imagine this: the actor is acting a scene in which there is supposed to be a fire ... It is his role to imitate as persuasively as he can a man who is trying to warn others of a fire. "Fire!" he screams. And perhaps he adds, at the behest of the author, "I mean it! Look at the smoke!" etc. And now a real fire breaks out, and the actor

> tries vainly to warn the real audience. "Fire!" he screams. "I mean it! Look at the smoke!" etc.[27]

In this scenario, the actor has been disabled from performing the illocutionary act of warning the audience when a real fire breaks out. He utters various exclamations that would normally be constitutive of a warning, but the special circumstances of the theatrical conventions keep the members of the audience from recognizing that those exclamations do indeed constitute an attempt to warn them. Because the sway of the conventions has deprived the actor of the ability to perform the illocutionary act of issuing a warning, he has of course also been deprived of the ability to achieve the perlocutionary effects that would be sought through such an act.

Langton argues that, notwithstanding the differences between histrionic conventions and the marketing of pornography, the prevalence of pornographic materials in a society can comparably afflict women with illocutionary disablement in the socio-sexual arena. Whereas the actor in Davidson's vignette has been disabled from conveying a warning to the spectators in the theater, a woman in a society marked by the widespread distribution of pornography is disabled from conveying to any avid consumer of the pornography her refusal to engage in sexual intercourse with him. She will probably not be prevented from uttering words of refusal in most contexts, but those words will not be correctly construed as rebuffs. Instead, her efforts to refuse sexual intercourse will be misconstrued as coquettish inveiglements or as straightforward expressions of acceptance.[28] Because a woman's "no" is so often portrayed as meaning "yes" in hard-core pornography, the men who view or read such pornography will be all too prone to perceive "no" as "yes" when they interact with women in real-life sexual encounters. Thus, although the women who interact with those men will not have been prevented from saying "no," they will have been silenced in that their refusals are not registered as such. Their words of rejection will be heard as words of acceptance or enticement. In many sexual contexts, these women will have been disabled from performing illocutionary acts of refusal. As Langton writes(2009, 31, emphasis in original): "Some speech acts are *unspeakable* for women in some contexts: although the appropriate words can be uttered, those utterances fail to count as the actions [of refusal] they were intended to be."

Langton's contentions about the silencing of women by pornography are of course partly empirical hypotheses that have to be substantiated empirically. Still, difficult though it is to answer the question whether the widespread marketing of

[27] Davidson 2001, 269–70, quoted in Langton 2009, 49. Though neither Davidson nor Langton mentions as much, there is a bit of dialogue in Act II of Tom Stoppard's *Rosencrantz and Guildenstern are Dead* that very roughly corresponds to what is depicted in Davidson's scenario.

[28] For a catalogue of sundry ways in which a woman's refusals might be misconstrued by men who avidly consume pornography, see McGowan 2017. Although a few of McGowan's distinctions are rather elusive, her taxonomy overall is valuable.

pornography increases the frequency with which women's attempts to refuse sexual advances are misinterpreted, I have already made clear that this chapter is not concerned with such empirical cruxes. Instead, we shall focus here on some ethical matters and some matters of speech-act philosophy. Before we probe a few dubious aspects of Langton's claims, we should glance at one of their great strengths. Although this chapter will contest some of the specific ways in which Langton presents her critique of the silencing of women, and although I will submit that her critique lends no support whatsoever to proposals for the outlawing of pornography, her insights into the intricacies of silencing are commendable.

5.4.2 A Contemporary Application

As will be noted again in my next chapter, nearly all of the recent philosophical work on the perniciousness of hatefully bigoted utterances has grappled solely with invective that stems from the far right of the political spectrum. In the present-day United Kingdom, however, many of the worst such utterances emanate from the far left of that spectrum. In 2015, one of the two main political parties in the United Kingdom—the Labour Party—was taken over by Jeremy Corbyn and other left-wing extremists. Corbyn at the time was perhaps most notorious for his longstanding support of Irish republican terrorism and for his effusive tributes to anti-Western tyrannies, but he also had a lengthy and unlovely history of associating himself warmly with rabid antisemites.[29] During his four-and-a-half years as the leader of the Labour Party, the level of antisemitism within the organization surged and prompted numerous Jews to leave the party after having been affiliated with it throughout their adulthood. One of the most galling features of the bigotry unleashed by Corbyn was the way in which his supporters most commonly responded when Jews and others complained about the myriad of serious antisemitic incidents within the Labour Party. Again and again, those supporters alleged that the complaints either were attempts to shut down criticism of Israel or were attempts to vilify Corbyn and his fellow far-leftists in order to undo their control of the Labour Party. These sneeringly crass ripostes to the objections that were mounted against the torrent of antisemitic abuse in Corbyn's Labour Party perfectly exemplified the infliction of the illocutionary disablement which Langton has recounted. Although many of the retorts by Corbyn's supporters were undoubtedly disingenuous, some of the retorts were sincere though egregious misinterpretations of the worries that had been voiced by Jews and others about the swell of antisemitism in the Labour Party. Because the outlooks of quite a few admirers of

[29] For two powerful studies of the antisemitism that has pervaded the far left of the political spectrum in the contemporary United Kingdom, with extensive attention to Corbyn's malign influence, see Hirsh 2018 and Rich 2018.

Corbyn had been warped by their immersion in poisonous ideologies—not least in the antisemitic canards propagated by the Soviet Union during the era of the Cold War (Tabarovsky 2019)—those admirers persistently and odiously misconstrued the remonstrations that were addressed to them by opponents of antisemitism.

When the opponents of antisemitism tried to perform speech-acts of complaint about the Jew-hatred that permeated the Labour Party under Corbyn, his minions took those opponents instead to be performing speech-acts of defiance through which they balked at his ascendance within the party or at his relentless hostility toward Israel. Speech-acts of complaint and speech-acts of defiance are alike in belonging to the category which Austin labeled as "behabitives" (1975, 160–1), but in this context the bearings of the former speech-acts are very different from those of the latter. Corbyn's votaries mistook the former for the latter by attributing to Jews some of the traits which antisemites over the centuries have so often associated with Jewishness: craftiness, self-interestedness, dual loyalties. With these antisemitic responses to protests against antisemitism, the devotees of Corbyn silenced Jews—not usually by preventing Jews from speaking, but instead by continually failing to hear Jews' speech-acts for what they were. In that regard, the relationship between Corbyn's acolytes and Jews was analogous to the relationship between the male consumers of pornography and women. Just as the outlooks of the consumers of pornography have been befogged by their immersion in hardcore filth, the outlooks of the followers of Corbyn have been befogged by their immersion in the swamp of far-left dogmatics.

5.4.3 The Matter of Uptake

Perceptive though Langton's analysis of silencing is, it is open to question in certain respects (beyond any queries about empirical matters, from which I have here prescinded). Most notably, the distinction between illocutionary disablement and perlocutionary frustration is far from clear-cut. Langton maintains that, when a man who consumes pornography has misconstrued a woman's insistent "no" as a welcoming "yes" in a sexual context, he has silenced the woman by inflicting illocutionary disablement upon her. He has prevented her from performing a speech-act of refusal, because he has failed to register correctly the type of speech-act that she has endeavored to perform.

Now, notwithstanding that there is a clear sense in which a man who misinterprets a woman's act of refusal as an act of acceptance has thereby silenced her, what is far less clear is that the silencing has kept her from performing an act of refusal at all. In other words, what is not clear is that the woman has suffered illocutionary disablement rather than perlocutionary frustration. Of course, the perlocutionary frustration in this situation would be different from the perlocutionary frustration in a situation where a man recognizes a woman's act of refusal as such and where he nonetheless disregards it in order to indulge his own sexual impulses. Still, in spite of the differences between these species of perlocutionary frustration, the key point in each of them is that the performance of a speech-act of refusal has aimed to produce certain effects on an addressee's outlook and has failed to produce those effects. In each case, that is, the misadventure appears to be perlocutionary rather than illocutionary. Instead of pertaining to anything which a speaker of some words of refusal has omitted to do, each misadventure pertains to the fact that an addressee has not properly taken on board those words.

For Langton, however, the distinction between illocutionary disablement and perlocutionary frustration hinges partly on whether an addressee has correctly discerned the nature and content of the relevant speech-act. If the addressee has misconstrued that nature or content—for example, by presuming that a speech-act of refusal is instead a speech-act of assent—the person seeking to perform the speech-act has been thwarted from doing so. She has been illocutionarily disabled, or so Langton contends. By contrast, if the addressee has correctly perceived the nature and content of an act of refusal but has chosen to behave at variance with it (whether out of sadism or out of overweening self-indulgence), the person seeking to perform the speech-act of refusal has managed to do so but has not managed to achieve the perlocutionary effects which she has sought. She has undergone perlocutionary frustration.

By drawing the distinction between illocutionary disablement and perlocutionary frustration in this fashion, Langton follows a certain strand in Austin's own analysis of the illocutionary and perlocutionary dimensions of speech-acts. After devoting quite a bit of time and ingenuity to the endeavor of differentiating between those dimensions, Austin somewhat blurred the clarity of the division between them in a way that bears directly on Langton's account of silencing:

> Unless a certain effect is achieved, the illocutionary act will not have been happily, successfully performed. This is not to say that the illocutionary act is the achieving of a certain effect. I cannot be said to have warned an audience unless it hears what I say and takes what I say in a certain sense. An effect must be achieved on the audience if the illocutionary act is to be carried out. How should we best put it here? And how can we limit it? Generally the effect amounts to bringing about the understanding of the meaning and of the force of the locution. So the performance of an illocutionary act involves the securing of *uptake*. (Austin 1975, 116–17, italics in original.)

Austin did not elaborate on his inclusion of uptake among the felicity conditions for the performance of any speech-act, and the import of his brief remarks on the matter has been a topic of controversy for decades among specialists in speech-act philosophy.[30] We will not delve into those controversies here, but we should note

[30] Some of the far-reaching controversies are helpfully discussed in Sbisà 2009.

that the Austinian position on the matter is central to Langton's analysis of the silencing of women by pornography. To be sure, even were the Austinian position rejected, Langton could maintain—subject to empirical confirmation—that the marketing of pornography tends to silence women. However, she would then have to accept that the silencing is perlocutionary rather than illocutionary. If she is to stand by her repeated claims that the silencing of women consists in the stymieing of their efforts to perform illocutionary acts of refusal, she has to establish that Austin was correct in his inclusion of uptake among the felicity conditions for illocutionary acts.

5.4.3.1 Two Clarifications

Before we ponder whether Langton can vindicate Austin's stance on the matter of uptake, two clarifications are in order. First, although Austin's stance does not eliminate the alignment between the illocutionary/perlocutionary distinction and the constitutive/causal distinction, it does somewhat complicate that alignment. The correspondence between the two distinctions has heretofore seemed clear-cut, because the elements of various speech-acts have heretofore seemed to include only conventions and circumstances and intentions and utterances. When certain utterances are undertaken with certain intentions in the presence of certain conventions and circumstances, those utterances are illocutionary acts that constitute certain effects. (Of course, usually the utterances are also perlocutionary acts that causally elicit responses in addressees.) This tidy picture, in which nothing causally downstream from an utterance is involved in endowing the utterance with its status as an illocutionary act, becomes somewhat less tidy when the matter of uptake is brought in. Uptake, consisting in an addressee's apprehension of the type and content of an illocutionary act that has been performed, is causally downstream from the utterance which constitutes that act. Thus, if uptake is a necessary condition for the performance of such an act, one of the elements constitutive of a speech-act is causally connected to the other such elements. Still, although the Austinian picture is somewhat more complex than it initially seems, the constitutive/causal dichotomy remains aligned with the illocutionary/perlocutionary dichotomy. When an utterance is undertaken in the presence of circumstances and conventions that endow it with illocutionary force, and when the utterance is met with uptake on the part of its addressee(s), those elements of an illocutionary act are together constitutive of the act itself and of anything that is integral to it (such as the subordination of black South Africans that is constituted by the enacting of the discriminatory statute which Langton recounts). By contrast, any responses in the addressee(s) beyond sheer uptake are causal effects of the utterance in its status as a perlocutionary act. In short, any states of affairs that follow from an utterance qua illocutionary act are constituted by the utterance, whereas any states of affairs that follow from an utterance qua perlocutionary act are causal effects thereof.

Second, in relation to the marketing of pornography, the silencing of women (if it occurs) is perlocutionary rather than illocutionary; it occurs through the causal impact of the pornography on the beliefs and attitudes of men.[31] Hence, when I contemplate here whether the silencing of women is illocutionary or perlocutionary, I am considering the silencing not in relation to the marketing of pornography but instead in relation to the efforts by women to perform speech-acts of refusal. An utterance whereby a woman seeks to rebuff the sexual advances of some man is both an illocutionary act and a perlocutionary act. The question to be mulled over here is whether the silencing described by Langton—silencing that consists in a failure of uptake—pertains to a woman's utterance qua illocutionary act or qua perlocutionary act. Is uptake an illocutionary feature or a perlocutionary feature of that utterance?

5.4.3.2 In Search of a Justification

Langton, of course, contends that uptake is an illocutionary feature of a woman's act of refusal. She believes that, without uptake on the part of any addressee of the words through which a woman rejects the addressee's sexual overtures, the woman has not performed an illocutionary act of refusal. An attempt to perform such an act has occurred, but the attempt has been scotched by the failure of the addressee to grasp that the words of rejection are indeed an instance of refusal. Or so Langton maintains. However, neither in *Sexual Solipsism* nor in any of Langton's other relevant writings is there a persuasive justification of her position on this matter. Langton does distinguish clearly between illocutionary disablement and perlocutionary frustration, and she succeeds in rebutting an ill-advised objection to her position by Daniel Jacobson,[32] but she never provides an adequate rationale for her insistence that an illocutionary act of refusal cannot be performed without the element of uptake.

5.4.3.2.1 Reciprocity in General

Langton's chief effort to supply such a rationale occurs in a chapter of *Sexual Solipsism* that is derived from an essay written in collaboration with Jennifer Hornsby. There Langton invokes the notion of reciprocity in support of her view – which she shares with Hornsby – that uptake is an essential ingredient of every illocutionary act. As she writes:

[31] This chapter will later highlight the full import of the fact that, when the silencing of women by the marketing of pornography does take place, it occurs by way of certain perlocutionary effects of that marketing. Of considerable significance for the principle of freedom of expression is that the silencing is remotely caused, rather than directly constituted, by the purveyance of pornographic materials.

[32] Langton, 2009, 83. Jacobson conflates the absence of a person's refusal with the presence of a person's consent. See Jacobson 1995, 77–8; 2004, 68.

> People who share a language have the capacity not simply to understand one another's words, but also to grasp what illocutionary acts others might be trying to make ... Language use then relies on a mutual capacity for uptake, which involves a minimal receptiveness on the part of language users in the role of hearers. This minimal receptiveness doesn't mean that a hearer will agree with what a speaker is saying: but it does mean that a hearer has a capacity to grasp what communicative act a speaker might be intending to perform.[33]

These quoted statements are unexceptionable and convincing, but they do not support the proposition that a woman undergoes illocutionary disablement on every occasion when her refusal of sexual advances has failed to elicit uptake on the part of the addressee of the refusal. What can be inferred from this quoted passage is that opportunities for people to engage in illocutionary acts are dependent on the sway of reciprocity along the lines described here by Langton. In the absence of linguistic practices that are marked by such reciprocity, people will not have acquired the communicative competences that enable them to perform illocutionary acts; and, in the absence of such practices, the conventions that vest sundry utterances with illocutionary force will not have emerged. Nevertheless, despite the vital role of reciprocity in making illocutionary acts possible, its sway does not require that *every* such act succeed in eliciting uptake. Provided that illocutionary acts typically involve uptake, there can be exceptional instances of such acts where no uptake is evoked. The general reign of reciprocity is consistent with the occurrence of those anomalous instances.

In maintaining as much, I am adopting a position that has elsewhere been espoused separately by Hornsby and by Langton. In a 1994 essay on which Langton draws quite heavily for the chapter in *Sexual Solipsism* from which I have quoted just above, Hornsby takes an aptly nuanced stance:

> [E]ven where there is an intended audience, the speaker may do some illocutionary act although the audience does not latch on to it. In fact we talk with some ambivalence about cases where an illocutionary attempt is not recognized. (There are examples which we might describe either with "She warned him, but he never realized the danger" or "She tried in vain to warn him.") ... [T]he idea of reciprocity can be essential to the idea of illocution, without the working of reciprocity's being essential to the isolated performance of any illocutionary act. (Hornsby 1994, 197–8)

Both when discussing illocutionary acts in general and when discussing specifically the attempts by women to perform illocutionary acts of refusal in response to

[33] Langton 2009, 78. Langton is here drawing heavily on Hornsby 1994. Hornsby further expounds her view of the matter in Hornsby 2011, 381–3.

sexual overtures, Hornsby rightly affirms that such acts are defective or less than fully successful when they do not elicit uptake (1994, 197–9). She pertinently writes that "where there is no [uptake] there is less than 'full success'" and that "performances of illocutionary acts in the absence of [uptake] are in some way defective." She explains that "such performances are not such as to further the usual communicative ends of language" (197, 198). We should admire these quoted remarks as entirely apposite, while accepting that a woman can perform an illocutionary act of refusal even if her firm words of rejection have not resulted in uptake on the part of the lustful man to whom the words are addressed. Such an act in those circumstances has been less than fully successful, but it has occurred. As Hornsby declares, "there can be an illocutionary act even when, the speaker having not been fully successful [through a failure of uptake], there is no 'perfect' illocutionary act" (1994, 199).

Langton too has elsewhere adopted a position that is more flexible than the one which she articulates in the chapter from which I have quoted in my penultimate paragraph above. She stakes out that capacious position in her reply to a quite recent article by Hornsby. In that latter article, Hornsby invokes a communicative conception of speech-acts in support of the view that the triggering of uptake is a feature of every illocutionary act. Though Hornsby should not have drawn any bolder conclusions from her communicative conception of speech-acts than from her earlier emphasis on reciprocity, we can leave that point aside at this juncture. Of direct relevance here instead is that she supplements her communicative conception with a conception focused on the alignment between the illocutionary/perlocutionary distinction and the constitutive/causal distinction. Under that latter conception of speech-acts, "[i]llocutionary acts are done *in* speaking: the [illocutionary] force is integral to the act of speaking. Perlocutionary acts, by contrast, are done by virtue of speaking's having effects in its turn" (Hornsby 2011, 383, italics in original). In reply, Langton "welcome[s] this expansion of the illocutionary to include speech acts that are not primarily communicative: for one thing, it seems truer to Austin's own pluralistic conception." She explains that "Austin wanted the idea of illocution for a number of purposes, one of which was to mark a contrast between the acts constituted by speech, and the effects of speech" (Langton 2011, 428). Now, although Langton applauds Hornsby's expanded understanding of illocution because she thinks that it is serviceable for her own account of the role of pornography in subordinating women, I applaud it here because it militates in favor of greater flexibility with regard to the matter of uptake.

Better than any doctrinaire position on the matter of uptake is the position which Hornsby has articulated in 1994. In other words, provided that uptake typically occurs when an illocutionary act of some type is performed,[34] there can

[34] The property of typicality to which I advert here is stronger than just a statistical property. It is a quasi-conceptual connection, homologous to the quasi-conceptual connection (which I have

be aberrant instances of that act-type where no uptake is elicited. Even within a single act-type, the differences between the situations in which people aberrantly perform and the situations in which people unsuccessfully attempt to perform are multifarious. Let us consider a pair of examples that together illustrate one of those differences. Suppose that Marion and Samuel are both competent speakers of English. If Marion engages in an utterance to indicate her rejection of sexual advances by Samuel, and if he altogether fails to hear her utterance—perhaps because, unbeknownst to her, he has temporarily gone out of the bedroom where she is—her attempt to refuse his advances has not yet resulted in an illocutionary act of refusal. She has tried to perform such an act but has not yet managed to do so (Hornsby 2011, 381 n3). By contrast, if Marion engages in an utterance to indicate clearly her rejection of sexual advances by Samuel, and if he hears her words but badly misconstrues them as her acceptance of his overtures, she has performed an illocutionary act of refusal despite the absence of uptake on the part of her addressee. Whether or not Samuel's misinterpretation is due to his having been led astray by hard-core pornography, the misinterpretation does not suffice to undo the occurrence of the illocutionary act of refusal as such. His misconstrual obviously foils the occurrence of certain perlocutionary effects that might otherwise have ensued from Marion's utterance, but it does not prevent the utterance from amounting to an illocutionary act of refusal.

Were we to perpend many other examples, we would find further subtle differences between situations in which an absence of uptake does preclude the performance of an illocutionary act and situations in which an absence of uptake does not preclude such a performance. Attentiveness to nuances, rather than a blanket insistence on the decisive role of uptake, is warranted in one's assessments of such examples. However, a caveat should be attached here. My brief discussion of Marion and Samuel has been explicitly premised on the assumption that uptake typically occurs when women utter words of refusal in response to sexual advances. If that assumption is false in some society or even in some locality within a broader society, the women there whose words of rebuff do not elicit uptake are thwarted from performing the illocutionary acts of refusal which they have sought to perform. In such circumstances, the reciprocity envisaged by Hornsby is so attenuated that it has largely given way to illocutionary disablement (at least with regard to the efforts of women to perform acts of refusal). Thus, if Langton can show that failures of uptake in response to women's attempts to refuse sexual advances are routine and pervasive rather than exceptional—in some society, or in some locality within a broader society—and if she can further show that such a state of affairs is due to the influence of pornographic materials and their repeated suggestions that a woman's "no" means "yes," then she will be able to sustain her thesis that those

expounded elsewhere) between moral judgments and moral motivations. On that latter connection, see Kramer 2009, 279–85; 2019b, 239–43.

materials have silenced women in the specified society by imposing illocutionary disablement upon them.

5.4.3.2.2 Jacobson's Example Redux

In support of the notion that uptake is an ingredient of every illocutionary act, Langton probes an example by Jacobson which ostensibly disconfirms that notion. His example, in a slightly abbreviated form, is as follows: "Suppose Bill, in the grips of some paranoid fantasy, thinks Sally has only sent him an invitation to her wedding in order to gloat—that she does not really want him to attend... We should say that Sally has invited Bill, despite the fact that he misconstrues her act" (Jacobson 1995, 73, quoted in Langton 2009, 82). Langton suitably rebuts Jacobson's line of reasoning, as she distinguishes between Sally's inviting someone to a ceremony and Sally's wanting the addressee of the invitation to accept it: "There is a difference between inviting someone to your wedding and wanting him to attend, and there is a corresponding difference between someone's believing that he is invited to a wedding and his believing that his attendance there is wanted" (Langton 2009, 82). Contrary to what Jacobson presumes, his scenario does not involve a failure of uptake on the part of Bill. Bill correctly grasps the nature and content of the illocutionary act—an act of invitation—which Sally has sought to perform. Bill incorrectly identifies the motive that has prompted her to undertake such an act, but his error on that point is consistent with the occurrence of uptake on his part. Langton is justified in maintaining as much, in her rejoinder to Jacobson.

However, the scenario of Sally and Bill can easily be tweaked to circumvent the riposte by Langton. Suppose that, when Bill receives and opens an invitation from Sally to her wedding, he glances at the writing on the stationery and surmises that it is a fancy note in which she expresses her gratitude for some work that he has recently carried out at her home. Feeling slightly embarrassed about being thanked effusively yet again by a customer for his labors, he crumples up the invitation and discards it. He gives no further thought to the matter. In these circumstances, there has clearly been no uptake by Bill. His skimming of the invitation has led him to misconstrue badly the nature and content of Sally's illocutionary act. All the same, Sally has performed the illocutionary act of inviting him to her wedding; she has undergone perlocutionary frustration rather than illocutionary disablement.

In short, although Jacobson's vignette in its original formulation does not tell against the proposition that the eliciting of uptake is an element of every illocutionary act, the vignette with a bit of tweaking is quite serviceable for impugning that proposition. The original version differs from the modified version in that only the former has portrayed a situation where there is uptake by Bill, but the two versions are alike in depicting the performance by Sally of an illocutionary act of invitation. Consequently, the occurrence of such an illocutionary act is not always marked by the occurrence of uptake.

5.4.3.2.3 The Ethical Upshot

What makes Langton's position on uptake so puzzling is that it lacks any apparent ethical rationale.[35] If any silencing of women brought about by the marketing of pornography does consist in illocutionary disablement, that silencing is deplorable; but likewise if any silencing of women by the marketing of pornography consists instead in perlocutionary frustration, that silencing too is deplorable. Obviously repugnant is a man's misconstrual of a woman's "no" as "yes" in a sexual context where rape ensues. Also repugnant, however, is the behavior of a man who understands a woman's rejection of his sexual advances and who disregards her refusal as he overpowers her with concupiscent vehemence. Perhaps worst of all is the conduct of a man for whom a woman's refusal is a stimulus to sexual conquest, as he experiences a surge of sadistic gratification from his awareness that he is acting so brutally against her will. Given that all of these modes of misconduct by men against women are odious, there is no evident reason for concentrating on one such mode more than on the others when we condemn the ways in which the marketing of pornographic materials may tend to silence women.

In particular, there are no reasons that pertain to the principle of freedom of expression. On the one hand, as will be argued shortly, the protection bestowed by that principle on the production and distribution of pornography is unaffected by the question whether the harm of silencing undergone by women should be classified as illocutionary disablement or as perlocutionary frustration. In either case the harm of silencing, insofar as it is attributable to the influence of pornographic materials, is an offshoot of perlocutionary effects caused by the marketing of those materials. As something diffusely and remotely caused rather than constituted by the availability of those materials, the silencing of women cannot justify the imposition of legal restrictions on that availability. Later in this chapter, we will return to this point at greater length.

On the other hand, the silencing of women by pornography—in any of the ways outlined in the penultimate paragraph above—is gravely wrong. Hence, the countering of such an effect is a major responsibility of any system of governance. As has been affirmed in §5.3.4.2.1 above, the legal permissibility of most types of pornography is fully consistent with a diverse array of measures that should be undertaken by any system of governance to avert the dismaying effects that can ensue from the widespread availability of pornography. Particularly grievous among those potential effects is the thwarting of women's efforts to decline sexual overtures. Accordingly, policies aimed at heading off such an effect—policies such as those recounted in §5.3.4.2.1 and in my next chapter—are crucial for the fulfillment of the moral obligations that are incumbent on every system of governance. They are crucial for the fulfillment of the paramount responsibility of any such system to

[35] Of clear relevance here is the discussion in Antony 2011, 398–9.

bring about the social and political and economic conditions under which every citizen can be warranted in harboring an ample sense of self-respect. What should be emphasized here is that this point about the adoption of such policies is vital irrespective of the forms in which the silencing of women might occur. In any of the forms mentioned in the penultimate paragraph above, and also in the form of locutionary stifling that has been sketched near the outset of §5.4, the silencing of women is an evil which a system of governance is morally duty-bound to combat. There is no ethical reason for singling out one of those forms of that evil above the others.

While acknowledging that perlocutionary frustration can occur in the absence of illocutionary disablement, Langton articulates an ethical rationale for her concentration on the latter (and for her insistence that uptake is an element of every illocutionary act):

> What is hoped for is a certain capacity to perform communicative illocutions, especially those of sexual communication. This illocutionary potential requires from hearers only a minimal receptivity, a capacity for uptake, a capacity to recognize the kind of thing a speaker may be trying to do with her words. The hope is modest: for example, successful refusal is no guarantee against rape, if it is illocutionary success we are speaking of. It is no guarantee that a refusal will be honoured, only that it will be recognized for the act it is intended to be. But illocutionary success, for these speech acts, is perhaps a minimum to hope for. Illocutionary success at least gives a speaker a fighting chance. (Langton 2009, 73)

While granting that the occurrence of uptake on the part of an addressee is not sufficient to ensure that a woman's refusal of sexual advances will induce the addressee to refrain from committing an act of rape, Langton here maintains that the occurrence of uptake is at any rate a necessary condition for inducing the addressee to refrain from such a crime. However, when we attend to the multiple ways in which a woman's illocutionary act of refusal might prove to be inefficacious, we can see that Langton has erred. If a man derives intense gratification from the sadistic thrill of forcing himself sexually on women against their wishes, and if he derives no comparable sense of ecstasy from consensual intercourse, his misinterpretation of a woman's words of refusal as words of consent could lead him to abstain from following through on his sexual advances. In that event, the absence of uptake on the part of the sadist has spared the woman from being raped and has thus given effect to her words of refusal. No doubt, situations of this kind are much rarer than situations in which failures of uptake during sexual encounters give rise to incidents of rape. Nevertheless, this scenario of the sadist is not outlandishly fanciful. In some credible circumstances, a failure of uptake rather than the occurrence of uptake is what "gives a speaker [specifically, a woman whose words are a rejection of sexual overtures] a fighting chance."

5.4.4 A Conflict within the Principle of Freedom of Expression?

As a transition to the final main section of this chapter, in which I will plumb the issues of freedom of expression that arise from Langton's work, we should here probe a set of attempts by Langton to invoke a version of the principle of freedom of expression in support of legal restrictions on pornography. Her invocation of a version of that principle pertains specifically to her claims about the silencing of women by the marketing of pornography. More than once—in Langton 2009, 29–30, 63; 2017, 28—Langton approvingly adverts to MacKinnon's contention that the elimination of such silencing through the imposition of legal bans on pornographic materials would be justifiable by reference to a version of the principle of freedom of expression. MacKinnon has formulated her thesis as follows: "[L]iberalism has never understood that the free speech of men silences the free speech of women. It is the same social goal, just other *people*. This is what a real inequality, a real conflict, a real disparity in social power looks like" (1987, 156, emphasis in original). Langton explicitly subscribes to MacKinnon's thesis: "The claim that pornography silences women expresses a ... conflict ... within liberty itself. Viewed thus, the [anti-pornography ordinance drafted by MacKinnon] poses an apparent conflict between the liberty of men to produce and consume pornography, and the liberty of women to speak" (2009, 30). Slightly later in her book, Langton reiterates her endorsement of MacKinnon's position. She declares that, if the marketing of pornography does indeed bring about the silencing of women, then "pornography poses a conflict between liberty and liberty: in particular between the free speech of men and that of women" (2009, 31).

Langton is concerned chiefly to demonstrate that the widespread availability of pornographic materials in a society can give rise to the silencing of women. Although I have impugned some of the specifics of her ruminations on that silencing—especially the sweepingness and inflexibility of her stance on the role of uptake in illocutionary acts—I do not doubt that the marketing of pornography can lead to instances of the silencing of women. Through any of the routes that have been delineated in this chapter, the silencing of women can result from the circulation of hard-core pornography in a society; and, even without any elaborate empirical studies, there are quite ample grounds for thinking that the influence of pornographic materials has sometimes heightened the incidence of the silencing of women through those routes. On that much, I concur with Langton and MacKinnon.

Far more dubious, however, is the notion that a system of governance which forbears from outlawing the distribution of pornography has thereby sacrificed the freedom of expression of women for the sake of upholding the freedom of expression of men. We here need to return to some distinctions drawn in my opening two chapters. As has been maintained in §2.2 of Chapter 2, the phrase "freedom of expression" (or any cognate phrase such as "freedom of speech" or "freedom of communication" or "free speech") is often understood in more than one way. In one major sense of that phrase, it denotes a principle of political morality that imposes some deontological limits on the purposes for which any system of governance can legitimately deprive people of their deontic or physical liberties to engage in communicative conduct. In another sense of "freedom of expression," that phrase denotes the deontic liberties of people to engage in communicative conduct and also the Hohfeldian immunities that normatively secure those liberties against efforts to extinguish or suspend them. In yet a further sense, the phrase "freedom of expression" refers to the physical and psychological and normative abilities of people to engage in communicative conduct. With these distinctions freshly in mind, we should explore the assertions by MacKinnon and Langton about conflicts between the freedom of expression of men and the freedom of expression of women.

5.4.4.1 "Freedom of Expression" as a Principle of Political Morality

Some of the wording in the pronouncements by MacKinnon and Langton seems to indicate that they are using the phrase "free speech" (or its cognates) to refer to the principle of political morality that has been mentioned in the final paragraph above. Particularly suggestive of this way of thinking is MacKinnon's declaration that "[i]t is the same social goal, just other *people*." Let us here leave aside the fact that the principle of freedom of expression is a deontological precept rather than an encapsulation of a consequentialist goal. MacKinnon appears to be alleging that that principle currently is applied selectively to favor men over women, and she is calling for the elimination of that inequity through the outlawing of pornography. She believes that, because the unrestricted distribution of pornography results in the silencing of women on matters that are central to their lives, the only way to uphold the principle of freedom of expression in application to women is to ban the pornographic materials that produce the silencing. If MacKinnon's message is indeed along these lines, then it bespeaks a far-reaching misconception of the principle of freedom of expression.

As has been mentioned briefly above, and as has been argued at length in my previous chapters, the principle of freedom of expression is a precept of self-restraint incumbent on every system of governance. It disallows any governmental measures that prohibit or restrict communicative conduct qua communicative conduct. Communicative activities of sundry kinds can be prohibited in keeping with the principle of freedom of expression, but only if the prohibitions are aimed against wrong-making properties of those activities that are not inherently communicative—and thus only if the forbidden activities constitute misconduct that can properly be outlawed on communication-neutral grounds. Now, the principle of freedom of expression protects most types of pornography against legal restrictions, because such restrictions would be directed against the communicative character or contents of the pornographic materials (as MacKinnon's anti-pornography ordinance in Indianapolis explicitly was). We shall explore this point at greater length hereafter. At the moment, the question to be addressed is whether the principle of freedom of expression similarly protects women against the silencing of their efforts to refuse the sexual advances of men.

As should be evident, the answer to the question just posed is negative. On the one hand, both morally and legally, women are indeed protected against the silencing of their efforts to rebuff sexual advances. However, the protection is conferred not by the principle of freedom of expression but instead by the moral principles and legal norms that prohibit sexual assault and rape. Those moral principles and legal norms bestow deontic protection, and the effective implementation of the legal norms will also bestow material protection. (Admittedly, the protection directly conferred by the implementation of the legal norms is typically punitive and *ex post* rather than anticipatory and preventative. However, the prospect of punishment normally gives rise to a deterrent effect that is operative *ex ante*.) Furthermore, as has been observed several times already in this chapter, any system of governance that fulfills its moral responsibilities will have undertaken diverse measures to counter the pernicious misapprehensions and stereotypes that can be fostered not only by pornography but also by other sources such as advertising and non-pornographic films and television programming. Those governmental measures, which are fully compatible with the principle of freedom of expression, provide further safeguards to women against the silencing of their words of refusal.

On the other hand, as has been stated, the security enjoyed by women against such silencing does not stem from the principle of freedom of expression. Although that principle does extend protection in some situations where the endeavors of individuals to communicate their views are interrupted or drowned out by the actions of other private individuals—as we have seen in Chapter 2's reflections on heckling and on hostile audiences—it does not extend protection in the situations where the negative responses of women to sexual overtures are misconstrued by men as affirmative responses. When the principle of freedom of expression does condemn an instance of disruptive interference by some private individual(s) with the speech of some other private individual(s), the interference is occurrent in public and is animated by hostility toward the content or communicative nature of the speech. Hecklers prevent the potential addressees of the speech from enjoying access to it. Moreover, the causal nexus between the actions of interference and the thwarting of the speaker's communicative endeavors is direct and particularized rather than remote and diffuse. If the actions of interference are themselves communicative, they are so only incidentally; they could equally well have unfolded as sheer noise-making or violence. In such circumstances, as Chapter 2 has observed, the acquiescence of governmental officials in the disruptive obstruction would amount to "an improper delegation of authority to the public to suppress messages it disfavors" (Kagan 1996a, 463). By contrast, the instances of silencing which Langton scrutinizes are not occurrent in public settings where potential addressees may have wished to enjoy access to what has been silenced. In addition, the causal links between the marketing of pornography and those instances of silencing are diffuse and remote rather than particularized and direct. Furthermore, the instances of silencing in themselves—in isolation from the acts of sexual assault or rape which they are so likely to impel—do not contravene the principle of freedom of expression at all. Only if some such instance of silencing is an element of sexual misconduct will it have become legally actionable; and then its actionability is due to its being such an element rather than to its having run athwart the principle of freedom of expression.

Suppose for example that, after making some sexual advances to Molly, Peter misconstrues her negative reply as an affirmative reply. By Langton's reckoning, Peter has disabled Molly from performing an illocutionary act of refusal. However, because Peter is so delighted about the perceivedly positive reaction from Molly, he does not need any further gratification and therefore does not follow through on his advances. He desists from pursuing Molly any further, and indeed he leaves her house in order to return to his own residence where he will fall asleep in blissful contentment. In this situation, even if Langton were correct in thinking that Molly has been stymied by Peter from performing an illocutionary act of refusal, there would be no basis for concluding that Peter or anyone else has contravened the principle of freedom of expression. There would indeed be no basis for concluding that Peter has done anything that should incur legal sanctions.

Of course, although the scenario of Peter and Molly is not ludicrously far-fetched, it is certainly not typical. Far more often, a man's misinterpretation of a woman's "no" as "yes" will lead to his committing an act of sexual assault or rape. In that event, the man's overall conduct—including his obtuse misjudgment about the type of illocutionary act which the woman has performed—will properly be subject to criminal sanctions. Though neither the man's misreading of the woman's illocutionary intentions nor any other aspect of his conduct has transgressed the principle of freedom of expression, his overall course of action has arrantly transgressed the woman's right to bodily integrity. Only as a constituent of that overall course of action, and thus only as a constituent of the transgression of the woman's right to bodily integrity, is the man's misreading properly susceptible to any legal penalties. Neither as such a constituent nor in isolation is his misinterpretation at odds with the principle of freedom of expression.

A fortiori, nothing done by pornographers in the production and distribution of their repellent materials is at odds with that principle. Even if the marketing of those materials does incline some men to think that the negative replies of women to sexual overtures are positive replies, the harm diffusely and remotely caused by the vending of the materials is an increased incidence of sexual assaults and rapes. Pornography-encouraged misconstruals of women's illocutionary acts of refusal may be involved in the increased incidence of such crimes, but—as has just been contended—the misconstruals, either in isolation or as elements of the aforementioned crimes, are not violative of the principle of freedom of expression.

What is contravened by the men who commit sexual crimes on the basis of such misconstruals is a principle that invests each person with a right to bodily integrity, rather than a principle that invests each person with a right to freedom of expression.

Hence, if the phrase "free speech" in MacKinnon's and Langton's declarations is to be understood as referring to the principle of freedom of expression, those declarations go awry in suggesting that that principle is applied unequally to the benefit of men and to the detriment of women when the marketing of pornography is legally permitted. Though a policy of legally permitting the distribution of most types of pornography is indeed required under the principle of freedom of expression, the sustainment of such a policy does not detract at all from the protection conferred by that principle on the communicative activities of women. Accordingly, the discontinuation of the legal permissibility of most types of pornography would not expand at all the protection provided to women by the principle of freedom of expression. Untoward causal effects of the marketing of pornography can include the silencing of some women's efforts to reject sexual overtures; but, although such effects are serious wrongs which any system of governance is morally obligated to counter, they do not attenuate in range or robustness the protection extended by the principle of freedom of expression to women's communicative conduct. In short, when MacKinnon's and Langton's thesis about a conflict within liberty is explicated as a thesis about a conflict within the principle of freedom of expression, it is unsustainable. We should therefore move on to ascertain whether MacKinnon and Langton can successfully resort to either of the other two ways of explicating their claims about a conflict within liberty.

5.4.4.2 "Freedom of Expression" as Deontic Liberties and Normative Immunities

Instead of denoting a certain principle of political morality—the principle of freedom of expression—the phrase "free speech" in MacKinnon's and Langton's pronouncements might refer to the deontic liberties and normative immunities which are bestowed by that principle. When their pronouncements are elaborated along these lines, MacKinnon and Langton are claiming that legal norms and decisions which uphold the legal liberties and immunities of pornographers are thereby eliminating some of the legal liberties and immunities of women. Because the pornographers exercise their legal liberties to manufacture and distribute materials that induce some consumers of those materials to misinterpret women's rebuffs as acceptances, the removal of those legal liberties is necessary to ensure that women can exercise their own legal liberties to communicate their views and wishes on matters of great importance. Such is the message to be gleaned from MacKinnon's and Langton's assertions, if they are glossed in this second way.

However, as is indicated by the shift in the foregoing paragraph from a proposition about the elimination of liberties to a proposition about the effective exercise of those liberties, the thesis about a conflict within liberty is not salvageable in this second manner. When a system of governance adheres to the principle of freedom of expression by legally permitting the production and distribution of most types of pornography, it does not thereby deprive women of any legal liberties or immunities. Admittedly, some of the remote causal effects of the policy of legal tolerance might lessen the ability of some women to exercise certain legal liberties effectively. However, as has been emphasized in my opening chapter, abilities to exercise deontic liberties are physical liberties; whereas deontic liberties such as legal liberties are permissions, physical liberties are abilities. Ergo, although some of the remote causal effects of the marketing of pornography might eliminate certain physical freedoms or certain combinations of jointly exercisable physical freedoms that would otherwise be retained by women, those effects do not eliminate any of the legal freedoms held by women. Women are legally at liberty to communicate their views and feelings on sexual matters or other matters, even in circumstances where they have been foiled from exercising some of their legal liberties-to-communicate. Consequently, if the phrase "free speech" in the quotations from MacKinnon and Langton above is glossed as referring to legal liberties and immunities, their quoted statements about a conflict within liberty are untenable. So glossed, their statements would be equivocating as they proceed from premises about physical unfreedoms to conclusions about deontic unfreedoms—that is, from premises about the inability of women to exercise certain deontic liberties to conclusions about the non-existence of those deontic liberties. We should thus turn to the final main way in which the statements by MacKinnon and Langton might be construed, to see whether they fare any better with it.

5.4.4.3 "Freedom of Expression" as Physical Freedoms

If "free speech" or "freedom of expression" is construed as referring to physical freedoms—abilities—then the statements by MacKinnon and Langton are declaring that the absence of restrictions on the abilities of pornographers to manufacture and distribute their unsavory wares will detrimentally affect the abilities of women to communicate their thoughts and sentiments. In particular, many women will undergo the loss or erosion of their abilities to communicate rejections of sexual advances, as their words of refusal are frequently taken to be words of acceptance. Langton does seem to be talking about physical freedoms in her assertions which I have quoted near the outset of §5.4.4, and also in the following assertion which appears later in her book: "If pornography silences women, it presents a conflict within liberty itself, between pornographers' right to speak and women's. If pornography silences women, women will have difficulty fighting subordinating speech with speech of their own" (Langton 2009, 63). Here the concern seems to be not that women will lose their legal liberties-to-communicate if the marketing of pornographic materials is legally tolerated, but instead that women will lose some of their key *abilities* to communicate. Many of them will lose their abilities to communicate their unwillingness to engage in sexual intercourse, and they will furthermore lose their abilities to communicate any remonstrations that would contest the deleterious influence of pornography. These appear to be the effects that Langton has in mind when she writes about a "conflict within liberty itself," and they are probably also the effects envisaged by MacKinnon when she denounces the silencing of the free speech of women by the free speech of men.

In some clear respects, this third approach to MacKinnon's and Langton's pronouncements is more promising than either of the other two approaches. Though questions about the actuality of the effects broached in the preceding paragraph are fiendishly difficult empirical matters, the likelihood that some such effects arise from the marketing of pornography is quite high. Note, moreover, that worries about those effects are not dependent on the correctness of Langton's analysis of the silencing that might be brought about by pornography. Even if that silencing is better analyzed as perlocutionary frustration than as illocutionary disablement, any pornography-fostered increase in the incidence of the silencing is to be viewed with consternation. Indeed, precisely because that effect and other related effects are so dismaying, I have highlighted the need for vigorous governmental measures to avert or counter them.

What is more, this third version of MacKinnon's and Langton's declarations about a conflict within liberty is in accordance with a broader line of thought that has emerged from time to time in the philosophical and legal literature on freedom of expression. Cass Sunstein, for example, has proclaimed:

> [M]any content-neutral laws have content-differential effects. They do so because they operate against a backdrop that is not prepolitical or just. In light of an unjust status quo, rules that are content-neutral can have severe adverse effects on some forms of speech. Greater scrutiny of content-neutral restrictions is therefore appropriate. Above all, courts should attend to the possibility that seemingly neutral restrictions will have content-based effects. (Sunstein 1992, 296, footnotes omitted)

Of course, Sunstein is here concerned chiefly with the ways in which legal prohibitions that are not aimed at limiting communications qua communications can nonetheless impinge disproportionately on the communicative abilities of people in some disadvantaged groups. However, his basic point can be extrapolated to laws that permit certain activities which in turn impinge disproportionately on the aforementioned communicative abilities. Accordingly, when MacKinnon's and Langton's statements about a conflict within liberty are understood as referring primarily to physical freedoms, those statements are presenting a specific variant of the wide-ranging point made by Sunstein.

Still, although this third construal of MacKinnon's and Langton's assertions is in some respects more promising than the previous two interpretations, it does not succeed as a justification for outlawing the production and distribution of most types of pornography. MacKinnon, as the co-author of the municipal prohibition on the marketing of pornography in Indianapolis, has long striven for the outlawing of most types of pornographic materials. Admittedly, Langton—as has been observed already in this chapter—is somewhat more hesitant about the matter of legal bans. Immediately after the most recently quoted statement by her about the conflict within liberty, she writes as follows: "Does this give us reason for thinking that MacKinnon may be right, not only in the two claims considered [about subordination and silencing], but in her view that pornography should be restricted by law? Perhaps. Or perhaps we need independent argument to bridge the gap." However, Langton straightaway adds: "Such an argument is beyond my project here, but it may not be too hard to find" (2009, 63). Thus, we are proceeding germanely when we ponder whether MacKinnon's and Langton's remarks about a conflict within liberty can justify legal restrictions on the vending of pornography. Let us consider three main reasons why the answer to this question is negative.

First is a consideration which has been broached already and which will be developed at length in the concluding principal section of this chapter. Insofar as the marketing of pornography does eventuate in the silencing of women in any of the ways contemplated by this chapter, it does so as a result of the messages and values that are conveyed by pornographic materials. It does so, in other words, because of the communicative character and contents of those materials. Hence, if a legal prohibition on the sale of pornography is imposed for the purpose of protecting women from being silenced, its purpose is not communication-neutral; such a prohibition is aimed at the communicative character and contents of pornographic materials and is therefore incompatible with the principle of freedom of expression. In precisely this respect, a prohibition on the marketing of pornography differs from legal restrictions on the unruliness of hecklers and hostile audiences. Legal constraints of the latter kind are aimed at the disruptiveness of the behavior of the hecklers or hostile audiences. As has already been noted, the disruptiveness can occur through communicative conduct but can equally well occur through outright violence or noise-making or arson. Hence, legal curbs aimed at limiting the obstreperousness of hecklers can be communication-neutral and can thus be in compliance with the principle of freedom of expression. Not similarly in compliance with that principle are legal bans designed to squelch the distinctively communicative effects of pornographic materials.

Second, if the conflict within liberty to which MacKinnon and Langton advert is a conflict between the exercised physical freedoms of pornographers and the physical freedoms of women, it is one manifestation of a vast welter of such conflicts. This point has been suggested in the extract from Sunstein above. However, exactly because the problem of conflicts between physical liberties is sweepingly comprehensive rather than confined to one context or set of contexts, any efforts to come to grips with it through the imposition of legal curbs will give rise to imponderable difficulties. As has been repeatedly and powerfully emphasized by Larry Alexander in his book on freedom of expression (2005), all laws—laws whose purposes are communication-neutral as well as laws whose purposes are communication-focused—affect the communicational abilities of people, often in far-reaching ways. Alexander observes that "all laws affect what gets said, by whom, to whom, and with what effect. In short, all laws have what I shall call 'message effects'" (2005, 17, italics deleted). He writes:

> For example, laws determining who owns what property under what restrictions or the price and availability of various resources will also determine what gets said, by whom, to whom, and with what effect—that is, such laws will have message effects. A change in the law of any region of the corpus juris will have message effects. Laws equalizing income would surely have dramatic message effects. (17)

Any legal prohibitions introduced to address certain message effects will generate further message effects which in turn have to be addressed. As Alexander remarks:

> [A]ll laws have message effects – they affect what gets said, by whom, to whom, and with what effect ... [A] ... freedom of expression challenge to a law or group of laws is a demand that the laws be changed; but every change in the laws will have message effects, so that ... freedom of expression claims are always aligned against each other. Thus, testing challenged laws by the [prevailing standard for constitutionality] will entail testing all of their alternatives by that test. (18)

The point which Alexander advances here, and at a number of other junctures in his book, is that an approach to freedom of expression which tries to resolve conflicts between people's respective communicational abilities—by reference to egalitarian standards or other ideal standards—will land itself in utterly open-ended consequentialist calculations. Because the resolution of any of the multitudinous conflicts will affect the ways in which all the other conflicts are to be resolved, they all have to be tackled at once. The preposterousness of such an endeavor is familiar from the general philosophical literature on consequentialism (Finnis 1980, 111–18).

Third, as this chapter has already emphasized, the noxious effects that might ensue from the marketing of pornographic materials are to be averted or counteracted not through bans on most types of pornography but instead through a variety of educational measures and other measures. A system of governance is not fulfilling its moral responsibilities if it outlaws the distribution of most types of pornography, but it is likewise not fulfilling its moral responsibilities if it takes no adequate steps to cultivate and sustain an ethos of respect for the values of liberal democracy. Because some of those values (such as the ideal of human equality) are rebarbatively challenged in the films and books and magazines and photographs produced by pornographers, a system of governance that complies with its moral duty to promote the aforementioned ethos will be pitting itself against the manufacturers and vendors of pornography. However, it will be doing so not through legal restrictions—which would be at variance with the principle of freedom of expression—but instead through more speech, in the expansive sense of "more speech" that has been limned in §5.3.4.2.1 above. Hence, while adhering resolutely to the principle of freedom of expression which would be blatantly contravened by laws such as MacKinnon's anti-pornography ordinance, the overall operations of the system of governance envisaged here will be sustainedly addressed to the concerns that motivate such an ordinance.

5.5 Pornography and Freedom of Expression

In this final main section of Chapter 5, we should mull over the reasons why every system of governance is morally obligated to leave most types of pornography legally unrestricted. We should do so, moreover, with reference to the harms of subordination and silencing that might ensue from the widespread availability of pornography. Although this chapter has shown that Langton's claims about the illocutionary-constitutive subordination of women by pornography are untenable, it has allowed that the subordination of women through various perlocutionary effects of pornography (and various perlocutionary effects of some non-pornographic materials) might be occurring. Similarly, although this chapter has contested Langton's characterization of the silencing of women that might be induced by pornography, it has allowed that the silencing of women might indeed be induced in several ways by the production and distribution of pornographic materials. Given that these harmful effects of the availability of pornography might quite credibly materialize, why is the legal proscription of pornography not a measure that can legitimately be undertaken by any system of governance?

As has already been suggested in this chapter, the answer to this question lies in the fact that a legal prohibition on the marketing of pornography would not be communication-neutral. Indeed, it would not even be viewpoint-neutral. Such a prohibition would be aimed at pornographic materials qua modes of communication, and would thus be at odds with the principle of freedom of expression. Let us begin here by distinguishing this key point from a line of thought with which it might be conflated.

5.5.1 Easterbrook's Inadequate Rationale

In the judgment by the U.S. Seventh Circuit Court of Appeals that invalidated MacKinnon's anti-pornography ordinance in Indianapolis, Judge Easterbrook—as has already been noted in this chapter—accepted *arguendo* that the widespread availability of pornography in a society will tend to generate perlocutionary effects that exacerbate the incidence of sundry harms and indignities against women. In explaining why any ban on the marketing of pornographic materials would nonetheless be inconsistent with the First Amendment, Easterbrook declared: "Yet this simply demonstrates the power of pornography as speech. All of these unhappy effects depend on mental intermediation. Pornography affects how people see the world, their fellows, and social relations. If pornography is what pornography does, so is other speech" (*American Booksellers Association v Hudnut* 1985, 329).

Justified though the invalidation of the anti-pornography ordinance was, Easterbrook's rationale for the invalidation is badly misguided. As a matter of American constitutional law, the cardinal snag is that his rationale applies to numerous types of communications—such as fraud, libel, incitement, solicitation to crime, advertising of illegalities, perjury—that can be legally proscribed, and have been legally proscribed, in consistency with the First Amendment (Koppelman 1996, 234). All of those types of communications "depend on mental intermediation" for their "unhappy effects," yet none of them is shielded by the First Amendment against being outlawed. As a matter of political philosophy, equally, the rationale articulated by Easterbrook is misconceived. As has been argued in Chapter 3, legal restrictions on the types of communications just listed are consistent not only with the First Amendment but also with the moral principle of freedom of expression. My discussions in that earlier chapter will help to shed light here on why the marketing of pornographic materials is not similarly susceptible to being banned, for the considerations adduced there in support of legal prohibitions are not applicable to pornography. Unlike the justification invoked by Easterbrook, the considerations from Chapter 3 will enable us to discern why the principle of freedom of expression shields pornography against legal curbs while leaving perjury and incitement and fraud unshielded. A focus on the involvement of mental intermediation—a focus on something that is involved in the unhappy effects of perjury and incitement and fraud as much as in the unhappy effects of pornography—would leave utterly mysterious these differences in the protection conferred by the principle of freedom of expression.

5.5.2 Directness and Proximity versus Diffuseness and Remoteness

As has been suggested already in this chapter and in earlier chapters, the pivotal question to be addressed is whether the marketing of pornography can be legally forbidden in a communication-neutral manner. If the only purposes credibly ascribable to legal bans on the production and distribution of pornographic materials would be directed against the communicative character or contents of those materials, then such bans would contravene the principle of freedom of expression. Now, given the types of harms that might credibly be occurring partly as a result of the widespread availability of pornography, the answer to the pivotal question about communication-neutrality is negative. Any law that proscribes the production or distribution of pornographic materials would fail to be communication-neutral or even content-neutral. Consequently, any such law would violate the principle of freedom of expression. (Recall here that child pornography and any pornographic materials produced through violent coercion are outside the scope of my discussion.)

Although the harms that might credibly arise partly as a result of the availability of pornographic materials would be due to perlocutionary effects induced by those materials, that fact alone is scarcely sufficient to establish that the materials in question cannot properly be outlawed. After all, the mental intermediation highlighted by Easterbrook is what speech-act theorists have labeled as "perlocutionary effects." Yet, as has been observed, the fact that the harmful consequences of various types of communications cannot occur without mental intermediation is not per se something that morally exempts those types of communications from being legally forbidden. An additional factor is needed.

To answer the pivotal question that has been posed above, we have to consider the additional question whether the distribution of pornography constitutes wrongdoing that is communication-independent. Now, although this additional question refers to the constituting of *wrongdoing*, the connection to *harm* does not have to be constitutive; it can be causal. Indeed, for most types of communicative conduct about which the additional question might be asked (*mutatis mutandis*), the connection to harm will indeed be causal rather than constitutive.

Consider a striking example propounded by Jed Rubenfeld.[36] Suppose that Timothy maintains a lookout while his three partners in crime enter a bank to commit an armed robbery. When Timothy notices that several police cars are approaching, he uses a mobile phone or a walkie-talkie to inform his colleagues that they should exit the bank as rapidly as they can. His imparting of this information constitutes his participation in the armed robbery of a bank, which is a very serious type of wrongdoing that can legitimately be outlawed. In any typical circumstances the purpose of legally forbidding Timothy's conduct is not focused on the fact that the conduct is communicative, but is instead focused on the fact that his conduct constitutes his participation in an armed robbery. As Rubenfeld writes: "[T]hrough [his] speech, [Timothy] participated in a prohibited (and prohibitable) course of conduct. So long as the state bans bank robbery in general, it can constitutionally punish everyone who participates in a bank robbery—including people who participate in a bank robbery *through words*" (2001, 828, emphasis in original). At

[36] Rubenfeld 2001, 828. See also Schauer 2019a, 42–3. Many similarly striking examples are probed in Greenawalt 1989.

the moment, we should simply note that Timothy's conduct is causally rather than constitutively connected to any harm that it helps to bring about. What is constituted by his conduct is his direct participation in an instance of serious wrongdoing that can legitimately be proscribed on communication-neutral grounds.

Thus, instead of concentrating chiefly on the distinction between the constituting of harm and the causing of harm, we should be concentrating on a distinction between direct participation in legally actionable misconduct and diffuse or remote involvement in such misconduct. Let us recall that a classic way of drawing this latter distinction, specifically in connection with the difference between incitement and advocacy, was articulated by the U.S. Supreme Court in the landmark case of *Brandenburg v Ohio* (1969). As has been recounted in Chapter 2, the *Brandenburg* Court laid down the following standard for differentiating between constitutionally protected advocacy and constitutionally unprotected incitement:

> [T]he constitutional guarantees of free speech and free press do not permit a State to forbid or proscribe advocacy of the use of force or of law violation except where such advocacy is directed to inciting or producing imminent lawless action and is likely to incite or produce such action. (*Brandenburg v Ohio* 1969, 447)

As Chapter 2 has remarked, three elements are central to the U.S. Supreme Court's conception of incitement. The communicated statements are *intended* to bring about unlawful activity, and they are *likely* to bring about such activity, and the activity in question is *imminent* rather than temporally distant. Rubenfeld aptly encapsulates the significance of the *Brandenburg* standard: "What is decisive about the *Brandenburg* formulation is that it allows speech to be prohibited not because of its harmfulness, but because the speaker seeks there and then to bring about a particularized, prohibited, and prohibitable course of conduct" (2001, 827, italics omitted). As he adds, with reference to the three elements that are integral to the *Brandenburg* criterion for incitement: "When someone *intentionally* uses speech to bring about *imminent* unlawful conduct, and it is *likely* that this result will ensue, he is properly treated as having engaged himself in, as having participated in, that course of conduct."[37]

Of course, the appropriate interpretation of each of the main elements in the *Brandenburg* standard—especially of the second and third elements—will to some extent be a context-specific matter. For example, although the feature of imminence will often consist in virtual immediacy, it can sometimes extend over longer periods. Suppose for instance that a Christian priest delivers an incendiary sermon in a community where antisemitic bigotry is widespread. In the sermon, the priest alleges that the Jewish inhabitants of the community have mistreated Christian

[37] Rubenfeld 2001, 828, emphases in original. See also Rubenfeld 2002b, 758.

children ghoulishly, and he invokes the closing portion of Luke 22:36 ("And let him who has no sword sell his mantle and buy one") in support of his call for retaliatory measures. Although the priest's tirade does not trigger any immediate pogroms—because the tirade is followed by other portions of the Christian ceremony over which the priest presides, and because the residences of Jews are at a distance from the church—it does result in several attacks against Jews later in the day and during the evening. In this situation, the *Brandenburg* requirement of imminence has been met. By intentionally instigating the pogroms in circumstances where the instigation was likely to be effective, the priest has involved himself directly as a participant in those hideous attacks. His inflammatory preaching would not be protected by the First Amendment to the American Constitution, and it is not protected by the principle of freedom of expression.[38]

5.5.3 The Status of Pornography

For the current chapter's enquiry into the status of pornography, then, we need to ask whether the activities of pornographers in producing and marketing their wares are so closely connected to properly criminalizable misconduct that the pornographers can correctly be classified as participants in the misconduct. If the answer to this question were affirmative, then the production and distribution of pornographic materials could credibly be outlawed in a communication-neutral fashion—since misconduct is properly criminalizable only if it can credibly be outlawed on communication-independent grounds. In other words, if the answer to this question were affirmative, then some legal bans on the production and marketing of pornographic materials could credibly be aimed not at the communicative character or contents of those materials but instead at their roles as components of communication-independent misconduct.

In fact, however, the answer to this question is negative. Neither the possible role of the dissemination of pornography in bringing about the subordination of women nor the possible role of the dissemination of pornography in bringing about the silencing of women is sufficient to warrant the classification of pornographers as participants in the serious wrongs that might be encouraged by their products. Probably none of the requirements in the *Brandenburg* standard is satisfied, but we should concentrate here on the requirement of imminence or proximity.

On the one hand, as has already been sketched, this requirement can sometimes be fulfilled even if the wrongdoing that is fostered by certain utterances does not

[38] Thus, contrary to what is suggested by Peter Molnar (2012, 194), some utterances in extreme circumstances are properly classifiable as incitement even though "the hearers cannot act in the very place where they are under the direct influence of the inciting speech." Indeed, Molnar himself goes on to report such an example of incitement (2012, 194–5) – though the incident which he describes is perhaps better classified as an example of solicitation to commit a crime.

occur immediately after those utterances. Similarly, the requirement of imminence or proximity can sometimes be fulfilled even without any geographical propinquity between the people whose utterances set some wrongdoing afoot and the people who carry out the subsequent stages of the wrongdoing under the influence of those utterances. Especially in an age of high-speed electronic communications, someone can participate directly in wrongdoing that takes place many miles away.

On the other hand, even though temporal immediacy and geographical closeness are not always indispensable for the subsumability of utterances into communication-independent wrongdoing, any causal links that might arise between the activities of pornographers and the subordination or silencing of women are far too tenuous for any such subsumability. Reprehensible though the activities of the manufacturers and distributors of hard-core pornography are, those activities are not direct components of any serious communication-independent misdeeds—such as rapes or sexual assaults—that might ultimately be inspired by the products of those activities. Were such products to be outlawed, the legal proscription of them would not credibly be aimed at them qua elements of serious communication-independent misconduct; instead, it would be aimed at them qua communications which might prompt (or which have prompted) the perpetration of such misconduct. Accordingly, the imposition of a legal ban on the production or distribution of pornographic materials would transgress the principle of freedom of expression.

5.5.4 Points of Contrast

To see why the requirement of imminence or proximity is not met, we should contrast the activities of pornographers with the modes of behavior depicted in a few scenarios that are broached by Langton. First is a very brief scenario invoked by Langton in a somewhat different context. Echoing MacKinnon (1987, 156), Langton portrays a situation in which the handler of a ferocious guard dog utters the instruction "Kill" in order to impel the dog to attack somebody else (Langton 2009, 105). In the present context, let us assume that the handler issues his instruction despite the fact that he has no legitimate reason—such as the defense of himself or of other people—for doing so. In that event, his utterance amounts to very serious misconduct that can properly be outlawed on communication-neutral grounds. An apt prohibition on such an utterance will be aimed at it not as an instance of communication but instead as the wielding of deadly force. The wrongful wielding of such force can legitimately be proscribed, even when it occurs through an utterance rather than through some non-communicative act such as the pulling of a trigger or the lighting of a fuse. Though some instances of communication fall within the scope of a ban on the wrongful plying of lethal force, their inclusion in that scope is entirely consistent with the principle of freedom of expression; they are included not because of their communicative character but because of what they have in common with non-communicative instances of the wrongful plying of lethal force. What makes this scenario of the dog handler so straightforward is that it so obviously satisfies the requirements laid down by the *Brandenburg* standard. There is virtually no interval between the utterance by the handler and the fatal attack by the dog which the utterance designedly instigates.

Second, Langton twice refers to a scenario which I have broached in some of my previous chapters: namely, John Stuart Mill's vignette about a firebrand speaker who venomously delivers an oration to a mob gathered outside the home of a corn-dealer (Langton 2009, 86–7, 306). Whipping up the fury of his audience, the speaker declaims to them about the exploitativeness of corn-dealers that is the source of their economic woes. As has long been recognized, Mill's vignette depicts a paradigmatic instance of incitement. Differentiating between incitement and mere advocacy is precisely the point of the *Brandenburg* criterion, and all the features specified by that criterion are straightforwardly present in Mill's scenario. Like the interval between the issuance of the instruction by the dog handler and the attack by the dog, the interval between the harangue of the orator and the rampaging of the mob is so brief as to be virtually non-existent.

Third, when seeking to recount how the circulation of pornographic materials in a society can silence women, Langton adverts more than once to the drowning out of speakers by hecklers (2009, 66, 72, 101). She declares: "On the feminist argument [about silencing], pornography acts like the heckler" (66). However, as has already been remarked in this chapter and in Chapter 2, heckling that disrupts the delivery of a speech by somebody else is very different from the marketing of pornography. Such heckling is only incidentally communicative, for it can equally effectively take the form of violence or of sheer noise-making with cacophonous machinery. Moreover, the link between the conduct of the heckler and the silencing of the harried speaker is virtually instantaneous. Heckling is a highly focused and direct way of bringing about the wrongful result for which it is undertaken. Although the *Brandenburg* standard is concerned specifically with incitement rather than with heckling, the requirements propounded in that standard are patently fulfilled by any disruptive instance of heckling.

Fourth, again in connection with her thesis that pornography tends to bring about the silencing of women, Langton refers several times to the set of facts in the infamous 1975 English case of *DPP v Morgan*.[39] After a night of drinking, the defendant invited three colleagues home with him to engage in sexual intercourse with his wife. He told them that his wife enjoyed being overpowered by her sexual partners and that they should not heed any ostensible refusals or protests on her part. When the men reached the defendant's home, they all proceeded to rape his

[39] See Langton 2009, 71–2, 254 n28; 2011, 431. See also Antony 2011, 399.

wife and to disregard her vigorous resistance. Although in actuality the defendant himself along with his colleagues engaged in forcible intercourse with his wife, we should suppose here counterfactually that his only role in the despicable proceedings consisted in inviting his friends and in misinforming them about his wife's sexual predilections. Even so, he was clearly a full participant throughout. With his invitation and misinformation and encouragement, he brought about the multiple rapes of his wife in a manner that unequivocally satisfied the requirements in the *Brandenburg* criterion. He intended to induce those rapes, and he made their imminent occurrence highly likely. His words, like the wrongful issuance of the instruction "Kill" to the guard dog by the handler, were unprotected by the principle of freedom of expression. In each case, the words were subsumed into the wrongs provoked by them.

5.5.5 Back to Pornography

With the foregoing quartet of scenarios in mind as points of contrast, we should return to mulling over the status of pornography. As should be apparent, the connections between the marketing of pornography and the perpetration of sexual assaults are far more tenuous than the connections between speech and prohibitable wrongdoing in any of the four vignettes above. This conclusion is especially obvious in relation to the situation of heckling, where the disruptive jeering is itself the serious misconduct. However, it is nearly as obvious in relation to each of the other situations, where the causal ties between speech and serious misconduct are highly direct and focused.

Nothing comparable ensues from the production and distribution of pornographic films and magazines. Indeed, unless we suspend the third *Brandenburg* requirement—the requirement of imminence or proximity—we cannot plausibly maintain that the second *Brandenburg* requirement, the requirement of likelihood, is met by the production and distribution of pornographic materials. Empirical studies might eventually show conclusively that, in some societies, the widespread availability of pornography is responsible for increased levels of very serious misconduct such as rapes and sexual assaults. However, such studies will be charting the effects of long-term operations involving a multitude of activities by diffuse producers and marketers of pornographic materials. The studies will not be showing that any particular activities of those producers and marketers are aimed at giving rise to imminent instances of the misconduct just mentioned. Yet the intentional generation of a high likelihood of imminent wrongdoing is what is required under the *Brandenburg* standard. Since the standard laid down by the *Brandenburg* judgment is not only a precept of American constitutional law but is also a corollary of the moral principle of freedom of expression, the conclusion follows that legal bans on most types of pornography are in contravention of that moral principle.

Proponents of such bans are apt to think that an insistence on conformity to the *Brandenburg* standard bespeaks a naively inadequate conception of causation. We shall encounter such an allegation by Waldron in my next chapter, when we examine his attempt to vindicate legal curbs on the expression of hatefully bigoted sentiments. However, as we shall see there, he draws upon MacKinnon's work at that very juncture in his theorizing. MacKinnon does indeed inveigh against the understanding of causation which she imputes to the opponents of her stance on the matter of pornography. As we approach the close of this chapter, we should ponder a lengthy quotation from her complaints about that understanding of causation:

> First Amendment logic, like nearly all legal reasoning, has difficulty grasping harm that is not linearly caused in the "John hit Mary" sense ... Notice that the specific idea of causality used in obscenity law dates from around the time that it was first "proved" that it is impossible to prove that pornography causes harm ... [T]he view became that pornography must cause harm the way negligence causes car accidents or its effects are not cognizable as harm. The trouble with this individuated, atomistic, linear, isolated, tortlike—in a word, positivistic—conception of injury is that the way pornography targets and defines women for abuse and discrimination does not work like this. It does hurt individuals, not *as* individuals in a one-at-a-time sense, but as members of the group "women." Harm is caused to one individual woman rather than another essentially the way one number rather than another is caused in roulette. But on a group basis, as women, the selection process is absolutely selective and systematic. Its causality is essentially collective and totalistic and contextual. To reassert atomistic linear causality as a sine qua non of injury—you cannot be harmed unless you are harmed through this etiology—is to refuse to respond to the true nature of this specific kind of harm. (MacKinnon 1987, 156–7, emphasis in original)

MacKinnon speculates that the conception of causality which she deplores has been embraced by defenders of the First Amendment in order to ensure that gender-based inequalities cannot be redressed through constitutionally valid laws (157).

As should be manifest from the present chapter and from earlier chapters in this book, MacKinnon's broadsides are misdirected. When champions of the principle of freedom of expression adhere to the *Brandenburg* standard as they gauge whether certain communicative activities can legitimately be outlawed, they are not exhibiting a pre-modern mentality. Even less are they engaging in a sinister and unavowed endeavor to perpetuate gender-based inequalities. Rather, they are giving effect to the principle of freedom of expression by insisting that communicative activities cannot legitimately be banned qua communicative activities. Any legitimate prohibition on such activities has to be directed at them qua serious misconduct whose wrongness is communication-independent. An anti-pornography law of the kind advocated by MacKinnon is not legitimate, then.

Such a law is aimed at the cumulative effects of pornographic materials in forming and reinforcing an ethos of male domination and female subordination. As that ethos becomes and remains ensconced in a society, its influence on the outlooks of men will incline many of them to perpetrate or countenance sexual wrongdoing. Although the instances of such wrongdoing are hardly ever discretely traceable to items of pornography that have been intended and likely to bring about the wrongdoing imminently, a high or increased aggregate level of such misconduct can be traceable to the role of pornographic materials in cumulatively poisoning the attitudes and beliefs that are widely harbored among the men in a society where those materials are prevalently available. To arrest and reverse that cumulative poisoning, legal constraints should be imposed on the production and distribution of pornography. Such is the approach for which MacKinnon is arguing in the lengthy passage quoted above. Let us leave aside the difficulties of substantiating the large-scale empirical claims which she makes in support of her approach. Even so, the fatal problem is that she is calling for the proscription of pornographic enterprises qua communicative activities. After all, the noxious effects which she associates with the marketing of pornography derive from the messages and values that are communicated by pornographic materials to the consumers of those materials. The cumulative poisoning of men's outlooks is due to the cumulative dissemination of those warped messages and values by the manufacturers and distributors of pornography. Hence, to advocate the imposition of legal curbs on the production and vending of pornography—where the purpose of the curbs is to halt the aforementioned cumulative poisoning—is to advocate the imposition of such curbs on communicative endeavors qua communicative endeavors. Any such approach is squarely at odds with the principle of freedom of expression. Not only does it fail to be communication-neutral; it likewise fails even to be viewpoint-neutral.

By contrast, communicative activities that do fall under the ambit of the *Brandenburg* standard are susceptible to being proscribed in a communication-neutral fashion. Such activities are subsumed into the very serious misconduct which they are intended to induce imminently. They can legitimately be forbidden as the opening stages of such misconduct. Somebody who engages in any of those activities is rightly classifiable as a participant in the wrongdoing which he instigates, and his conduct can thus appropriately be subjected to legal sanctions just as much as can the conduct of the other participants in that wrongdoing. The fact that he participates through utterances (like the bank robber whose task is to issue a warning when the police are coming) is incidental; what is decisive for his susceptibility to legal sanctions is his having participated directly in very serious misconduct. That feature of his behavior distinguishes him from pornographers, who are not similarly participants in the misdeeds that might ultimately be inspired by some of their wares. Though an inciter's provocations can aptly be outlawed as very serious misconduct whose wrongness is communication-independent, the rationale for any ban on the materials produced and distributed by pornographers would be aimed precisely at the communicative contents of those materials. Consequently, whereas the outlawing of the provocations can be in accordance with the principle of freedom of expression, the outlawing of pornographic materials cannot.

In short, notwithstanding MacKinnon's emphatic assertions to the contrary, an insistence on the *Brandenburg* standard by defenders of the principle of freedom of expression is attributable neither to a naïve conception of causation nor to any nefarious countenancing of gender-centered inequities. Rather, it is attributable to one's determination to implement the principle of freedom of expression by differentiating between communicative activities that are aptly prohibitable on communication-neutral grounds and communicative activities that are not credibly prohibitable on any such grounds. The justification for adherence to the principle of freedom of expression itself by any system of governance has been supplied in Chapter 4, and that justification is operative in the context of debates over pornography as much as in other contexts.

This chapter should close by emphasizing afresh that, instead of being bound up with any condonation of gender-based injustices, a satisfactory defense of the principle of freedom of expression is bound up with an insistence on measures to combat and avert such injustices (and other injustices). The rationale for upholding that principle—a rationale focused on the paramount moral responsibility of every system of governance to bring about the political and social and economic conditions under which everyone can be warranted in harboring an ample sense of self-respect—is incompatible with connivance at the subordination or silencing of women. Any system of governance that operates in conformity to that rationale will not only tolerate the production and distribution of most types of pornography, but will also strive to prevent or remedy any baneful effects that might result from the widespread availability of pornography. It will strive to counter the values and messages that are conveyed by hard-core pornographic materials. Far from exhibiting any inconsistency or befuddlement, the adoption of this combination of approaches by a system of governance is essential for the system's upholding of the precepts of liberal democracy.

6
Hatred, Dignity, and Freedom of Expression

Having examined at length some powerful feminist arguments that may have seemed to tell in favor of legal restrictions on the vending of pornography, we should now scrutinize a sustained line of reasoning by Jeremy Waldron in favor of legal restrictions on the expression of hateful sentiments. Whereas Rae Langton and other feminist philosophers have in recent years turned their attention to hateful utterances as much as to pornography, the insights which they have marshaled from the philosophy of language do not figure prominently in Waldron's *The Harm in Hate Speech* (2012). Indeed, the only feminist theorist with whom Waldron engages in that volume is Catharine MacKinnon. Instead of drawing sustainedly on the philosophy of language for his approach to the problem of hatefully bigoted forms of communication, he draws chiefly on political philosophy and on legal and political theory. His approach is marked particularly by his concern with "political aesthetics"—namely, a concentration on the visual and aural and tactile appearances of a society. Waldron contends that the appearance of a society is disfigured by expressions of hateful attitudes in public settings, especially when the expressions are durably present as signs or recordings or statues or Web sites or other such lasting encapsulations of bigotry. Though the ugliness of the disfigurement is partly aesthetic, it is predominantly ethical; the presence of such items in public settings will have undermined a political community's provision of a major public good that is central to the very decency of the community. That public good consists in the assurance supplied (mainly implicitly) to every reasonably law-abiding member of the community that he or she is fully entitled to pursue his or her daily activities and long-run objectives on the same basic terms as everyone else. Such an assurance is weakened if not destroyed by the proliferation of hateful displays. Consequently, Waldron maintains, laws that prohibit certain types of bigoted utterances can be justified in a liberal democracy as means of preserving the vital public good which those utterances would cumulatively subvert.

This chapter will examine Waldron's reasoning in some depth, in order to impugn his general conclusion and many of his specific conclusions. Before we turn to peruse the details of his arguments, however, we should take account of some points that are not at issue in my resistance to his positions. Readers who are not already conversant with the principle of freedom of expression could easily gain from Waldron's book a highly misleading impression of that principle. Thus, to try to forestall any such misleading impression, this chapter will begin its critique of

Freedom of Expression as Self-Restraint. Matthew H. Kramer, Oxford University Press (2021). © Matthew H. Kramer.
DOI: 10.1093/oso/9780198868651.003.0006

Waldron with a preliminary section aimed at making clear that certain propositions are not genuinely in dispute between him and his opponents.

6.1 Points Not in Controversy

By averting some possible misapprehensions about what is in contention between Waldron and his opponents, this chapter can then proceed to home in more effectively on the actual points of contention.

6.1.1 Fighting Words and True Threats

As has been observed in §5.3.4.2.1 of Chapter 5, Mary Kate McGowan has explicitly submitted that expletive-laced racist diatribes directed against particular individuals at close range are viewed by liberals as protected modes of communication under the First Amendment to the American Constitution. Waldron does not advance any explicit suggestion along those same lines, but conversely he does not make any effort to inform his readers that diatribes of the kind just mentioned are not at issue between himself and his opponents. Such harangues are not at issue, because the outlawing of them can be fully consistent both with the First Amendment and with the moral principle of freedom of expression. A racist tirade directed against some particular individual(s) at close range will normally be classifiable as "fighting words" or as a "true threat" and will therefore not be legally protected by the First Amendment or morally protected by the principle of freedom of expression. As has been remarked in Chapters 3 and 5, such an outburst is unprotected because it constitutes an attempt to provoke a violent scuffle or because it constitutes an attempt to place someone else in fear of the immediate infliction of a violent attack. An attempt of either of those kinds can occur through non-communicative conduct as well as through communicative conduct; hence, when such an attempt does occur through communicative conduct, it can nonetheless be subject to legal sanctions on communication-independent grounds. It is legitimately proscribable because of the wrong-making properties which it shares with non-communicative instances of the crime or tort which it constitutes.

Though Waldron does not expressly allege that liberal defenders of the principle of freedom of expression would resist the imposition of legal sanctions for misconduct of the sort just delineated, he likewise does not expressly affirm that the defenders of that principle would in fact readily countenance the imposition of such sanctions. Moreover, some passages in his book could easily incline unwary readers to infer that the hateful utterances protected by the First Amendment and by the principle of freedom of expression do include philippics that are properly classifiable as "fighting words" or as "true threats." For example, Waldron at one juncture recalls an eloquently poignant comment made by Lyndon Johnson at the time when Johnson was prevailing upon the U.S. Congress to enact major civil-rights legislation:

> David Bromwich once quoted a remark that President Lyndon Johnson made in response to a question about the moral necessity of the 1964 Civil Rights Act. The president's response? "A man has a right not to be insulted in front of his children." It is a telling image of the ugliness and distress that the details of discrimination inflict upon people; and it is security against interactions of this kind in the ordinary dailiness of life, as much as the upholding of any grander constitutional right, that is at stake when we ask about the assurances that a well-ordered society holds out for its citizens. (Waldron 2012, 84, endnotes omitted)

Waldron adds that the assurances to which he here refers—assurances which he believes to be dependent on the operativeness of laws that prohibit hatefully bigoted utterances—will have supplied the requisite "security ... for each person's proper pride and dignity against the soul-shriveling humiliation that a discriminatory rebuff can give rise to" (84).

When Waldron writes in these quoted statements about being insulted in front of one's children and being subjected to the humiliation of discriminatory rebuffs, he conveys the impression that torrents of individually targeted invective delivered at close range are among the utterances which the introduction of hate-speech laws will newly proscribe. (Alternatively or additionally, he conveys the impression that the newly proscribed utterances will include forms of communication that are constitutive of acts of discrimination. Such forms of communication are discussed in my next subsection.) Let it be noted, then, that most instances of individually targeted racist invective delivered at close range are already subject to being legally prohibited under the category of "fighting words" or "true threats." To be sure, if the legal constraints on such utterances were imposed by the hate-speech statutes which Waldron commends, the constraints would contravene both the First Amendment and the moral principle of freedom of expression—because statutes of that sort, at least as they have typically been interpreted and applied, are not communication-neutral or even viewpoint-neutral. Nevertheless, utterances that constitute fighting words or true threats can legitimately be prohibited by laws that are communication-neutral. Such laws, both in their purposes and in their implementation, would be aimed at those utterances on the communication-neutral grounds that have been sketched in the opening paragraph of this subsection. Thus, given that those utterances can be outlawed in accordance with the principle of freedom of expression (and in accordance with the First Amendment), their susceptibility to being outlawed is not at issue between Waldron and me. Anyone who mulls over Waldron's arguments for hate-speech statutes should always keep in mind that such statutes are not necessary for the imposition of legal restrictions on fighting words and true threats. A liberal-democratic system of governance should impose communication-neutral legal restrictions on those utterances while eschewing Waldron's hate-speech statutes.

6.1.2 Acts of Discrimination

Although Waldron acknowledges at a few junctures that the principles of liberal democracy are fully consistent with legal curbs on acts of racial or ethnic or religious discrimination in public and commercial services, he occasionally writes as though liberals believe that utterances constitutive of acts of discrimination are somehow exempt from legal curbs. Of course, the distinction between utterances that are constitutive of such acts and utterances that are not so constitutive is sometimes quite fine and is often heavily context-specific. Consider, for example, a sign mentioned by Waldron: "Muslims Out" (2012, 59). Displayed by a bigot who is marching in a political rally or strolling in a public square, the sign would be protected by the First Amendment and by the principle of freedom of expression. Reprehensible though such a sign clearly is, it would not legitimately be subject to legal proscription in such circumstances. In those circumstances, the bigot would be advocating discrimination rather than practicing discrimination. By contrast, if such a sign is posted on the door of a shop to indicate that Muslims will not be served or will not be allowed to enter, the posting of the sign is an act of discrimination that can legitimately be subjected to penalties under an antidiscrimination law. Though the display of the sign is of course an instance of communicative conduct, a legitimate prohibition on it will be aimed at the wrong-making properties which that display has in common with non-communicative acts of discrimination. Such a prohibition is communication-neutral and is therefore straightforwardly in keeping with the principle of freedom of expression.[1]

Similar points apply to other signs mentioned by Waldron: "No Blacks Allowed" and "Christians Only" (2012, 59). Though there are some contexts in which such signs would not be constitutive of acts of discrimination, they would be so constitutive in most credible contexts in which they might be posted. Waldron specifically adverts to shops and hotels as places where "Christians Only" signs used to be posted in parts of the United States to indicate that Jews would not be served as customers. Were those signs to be displayed in such places nowadays, they would rightly be open to sanctions under applicable antidiscrimination laws.[2]

[1] For a failure to recognize this point, see Suk 2012, 147, 148 n14.

[2] Even when "Christians Only" signs are constitutive of acts of discrimination, there are some contexts in which the discrimination is not properly susceptible to legal sanctions. For example, such a sign might appear at the entrance of a portion of a church that is reserved for Christian believers. Unlike a shop or a hotel or a governmental agency, a church should not be subjected to legal penalties for practicing religious discrimination of this kind. However, the moral basis for exempting the sign in those

Waldron quite plainly thinks that liberal defenders of the principle of freedom of expression believe that any signs which announce practices of bigoted discrimination are themselves exempt from legal restrictions. In the following passage, which should be quoted in full, he employs free indirect discourse to encapsulate what he takes to be the liberal view of this matter:

> Of course, if the racist appearances correspond to a racist reality, then things are different. If the signs saying "Christians Only"—or, in the more [discreet] form that used to be seen in Miami, "Churches Nearby"—are accompanied by discriminatory practice against Jews, then there *is* something to worry about. Or if Muslims are actually beaten up in the street, if minority members are not protected against the discrimination advocated in racist posters, or if those in power treat people in the unequal and degrading ways that the racist leaflets call for—*that* would show that the society was not well-ordered. But if it's just signage, they [the defenders of the principle of freedom of expression] say, there is nothing to worry about. And even if we act against the discrimination, the beatings, and the inequality, still—they will add—we should leave the signage in place.

One remarkable and dismaying feature of this passage will receive attention later in this chapter: namely, the way in which Waldron resorts to phrases such as "there is nothing to worry about" in order to discredit his opponents by suggesting that an insistence on liberal toleration is a stance of feckless indifference or condonation. At the moment, we should concentrate instead on the untenability of the distinction which Waldron tries to draw in this excerpt. If a bigoted sign is displayed in a context in which it constitutes an act of invidious discrimination, its constituting of such an act is independent of whether it is combined with further discriminatory practices. Suppose for example that a "No Blacks Allowed" or "Christians Only" sign has been affixed to the entrance of a shop or hotel or bus, and suppose that black people or identifiably Jewish or Islamic people would be served as customers if they were to disregard the sign and seek entry. Even so, the displaying of the sign in such circumstances is an act of discrimination that can legitimately be subjected to sanctions under an antidiscrimination law. It constitutes an effort to keep certain people—singled out on grounds of race or religion—from making use of a commercial service that is open to the public. Such an effort is an act of discrimination, whether or not it is backed up by further invidious steps that are likewise aimed at keeping out the disfavored people. Waldron is quite wrong in thinking that liberal defenders of the principle of freedom of expression would hold that such a sign is exempt from legal restrictions. (Waldron in the quoted passage could conceivably

circumstances from such penalties is not the principle of freedom of expression; rather, it is the principle of freedom of association coupled with the principle of freedom of religion.

be read as invoking the distinction which I have drawn in the opening paragraph of this subsection, between contexts where bigoted signs are constitutive of acts of discrimination and contexts where such signs are not so constitutive. However, the extract is much more readily construable as distinguishing instead between any bigoted signs that are constitutive of acts of discrimination and any further invidious practices that would give effect to those signs.)

Contrary to what Waldron later states in a somewhat different context, the point here is not that the "concerns of this kind [about discrimination] must be able to prevail over First Amendment considerations" (Waldron 2012, 117). That way of framing the matter is redolent of the consequentialism which permeates Waldron's approach to the problem of hateful utterances. Waldron believes that the importance of combating racist discrimination has to be balanced against the importance of upholding the freedom of people to express themselves, and that the former desideratum should sometimes be deemed to outweigh the latter. We shall return hereafter to his consequentialism and his attendant emphasis on balancing. At present, what should be underscored—in line with the patterns of argumentation in my previous chapters—is that I have not engaged in consequentialist balancing at all when I affirm that there can be morally legitimate prohibitions on any signs that are constitutive of acts of invidious discrimination. Rather, a prohibition on such signs can be morally legitimate because it can be communication-neutral; when a law that forbids such signs is indeed legitimate, it is aimed at them not as instances of communication but as instances of discrimination. Although a bigoted sign designed to exclude certain people from public or commercial services is of course communicative, its characteristics for which it can legitimately be banned are those which it shares with non-communicative instances of discriminatory exclusion. Hence, there is no occasion for the consequentialist balancing which Waldron envisions. When a legal ban is directed against racist or antisemitic signs qua acts of discrimination rather than qua acts of communication, it is entirely consistent with the principle of freedom of expression. Moreover, contrary to what Waldron contends, a liberal defender of the principle of freedom of expression will readily accept that such signs can constitute prohibitable acts of discrimination even when the signs are not combined with further exclusionary practices.

6.1.3 Targeted Harassment

An extended series of communicative interactions by somebody with someone else can amount to proscribable harassment even if no single communication within the series has amounted to "fighting words" or a "true threat." If the persistent communicative interactions are denigratory or importunate, and if they are targeted at some particular individual(s), they can legitimately be subjected to legal restrictions. Such restrictions are consistent with the principle of freedom of expression if the purpose that underlies them is communication-neutral. Underlain by such a purpose, the restrictions are aimed at the communicative interactions not qua instances of communication but qua instances of targeted harassment. Those interactions are susceptible to being legally curbed because of the features which they have in common with non-communicative instances of harassing behavior.

Targeted harassment is especially a problem in settings where multiple encounters are highly probable, such as workplaces or schools or universities or small neighborhoods. In many such settings, a spirit of camaraderie or collaborative cohesion is vital for the attainment of various institutional objectives. Particularly in these settings, though also more broadly, people can legitimately be required to refrain from behavior—whether the behavior be communicative or non-communicative—that is likely to make the addressees of the behavior reasonably feel that they are being singled out for sustained persecution or for unwanted sexual attentions or for other forms of mistreatment that are apt to overwhelm those addressees with the sense of being under siege.

When targeted harassment occurs in the workings of institutions like those mentioned above, it is usually best handled through the disciplinary procedures and mechanisms of the institutions themselves.[3] However, when cases of harassment are severe, and when they have not been adequately remedied through the aforesaid procedures and mechanisms (perhaps because the harassment has occurred outside any institutional settings), they can fittingly be regulated through legal channels. Though hatefully bigoted utterances focused on a particular individual are more likely to amount to "fighting words" or "true threats" than to a pattern of harassment, there can undoubtedly be circumstances in which a series of such utterances—each of which is at the lower end of inflammatoriness—would cumulatively be classifiable as a pattern of harassment. In such circumstances, legal sanctions can be a legitimate response to the series of utterances. Such sanctions, if legitimate, are directed at the wrong-making characteristics that are possessed both by the pattern of utterances and by any pattern of targeted harassment that is conducted through non-communicative means.[4]

Major social-media platforms, such as Facebook and YouTube and Twitter, are on the frontier of controversies pertaining to harassment and bullying. Though a full exploration of the problems posed by such platforms is well beyond the scope of this chapter,[5] we should fleetingly glance here at a few relevant considerations. On

[3] For an interesting discussion of this matter, see Jacobson and Schlink 2012, 219–27.

[4] Susan Brison asserts that "even if hate speech constitutes a form of harassment or race or sex discrimination, it is protected under the First Amendment" (1998, 315). See also Gelber and Brison 2019, 14. However, the principal case which Brison cites in support of her assertion—the 1989 case of *Doe v University of Michigan*—rightly affirms the opposite of what she contends. The code of conduct at issue in *Doe v University of Michigan* was struck down as unconstitutional not because hateful utterances that constitute targeted harassment are protected by the First Amendment, but because the code was overbroad (both in its formulation and in its application) and unconstitutionally vague.

[5] For a stimulating collection of essays on a variety of such problems, see Brison and Gelber 2019. See especially Citron 2019. Likewise thought-provoking are the essays in Part Four of Bollinger and

the one hand, individually targeted abuse perpetrated through Facebook or Twitter is not delivered at close range and is therefore unlikely ever to amount to fighting words. On the other hand, in some extreme cases it could amount to true threats or to incitement. More plausibly, it can amount to harassment in cases where the relevant communications are prolonged. All the operators of social-media platforms have promulgated some standards to regulate misconduct of this sort, and they are the parties chiefly responsible for remedying it. Although they are private corporations, the platforms which they manage have become immensely important public fora. Consequently, the principle of freedom of expression is applicable to their decisions and to the communications that unfold on their platforms. Still, as has been observed, the principle of freedom of expression is consistent with curbs on campaigns of targeted harassment. In a situation where such a campaign is severe in its scurrility or protractedness or scale, the operator of a social-media platform can be justified in taking steps to put an end to the abuse. Those steps are especially warranted—and, in extreme cases, urgent—where the target of a pattern of harassment is a youngster.

6.1.4 The Protectedness of Offensive Communications

While arguing that laws which forbid hatefully bigoted utterances can be legitimate as means of upholding the basic dignity of each person in a society, Waldron takes pains to differentiate between utterances that assail the basic dignity of other individuals and utterances that merely cause offense to other individuals (2012, 105–43). He believes that legal prohibitions on utterances of the former type can be morally justified, whereas he contends that legal prohibitions on utterances of the latter type are not similarly justifiable. Although this chapter has not yet fully expounded Waldron's understanding of dignity, his distinction between protecting people's dignity and protecting people from offense is broadly as follows. Dignity consists in one's status as an equal member of a society who carries the same fundamental entitlements and obligations as every other largely law-abiding member. Possessed of dignity, a person is entitled to participate in processes of democratic decision-making and is legally protected against multifarious forms of mistreatment. Whereas dignity is primarily an objective matter of status and only secondarily a matter of one's feelings about one's status, offense is primarily a subjective matter of feelings. When somebody is offended by the sentiments or beliefs or lifestyles or activities of other people, she experiences consternation or distress in response to what offends her. Reactions of offense can range from mild vexation or distaste to outrage or revulsion, but—regardless of the intensity of those

Stone 2019. Some of the problems explored are accentuations of difficulties surrounding the older mass media; on such difficulties, see for example Baker 1994. See also Kenyon 2014.

reactions—"[i]t is not the function of racial or religious hatred laws to protect against hurt feelings" (Waldron 2012, 111).

Waldron explores many complexities surrounding the distinction which he endeavors to draw, and he is aware that the demarcation between safeguarding people's dignity and shielding people against offense is elusive in quite a few contexts. However, he contends that the demarcation is sufficiently clear and robust to render morally tenable the imposition of legal prohibitions on utterances which oppugn the basic dignity of individuals. Laws that forbid such utterances can be justified even though any laws designed to protect people from affronts to their sensibilities would not be justified. Waldron asserts—repeatedly—that his opponents have inappositely assumed that the hate-speech statutes which he favors are laws of the latter kind. Somewhat stridently, he declares that animadversions on the idea of legally protecting people from being offended are "a distraction ... which is introduced gratuitously into the discussion of hate speech laws by those intent on discrediting them" (Waldron 2012, 111). He submits that his opponents are guilty of "studied obtuseness" when they suggest that "the only purpose of [hate-speech] laws is solicitude for people's hurt feelings" (112).

Comparably pugnacious allegations of disingenuousness and obtuseness abound in Waldron's tome on hateful utterances, but they should not distract readers from his highlighting of the differences between laws that forbid attacks on people's basic dignity and laws that protect people against being offended. My critique of Waldron in this chapter will not presume that the purpose of the hate-speech statutes which he defends is to protect people from affronts to their sensibilities. Though (as Waldron acknowledges) there have undoubtedly been some efforts by adherents of various religions to persuade judges to hold that those statutes do expansively cover the causing of offense, the statutes are not most plausibly interpreted in that fashion. I will not be so interpreting them in this chapter. Rather, I will take as given that Waldron is correct in ascribing to hate-speech laws the purpose of upholding the basic dignity of individuals, and I will maintain that those laws—endowed with such a purpose—are morally illegitimate as contraventions of the principle of freedom of expression.

6.1.4.1 A Genuine Distinction

Before we move on, three comments should be added to what has been said here. First, my acceptance of the distinction between upholding the basic dignity of individuals and shielding the sensibilities of people from offense is not merely for the sake of argument. Rather, that dichotomy is perfectly genuine and is of far-reaching importance. Whereas every system of governance is morally obligated to secure the basic dignity of individuals, the cushioning of people's sensibilities from offense is not a legitimate function for any system of governance. On the one hand, this chapter will argue that the hate-speech laws commended by Waldron are not morally permissible even as means for furthering the aim of upholding the basic social dignity of individuals. On the other hand, in line with what has been remarked at several junctures in Chapters 4 and 5, the present chapter will emphasize that the cultivation of an ethos of respect for the dignity of individuals is a central responsibility of every system of governance. As will be discussed later, the fulfillment of that responsibility can occur through educational measures and sundry other measures that are consistent with the principle of freedom of expression. Whereas Waldron repeatedly insinuates that the lone alternative to his favored legal restrictions is a policy of doing nothing in response to the utterances of bigots and extremists, those utterances can in fact be countered through an array of techniques. Such techniques are collectively a liberal-democratic alternative both to Waldron's illiberality and to the irresponsibility of taking no steps that will thwart the spread of the outlooks which the bigots and extremists seek to propagate.

6.1.4.2 A Different Justification

Second, although I concur with Waldron that the sparing of people from hurt feelings is not properly a function for any system of governance, my grounds for taking such a position are quite different from his. In keeping with the consequentialism that suffuses his approach to communicative liberties, Waldron submits that the conditions for effective democratic decision-making would be undermined if a system of governance were seriously to endeavor to safeguard people from affronts to their sensibilities (2012, 126–36). His discussion of the matter is quite convincing as far as it goes, but—like any consequentialist justification—it does not support an absolute constraint on the purposes that can legitimately be pursued by a system of governance. As Waldron himself concedes, his justification is hostage to empirical contingencies.

By contrast, in keeping with the deontological approach to freedom of expression that runs throughout this book, my basis for insisting on the impermissibility of legal mandates which proscribe offensive modes of expression is that such mandates would detract from the level of self-respect that is warranted for each person in the society where the mandates have been adopted. Like other departures from freedom of expression as self-restraint, legal curbs on the causing of offense would be both overweening and degrading for the system of governance that imposes the curbs. As can be inferred from Chapter 4, such measures would be overweening as efforts by a system of governance to direct the patterns of discourse in the society over which the system presides, and they would be degrading as ways of making the success of the system dependent on the non-occurrence of some patterns of discourse whose occurrence could readily be tolerated if the system and the ethos of its society were ethically robust. Legal barriers against the offending of sensibilities would presuppose the viciousness of the society in which the barriers are thought to be necessary. They would presuppose the absence there of the live-and-let-live ethos that should prevail when nothing more than offensiveness is involved. They would consequently presuppose the failure of the regnant system of governance to carry out its paramount moral responsibility: namely, its responsibility to bring about the political and social and economic conditions under which everyone within its jurisdiction can be warranted in harboring an ample sense of self-respect.

Of course, the remarks in the foregoing paragraph are a bare adumbration of a justification rather than a full presentation thereof with supporting arguments. However, the full justification for my opposition to legal safeguards against the offending of sensibilities will be apparent not only from Chapter 4 but also from much of the argumentation in the rest of this chapter—since the basis for my discountenancing of such safeguards is largely parallel to the basis for my discountenancing of the hate-speech restrictions that are championed by Waldron. In each case, the rationale for my defense of the principle of freedom of expression is deontological and thoroughly ethical rather than consequentialist and partly empirical. Thus, although Waldron and I converge in looking askance at the imposition of legal prohibitions on offensive utterances, there is a marked divergence between the rationales that respectively underlie our positions. That divergence becomes manifest when the focus shifts from offensive utterances to the hatefully bigoted utterances on which he principally trains his scrutiny.

6.1.4.3 The Pragmatics of Communications

Notwithstanding the genuineness and significance of the contrast between utterances that assail the basic dignity of individuals and utterances that merely rile the sensibilities of individuals, the communications which straddle that contrast are even more troublesome and numerous than Waldron allows. Let us briefly mull over two examples. Each of them pertains to hatefully bigoted pronouncements that have emanated from the left of the political spectrum in the United States or the United Kingdom. (Like the feminist political philosophers whose work I have examined in Chapter 5, Waldron focuses solely on the far right of the political spectrum in his reflections on hateful utterances.)

One of the most vitriolic antisemites in the United States during the past several decades has been Louis Farrakhan, an African-American preacher who heads the sinister Nation of Islam. Though Farrakhan is not easily locatable on the political spectrum, his supporters are primarily on the left. Over the years, he and his acolytes have spread a myriad of inflammatory insults and poisonous falsehoods about Jews. However, in one of his most famous screeds, he inveighed not only against Jews but also against Judaism. In a sermon delivered in 1984, which was partly recorded by a Chicago reporter, Farrakhan included the following fulmination: "Now that nation called Israel never has had any peace in forty years and she will never have any peace because there can be no peace structured on injustice, thievery, lying and deceit and using the name of God to shield your gutter religion under His holy and righteous name" (Shipp 1984). Let us concentrate here exclusively on the characterization of Judaism as a "gutter religion," as if that characterization had occurred in isolation from remarks directed explicitly against Jews. Given the sharp division which Waldron tries to maintain between attacks on the basic dignity of individuals and attacks on the doctrines or ideas that are espoused by individuals, he seems to have committed himself to concluding that the disparagement of Judaism as a gutter religion is not an assault on the basic dignity of Jews. Yet that disparagement is best construable as just such an assault. Notwithstanding that it is framed as a denunciation of a certain creed rather than overtly as a denunciation of the people who subscribe to that creed, its venomousness effaces the difference between those two foci. Even Jews who do not believe in the God of the Hebrew Scriptures (or in any other god) can rightly feel that the phrase "gutter religion"—applied to the faith at the heart of Jewish life for centuries—is a broadside against them.

As the example of Farrakhan suggests, we generally need to take into consideration the pragmatics of an utterance as well as its semantics when we assess whether it is a barrage against the dignity of individuals or instead only a barrage against certain ideas or activities that have been embraced by individuals. That is, we need to take into consideration not solely the meanings of the phraseology of an utterance but also the purposes pursued through the use of that phraseology. Only by attending to the pragmatics as well as to the semantics do we grasp the full content that has been conveyed by some instance of communication. Now, even if we prescind from the fact that Farrakhan has vilified Jews expressly on numerous occasions, his choice of the phrase "gutter religion" as a designation for Judaism conveys a clear message of contempt for Jews as well as for the faith to which many of them adhere. The semantics of his terminology may be solely about Judaism, but the full content conveyed by his selection of that terminology is equally about Jews.

Attentiveness to the distinction between semantics and pragmatics is again crucial as we ponder a second example of contemporary left-wing antisemitism. As has been recounted in §5.4.2 of Chapter 5, the Labour Party in the United Kingdom—one of the country's two foremost political parties—was taken over in 2015 by Jeremy Corbyn and other left-wing extremists who oversaw a huge surge of antisemitic slurs among the party's activists. One technique often employed by quite a few of those activists was to rant about Zionism and Israel rather than overtly about Jews (who were typically labeled as "Zionists"). Zionism is a multifaceted array of theories centered on the idea of national self-determination for Jewish people.[6] Hence, if the declamations about Zionism by the fanatics in the Labour Party were to be taken at face value, and if Waldron's duality between derision of individuals' dignity and derision of individuals' creeds were to be applied woodenly to those declamations taken at face value, we would conclude that the declamations were located on the latter side of that duality—even though

[6] For some perceptive expositions of Zionism, see Almog 1987; Avineri 1981; and Gans 2008.

many of them were imbued with the lurid language and imagery of traditional antisemitism. In fact, of course, we should not be focusing solely on the semantics of the utterances in question. Such a blinkered approach would overlook much of what was being imparted by those utterances, which served as vehicles for the conveyance of antisemitic sentiments from Corbyn's myrmidons to one another and to the Jews against whom the sentiments were directed. Like the much more explicit statements of Jew-hatred that became rife among members of the Labour Party during Corbyn's leadership,[7] the statements by those members that railed against Zionism were very often attacks on the dignity of Jews.

Again, the examples in this subsection do not cast doubt upon the genuineness of the division between assaults on basic dignity and assaults on ideas or creeds. Rather, they suggest that the application of that dichotomy to sundry utterances is even more complex than Waldron seems to envisage. Matters of pragmatics, some of which are highly context-specific, are oft decisive in determining how the sundry utterances should be classified. For Waldron, these complications are considerably more problematic than for me. For him, the divide between attacks on basic dignity and attacks on ideas or creeds is a distinction between some modes of communication that can legitimately be proscribed by law and some modes of communication that cannot legitimately be so proscribed. In his scheme of things, then, courts or other adjudicative bodies will have to grapple with the frequently subtle matters of pragmatics to which I have referred here. For me as a defender of the principle of freedom of expression, by contrast, the difference between attacks on basic dignity and attacks on ideas or creeds is not tantamount to a distinction between what is legitimately censorable and what is exempt from censorship. Under the principle of freedom of expression, no attack of either kind is morally susceptible to legal prohibitions (save in circumstances where someone's vituperation constitutes an act of wrongdoing, such as incitement, that can legitimately be forbidden on communication-neutral grounds). Hence, the difficulties of differentiating between those two types of attacks will not have to be shouldered by courts or other adjudicative bodies as they gauge whether utterances are subject to the interdictory sway of a system of governance.

6.1.5 Political Parties

Although Waldron does not say anything about political parties in *The Harm in Hate Speech*, my remarks on the United Kingdom's Labour Party in the preceding subsection warrant some brief reflections on such organizations here. Whereas a system of governance cannot ever properly impose sanctions or disadvantages on

[7] See, for example, Harpin 2019.

people for reasons that are not communication-neutral, a political party can legitimately proceed on the basis of content-specific considerations when it determines whether people are fit to belong to it as members.[8] Such a party is an organization which numerous people voluntarily enter in order to collaborate with others who are largely like-minded on an array of political issues (or on broader political ideals). A party will generally not be very successful in a liberal democracy unless it encompasses quite a wide range of viewpoints, but no party would be ideologically coherent if it sought to embrace all viewpoints. A political party cannot credibly present itself as devoted to the values of liberal democracy, if it welcomes Stalinists and Nazis and Islamist fanatics into its ranks or if it declines to discipline or expel such people when their presence among its ranks is discovered. A party cannot credibly profess to be opposed to racism and other forms of prejudice if it welcomes myriad antisemites and other bigots into its ranks, or if it declines to discipline or expel such people when their presence among its ranks is revealed. As an ideological grouping, a political party can legitimately discipline or expel its members for some utterances that would not be legitimately prohibitable by a system of governance—where the utterances in question, if left unaddressed, would tend to bring the party into grave disrepute and would significantly impair the believability of its commitments to certain aims and values. Thus, although most of the antisemitic utterances that abounded among members of the Labour Party during the leadership of Corbyn were not legitimately susceptible to the imposition of sanctions by a system of governance, nearly all of those utterances were properly open to disciplinary steps by a political party that purports to be opposed to bigotry. It was therefore greatly to the discredit of Corbyn and his henchmen that so few such steps were taken by the Labour Party under his dominion.

6.1.6 Hiring Decisions

Even when a prospective employer is a public organization within a system of governance, the constraints incumbent on such a system under the principle of freedom of expression allow the employer to conclude that some utterances by an applicant for a job have revealed him or her to be unfit for the position under consideration. For example, the members of a hiring committee in a police force would be grossly irresponsible if they were to ignore the fact that an applicant for a position as a constable in a multiracial community has spoken admiringly of violent and discriminatory tactics wielded in the past by the police against certain racial minorities. Similarly, the members of a hiring committee in an agency entrusted with national security would be egregiously remiss if they were to ignore the fact

[8] On this point, I agree with Rubenfeld 2001, 814–15; Scanlon 2003, 194–5; Shiffrin 2014, 109.

that an applicant for a position as a defense analyst has spoken admiringly of efforts by Communist radicals to overthrow the prevailing system of governance. Indeed, assertions of these sorts can legitimately be acted upon by the police force or the defense agency not only at the point of hiring but also at subsequent stages of employment. Utterances that bespeak the wholesale unsuitability of someone for his or her job can properly be treated as grounds for discipline or dismissal by an employer. In that respect, such utterances are like any other factors that disqualify someone for employment in a certain position.

At the point of hiring, statements made by applicants in various settings can sometimes legitimately be taken into account even though the statements do not bear directly on the likely proficiency of the applicants in the roles which they are seeking. For example, suppose that Herman applies for a research fellowship in mathematics at a public university, and suppose that the members of the appointments committee become aware that Herman in several settings has spoken favorably about the aims and methods of the Ku Klux Klan. Although his odious pronouncements would probably not bear directly on his prowess as a mathematician, the members of the appointments committee can legitimately take account of those pronouncements when deciding whether to confer upon him a fellowship that will make him a member of the broader university. They might reasonably worry that the attitudes betokened by his statements would tend to vitiate his manner of interacting with other members of the university. His benighted utterances can permissibly be taken into consideration in this fashion at the stage where his appointment is under deliberation, even though they cannot permissibly be treated by an employer as grounds for disciplining or dismissing him after he has taken up his position. Of course, if Herman gains the position, and if the attitudes evinced by his utterances do dismayingly affect the ways in which he interacts with other members of the community, he can permissibly be disciplined or dismissed. However, at that juncture, the permissible grounds for proceeding against him will consist not in his having made the repugnant pronouncements but instead in his having behaved objectionably toward others during his fellowship.

6.1.7 Unfitness for Employment

Overlapping with some of the situations discussed in the preceding subsection is any situation where someone has made statements that reveal and render him to be unfit for his job, as the statements constitute gross abuses of his position of employment. Waldron refers at several points to the 1990 Canadian case of *R v Keegstra*, in which the Supreme Court of Canada upheld the constitutionality of the country's hate-speech legislation (Waldron 2012, 57–8, 84–5, 154, 242 n18). Although the reasoning adopted and the outcome reached by the Court were at variance with the principle of freedom of expression, the facts of the case are what should receive some attention here. Those facts could and should have been handled adequately without any recourse to hate-speech legislation.

Through his position as a teacher in a public high school in Alberta during the 1970s and early 1980s, James Keegstra repeatedly engaged in antisemitic diatribes wherein he contended that all Jews are evil and that all evil people are Jewish. Among the derogatory terms applied by him to Jews on numerous occasions in his classroom were "barbaric," "subversive," "sadistic," "child killers," "money-loving," "power-hungry," "manipulative," "deceptive," "treacherous," "impostors," and "communists." He told his students that Jews are striving to destroy Christianity and that they are responsible for all wars and depressions and upheavals. He asserted that Jews "created the Holocaust in order to gain sympathy." He required his students to endorse his antisemitic claims in their essays and examinations. Students who parroted his views were awarded high marks, whereas students who dissented from those views were awarded low marks.

Not clear from the judgments issued in the case is how Keegstra managed to continue in his position as a schoolteacher for approximately a decade before his dismissal in 1982.[9] Even a small proportion of his antisemitic onslaughts would have amounted to sufficient grounds for dismissal and for disqualification from any future employment as a teacher. Proceedings against him by his school and by any relevant teaching-accreditation authority could and should have been undertaken not as a way of policing the tenor of public discourse but instead as a way of monitoring and maintaining the quality of the pedagogy provided in the Albertan educational system. Keegstra, through his multitude of scurrilous attacks on Jews and through his corrupt practices of awarding grades, displayed a lack of elementary competence as a teacher of social studies. Any school that employed him for more than the briefest period was egregiously in dereliction of its responsibility to educate students and to shield them from abuse, and any accreditation authority that left him in possession of his formal pedagogical qualifications was likewise in dereliction of its responsibilities. Dismissal and disqualification were both morally obligatory and morally permissible as measures to be administered in response to Keegstra's misfeasance. Specifically in connection with his perversion of the process of grading his students, further sanctions for his abuse of a position of public trust would also have been morally permissible.

Unlike the hate-speech legislation under which Keegstra was prosecuted, laws that authorize and require the measures outlined in the preceding paragraph are consistent with the principle of freedom of expression. Keegstra's school could and should have taken action not as a censor of public discourse but as an employer entrusted with the responsibility of supplying education to high-school students in an Albertan town. Bearing such a responsibility, a school is accordingly duty-bound to

[9] For some suggestions of answers to this puzzling question, see Benton-Evans 1997, 126–8.

ensure that the teachers whom it employs are competent to carry out their roles as teachers. It is not fulfilling that duty if its administrators omit to take prompt steps when they discover that a teacher is regularly imparting preposterous and irrelevant falsehoods to students in their lessons. The administrators are morally permitted to take such steps—under the principle of freedom of expression—because their handling of the matter, if properly conducted, is communication-neutral. Though the conduct that manifests the incompetence of someone as a teacher can of course be communicative (as it obviously was in Keegstra's case), pedagogical incompetence can be manifested in many other ways as well. For example, a teacher might persistently let the children chat among themselves in lieu of undergoing any lessons, or he might persistently assign grades to students through aleatory procedures, and so forth. Had Keegstra's conduct been addressed properly by his school, his actions would have resulted in his dismissal because of the properties which those actions had in common with these other ways of manifesting pedagogical ineptitude.

Not in dispute between Waldron and me, then, is the proposition that Keegstra's conduct warranted the imposition of sanctions. However, we disagree over the appropriate nature and source of the sanctions. Waldron applauds the imposition of criminal penalties under the provisions of the hate-speech legislation that were brought to bear on Keegstra for his invective. Now, notwithstanding the grotesqueness of that invective, the imposition of such penalties was clearly in contravention of the principle of freedom of expression—for, like the hate-speech legislation under which the imposition occurred, it was not communication-neutral and was indeed not even viewpoint-neutral. Very different is the approach to Keegstra's misconduct which I have proposed in this subsection. Instead of being subjected to a criminal prosecution under a hate-speech statute, Keegstra should have been promptly dismissed by the public school that employed him, and he should have been deprived of his formal qualifications as a schoolteacher by the relevant accreditation authority. Those sanctions would have been communication-neutral, since they would have been imposed in response to his pedagogical incompetence rather than in response to the odium of his expressions of bigotry. Thus, whereas the principle of freedom of expression disallows the sanctions which Waldron favors, it is fully compatible with the sanctions recommended here.

6.1.8 Incitement

In several previous chapters, I have recounted the criterion articulated by the U.S. Supreme Court in *Brandenburg v Ohio* for the classification of communicative conduct as incitement that is not protected under the First Amendment to the American Constitution. As has been stated, the terse *Brandenburg* judgment laid down three requirements for such a classification: the communication in question is *intended* or directed to bring about some seriously unlawful activity, and it is *likely* to bring about such activity, and the probable occurrence of the unlawful activity is *imminent* rather than remote. When those features of incitement are correctly predicable of any of the hatefully bigoted utterances on which Waldron trains his scrutiny, the utterances can be proscribed by law on communication-neutral grounds. Legal sanctions imposed on the people who engage in utterances of incitement can be straightforwardly consistent with the principle of freedom of expression.

As explicated by the U.S. Supreme Court, the category of incitement is rightly distinguished from the category of advocacy. In several of the hate-speech statutes that are operative today in the United Kingdom, the term "incitement" is used more expansively to cover quite a bit of communicative conduct that would be classified as advocacy under the *Brandenburg* standard. As has already been argued in some of my previous chapters, the *Brandenburg* Court's understanding of the distinction between incitement and advocacy—unlike the understanding of that distinction exhibited in the British hate-speech laws—is in conformity with the principle of freedom of expression. When the requirements for the classification of an utterance as an instance of incitement under the *Brandenburg* standard are satisfied, the utterance is subsumable into the serious wrongdoing which it is designed to instigate imminently. Such an utterance by somebody is an opening stage of the wrongdoing which the inciter is endeavoring to provoke; it constitutes his participation in that wrongdoing. (Of course, if the provocation is unsuccessful, the utterance of incitement constitutes an *attempt* to participate in such wrongdoing rather than an instance of actual participation therein.) Hence, a legal sanction levied on somebody for engaging in incitement can be communication-neutral—and will be communication-neutral if it is properly levied. Aptly oriented, the sanction is imposed because the inciter is a perpetrator of the violence or other misconduct which his utterance has impelled. So oriented, the sanction is a response to the utterance qua act of violence rather than qua act of communication.

Though the *Brandenburg* Court's correct understanding of the category of incitement is significantly narrower than the understanding that is operative in British hate-speech legislation, there is of course a considerable overlap between them. Hence, quite a few of the hideous utterances that would be banned under Waldron's favored hate-speech legislation are prohibitable in compliance with the principle of freedom of expression. Of course, given that Waldron's favored hate-speech laws are not communication-neutral, the banning of the aforementioned hideous utterances under those laws is in contravention of the principle of freedom of expression. Nonetheless, the utterances can legitimately be proscribed in accordance with that principle under laws that are suitably communication-neutral.

Waldron occasionally obscures the fact that instances of incitement (in the *Brandenburg* sense) are legitimately prohibitable under communication-neutral laws, for he sometimes writes as though the hate-speech laws which he champions are necessary for the banning of incitement. For example, he declares that the suitable formulation and implementation of hate-speech laws

> might not require the suppression of every word or epithet that counts colloquially as hate speech. It may require us to attend to the most egregious forms of group libel, particularly when the threatening or abusive form in which it is presented makes the destructive intention of the [speaker's] self-disclosure more or less explicit. (Waldron 2012, 172)

This quoted wording is rather vague, but the communications envisaged here by Waldron appear to include all or most instances of racist "true threats" and racist "fighting words" and racist incitement. Perhaps very few other communications are included. Now, of course, true threats and fighting words and incitement can be subjected to legal sanctions in conformity with the principle of freedom of expression under communication-neutral laws. Thus, were Waldron always as restrained as he is in this quoted passage, the prohibitory reach of his favored hate-speech laws would not be much different from the reach of some properly communication-neutral restrictions. (Having said as much, I should add that Waldron is not always so restrained, and in any event his favored hate-speech laws are not communication-neutral.)

6.1.9 Philosophy Rather Than Constitutional Theory

Waldron explicitly and repeatedly acknowledges that his position on the regulation of hatefully bigoted utterances is at variance with the First Amendment to the American Constitution. He makes virtually no effort to accommodate sundry distinctions that have been established under the First Amendment over the decades by the U.S. Supreme Court and other American courts. Indeed, he writes quite mockingly or quizzically about some of those distinctions. Instead of trying to contribute to the constitutional theory of the United States or of any other country, Waldron is endeavoring to contribute to political philosophy. He is attempting to distill the values of liberal democracy which he believes to be furthered by the imposition of legal restrictions on hatefully bigoted utterances. Having expounded those values and assessed their relative importance, he does not concern himself with the question whether his understanding of those values and of their relative importance tallies with the regnant understanding among experts in the law of the First Amendment. As he proclaims: "[*The Harm in Hate Speech*] is not intended as a study in American constitutional law" (Waldron 2012, 152).

Like Waldron's tome on hate speech, my book on freedom of expression is not an exposition of American constitutional law. It is a contribution to political philosophy rather than to the constitutional theory of the United States. I draw quite frequently on the doctrines and distinctions of American constitutional law when they accord with the requirements and implications of the principle of freedom of expression, but I draw upon them for illumination rather than for their authority, and I depart from them whenever they are at odds with the requirements and implications of the moral principle of freedom of expression. This aspect of my book has been clear since my opening chapters. Thus, it is no part of the purpose of this chapter to criticize Waldron for writing as a political philosopher rather than as a lawyer. Quite the contrary.

Nevertheless, Waldron does go astray in some of his comments on facets of American constitutional law. A political philosopher is of course well advised to eschew many of the details of that law, but is also well advised to try to fathom the rationales for major doctrines therein. In that respect, one juncture at which Waldron particularly stumbles is his effort to explicate the distinction between content-neutral and content-focused restrictions on communications. Because his error on this point is directly relevant to the fundamental orientation of my book on freedom of expression, we should examine his misstep at some length. He writes as follows:

> The distinction [between content-neutral and content-focused restrictions] is no doubt a subtle one. I have heard it argued that Oliver Wendell Holmes's famous example, the [malicious or reckless] shouting of "Fire!" in a crowded theater, is not really prohibited on account of its content; it is prohibited for the likely effect of this content—as Holmes puts it, "causing a panic." One could engage in similar casuistry for the case of hate speech. One could argue that racist speech or the defamation of some racial, ethnic, or religious group is prohibited (where it is) not because of its content per se, but either because of the way it is expressed or because of the likely effect of what is said or published upon society's maintenance of the basic dignity of the members of the targeted group. One could make this argument if one wanted to take the American distinction between content-based and non-content-based prohibitions extremely seriously. (Waldron 2012, 151, endnote omitted)

Far from taking the American distinction very seriously, somebody advancing the line of argument broached here by Waldron would be misunderstanding that distinction ludicrously. We should scarcely be surprised that Waldron himself brusquely rejects the postulated line of argument, as he forthrightly acknowledges that the hate-speech laws which he champions are content-focused:

> If we start drawing such distinctions [between a prohibition directed against the content of an utterance and a prohibition directed against the probable effects of the content of an utterance], then we will have to conclude that precious few proposals for content-based restrictions will ever be oriented *purely* toward content,

> to the exclusion of any interest in what happens as a result of the publication of content. Better to admit that hate speech ... is forbidden, where it is, because of the effect *of its content* in helping to undermine the assurance that members of vulnerable groups are supposed to be able to draw from the public affirmation of their dignity. (Waldron 2012, 151, emphases in original)

Waldron reiterates: "Better ... just to acknowledge straight up that a restriction on hate speech or on group defamation is a restriction on speech on account of its content, and that it is the content that explains the restriction" (152).

Not at all startling is the conclusion reached here by Waldron. In fact, the hate-speech statutes which he lauds are paradigmatic instances of content-focused prohibitions. Like the anti-pornography ordinance introduced into the city of Indianapolis by MacKinnon in the 1980s, the hate-speech legislation favored by Waldron is content-focused not only in its underlying purpose but also in its explicit wording. Thus, the acknowledgment by Waldron of the content-focused character of that legislation is the only plausible conclusion at which he could have arrived. What *is* startling is that he apparently thinks that there might be some doubt about the matter among his opponents. His perception of a need to dispel such doubt is rooted in his having heard—from some unnamed interlocutor, with reference to a ban on the malicious shouting of "Fire" in a crowded theater—that the distinction between a content-focused prohibition and a content-neutral prohibition is to be cashed out as a distinction between a prohibition directed against the content of an utterance and a prohibition directed against the probable effects of the content of an utterance. Waldron correctly retorts that such a ridiculous way of explicating the content-focused/content-neutral distinction would effectively eliminate that distinction by reclassifying every prohibition as content-neutral. Remarkably, however, he does not broach or contemplate any other way (a far more sensible way) in which that distinction might be cashed out.[10]

As should be evident from several previous chapters of this book, a proper legal ban on the malicious or reckless shouting of "Fire" in a crowded theater is content-neutral because it is directed against such an utterance not qua instance of communicative conduct but instead qua wrongful effort to induce a dangerous public disturbance. A legal prohibition on deliberately or recklessly bringing about a dangerous public tumult, or on attempting to bring about such a tumult, will of course extend to some instances of conduct that are communicative. Some wrongful efforts to engender situations of dangerous public disorder proceed by way of communicative conduct; the malicious shouting of "Fire" in a crowded theater is an

[10] Waldron does ponder a couple of reasons adduced by Geoffrey Stone for taking special exception to content-focused restrictions on communications. See Waldron 2012, 152–7. However, he never broaches any other way of drawing the content-focused/content-neutral distinction itself. (Later in this chapter, I will look at Waldron's remarks on one of Stone's two rationales.)

obvious example. However, the specified prohibition will likewise extend to any instances of non-communicative conduct that constitute wrongful efforts to engender situations of dangerous disorder. When the prohibition extends to the communicative instances of conduct that constitute such efforts, it is directed against the wrong-making properties which they have in common with the non-communicative instances of conduct that constitute such efforts. It is therefore a communication-neutral law. Its purpose resides not in disallowing the communication of certain types of messages or sentiments, but instead in disallowing the perpetration of violent misconduct.

6.2 Waldron's Case in Favor of Hate-Speech Laws

As has been mentioned at the outset of this chapter, Waldron in his defense of hate-speech legislation concentrates on the tendency of hatefully bigoted modes of communication to disfigure the societies in which they emerge. Those modes of communication create a social environment whose ugliness puts into question certain assumptions and assurances which people ought to be able to take for granted. Every reasonably law-abiding member of a society ought to be able to presume with confidence that he or she is endowed with the same basic entitlements and encumbered with the same basic responsibilities as is every other reasonably law-abiding member of the society. In a flourishingly liberal-democratic society, that confidence is normally so strong and resilient and pervasive that it is left implicit on most occasions. It is a sense of assurance cultivated by the interaction of people who recognize one another as equals. Everyone knows that she herself is fundamentally on a par with each of her fellow citizens, and she knows that each of them recognizes her parity with everyone else. Such knowledge on the part of everyone in relation to everyone is only quite rarely summoned to conscious reflection by anybody, since it usually functions instead as the background to countless everyday interactions that are imbued with an elementally reassuring quality because of the operativeness of that knowledge. Those everyday interactions take their character in part from the pervading sense of reassurance that has been bred by past interactions, and they help to project that sense of reassurance into the future by bolstering afresh its benignly unspoken grip on the outlook of virtually every member of the society in which the interactions occur.

Hatefully bigoted speeches and placards are aimed at fraying the blanket of reassurance that enwraps the citizens of a liberal-democratic society. Hatemongers target certain groups for opprobrium, as they insist that every member or nearly every member of any group under attack is reprehensible. Features that are characteristic of an assailed group—such as skin color or religious faith or ethnic origins—are conflated with features such as criminality and bestiality and stupidity. Those conflations, which are given enduring expression in regularly displayed signs and in Web sites and in other such vehicles for the spewing of bigoted venom, are designed to undermine the sense of comfort and acceptance that would otherwise permeate the social and economic and political relations of a liberal democracy. Though no single such outpouring of defiant hatred will discernibly undermine the sense of security that informs the interactions of a thriving liberal democracy, many such outpourings over time can cumulatively sap that very sense. Those outpourings together form a dissonant chord in the social environment, by conveying a sinister message to the members of any disfavored racial or religious or ethnic group: namely, the message that they are neither welcome nor safe. At the very least, the people targeted by the hatemongers are no longer able to take utterly for granted that their fellow citizens all readily accept them as belonging to their society fundamentally on a par with everybody else. Even if those contemned people continue to feel generally secure, their sense of assurance is now tinged with self-consciousness and traces of doubt. They can no longer feel fully at home in the society that encompasses the tirades against them. Gradually, the nagging doubts become corrosive as the vilified people start to wonder whether even their amicable exchanges with others are to be taken entirely at face value. In the estimation of such people, quotidian transactions come to be tainted with an undertow of unease. Like the jealousy-inducing chicanery practiced on Othello by Iago, the apprehension-inducing fulminations of the hatemongers are "in their natures poisons,/Which at the first are scarce found to distaste,/But with a little act upon the blood/Burn like the mines of Sulphur" (*Othello*, III. iii. 326–9). With the diatribes of the bigots as a lasting part of the social environment in which everyday life is pursued, the peace of mind that should be felt by every upstanding citizen in a liberal democracy—the peace of mind that is the hallmark of a person's dignity as such a citizen—is no longer straightforwardly available to the members of any group reviled in those diatribes. As Waldron writes:

> The point of the bigoted displays that we want to regulate is that they are not just autonomous self-expression. They are not simply the views of racists letting off steam. The displays specifically target the social sense of assurance on which members of vulnerable minorities rely. Their point is to negate the implicit assurance that a society offers to the members of vulnerable groups—that they are accepted in society, as a matter of course, along with everyone else; they aim to undermine this assurance, call it in question, and taint it with visible expressions of hatred, exclusion, and contempt. And so it begins: what was implicitly assured is now visibly challenged, so that there is a whole new set of calculations for a minority member to engage in as he sets out to do business or take a walk in public with his family. (Waldron 2012, 88–9)

One principal set of addressees of the invective poured forth by racists and other bigots, then, is any group of people who are the targets of the invective. Unnerving those people is a cardinal objective of the extremists who engage in hateful utterances. A further principal aim of the extremists is to communicate with one another through these utterances. While seeking to fill the targets of their loathing with consternation and trepidation, the bigots also endeavor to inspire one another with feelings of optimism and solidarity. Their besmirching of the social fabric with their hate-drenched displays is *pari passu* a means of building a network of like-minded people. They attenuate their society's provision of the public good of assured equality and dignity, by partly replacing the society's liberal-democratic ethos with the ugliness of their own prejudices. Through their posters and Web sites and public proclamations, they communicate those prejudices to their fellow bigots as well as to their victims and to the world at large. They thereby establish among themselves a counter-culture of turpitude to assail and unsettle the dominant liberal-democratic ethos in their society. Waldron quite vividly captures the role of hatefully bigoted utterances as signals conveyed by the votaries of such a counter-culture to people of a similar bent:

> Hate speech doesn't just seek to undermine the public good of implicit assurance. It also seeks to establish *a rival public good* [or, rather, a public evil] as the wolves call to one another across the peace of a decent society. The publication of hate speech, the appearance of these symbols and scrawls in places for all to see, is a way of providing a focal point for the proliferation and coordination of the attitudes that these actions express, a public manifestation of hatred by some people to indicate to others that they are not alone in their racism or bigotry. (Waldron 2012, 94–5, emphasis in original)

As has already been suggested in this chapter, Waldron understands the property of dignity as a status attaching to every member of a liberal-democratic society who is reasonably law-abiding. It is a status of fundamental equality, whereby everyone endowed with it possesses the same basic rights as everyone else and bears the same basic duties as everyone else. It is partly a *legal* status of equality, but is even more importantly a *social* status engendered and sustained by the myriad of everyday encounters in which people interact with one another as equals. Each person in such encounters is routinely recognized as somebody who cannot permissibly be excluded from any place that is open to the public at large. The routineness of the recognition is a key aspect of it, for dignity consists partly in being able to proceed through one's mundane activities while confidently presuming—with assurance that is all the stronger for being largely unreflective—that one will not be subjected to violence or humiliation or invidious discrimination. That taken-for-granted confidence is a product of the flow of social intercourse in a liberal democracy, which both presupposes and reinforces the appropriateness of such an attitude.

Now, given this understanding of dignity as a status of elementary equality, the hateful pronouncements that emanate from bigots are aimed at denying and counteracting the sway of dignity in the social and political relations of their society. Their pronouncements directly call into question the dignity of some of their fellow citizens, and they seek to induce the removal of the dignity of those citizens altogether by influencing the attitudes of others. Hence, the role of hate-speech laws in Waldron's reckoning is to avert and repel such assaults on dignity. By restricting the latitude of hatemongers to inject the poison of their ranting into public discourse, those laws uphold the dignity of every member of the society. Such laws on their own terms are expressive of that common dignity, and they give material effect to it by deterring or penalizing the efforts of venomous people to disfigure the landscape of their society with the displays and utterances of hatred. Such laws help to preserve a social environment in which the members of vulnerable minority groups can go about their daily activities with the same equanimity as everyone else. When a well-ordered environment of that kind does obtain throughout a society, the throngs of transactions among people that make up everyday life will both presuppose and implicitly consolidate the dignity of everyone involved. Such a happy state of affairs is what the imposition of legal restrictions on the expression of bigotry can be designed to achieve. According to Waldron's defense of such restrictions, the affirmation or consolidation of individual dignity in this fashion is the purpose that vindicates the limits which the restrictions place on freedom of expression.

Waldron is not unattuned to the fact that hate-speech laws involve certain drawbacks. On the one hand, he says very little about the ways in which such laws have lent themselves to being misapplied in the various Western countries—including the United Kingdom and Canada—where they have been enacted (Greene 2012, 95–7; Minow 2000, 1264–7; Rosenfeld 2012, 244, 264–5; Skillen 1982, 142–3; Strossen 2001, 266–71; 2018, 26–9; Strossen and Molnar 2012, 390–1). On the other hand, Waldron readily allows that bans on hateful displays and utterances are in tension with certain liberal values. However, proceeding in the consequentialist vein of philosophizing that runs throughout *The Harm in Hate Speech*, he maintains that the considerations which tell against the introduction of hate-speech laws are to be placed in a balance alongside the considerations which tell in favor of such laws. As he writes in one of the many passages where he states explicitly the consequentialist character of his approach to the issue: "What I argue . . . is not that we should dismiss [the interest of every individual in autonomous self-disclosure through communicative conduct], but that it must be balanced against other interests at stake in the situation" (Waldron 2012, 140). Slightly later in his book, he furnishes a somewhat more expansive summary of the consequentialist balancing which he commends to his readers:

> We recognize, in general, that the considerations which argue in favor of the broad importance of free speech *do* extend to speech attempting to stir up racial or religious hatred; but we say that nevertheless such speech must be regulated,

> and in extreme cases prohibited, because of the harm that it does. And we acknowledge that the harm in prospect must be grave—more serious than the harm that would justify regulation where such speech was not an issue—on account of the value of free speech that has to be outweighed on the other side. (147, emphasis in original)

He recapitulates his consequentialist approach as follows:

> I believe we should stick with the balancing model ... weighing the importance to individuals of ... autonomous self-disclosure ... against the importance of the social and individual values that are compromised when the act of self-disclosure [by a racist or some other bigot] goes public ... There is, in my view, no way of avoiding this need for balance. There really are rival values in play here. (171–2)

On the whole, Waldron is inclined to strike the balance in favor of hate-speech legislation of the sort that has been enacted in many Western liberal democracies.

6.3 A First Rejoinder to Waldron: Not Doing Nothing

In the rest of this chapter, I will undertake a number of ripostes to Waldron's defense of hate-speech laws. One point that will not be pursued here is something mentioned fleetingly in §6.2 above: that is, the fact that such laws have lent themselves to being misapplied frequently. My objections to legal curbs on hatefully bigoted utterances are concerned with matters of principle rather than with matters of implementation, notwithstanding the importance of the latter matters. Moreover, any tweaking of the hate-speech laws to try to render them less susceptible to overinclusive applications would in many respects make them even more blatantly violative of the principle of freedom of expression—since it would accentuate their inconsistency with the ideals of subject-neutrality and viewpoint-neutrality. Hence, although opponents of the statutes which Waldron champions are justified in lamenting the occasions on which such statutes are wielded against people who are supposed to benefit from them, this chapter will not be focusing on those problems.

Instead, my first main rejoinder to Waldron contests an assumption which underlies his whole defense of hate-speech laws and which is often explicitly voiced in the course of that defense. A comparable assumption (*mutatis mutandis*) also informs some feminist writings on pornography, and I am therefore returning to a topic which I have addressed intermittently in Chapter 5. That is, Waldron assumes and frequently states that the sole alternative to the enactment of hate-speech legislation is a posture of feckless acquiescence in the rantings of bigots. He first sounds this theme near the outset of his book, when he writes that some unnamed opponents "say that people like [themselves], who detest hate speech, should learn to live with it." According to him, these opponents are inclined to add that people who belong to the racial or religious or ethnic groups vilified in the posters and leaflets of hatemongers "should also learn to live with these signs." Using free indirect discourse, Waldron synopsizes the views of these unnamed opponents as follows:

> [T]he bigoted invective that defiles our public environment . . . should be no concern of the law, they say. People are perfectly within their rights, publishing stuff like this. There is nothing to be regulated here, nothing for the law to concern itself with, nothing that a good society should use its legislative apparatus to suppress or disown. The people who are targeted should just learn to live with it. (Waldron 2012, 3)

Time and again, Waldron reiterates this suggestion that anyone who discountenances the "use [of a] legislative apparatus to suppress" the advocacy of repugnant creeds is thereby counseling in favor of a learn-to-live-with-it stance of ignominiously meek resignation and passivity.

For example, he admonishes his readers that racists "may not harm the people who call for their toleration, but then few of *them* [that is, few of the people who call for toleration] are depicted as animals in posters plastered around Leamington Spa . . . We should speak to those who are depicted in this way, or those whose suffering or whose parents' suffering is mocked by [the Skokie neo-Nazis], before we conclude that tolerating this sort of speech builds character" (Waldron 2012, 7, emphasis in original). Even leaving aside the inaccuracy of Waldron's insinuation that the defenders of the principle of freedom of expression are calling for a lie-back-and-take-it response to bigoted ravings, his pronouncement is especially ill-judged because many of those defenders are Jews. Unlike Waldron, they belong to a religious-ethnic group that is one of the most frequent targets of the hatemongers. Indeed, Waldron's reference to the proposed march of neo-Nazis in the Illinois city of Skokie during the 1970s is particularly ironic, because the neo-Nazis in the ensuing litigation were represented by the American Civil Liberties Union; the general counsel of that organization at the time was Aryeh Neier, a Jew who as an infant had escaped from Nazi Germany with his family.[11]

Throughout *The Harm in Hate Speech*, Waldron pits himself against what he regards as the lackadaisicalness and irresponsibility of his opponents. For instance, he feels a need to deny that the basic dignity of the members of vulnerable minority groups is "a matter of purely private belief, with which the law should have no concern" (2012, 30). He attributes to his opponents the view that, if members

[11] For an interesting discussion of Neier's role in the litigation, see Bollinger 1986, 97–100.

of vulnerable minority groups are not subjected to violence or invidious discrimination and are instead simply surrounded by posters and banners in which their groups are reviled, then "there is nothing to worry about" (68). Startlingly, he even alleges that his opponents applaud the hatefully bigoted invective itself—rather than merely the legal tolerance of such invective—as something that enhances public discourse. He writes:

> [T]hey love the richness and untidiness of the marketplace of ideas: let a thousand flowers bloom, they say, even the poisonous ones. For of course some of the ideas are foul and distasteful. But if you blur your eyes a bit, what you see is a glorious splash of moving and variegated color—ideas interacting openly and unpredictably with one another in full public view. *That*, they will say, is surely a feature of a well-ordered society—even if the men, women, and children who are the targets of these foul and distasteful messages of hate have difficulty in maintaining this lofty perspective. (Waldron 2012, 67, emphasis in original)

Waldron asserts that the point of contention between himself and his opponents is "whether the law should be *indifferent* to [the impact of hateful fulminations] on what our society looks like and what it is for the members of certain groups to have to try and make a life in a society that looks like that" (2012, 77, emphasis added). He informs his readers "that the damage [inflicted by hatefully bigoted utterances upon the fabric of a society] is serious and that we cannot assume that a social system can simply shrug it off" (157–8), and he chidingly declares that it is "wrong to ignore the harm to minorities in particular" (158). A bit later in his book, he again contends that "the evils that are constituted by [racist speech-acts] cannot be ignored" (167). He goes on to complain that, if the First Amendment disallows the imposition of legal bans on the advocacy of racist doctrines, then it "requires us to turn a blind eye to these matters" (181). In a rhetorical question, he encapsulates his animus toward what he perceives as the cavalier irresponsibility of liberals who insist upon the principle of freedom of expression (196–7): "Are we really in need of such robust debate on racial ontology that we have no choice but to require individuals and families within minority groups to bear the costs of such humiliating attacks on their social standing?"

In these and other passages, Waldron repeatedly conveys the impression that everyone who disagrees with his position on hate-speech legislation is in favor of abjectly doing nothing in response to the ugly displays and utterances of hatemongers. Waldron seems to think that the defenders of the principle of freedom of expression believe that any harms which ensue from such displays and utterances are to be discounted as negligible. According to him, those defenders callously expect the members of vulnerable minority groups to learn to live with the contumely that is heaped upon such groups.[12] These numerous accusations

[12] For some criticism of Waldron on this score, see Heinze 2016, 111–12, 211–12. See also Strossen and Molnar 2012, 382, 385, 387–90.

and insinuations by Waldron do not tally with the views actually articulated by any responsible defenders of the principle of freedom of expression. As is evident from Chapters 4 and 5, the very basis for upholding that principle is inconsistent with the notion that the members of reviled groups are appropriately left by a system of governance to fend for themselves in the face of bigoted signage and speeches. Any system of governance that adopts a posture of meek acquiescence in such bigotry is thereby failing to fulfill its paramount responsibility to bring about the political and social and economic conditions under which every member of a society can be warranted in feeling an ample sense of self-respect. To say as much, however, is not at all to endorse Waldron's stand on the propriety of hate-speech legislation.

Instead of imposing some legal prohibitions that contravene the principle of freedom of expression, a system of governance should strive to counter the advocacy of hateful credos by marshaling the sundry techniques that have been outlined in Chapter 5. When Waldron repeatedly asserts that any system of governance which legally tolerates the advocacy of those noxious credos is thereby turning a blind eye to the harms that such advocacy tends to bring about, he is making a mistake which I have criticized in Chapter 5. He is viewing some aspects of the operations of a system of governance in isolation from the other aspects thereof. If we look only at the prohibitions imposed by the criminal law and tort law in a given jurisdiction, and if we do not there find any prohibitions on the advocacy of racist doctrines, we might be tempted to conclude that the system of governance which presides over the jurisdiction is failing to come to grips with the malevolence of such doctrines. We might be tempted to conclude that no adequate steps are being taken to counteract the effects that can flow from the public espousal of bigotry. However, if the prevailing system of governance is fulfilling the basic moral responsibilities incumbent on it as a liberal democracy, any conclusions along these lines will be distortively blinkered. Such a system will not only be abiding by the principle of freedom of expression, but will also be acting on numerous other fronts to promote and fortify an ethos of liberal-democratic values. Whereas the principle of freedom of expression obligates a system of governance not to clamp legal restrictions on the advocacy of hateful ideas and the expression of hateful sentiments, the broader moral duties incumbent on the system require it—in full consistency with the principle of freedom of expression—to counter the propagation of such ideas and sentiments in any number of ways.

One of the foremost means by which any system of governance can legitimately stanch the spread of noisomely illiberal outlooks is its network of schools and other educational programs. Whether in the public sector or in the private sector, every school should be legally required to include in its curriculum some lessons and activities that are at least partly designed to foster the understanding and acceptance of elementary values of liberal democracy. Such lessons and activities should of course leave ample room for multifarious viewpoints along the political spectrum and for diverse perspectives on the underpinnings of the values of liberal democracy. For example, they should leave abundant room both for religious outlooks and for non-religious or irreligious outlooks, and they should likewise leave abundant room for attachments to any political parties that are not centered on odiously illiberal objectives. Lessons and educational activities undertaken for the purpose of solidifying a society's liberal-democratic ethos are grossly abused if they are channeled into partisan or sectarian narrowness. Still, provided that such narrowness is sedulously avoided, the boundaries highlighted and clarified by these educational endeavors are vital for the flourishing of the aforementioned ethos. Those boundaries, which mark the divisions between liberal democracy and viciously illiberal creeds, should be accentuated in the minds of students through the curricular and extracurricular programs in schools.

Educational offerings in schools have to be accompanied by a host of other governmental efforts, and also by the efforts of private individuals and organizations. Indeed, one crucial way in which a system of governance should operate to strengthen the embrace of fundamental liberal-democratic ideals is the provision of financial and logistical support to suitable anti-extremist groups. Such groups employ a diversity of techniques designed to avert the radicalization of youngsters or adults who might succumb to noxious ideologies, and to redeem individuals who have already fallen under the sway of such ideologies, and to monitor and expose the machinations of hatemongers, and to compile publicly available profiles of the hatemongers' activities, and to enlist widely admired people (such as athletes and entertainers) who can speak out forcefully against the allures of extremist doctrines, and to organize musical and dramatic events that can serve in part as statements against racism or other forms of extremism, and to mobilize consumer boycotts of companies that are associated with extremism, and so forth. Though many of these techniques can and should also be plied directly by a system of governance, they can often be employed more subtly and cogently by non-governmental groups which specialize in such matters and which have extensive connections to communities whose members are particularly susceptible to the wiles of hatemongers. Thus, frequently a system of governance can proceed most effectively by establishing an overarching framework of funding and coordination within which these heterogeneous anti-extremist groups can pursue their projects.

Beyond the overtly educational settings of schools, a system of governance plays a central pedagogical role in the broader society over which it presides. Statements made by officials at every tier of such a system are of major importance in setting the moral tone of a society. One high-profile example occurred during September 2001 in the aftermath of the atrocities committed in New York and Washington by Islamist terrorists. In several televised public pronouncements made in the hours and days that followed those heinous crimes, the American President George W. Bush took pains to underscore the distinction between Islam and Islamism. In so doing, he undoubtedly contributed to keeping low the incidence of retaliatory acts of violence against Muslims by other Americans within the United States.

Although the Bush Administration deserves excoriation for its countenancing of the use of torture in its subsequent war against terrorism,[13] Bush deserves credit for having recognized the pedagogical and hortatory import of his position at a moment of searingly high pressure in the country at large. In less prominent and far-reaching ways in a variety of contexts, officials at all levels of a system of governance can influence social mores salutarily (or detrimentally, if they misuse their positions by pandering to bigotry in their pronouncements).

Of course, unless the statements of officials are backed up by actions in some contexts, they are likely to seem hollow and even cynical. Any salutary influence that might be exerted by those statements would dissipate. However, we would go astray badly if we were to assume that the only germane actions in support of those statements are instances of prohibition and enforcement, or if we were to assume that the vital contexts for measures of prohibition and enforcement are the contexts to which hate-speech legislation is distinctively applicable. Rather, the decisive contexts for the effectuation of legal restrictions are those in which the hatemongers have moved beyond advocating their repellent beliefs and sentiments. Whenever the hatemongers have proceeded to engage in incitement or in targeted harassment or in fighting words or in practices of invidious discrimination or in acts of bigoted violence, they have breached the legal curbs on such modes of behavior. Those curbs should be enforced vigorously by a system of governance through its institutions of criminal law and tort law. Strong condemnations by relevant officials in response to crimes of these kinds are crucial, but they have to be backed up by the imposition of sanctions (within any applicable constraints of procedure and evidence).

Vigorous enforcement of the legal prohibitions just mentioned is indispensable partly because of the censorious messages which it conveys both to the offenders and to the public at large. Statements of condemnation by officials convey such messages as well, of course, but the levying of legal penalties will have valuably underscored the sincerity and meaningfulness of those statements. Such penalties will have shown that the prevailing system of governance practices what it preaches. Moreover, in line with what retributivists maintain, the administering of sanctions will amount to a public vindication of the dignity of any victims. It will thereby reaffirm the values of liberal democracy that have been flouted by bigots through their mistreatment of those victims. In addition, the preparedness of a system of governance to react robustly to hate-driven crimes will help to deter the perpetration of those crimes. Despite the shortcomings of the deterrence-oriented conception of punishment as a general rationale for the imposition of criminal sanctions,[14] there is no doubt that the deterrent impact of such sanctions can be

[13] For citations to a welter of writings about the Bush Administration's deplorable policies on the use of interrogational torture, see Kramer 2014, 34 n3.

[14] For an extended discussion of the shortcomings of the deterrence-oriented rationale for capital punishment, see Kramer 2011, 19–68.

morally salutary in lowering the incidence of grave misconduct. In all these ways, the workings of the institutions of criminal justice in an overarching system of governance are invaluable for countering the attempts by hatemongers to undermine the ethos of a liberal democracy. Those institutions, when oriented properly and operating effectively, serve to fortify that ethos by upholding its integral values both retrospectively and prospectively.

Of course, the principle of freedom of expression requires that the imposition of criminal-law or tort-law sanctions not be undertaken in contexts where the hatemongers have confined themselves to advocating their rebarbative ideas and sentiments. Any levying of sanctions in such contexts would not be communication-independent. However, with a modicum of imagination, officials can back up their disapproval with actions even in such contexts. An example of such an approach was evident at Logan Airport in Massachusetts during the late 1970s and early 1980s.[15] During that period, a virulently antisemitic sect that disingenuously designated itself as the "Liberty Lobby" was allowed by law—in accordance with the principle of freedom of expression—to distribute its leaflets and newsletters alongside the other political groups that were legally entitled to avail themselves of the airport as a public forum. In the proximity of the area that was set aside for the Liberty Lobby's representatives, the airport officials had positioned an unusually large number of receptacles for rubbish. Passersby on whom the buffoons from the Liberty Lobby foisted their materials were thus able to deposit those materials promptly into appropriate bins. Quite a few of the recipients of the Liberty Lobby's documents ostentatiously ripped them up before so depositing them. Hence, an endeavor by extremists to gain currency for their warped outlook instead became an array of occasions for mockery of that outlook. As should generally happen in a society with a robust liberal-democratic ethos, the espousal of a doctrine of bigotry and hatred brought scorn upon the proponents of that doctrine rather than upon its targets.

In a multitude of ways, then, a system of governance that abides firmly by the principle of freedom of expression can operate to avert and counter the deleterious effects that might otherwise ensue from the advocacy of pernicious ideas by extremists. As has been suggested, some of the techniques involve the government's facilitation of various activities that are pursued by private individuals and organizations, while other techniques proceed through the workings of governmental institutions and agencies directly. With a medley of such approaches, a system of governance can fulfill its moral responsibility to sustain a robust liberal-democratic ethos in the society over which it presides. Far from doing nothing to combat the hateful ideologies whose proselytizers are legally tolerated insofar as they confine themselves to the advocacy of their grotesque ideas and aspirations, a system of

[15] The observations in this paragraph derive from what I witnessed at Logan Airport on a number of occasions during the specified period.

governance that does carry out its moral responsibilities in this fashion will be striving to keep the miasma of those ideologies very firmly in check. We can discern as much when we survey the operations of the system in their full range, instead of focusing on some aspect of them distortively in isolation. When we do take a synoptic view, we can readily see that an insistence on legal toleration in compliance with the principle of freedom of expression is hardly a policy of turning a blind eye to the poisonousness of hateful utterances. Nor is it a policy of leaving the members of vulnerable minority groups to fend for themselves. Doing nothing is scarcely the lone alternative to the illiberality of hate-speech laws.

6.4 A Second Rejoinder to Waldron: The Demeaningness of Hate-Speech Legislation

Whereas all the techniques for countering extremism that have just been outlined are in accordance with the principle of freedom of expression, the hate-speech legislation which Waldron champions is squarely in contravention of that principle. Such legislation, though doubtless well-intentioned, is in fact deeply demeaning. It bespeaks the failure of a system of governance to bring about the political and social and economic conditions under which every member of a society can be warranted in sustaining a high level of self-respect. The degradingness of hate-speech laws is indeed abundantly apparent from the rationale for them which Waldron elaborates.

Waldron more than once assures his readers that the legal prohibitions which he favors are not designed to control people's thoughts (2012, 33, 35, 38, 100). However, when he advances those assurances, he has in mind the hatemongers to whose utterances the legal prohibitions might be applied; he is indicating correctly that the prohibitions are targeted at certain oral or written pronouncements by such people, rather than at the sentiments which they harbor in their hearts. Yet if we train our scrutiny instead on the members of the public at large to whom those nasty pronouncements would be addressed, we can detect a straightforward sense in which the hate-speech restrictions are designed to control people's thoughts.

Among the addressees of the utterances issued by hatemongers are people in whom those purveyors of extremism hope to elicit bigoted attitudes. As Waldron recounts, the utterances of the hatemongers are designed to intimidate certain minorities and to salute fellow bigots and to inveigle members of the public at large. Of central importance to the hate-speech statutes which Waldron commends are the people in the last-mentioned group: the members of the public at large, whom the hatemongers aspire to persuade. As Waldron remarks, all of those statutes "are concerned with the use of words which are ... directed at members of vulnerable minorities, *calculated to stir up hatred against them*" (2012, 8–9, emphasis added). Were the ravings of the bigoted fanatics communicated only to the people whom the fanatics despise, and were those ravings inaccessible to third parties, the concern of the hate-speech statutes about the stirring up of hatred against the targets of the fanatics' vitriol would not be triggered. That concern is activated only insofar as the vitriol is disseminated to third parties.

Moreover, the centrality of the role of the public at large in the rationale for hate-speech laws is evident from Waldron's whole justification of those laws. As has been observed in §6.1.4 of this chapter, Waldron is careful to distinguish between the impairment of dignity and the causing of offense. By his reckoning, hate-speech laws tackle the former matter rather than the latter. Dignity, as Waldron explicates it, is an elementary social status. It consists in the social reputation of a person as a member of his or her society in good standing. In other words, it consists in a person's being prevalently regarded by his or her fellow citizens as someone who possesses the same basic entitlements and who bears the same basic responsibilities as any other member of the society in good standing. When something impairs the dignity of a person, it lowers or weakens her social reputation by inclining her fellow citizens to doubt whether they have been correct in perceiving her as a member of their society in good standing. A hatemonger tries to produce such an effect by imputing various negative characteristics to everyone in a certain racial or ethnic or religious group. In addition to seeking to dismay the individuals whose ethnic or racial or religious affiliations are the targets of his invective—and in addition to seeking to hearten and galvanize his fellow bigots by signaling his allegiance to their cause—the hatemonger seeks to sway the opinions of members of the public at large. It is the opinion-shaping ambition of the hatemonger that chiefly warrants the classification of his malign jeremiads as attacks on the dignity of the people whom he vilifies.

Given the centrality of the role of the public at large in Waldron's rationale for hate-speech laws, two conclusions are appropriate here. First, contrary to Waldron's claims that such laws are not designed to control people's thoughts, one of the prime purposes thereof is to guard against any debasing of people's outlooks through their exposure to the effusions of extremists. The realization of that purpose sustains the dignity of the individuals who belong to the religious or ethnic or racial groups that would be traduced by those effusions. Since the sustainment of the dignity of the individuals who belong to those vulnerable minority groups is the raison d'être of hate-speech legislation by Waldron's reckoning, his understanding of that legislation presents it as a form of thought-control. As has been stated above, we can see this point clearly when we turn our attention from the minds of the speakers to the minds of the addressees of the speakers. Unless the thoughts of the addressees are successfully controlled by hate-speech laws, those laws will fail to achieve the aim which Waldron ascribes to them and which he believes to be sufficient to justify them: namely, the aim of upholding the fundamental social reputations of the individuals who belong to the groups that would be reviled by the hatemongers.

A second conclusion, in line with what has already been suggested, is that the hate-speech legislation supported by Waldron is deeply demeaning for any society in which it is enacted. Such legislation presupposes the moral viciousness of the members of the public in that society. It therefore presupposes that the prevailing system of governance has woefully failed to bring about the social and political and economic conditions under which every member of the society can be warranted in harboring an ample sense of self-respect.

This claim about a presupposition of moral viciousness is of course not centered on the fact that the hate-speech legislation takes as given that there are very likely some people in the society who will be inclined to engage in hateful public pronouncements if such utterances are legally tolerated. In that regard, the hate-speech legislation no more demeans a society than does a legal prohibition on murder or arson. In each case, although the introduction of the specified legal restriction does not necessarily rest on the premise that the forbidden misconduct is likely to be perpetrated by some people in the absence of legal constraints,[16] it is most plausibly construable as resting on just such a premise (Hart 1994, 197–8). Yet the fact that such a premise undergirds the legal proscription of murder or arson does not demean the public at large. Members of the general public are not belittled when legal-governmental officials recognize that some nefarious people among those members would be strongly inclined to perpetrate murders or acts of arson if no legal sanctions were in prospect. Similarly, members of the general public are not belittled by the sheer fact that legal-governmental officials have recognized that the extremists among those members would be strongly inclined to express repellent ideas and sentiments if no legal sanctions were in prospect.

What does demean a whole society, however, is a further presupposition which underlies any hate-speech statutes that are grounded on the rationale supplied for them by Waldron. No such further presupposition underlies a statute that forbids murder or arson or theft. If hateful pronouncements by bigots were to produce any dignity-impairing effects, they would do so principally through the reactions of third parties. As has been observed already, reactions of third parties in sympathy with the pronouncements are what would damage the basic social status—the basic dignity—of the people in the vulnerable minority groups against whom the bigots inveigh. Were substantial numbers of third parties to be convinced by the vituperation of the hatemongers, the dignity-undermining effects of the vituperation would be significant. By contrast, if the ethos of a society is robustly liberal-democratic, the vitriol of the hatemongers will convince hardly anyone (especially given that the system of governance in such a society will be undertaking diverse measures to avert any proliferation of bigotry). In that event, any dignity-attenuating effects of the vitriol will be negligible. Instead of arousing any

[16] On this point, see Waldron 2012, 80–1. Waldron draws there on Rawls 1999, 211.

significant hostility toward the people in vulnerable minority groups, the purveyors of hate will arouse contempt toward themselves. Accordingly, when hate-speech laws are enacted on the grounds which Waldron adduces in favor of them, they presuppose that the ethos of the relevant society is not robustly liberal-democratic. They presuppose that substantial numbers of people in that society are highly receptive to egregiously malevolent doctrines. In other words, the hate-speech laws presuppose that the overall tenor of the society is morally vicious.

6.4.1 Group Libel versus Individual Libel

This observation about the degradingness of Waldronian hate-speech statutes is connected to a distinction that can shed light on one major aspect of *The Harm in Hate Speech*. In the third chapter of that book, Waldron seeks to revive the designation of "group libel" for the bigoted invective that would be banned under the aforementioned statutes. Although that designation was employed by the U.S. Supreme Court and many American legal scholars in the mid-twentieth century, it has since fallen largely out of favor in the United States. However, it continues to be used in quite a few European countries (Waldron 2012, 39–40), and Waldron is keen to reclaim it in the American context.

On the one hand, despite the designation, the harm inflicted by group libel—as Waldron understands it—is ultimately incurred by each member of some racial or religious or ethnic group. It consists in the damaging of the basic social reputation of each such person. On the other hand, that harm is incurred because of obloquy directed against the group to which the various members belong. The social standing of each of them is impaired through calumnies that are focused on what they have in common. As Waldron writes:

> In all of this, though we are talking about group dignity, our point of reference is the individual members of the group, not the dignity of the group as such or the dignity of the culture or social structure that holds the group together. The ultimate concern is what happens to individuals when defamatory imputations are associated with shared characteristics such as race, ethnicity, religion, gender, sexuality, and national origin. (Waldron 2012, 60, endnote omitted)

Group libel differs from individual libel in that the latter resides in unfounded and pejorative allegations about some person where the allegations do not ascribe negative characteristics to any racial or ethnic or religious group of which the person is a member. Individual libel concentrates on what the person himself has supposedly done or said or believed, rather than on the putative depravity of any race or religion or ethnicity to which the person belongs. Waldron contends that, although the nature of the legal sanctions imposed for group libel should differ from the nature of the legal sanctions imposed for individual libel, there should indeed be legal sanctions in prospect for each of those types of misconduct. Whereas the sanctions imposed for individual libel should generally be awards of damages in tort-law proceedings, the sanctions imposed for group libel should generally be fines or terms of imprisonment in criminal-law proceedings. That divergence between the types of remedies available is reflective of the divergence between the types of wrongs perpetrated. As Waldron declares:

> [T]he law has traditionally pursued two complementary concerns in this domain. On the one hand, there is the concern for personalized reputation in civil cases. On the other hand, there is a concern for the fundamentals of *anyone's* reputation or civic dignity as a member of society in good standing. The latter has been the concern of the law of criminal libel. Unlike civil libel, criminal libel has traditionally been interested not in protecting the intricate detail of each individual's personalized reputation and that person's particular position in the scale of social estimation, but in protecting the foundation of each person's reputation. (Waldron 2012, 52, emphasis in original)

Now, as we have beheld in §3.2.4 of Chapter 3, the availability of tort-law sanctions for some instances of individual libel is reconcilable with the principle of freedom of expression. By contrast, the present chapter will be arguing that the imposition of legal sanctions for any instances of group libel—where none of the categories discussed in §6.1 of this chapter is applicable—is always squarely at odds with the principle of freedom of expression. The cardinal reason for the protectedness of group libel under that principle and the unprotectedness of some instances of individual libel is that legal restrictions on the former are not communication-neutral whereas legal restrictions on the latter can be communication-neutral. We are able to see that point clearly when we compare §3.2.4 in Chapter 3 with §§6.1.9 and 6.5 in the current chapter. Here, however, we should ponder an ancillary reason why the principle of freedom of expression does exempt group libel from legal sanctions and sometimes does not exempt individual libel. This ancillary reason is directly connected to what has been said already about the demeaningness of hate-speech laws. In other words, we are here encountering a further ground for maintaining that such laws presuppose the moral viciousness of any society in which they are enacted.

When an individual is defamed as a child molester or a thief or a murderer on the basis of colorable factual assertions that will eventually turn out to be unfounded, reasonable third parties will be apt to lower their opinions of the traduced person. At least until the baselessness of the assertions is exposed (if it is ever exposed), and probably to some degree thereafter, the reputation of the person will suffer considerably. Perhaps a third party is unreasonable if she firmly credits the allegations against the libeled person before that person has had an adequate opportunity to rebut them, but no unreasonableness is involved in arriving more rapidly at the conclusion that the allegations might be true. Since even that milder and more tentative conclusion will be seriously damaging to the reputation of the person who has been maligned, the widespread adoption of such a view of the matter will detract greatly from the esteem in which the person is held by the other members of his community. Consequently, the severe impairment of a person's reputation by defamatory accusations is consistent with the reasonableness of the third parties whose reactions constitute that impairment. Hence, a law that safeguards individuals against such accusations does not perforce presuppose that the members of the society in which that law obtains are unreasonable. Without being unreasonable, members of the public can widely be inclined to adjust downward their appraisals of a person who has been baselessly but plausibly defamed.

Much the same is true when an instance of "individual" libel is committed against an organization such as a business corporation. Suppose that a corporation is falsely but colorably alleged to engage in highly exploitative labor practices or to use adulterated ingredients in the manufacturing of its food products or to neglect elementary safety procedures with cavalier remissness. Until the unfoundedness of the allegations has been solidly established, many people may reasonably be disposed to give some credence to them. Unless the allegations are propounded in a fashion that makes clear from the outset their untrustworthiness, one's crediting of them to some degree by lowering one's esteem for the besmirched corporation does not in itself bespeak any viciousness in one's outlook. Thus, a corporation can incur serious damage to its reputation through baseless charges against it even if all or virtually all members of the relevant society are ethically and epistemically reasonable. That damage will occur if the charges are widely credited among the people in the society, and—as has just been maintained—such a development can materialize without any unreasonableness on the part of those people. Accordingly, when a law safeguards businesses against the reputational harm that can be inflicted by spurious imputations, it does not thereby presuppose the moral viciousness of the members of the society in which that law has been enacted.

Group libel, as the bigoted vitriol that is covered by hate-speech laws, is quite different. Suppose that a hatemonger distributes a leaflet which proclaims that all Muslims are bomb-planting terrorists or that all Hispanics are murderers and rapists or that all Catholics are paedophiles. Or suppose that the leaflet is a display of pictures in which black people are portrayed as apes or in which Jews are portrayed as blood-sucking parasites. Can the recipients of the leaflet, on whom the hatemonger foists it, reasonably give credence to its invective? As is evident, the answer to this question is negative. No one could reasonably credit any of the propositions just broached or any similar propositions that might be conveyed by the filth which the hatemonger disseminates. Anybody who does credit any of those propositions—however tentatively—is *pro tanto* evincing moral viciousness. Yet the elementary social reputations of Muslims or Hispanics or Catholics or blacks or Jews will be weakened by the distribution of the hatemonger's literature only if substantial numbers of third parties are inclined to be persuaded by the views expressed in that literature. Ergo, the weakening of the elementary social reputations of the individuals who belong to any of those religious or ethnic or racial groups will occur only if substantial numbers of people in the hatemonger's society are morally vicious.

Now, Waldron contends that the purpose of hate-speech laws is to avert the erosion of the basic social reputations of the members of vulnerable minority groups. Such erosion would be brought about by the harangues of bigots in a given society only if substantial numbers of people there would respond approvingly to those harangues. In other words, the rationale for hate-speech laws elaborated by Waldron presupposes that substantial numbers of people in a given society are receptive to the venom of extremists. His rationale presupposes that substantial numbers of people in that society—and thus the society itself as an overarching entity—are morally vicious. Any hate-speech laws enacted on the basis of Waldron's rationale are vested with a similar presupposition.

6.4.2 The Robustness of a Liberal-Democratic Ethos

Waldron bewails the absence of hate-speech laws in the United States. He therefore presumes that the liberal-democratic ethos in the United States is tenuous and that the country as an overarching entity is morally vicious. In *The Harm in Hate Speech*, he does in fact quite often write as if the ethos of liberal democracy in the United States is highly precarious. His position on that point is greatly accentuated by his very frequent suggestions that the sole alternative to the enactment of hate-speech laws is to do nothing about public expressions of bigotry.

6.4.2.1 An Impression of Precariousness

One way in which Waldron conveys the impression of the United States as a powder-keg country is that he sometimes refers to examples of explosively illiberal societies as if they shed light on the situation of contemporary liberal democracies. For instance, he twice refers to the radio broadcasts in Rwanda in the spring of 1994 that called for the perpetration of genocide by Hutus against the Tutsis.[17] Many of those repugnant broadcasts, which were abetted by the Rwandan government in the aftermath of the assassination of the country's President, were properly classifiable as state-supported incitement and were thus rightly liable to severe punishments. Their hideousness sheds little light on the types of invective

[17] Waldron 2012, 34, 71. The horrific radio broadcasts before and during the Rwandan genocide are discussed at a number of junctures in Gourevitch 1998. See also Cotler 2012, 439–45; Mengistu 2012, 360–1, 372–4; Somerville 2012; Strossen 2018, 66.

that are at issue between Waldron and his opponents in debates over the introduction of hate-speech laws. In those debates, the invective at issue does not amount to incitement—for any vitriol that does amount to incitement is covered by already-existent legal restrictions. Nor, of course, does the system of governance in the contemporary United States sponsor the fulminations of extreme bigots.

Elsewhere in his book, Waldron adverts to the ferocious antisemitism among Christians in eighteenth-century England and in medieval Europe (2012, 204–7, 232). Such antisemitism remained fierce in western Europe long into the twentieth century, and it has to some degree lingered in eastern European countries such as Poland and Hungary and Austria. Still, in the modern-day United States and United Kingdom—the two countries to which Waldron devotes most of his attention—Christian antisemitism has dwindled to an untroubling level. The antisemitism that persists in those countries is to be found chiefly among certain Muslims and on the far left and far right of the political spectrum. Though Jeremy Corbyn's takeover of the Labour Party in the United Kingdom considerably exacerbated the problem of Jew-hatred in that country, the incidence of animosity toward Jews among people in the political mainstream is far short of what it was in bygone centuries.

Apart from occasionally referring to some tendentious examples, Waldron more directly depicts the modern-day United States as a country in which every instance of racist vituperation is sufficient to jeopardize the basic social standing of the individuals who belong to any targeted minority group. For instance, he writes: "[R]acial segregation, second-class citizenship, racist terrorism (lynchings, cross-burnings, fire-bombings of churches) are living memories in the United States … and those memories of racial terror are nightmarishly awakened each time one of these postings or pamphlets is put out into the public realm" (Waldron 2012, 31). Waldron is of course accurate in referring to the shameful history of racist domination and persecution in the United States. Precisely because of the ghastliness of that history, and because of the grimness of the history in every other country that is now properly classified as a liberal democracy, the measures commended in §6.3 to counter the blandishments of extremists are particularly pressing. However, one's awareness of the atrocities in quondam centuries—with the inequalities that persist to this day as their legacy—should not lead one to endorse Waldron's suggestion that the ethos of liberal democracy in the present-day United States is threatened whenever a hatemonger distributes a pamphlet full of vile racist claptrap.

Waldron begs to differ. On the one hand, he allows that the "actions [of hatemongers] may not seem all that significant in themselves; an isolated incident here, a forlorn Nazi procession there, some ratty racist little leaflet." On the other hand, he retorts that "precisely because the public good that is under attack is provided in a general, diffuse, and implicit way, the flare-up of a few particular incidents can have a disproportionate effect" (Waldron 2012, 94). He articulates a similar view at a slightly earlier juncture in his book, in a passage which I have already quoted at greater length. There he asserts that the aim of racists or antisemites with their bigoted posters and leaflets is

> to undermine this assurance [of equal dignity which a society offers to the members of vulnerable groups], call it in question, and taint it with visible expressions of hatred, exclusion, and contempt. And so it begins: what was implicitly assured is now visibly challenged, so that there is a whole new set of calculations for a minority member to engage in as he sets out to do business or take a walk in public with his family. (Waldron 2012, 88–9)

Waldron explains that "the necessary implicitness of this assurance makes it tremendously vulnerable" (88).

6.4.2.2 Waldron in a Different Key

If the ethos of a liberal democracy in the contemporary United States were as thin and fragile as Waldron represents it in the passages quoted above, the American system of governance would have failed miserably to bring about the political and social and economic conditions under which every citizen can be warranted in feeling a strong sense of self-respect. In a society where the moral obligation to bring about such conditions has been fulfilled by the prevailing system of governance, and where the ethos of a liberal democracy is therefore robust, any hatemongers with their rants bring disgrace upon themselves rather than upon the minority groups whom they deride. Waldron conveys the clear impression that no such robust ethos has evolved in the American context, on which he predominantly focuses. He thereby conveys the impression that the system of governance in the United States has woefully failed to meet its fundamental moral responsibilities.

To query whether the situation is as bleak as the quoted passages suggest, we do not have to have recourse to any elaborate empirical studies. We can turn instead to other passages in *The Harm in Hate Speech*. At a couple of important junctures in his book—both of which, as it happens, are junctures at which he is arguing against Ronald Dworkin—Waldron acknowledges forthrightly that the ethos of liberal democracy in the contemporary United States is much more solid than might be inferred from other portions of his text.

At the first of those two junctures, Waldron points out that the success of the U.S. federal government in implementing the various American constitutional provisions and statutes that prohibit invidious discrimination has been due in large part to the strength of the aforementioned ethos:

> The law does not have the resources to provide an armed escort for every minority member who wants to approach and enter a school, or university, or other public accommodation without fear of being turned away and humiliated on

> racial grounds ... States don't have the coercive resources to do this in any but a very few cases, and anyway it is hardly a satisfactory provision of justice when an individual has to proceed under armed escort. Even routine enforcement efforts by the Department of Justice against routine discrimination can handle only a handful of cases. By and large, the law has to rely in this area—as in almost every area—on self-application by ordinary citizens. And this means that any citizen who relies upon the *law* is, in the last analysis, relying indirectly on the voluntary cooperation of his or her fellow citizens. (Waldron 2012, 98–9, emphasis in original)

As Waldron sums up the matter, with reference to most of the responsibilities of justice that are incumbent on any system of governance: "The discharge of some governmental responsibilities is impossible without the whole-hearted cooperation of members of the public" (100).

Admittedly, Waldron's ruminations here are consistent with the proposition that the whole-hearted cooperation of Americans in effectuating the requirements of antidiscrimination laws is due to the esteem of Americans for legal mandates rather than to their esteem for any of the liberal-democratic values embodied by those mandates. Such a proposition is far from compelling, but it is not strictly inconsistent with what Waldron has said here. Even more important, then, is a second juncture at which he proclaims that Americans act in accordance with the values of liberal democracy. At that later juncture, he makes clear that the patterns of behavior which he describes are attributable to the pervasive acceptance of liberal-democratic values by people in the United States. A lengthy quotation is warranted:

> And maybe there was a time when we needed to have a great national debate about *race*—about whether there were different kinds of human beings, inferior and superior lines of human descent, ranked in hierarchies of capability, responsibility, and authority, and, if there were, what the implications would be for justice, morality, and public policy. Maybe there was a time when social policy generally—and perhaps immigration policy and cultural policy, in particular—could not adequately be debated without raising the whole issue of race in this sense. But that is not our situation today. It would be fatuous to suggest that our political community is in the throes of such a debate right now—a vital and ongoing debate crucial to the legitimacy of public policy. It would be fatuous to suggest that it is the importance of our continuing engagement in a debate of this kind that requires us to endure the ugly invective of racial defamation in the marketplace of ideas. In fact, the fundamental debate about race is over—won; finished. There are outlying dissenters, a few crazies who say they believe that people of African descent are an inferior form of animal; but for half a century or more, we have moved forward as a society on the premise that this is no longer a matter of serious consideration. (Waldron 2012, 195, emphasis in original, endnotes omitted)

This passage is remarkable in a book where Waldron has been declaring that any distribution of leaflets or pamphlets with portrayals of black people as apes would pose a threat to the basic social standing of black people. Since the basic social standing of anyone resides in the attitudes of members of the public at large, the threat envisaged by Waldron will be nontrivial only if numerous members of the public are inclined to credit the despicable canards in the racist leaflets or pamphlets. Yet here Waldron forcefully and rightly denies that members of the American public—beyond the ostracized "crazies" who distribute the leaflets or pamphlets—are so inclined. He drives this point home further in a lengthy endnote where he expands on the passage just above:

> It is not merely the fact that serious debate has died away on these topics. We regard them as settled also in the sense that we have erected whole swaths of social policy on their settlement. The falsity of the racist's claim, for example, is one of the fundamentals of our scheme of justice, not only in the sense that we take it for granted but in the sense that we feel entitled to build great edifices of law and policy on its foundation—education policy, strategies for equal opportunity, permanent mechanisms for securing equal concern and respect. And we most emphatically do not think we have to regard these edifices as temporary, liable to be dismantled next year or the year after, depending on how the debate about race comes out. We treat the falsity of the claim about race as one of the fundamentals of our approach to justice, and we distinguish it now from contestable elements like economic equality, affirmative action, progressive taxes, social provision in the public realm, and so on. (270 n34)

6.4.2.3 Philosophy Rather Than Social Science

Like Waldron's *The Harm in Hate Speech*, the present book is a work of philosophy rather than a work of social science. On the one hand, as is doubtless apparent, I generally concur with the most recently quoted passages and their favorable remarks on the breadth and depth of Americans' allegiances to the ideal of liberal equality in opposition to racism. Those allegiances, which have solidified during the decades since the civil-rights campaigns of the 1960s (as Waldron observes), are of course marked by significant variations among people's understandings of what the ideal of liberal equality requires and permits. Nevertheless, the Americans who still reject that ideal outright—to the extent of regarding black people as apes—are on the extreme fringes rather than in the mainstream. To be sure, in the years since the publication of Waldron's book on hate speech, there occurred the calamity of the election of Donald Trump to one term as President of the United States. Yet even Trump, the first major-party Presidential candidate for decades to engage in overt race-baiting while campaigning, did not clearly weaken the attachments of Americans to the values of liberal democracy. Although his demagoguery invigorated many of the bigots who were already on the extreme fringes, and although that demagoguery was associated with some year-to-year increases in hate crimes (Edwards 2020, 312), the statistical analysis in one major study concludes that the loyalties of ordinary Americans to the aforementioned values were strengthened rather than weakened during the grotesque Presidency of Trump (Hopkins and Washington 2020).

This predominantly favorable account of the views of contemporary Americans on matters of race is connected to a point that is obscured in Waldron's musings with his quite heavy reliance—throughout the fourth chapter of his book—on John Rawls's conception of a well-ordered society. As Waldron remarks (2012, 78), Rawls held that compliance with liberal requirements of justice is universal among the members of a well-ordered society. Instead of only partial compliance, there is full compliance. Rawls had his own theoretical reasons for posing a distinction between full compliance and partial compliance, but that dichotomy is mainly unhelpful for broader philosophical purposes. In any actual situation, the prospect of full compliance is overwhelmingly unlikely and is in any event unnecessary for the robustness of the liberal-democratic ethos in a society. Thus, instead of focusing on the desideratum of full compliance, we should be focusing on the desideratum of preponderant compliance. If the large majority of people in a society uphold the basic requirements of liberal equality, and if the system of governance in that society actively carries out measures of the kinds that have been adumbrated in §6.3 of this chapter, the aberrant people on the fringes who reject the fundamental requirements of liberal equality will not appreciably impair the ethos of decency that prevails in the society. Fortified by the measures just mentioned, that robust ethos can comfortably withstand the maunderings of the bigots along the fringes whose expressions of contempt for others bring contempt upon themselves. Such a society is rightly classifiable as well-ordered even though it lacks the thoroughgoing unanimity (on basic matters of justice) that is to be found nowhere outside a cemetery.

On the other hand, even if Waldron were correct in the passages where he writes pessimistically about the extraordinary fragility of the ethos of liberal-democratic values in the United States, my main conclusions in this chapter would be unaffected. Those conclusions are not hostage to social-scientific findings. Even if the arrangements that sustain the basic dignity of the members of vulnerable minority groups were as frail in the United States as Waldron ofttimes contends, the hate-speech laws advocated by him would be doubly degrading if they were introduced there. In the first place, as has already been argued, those laws presuppose the moral viciousness of any society that adopts them. Such laws enacted in the United States on the basis of Waldron's rationale would presuppose the correctness of his admonitions about the insolidity of the liberal-democratic ethos there, and would thus presuppose that morally vicious outlooks are very widespread in the United States. Such laws would bespeak the failure of the American system of governance to discharge its paramount moral obligation—its obligation to secure the social and political and economic conditions under which everyone in the United States can be warranted in sustaining a hearty sense of self-respect. Furthermore, as will be argued in the next section of this chapter, the hate-speech laws favored by Waldron are blatantly in contravention of the principle of freedom of expression. As has been maintained in my fourth chapter, the adherence by a system of governance to that principle is itself a key element of the conditions under which everyone in a society can be warranted in harboring a strong sense of self-respect. Consequently, the hate-speech laws extolled by Waldron would further detract from those conditions. In relation to the paramount moral obligation of every system of governance, such laws would be both a symbol of failure and a perpetuator of failure.

At the very best, those laws in some extreme circumstances might be less gravely wrong than would the non-enactment of them. In a situation where a system of governance has miserably fallen short of promoting a robust ethos of liberal-democratic values in the society over which the system presides, the dissemination of malicious falsehoods about some vulnerable minority group might very seriously jeopardize the basic dignity of the members of that group—even where the *Brandenburg* standard for incitement is not satisfied. In such a quandary, the enactment of some legal restrictions on the dissemination of those falsehoods might be less gravely wrong for a certain period than would the continuation of a policy of legally permitting the dissemination. As Chapter 1 has explained, conflicts of this type can arise between the principle of freedom of expression and some other moral requirements in extreme circumstances. When such a moral conflict does occur, a system of governance is under a moral obligation to abide by the principle of freedom of expression and is simultaneously under a moral obligation to deviate from that principle. Moreover, notwithstanding that the former obligation is always dauntingly stringent, it can be less stringent in some conceivable situations than the latter obligation. Although the moral constraints imposed by the principle of freedom of expression on any system of governance are absolute in that they are always and everywhere binding, their absoluteness—as Chapter 1 has recounted—is weak rather than strong. Formidably stringent though the principle of freedom of expression is, there can be extreme circumstances in which a conflicting moral requirement is even more so. Nonetheless, as Chapter 1 has emphasized, a moral obligation that has been overtopped in stringency by a conflicting moral obligation is still binding. Hence, even in the truly exceptional situations where the principle of freedom of expression has been so overtopped, it remains fully binding. Contraventions of it are morally wrong even when they are morally optimal. Hate-speech laws adopted in contravention of that principle are doubly degrading in the ways just expounded, whether or not a contrary course of action would have been even worse. At their very best, then, hate-speech laws are lamentable.

6.5 Riding Roughshod over Freedom of Expression

Laws that prohibit the articulation and distribution of hateful screeds—where none of the categories explored in §6.1 of this chapter is applicable—are squarely in violation of the principle of freedom of expression. Indeed, it is to the credit of Waldron that he does not pretend otherwise. He acknowledges straightforwardly that hate-speech laws are not content-neutral, as he avows that "the kind of restriction we have in mind operates and is envisaged explicitly as a limitation based on content." He adds:

> As [a content-focused restriction], it flies directly in the face of one of the pillars of American free-speech doctrine—namely, the principle that an exception may not be based on the content of what is said or published, or on the distance between what is said or published, on the one hand, and, on the other hand, some official orthodoxy which everyone in society is supposed to subscribe to in public. (Waldron 2012, 150)

With refreshing candor, in a sentence which I have quoted in §6.1.9 above, he goes on to proclaim: "Better to admit that hate speech ... is forbidden, where it is, because of the effect *of its content* in helping to undermine the assurance that members of vulnerable groups are supposed to be able to draw from the public affirmation of their dignity" (151, emphasis in original). Slightly later, in another sentence quoted in §6.1.9, he again accepts that it is "better just to acknowledge straight up that a restriction on hate speech or on group defamation is a restriction on speech on account of its content, and that it is the content that explains the restriction" (152).

One thing to be emphasized briefly here in response to Waldron's phrasing is that categories such as fighting words and true threats and incitement and targeted harassment are not *exceptions* to the principle of freedom of expression. On the contrary, they are *corollaries* of that principle. A straightforward implication of the principle of freedom of expression is that the communicative conduct covered by each of those categories is open to being legally restricted in a communication-neutral fashion. Waldron altogether misses this point when he writes disparagingly as follows:

> American First Amendment doctrine is mostly a tangled mess, as judges and legal scholars add byzantine epicycles to their basic principles in order to accommodate various exceptions that for one reason or another they are inclined to allow. Other countries have not allowed their free-speech doctrine to degenerate in this way, partly because their commitment to free speech is not presented as uncompromising in the first place, so that their departures from free speech are not the shamefaced lapses that Americans have to acknowledge. (Waldron 2012, 152)

Waldron here commits an error against which I have warned since my opening chapter. That is, he thinks that the absoluteness of the principle of freedom of expression entails the conclusion that every mode or instance of communicative conduct is exempt from legal restrictions.[18] No such conclusion in fact follows from the absoluteness of that principle. Consequently, the aforementioned categories in the jurisprudence of the First Amendment which are inconsistent with that conclusion—categories such as fighting words and true threats and incitement and targeted harassment—are not exceptions to the principle of freedom of expression. Much less are they "shamefaced lapses." Rather, as has just been stated, they are corollaries of that principle. As has been explained since my opening chapters, what the principle of freedom of expression absolutely disallows are legal prohibitions on communicative conduct that are not communication-neutral and content-neutral and speaker-neutral. Every such prohibition that transgresses any of those constraints of neutrality is morally impermissible, always and everywhere. However, a legal prohibition can be impeccably neutral in all the specified respects even though the scope of its interdictory sway encompasses many instances of communicative conduct. When a legal mandate is indeed neutral in all those respects, it is fully consistent with the principle of freedom of expression. Any types or instances of communication that fall within the prohibitory ambit of such a mandate are not exceptions to the principle of freedom of expression at all. Their being legitimately subject to sanctions because of their falling within that ambit is not something that detracts from the absoluteness of the principle of freedom of expression in any way.

All the same, Waldron is correct in acknowledging that the hate-speech laws which he champions are not content-neutral. They are directed against the viewpoints conveyed by certain modes of expression, even though those modes of expression do not constitute the perpetration of any misdeeds that are prohibitable on communication-independent grounds. Accordingly, the laws commended by Waldron are flagrantly at odds with the principle of freedom of expression. A system of governance that enacts them is thereby moving away from the conditions under which everyone can be warranted in sustaining an ample sense of self-respect. It does so by acting in a fashion that is simultaneously overweening and self-abasing. In so doing, it contravenes the paramount moral obligation that is incumbent upon every system of governance—as Chapter 4 has explained.

Waldron might respond in either or both of two ways. First, in keeping with the strongly consequentialist tenor of his theorizing throughout *The Harm in Hate Speech*, he is likely to regard the violations of the principle of freedom of expression as drawbacks that are to be balanced against the benefits of lowering the incidence of ugly racist invective in the public fora of a society. He will reckon that, if the

[18] For similar views, see Badamchi 2015, 909; Bollinger 1986, 176–9; Brison 1998, 318–19; Gelber and Brison 2019, 28 n8; Langton 2009, 5. See also Holmes 2012, 345–6. For a corrective, see Linde 1970, 1183 n66.

benefits substantially outweigh the drawbacks, the operativeness of hate-speech laws is both morally permissible and morally obligatory for a system of governance. However, as I have maintained throughout the present book, the principle of freedom of expression is deontological rather than consequentialist in character. Instead of articulating some consequentialist considerations that are to be balanced against countervailing consequentialist considerations in a cost/benefit calculation, it imposes some moral obligations that are binding always and everywhere on systems of governance. When such a system contravenes the principle of freedom of expression by adopting restrictions on communicative conduct that are non-neutral in one or more of the dimensions recounted above, it *pro tanto* undermines the political conditions under which everyone can be warranted in feeling a hearty sense of self-respect. Being always under a moral obligation to secure those conditions (along with the social and economic conditions under which everyone can be warranted in feeling such a sense of self-respect), a system of governance that contravenes the principle of freedom of expression is acting impermissibly regardless of any benefits that are attendant on its so acting.

A second retort of which Waldron avails himself is closely similar to the retort by MacKinnon which we have examined near the end of my fifth chapter. That is, drawing explicitly on MacKinnon's work at this juncture, Waldron fleers at his opponents for supposedly relying on a primitive conception of causation. He begins by drawing an analogy between his concerns about basic social dignity and the concerns of environmentalists: "In a way, we are talking here about an *environmental* good—the *atmosphere* of a well-ordered society—as well as the ways in which a certain ecology of respect, dignity, and assurance is maintained, and the ways in which it can be polluted" (Waldron 2012, 96, emphases in original). He then declares that anything along the lines of the clear-and-present-danger test, which is so frequently invoked by his opponents to differentiate between communicative conduct that can legitimately be banned and communicative conduct that is morally exempt from being banned, is hopelessly inadequate when we are determining whether the vituperations of bigots can legitimately be forbidden. After all, Waldron contends, the desideratum impaired by the ranting of the bigots is an environmental good that is damaged cumulatively over time rather than on each discrete occasion when such ranting is uttered or displayed. Hence, he concludes, the defenders of the principle of freedom of expression are perversely obtuse when they insist that no instance of spiteful invective can legitimately be subjected to sanctions unless the invective poses a clear and present danger to the basic dignity of members of vulnerable minority groups. Such an insistence by those defenders is indicative of their naively pre-modern understanding of causation:

> Imagine if we took that attitude toward environmental harms—toward automobile emissions, for example. Suppose we said that unless someone can show that *my automobile* causes lead poisoning with direct detriment and imminent harm

> to the health of assignable individuals, I shouldn't be required to fit an emission-control device to my car's exhaust pipe. It would be irresponsible to reason in that way with regard to environmental regulation; instead we figure that the tiny impacts of millions of actions—each apparently inconsiderable in itself—can produce a large-scale toxic effect that, even at the mass level, operates insidiously as a sort of slow-acting poison, and that regulations have to be aimed at individual actions with that scale and that pace of causation in mind. An immense amount of progress has been made in consequentialist moral philosophy by taking causation of this kind, on this scale and at this pace, properly into account, and it is odd and disturbing that older and cruder models of social harm remain dominant in the First Amendment arena. (Waldron 2012, 97, emphasis in original, endnote omitted)

Waldron follows MacKinnon in presuming that the defenders of the principle of freedom of expression, who adhere to the *Brandenburg* version of the clear-and-present-danger test, are guilty of intellectual backwardness. Like her, then, he fails to apprehend the import of the distinction between (1) direct and focused causal links that connect instances of communicative conduct to non-communicative misdeeds and (2) diffusely cumulative causal links that connect such conduct to such misdeeds.

In this chapter and in most of my previous chapters, we have glanced at sundry examples of direct and focused causal connections between communications and non-communicative misdeeds. Let us briefly recall three of them here: the participation of a gangster in a bank robbery through his issuance of warnings to his colleagues when he detects some approaching police cars in his role as a lookout; the incitement of a bloody riot at the home of a corn-dealer through the uttering of a diatribe there by a firebrand orator against the iniquity of corn-dealers; and a husband's inducement of a gang rape against his wife through his encouragement of the rapists and his misleading of them about the propensities of their victim. In each of these cases, and in each of the countless relevantly similar cases that could be adduced here, the direct and focused causal role of someone's communications in the perpetration of serious wrongdoing is constitutive of his participation in that wrongdoing.[19] His direct participation in criminality proceeds through his utterance of statements rather than through non-communicative conduct, but the sanctions justly imposable on him are directed against the wrong-making properties which his utterance of those statements has in common with the actions of

[19] This point is recognized by one of Shakespeare's low-life characters in *Henry IV, Part One*. After a highwayman Gadshill has summoned the chamberlain of an inn for information that will lead directly to the robbery of certain people who have stayed overnight at the inn, the chamberlain greets him: "At hand, quoth pick-purse" (II.ii.48). Gadshill replies: "That's even as fair as—at hand, quoth the chamberlain; for thou variest no more from picking of purses than giving direction doth from laboring: thou layest the plot how" (II.ii.49–52).

other people through which the criminality is perpetrated. Precisely because of the proximity and intentionality of the connections between his utterances and those actions of other people, the utterances are assimilable to those actions as elements of the criminality. Like the gangsters who wield guns in the bank, the gangster who watches out for the police is a participant in the bank robbery. Like the members of the mob who lynch the corn-dealer, the orator who stirs up the mob is a participant in the lynching. Like the friends of the husband who violently force themselves upon his wife in compliance with his exhortations, the husband is a participant in their raping of her. In each case, the man who has participated directly in criminality through communicative conduct can legitimately be punished on communication-neutral grounds.

By contrast, the causal connections envisaged by Waldron—like the causal connections envisaged by MacKinnon between the marketing of pornography and the perpetration of sexual crimes against women—are diffusely cumulative rather than direct and focused. Let us recall here that the disputes between Waldron and the defenders of the principle of freedom of expression are not focused on instances of vitriol that fall into any of the categories discussed in §6.1. When bursts of vitriol amount to incitement in the *Brandenburg* sense (or to fighting words or to true threats or to acts of discrimination or to targeted harassment), defenders of the principle of freedom of expression will readily accept that the hateful utterances can legitimately be subjected to sanctions on communication-independent grounds. Hence, the instances of bigoted vituperation at issue between Waldron and his opponents are those wherein hatemongers advocate hideous ideas or express hideous sentiments without inciting communication-independent misconduct or otherwise perpetrating such misconduct. Waldron's thesis is that, if those instances of vituperation are not curbed by hate-speech laws, they will cumulatively erode the basic dignity of people who belong to vulnerable minority groups. Yet that very thesis of his is about the communicative impact of the fulminations of the hatemongers; the diffuse processes of causation recounted in the thesis are processes of communicative influence. Waldron believes that, over time, the messages and sentiments conveyed by those fulminations will widely coarsen the outlooks of members of the public in ways that lower the basic social standing of people who belong to vulnerable minority groups. His thesis is about the fulminations qua acts of communication. Consequently, when he proposes the imposition of legal clamps on the utterances and placards of bigots through hate-speech laws, he is calling for the prohibition of certain acts of communication qua acts of communication. His proposals run directly athwart the principle of freedom of expression.

Of course, we should scarcely be surprised to arrive afresh at the conclusion that the hate-speech laws championed by Waldron are violative of the principle of freedom of expression. After all, Waldron himself unflinchingly acknowledges that those laws enacted on the basis of his rationale are content-specific curbs on modes of expression. Still, my point here is that the insistence by civil libertarians on the import of the distinction between the directly focused causation involved in incitement and the diffusely cumulative causation involved in advocacy is not—*pace* Waldron and MacKinnon—a product of pre-scientific benightedness. Rather, it is a recognition of the difference between a type of causation that can render communications assimilable to communication-independent misconduct and a type of causation that does not render communications so assimilable. Accordingly, it is a recognition of the difference between a type of causation that can render communications legitimately prohibitable on communication-neutral grounds and a type of causation that does not render communications so prohibitable. Patently, such a difference is of the utmost importance for the defenders of the principle of freedom of expression. Waldron and MacKinnon are not among those defenders, of course, but their unattunedness to that principle is evident when they submit that the only basis for one of its central distinctions is superstition or naiveté.[20]

What should be noted and emphasized in conclusion here is that the long passage from Waldron quoted most recently above is again suffused with his assumption that the sole alternative to the enactment of hate-speech laws is a policy of doing nothing about the advocacy of hateful doctrines by bigots. When he asserts there that "progress has been made in consequentialist moral philosophy by taking causation of this [gradually cumulative] kind, on this scale and at this pace, properly into account," he strongly conveys the impression that the defenders of the principle of freedom of expression—whom he is chiding—cannot and do not take such causation "properly into account." Yet, precisely because those defenders do take account of the pernicious long-term effects that would be likely to follow if the hateful utterances of bigots were not vigorously countered both by other citizens and by the system of governance that presides over a society, they urge the adoption of the sundry measures that have been outlined in §6.3 of this chapter. They grasp that doing nothing about those poisonous utterances is hardly the lone alternative to the enactment of hate-speech laws. They understand that the fulfillment of the responsibilities of a liberal democracy must comprise not only the legal toleration of hateful utterances (where none of the categories explored in §6.1 is applicable), but also an array of policies and procedures to render those utterances ineffectual and to lower their incidence. Such policies and procedures, which are implemented both through the endeavors of legal-governmental officials and through the endeavors of private citizens, help to endow a society and its system of governance with the ethical strength that is the very opposite of the

[20] Also unattuned to that principle is Bhikhu Parekh when he writes as follows: "It is therefore a mistake . . . to proscribe [hate speech] because or only when it is likely to [provoke serious public disorder]. What matters is its content—what it says about an individual or a group—and its long-term effect on the group and the wider society, rather than its immediate consequences in terms of public disorder" (2012, 41). See also Sunstein 2019, where the *Brandenburg* version of the clear-and-present-danger standard is assessed from an unremittingly consequentialist perspective that is blind to the deontological rationale for that standard.

fecklessness which Waldron repeatedly imputes to the defenders of the principle of freedom of expression. Endued with such strength, a liberal democracy that abides robustly by the principle of freedom of expression is a setting in which the leaflets and posters and pronouncements of bigots bring disdain upon them rather than upon the groups whom they target. It is a setting in which the confidence that accompanies and bolsters the commitment to liberal tolerance is far removed from the demeaning assumptions that underlie Waldron's espousal of hate-speech laws.

7

Conclusion: The Principle of Freedom of Expression in Practice

As this book has argued throughout, the principle of freedom of expression is a moral absolute. The general moral duties imposed by that principle on systems of governance are binding always and everywhere. Still, as a precept of political morality, the principle of freedom of expression is heeded to varying degrees by systems of governance throughout the world. Though that principle itself is invariant, the extent of the compliance with it by each of those systems is obviously something that varies substantially. Compliance is a scalar property. Egregiously illiberal systems of governance such as those in present-day China and North Korea abide by the principle of freedom of expression hardly at all, and even the liberal democracies that exist in quite a few parts of the world are not unswervingly perfect in their adherence to that principle. Even in the contemporary United States, where the level of conformity with the principle of freedom of expression is generally higher than in other countries, that level falls short of full compliance. Some of the deviations from the ideal of freedom of expression in the United States have been mentioned in earlier chapters.

What should be emphasized straightaway is that the contraventions of the principle of freedom of expression by all past and present systems of governance have not been inevitable. As has been remarked more than once in this book (especially in Chapter 4), the principle of freedom of expression is not extravagantly utopian. The moral duties imposed by that principle on systems of governance are not unrealistically demanding. On the one hand, to be sure, the exertion of the self-restraint involved in full compliance by any such system with the principle of freedom of expression is a wonderful collective achievement—as Chapter 4 has observed. Through self-restraint so exerted, a system of governance fulfills a major duty of justice and realizes one of the premier modes of excellence. On the other hand, the fulfillment of that duty and the realization of that mode of excellence are not preposterously difficult. Unlike an ideal that requires saintly outpourings of altruism or heroic feats of public-spiritedness from virtually everyone on a day-to-day basis, the ideal of freedom of expression can be attained without saintliness or heroism. It is a strenuous ideal, but not superhumanly strenuous. Provided that the officials in a system of governance have discharged their moral obligation to ensure

Freedom of Expression as Self-Restraint. Matthew H. Kramer, Oxford University Press (2021). © Matthew H. Kramer.
DOI: 10.1093/oso/9780198868651.003.0007

that the values of liberal democracy are embraced by a large majority of the people in their society, the implementation of the principle of freedom of expression will be largely straightforward even in application to the rebarbative modes of expression on which we have concentrated in Chapters 5 and 6.

All the same, notwithstanding that the ideal of freedom of expression can be fully realized in circumstances that are quite credible, it has not been fully realized in any past or present society. Such a state of affairs is due to several considerations. First, temptations to pursue shortcuts and adopt slipshod practices of governance are of course strong even in liberal democracies (and are far stronger in repressively illiberal systems of governance, naturally). Faced with such temptations, officials who are normally conscientious may occasionally succumb. Obviously, officials who are not generally conscientious will succumb with particular eagerness to the attractions of dubious shortcuts.

Second, even when the officials in a system of governance are keen to adhere to the values of liberal democracy such as the ideal of freedom of expression, they might misidentify the contents of those values. Indeed, such instances of misidentification are especially likely in circumstances where the officials have to judge whether certain modes of communication are properly subject to legal restrictions or not. Any judgment of that kind has to be based (implicitly if not explicitly) on an understanding of the content of the moral principle that determines whether legal curbs on communications are morally proper. Although the principle of freedom of expression recounted and defended in this book is the moral principle in question, I have used the phrase "versions of the principle of freedom of expression" from Chapter 2 onward to indicate that the applicable principle has been construed in multiple ways over the centuries. Even within a single country, philosophers and jurists and countless other people have frequently diverged in their perceptions of the content of that principle. Across countries, the divergences are all the more pronounced. Though most of the divergent understandings within any single country overlap considerably, the area of overlap does not extend to some major issues—such as the permissibility of banning hateful utterances qua acts of communication. Consequently, the noncompliance of sundry liberal democracies with some of the obligations imposed by the principle of freedom of expression is very often due not to a lack of conscientiousness on the part of officials, but instead to their being conscientiously under the influence of misapprehensions about the substance and implications of that principle.

In the context of this chapter, a third factor is at least as important as the first two. Officials in systems of governance are not philosophers who, from positions of relative detachment, contemplate matters at very high levels of abstraction. Officials must come to grips with problems posed by the situations on which they have to pass judgment in their capacities as administrators or adjudicators or legislators.

Those problems are not thought-experiments conjured up by the ingenuity of philosophers, but are instead real-world cruxes in regard to which the decisions of officials will directly affect the lives of the people involved. Confronted with those problems, the officials are frequently in the domain of non-ideal theory rather than in the domain of ideal theory.[1] In that former domain, where decisions have to be reached against a backdrop of past or present wrongs, the officials will sometimes encounter outright moral conflicts of the sort delineated in Chapter 1. That is, sometimes in a situation where the officials have to act, any course of conduct adopted by them will constitute a breach of a moral duty. In such circumstances, the perpetration of a moral wrong by the officials is unavoidable—for they are simultaneously under a moral obligation to φ and under a moral obligation not to φ. Such dilemmas are not commonplace, fortunately, but they do occasionally arise. As has been remarked in Chapter 1 and more briefly in a few subsequent chapters, moral conflicts can arise in some cases where the administrators and adjudicators in a system of governance are morally obligated by the principle of freedom of expression to nullify laws that impose restrictions on communicative activities qua communicative activities. In a case of that kind where a moral conflict is operative, the officials involved are under a moral duty to give effect to the principle of freedom of expression by disallowing the law that has been impugned; and, because of some countervailing moral considerations, they are simultaneously under a moral duty to deviate from that principle by countenancing the law in question. Moreover, in some exceedingly rare circumstances, the latter duty is more stringent than the former. Hence, even when the officials in a system of governance are fully conscientious and are clear-sighted in descrying the substance and implications of the principle of freedom of expression, they can be confronted with an extreme situation in which the morally correct course of action lies in departing from the requirements of that principle. Such a possibility has to be recognized when we have moved from the level of ideal theory to the level of non-ideal theory. (Let us recall here, in line with what has been emphasized in Chapter 1, that the morally correct course of action in the presence of a moral conflict is not morally permissible. It is only weakly permissible and is not strongly permissible. As a contravention of a moral obligation, it constitutes a wrong despite its being a less grave wrong than the fulfillment of that obligation would have been in the dire circumstances.)

[1] In modern philosophy, the distinction between ideal theory and non-ideal theory was drawn most influentially by John Rawls (1999, 7–8, 215–16, 308–9; 2001, 13, 64–6). For a very good overview of the distinction, see Stemplowska and Swift 2012. See also Adams 2020; Chahboun 2015; Farrelly 2020; Hamlin and Stemplowska 2012; Herzog 2012; Mills 2005; Robeyns 2008; Simmons 2010; Stemplowska 2008; Swift 2008; Valentini 2009; Volacu 2018.

7.1 Liberal Democracy and the Scalar Character of Compliance

Let us now explore tersely some of the matters broached in this chapter's opening remarks. First is the fact that the conformity of any system of governance with the principle of freedom of expression is a scalar property. Within any such system, that conformity occurs to a greater or a lesser degree. It can realistically amount to unfailing adherence, but it can alternatively obtain at any number of lower levels. Naturally, much the same is true of the compliance by a system of governance with any of the other main principles of liberal democracy.

On the one hand, the principle of freedom of expression and the other main principles of liberal democracy are deontological. The general moral obligations imposed by them on every system of governance are exceptionless. Hence, whenever any such system deviates from communication-neutrality or content-neutrality or speaker-neutrality, it falls short of realizing thoroughly the values of liberal democracy. On the other hand, the status of a system of governance as a liberal democracy does not hinge on the perfect realization of those values therein. If such a system complies with the principle of freedom of expression and with the other main principles of liberal democracy in most respects but not quite unswervingly, it qualifies as a liberal democracy in spite of its imperfections. Those imperfections are moral wrongs which the system is morally obligated to remedy (as will be discussed in the next section of this chapter), but they in their confinedness do not deprive the system of its character as a liberal democracy.

This point about the continued status of a system of governance as a liberal democracy is not simply a taxonomical matter. On the contrary, it extends to an array of issues in political philosophy. For example, as has long been recognized in the philosophical literature on the topic of political authority and political obligation, the capacity of any system of governance to impose moral obligations on citizens through its placing of them under legal obligations is largely determined by the overall moral character of the system.[2] A liberal-democratic system of governance possesses that capacity to a far greater extent than does a dictatorship. Indeed, that capacity is a scalar property that increases in proportion to the levels of conformity by a system of governance with the main principles of liberal democracy. Its scalar character is reflected in variations pertaining to both the range and the stringency of the moral duties of obedience which a system of governance is capable of engendering.

In the present book, however, a topic of even greater interest is the extent to which the members of any society can warrantedly take pride in the regnant system

[2] For a good recent discussion of some factors that bear on this topic, see Jubb 2019. For my own discussion of many such factors, see Kramer 1999, 254–308. For two high-quality general introductions to the topic, see Horton 1992 and Knowles 2010.

of governance. That extent directly bears, of course, upon the level of self-respect that is warranted for each of those members. Chapter 4 has shown why the adherence of a system of governance to the requirements set forth by the principle of freedom of expression is something that crucially affects the extent to which the system should elicit vicarious pride on the part of every generally law-abiding person in its jurisdiction. Because that adherence therefore partly determines the level of self-respect that is warranted for each such person, it is essential for the fulfillment of the paramount responsibility that is incumbent on any system of governance. Now, although Chapter 4 has argued that every deviation from the principle of freedom of expression goes against the fulfillment of the paramount responsibility to which I have just referred, it has readily allowed that a few minor transgressions of the principle will not suffice in themselves to prevent that responsibility from being performed. If a system of governance has carried out all or nearly all the other moral obligations that are binding upon it, then its handful of minor contraventions of the principle of freedom of expression will not have undone the political and social and economic conditions wherein everyone under the jurisdiction of the system can be warranted in harboring a sturdy sense of self-respect. Those contraventions as breaches of moral duties are wrongs which the system of governance is morally required to remedy, but their effects on its status as a liberal democracy and as an object of warranted pride for every generally law-abiding citizen are too slight to rule out the satisfaction of the system's paramount responsibility.

However, when a system of governance violates the principle of freedom of expression more and more frequently or more and more seriously, its standing as a liberal democracy becomes more and more tenuous. *Pari passu*, of course, its status as a collective achievement in which every generally law-abiding citizen can warrantedly take pride is more and more attenuated. As violations abound, the system loses its standing as a liberal democracy altogether, and its status as an object of warranted pride for each generally law-abiding person is consequently lost. Instead of being a source of warranted pride, it has become a source of warranted chagrin for each such person (independently of whether this or that individual has suffered material hardships as a result of the system's repressiveness). Lowering the level of self-respect that is warranted for anyone in its jurisdiction, the system of governance with its illiberality is operating strongly athwart the fulfillment of its paramount responsibility.

Chapter 4 has discussed at much greater length the ways in which the levels of self-respect warranted for the sundry people in a society are directly affected by the liberality or illiberality of the system of governance that presides over the society. What is added here, with my emphasis on the scalar character of the adherence of any such system to the principle of freedom of expression, is that the property of being a liberal democracy is a vague property in the technical sense.[3]

[3] In different contexts, I have discussed this matter of vagueness more rigorously and deeply—with citations to the germane philosophical literature—in several of my past writings. See Kramer 2007,

Hence, the property of being a source of warranted pride rather than warranted shame for every generally law-abiding member of a society is a vague property in that technical sense. That is, a system of governance which fulfills all or nearly all the requirements imposed on it by the main principles of liberal democracy (including, of course, the principle of freedom of expression) is determinately classifiable as liberal-democratic; a system of governance which fulfills very few of the requirements imposed on it by those principles is determinately classifiable as an illiberal tyranny; and a system of governance at some intermediate level of compliance with those requirements might not be determinately classifiable in either direction. Any vague property is such that, alongside the numerous cases in which it is determinately present or determinately absent, there are borderline cases in which it is neither determinately present nor determinately absent. The property of being a liberal-democratic system of governance—the property of being a system of governance that can warrantedly elicit pride among the citizens over whom it presides—is no different from other vague properties in this regard.

These complexities that pertain to any project of gauging the overall moral bearings of a system of governance are perfectly consistent with this book's affirmation of the absoluteness of the moral requirements established by the principle of freedom of expression. Every contravention of the requirement of communication-neutrality or content-neutrality or speaker-neutrality is a moral wrong that detracts from the overall moral bearings of such a system. Each of those requirements is binding always and everywhere. Nevertheless, when we are passing judgment on a system of governance as a whole—rather than seeking to ascertain the moral permissibility or impermissibility of some particular governmental measure—we have to take into account the complexities that have been sketched here. Those complexities relate not to questions about the applicability of the principle of freedom of expression nor to questions about the permissibility of particular laws or policies, but instead to questions about how badly the overall moral standing of a system of governance has been degraded by any contraventions of that principle. When we are addressing those last-mentioned questions, we are asking about the gravity of any contraventions (in their effects on the overall moral standing of the system) rather than about their classifiability as contraventions. Their gravity in debasing the system's overall stature has to be assessed holistically, as the severity of the impact of any given transgression is partly determined by the profuseness and egregiousness—or fewness and mildness—of other transgressions.

36–7, 70; 2009, 109–13, 260–1; 2011, 120–4, 194–5, 202–3, 252–6; 2018, 137–9. For the most sustained exploration of the problem of vagueness within the operations of legal systems of governance, see Endicott 2000. For an impressive recent collection of essays on the topic, see Keil and Poscher 2016.

7.2 Remedies for Contraventions

Every governmental measure that contravenes any of the requirements of neutrality laid down by the principle of freedom of expression—including the inaction of a system of governance in response to severely disruptive heckling—is a moral wrong and is therefore generative of some remedial obligation(s).[4] Any such remedial obligation is moral in character, but it should be given effect by the prevailing system of governance through some legal obligation(s) or some other appropriate step(s). Often left unaddressed in the philosophical literature on these matters is the topic of the remedies that are most fitting for any violations of the principle of freedom of expression. My own ruminations on that topic will be laconic. In part, the brevity is due to the fact that quite a few of the main considerations are broadly similar to those which I have lengthily pondered elsewhere in my reflections on apposite legal remedies for the perpetration of torture by governmental officials (Kramer 2014, 242–316). In addition, this book has already commented at several junctures on remedies that can serve to rectify breaches of the principle of freedom of expression. Even more, however, the terseness of this section is attributable to the fact that the topic of remedies is largely beyond the scope of the present volume. As will be discussed anew in the final section of this chapter, a number of important matters of procedure have been left aside in this book—because, despite their importance, my contemplation of them is not essential for the attainment of my chief objective herein. That objective is focused on predominantly substantive matters, as I have sought to explicate and defend the principle of freedom of expression and to investigate many of its substantive implications. Thus, although the procedural issues pertaining to the implementation of the ideal of freedom of expression are obviously of great significance, most of them can safely be pretermitted within the context of this book's aims. Sufficient here will be a glance at a few of the remedies that are suitable for that implementation.

7.2.1 Individual Wrongdoing by Officials

Especially in settings where laws have been given effect in morally objectionable ways, criminal-law proceedings or tort-law proceedings pursued against individual officials—as well as against the governmental agencies that employ them—can be morally justified. For example, suppose that some constables in a municipality enforce a breach-of-the-peace statute in a discriminatory manner against certain speakers whose messages are not to the liking of the constables. Some instances of discriminatory enforcement of this kind notoriously occurred

[4] I have elsewhere argued at length that every moral wrong—every breach of a moral duty—gives rise to remedial duties. See Kramer 2004, 249–94; 2005.

during the civil-rights campaigns in the southern half of the United States during the 1960s. Such instances of enforcement were morally wrongful partly because they invested hostile audiences with the authority to determine the range of communicative endeavors that would be legally countenanced, and partly because the overall pattern of enforcement was blatantly invidious. Hence, the marshaling of criminal or civil sanctions against the individual constables as well as against the police forces that employed them could be morally justified both under the principle of freedom of expression and under a principle of equal protection.

In Chapter 2 we have pondered the case of *Davis v Norman*, which may likewise have involved the morally dubious enforcement of a morally sound law. Although the record of facts in the case is not sufficient to warrant any firm confidence about the matter, the ordinance that prohibited the open-air storage of ruined vehicles may have been enforced against Mr Davis because the police took exception to the message which he was conveying through his display of his son's demolished truck. If so, then the availability of some sanctions as remedies is morally requisite. On the one hand, given that the enforcement of the ordinance consisted only in the removal of the truck rather than in any fines or other penalties, and given that it did not involve the ugly prejudices that were operative in some of the measures undertaken by constables against the civil-rights protestors in the southern half of the United States during the 1960s, the remedial obligations engendered by the removal of the truck—if the removal did indeed amount to a deliberate contravention of viewpoint-neutrality—would be quite modest. No terms of imprisonment for the individual police officers would be morally justified. On the other hand, some milder penalties (whether criminal or civil or institutional) imposed against the officers and against their employer could be so justified.

In the cases broached here, and in countless other relevantly similar cases, some administrative or adjudicative officials have given effect to just laws but have done so in ways that clash with the constraints of neutrality established by the principle of freedom of expression. In contexts where such officials have deliberately deviated from the terms of just laws instead of implementing them, the actions at variance with the aforementioned constraints of neutrality are even graver; consequently, the remedies that are morally vital for the rectification of those actions will be more onerous. Situations of this latter kind reveal especially clearly the moral requisiteness of holding law-enforcement officials individually responsible for some transgressions of the principle of freedom of expression. Although the officials qua officials are always acting on behalf of their system of governance and more specifically on behalf of the governmental body (such as a police force) that employs them, and although the responsibility for their actions performed within their roles as officials is therefore always collective as well as individual, there are some cases in which the wrongs constituted by transgressions of the principle of freedom of expression will not have been fully rectified without the imposition of sanctions on the individuals who have committed those wrongs.

7.2.2 Contraventions at the Level of General Laws

Although contraventions of the principle of freedom of expression at the level of law-application are not uncommon, the contraventions most frequently under scrutiny in high-profile litigation are at the level of general laws. In a liberal democracy, any remedies suitable for rectifying the wrongs perpetrated at that latter level are almost always directed against collectivities rather than against individuals (where a collectivity targeted by a remedy can be an entire system of governance or some organ of decision-making within that system). Moreover, very frequently the legal remedies pertinent for rectifying any contraventions of the principle of freedom of expression at the level of general laws are not sanctions.

As has been remarked in Chapters 1 and 2, the legal entitlements chiefly conferred on individuals and groups by constitutional free-speech guarantees such as the First Amendment are immunities. Those immunities shield individuals and groups against being deprived of their communicative liberties by laws that purport to remove or curtail such liberties. Now, as has been observed in Chapter 1, legal immunities are effectuated by administrative or adjudicative officials not through the imposition of legal sanctions but instead through the annulment of ostensible exercises of legal powers. Suppose for example that the U.S. Congress were to enact a statute which professes to bar everybody in the United States from discussing the matter of abortion in any location outside a private residence. Such a law would of course be challenged successfully in the courts, but the upshot of the challenge would not be the imposition of any penalties on the Congress or on any members of Congress. Rather, the upshot would be the invalidation of the statute, as the courts would declare that the attempt by the Congress to exercise its law-making powers had been of no avail. Instead of giving effect to any legal duty incumbent on the Congress, the courts would be giving effect to a legal disability that limits the Congress's legislative powers. That Hohfeldian disability is correlated with the immunity of each citizen against being deprived of communicative liberties by laws that contravene the First Amendment.

As is manifest from the exposition of the Hohfeldian analytical framework in Chapter 1, claim-rights and immunities are not equivalent. Similarly, of course, the duties that correlate with claim-rights and the disabilities that correlate with immunities are not equivalent. Hence, as has been stated in the preceding paragraph, the legal remedy that is most often suitable in response to a contravention of the principle of freedom of expression at the level of a general law—namely, the invalidation of that law either as a whole or in part—is not a legal sanction levied for a breach of a legal duty. Such a conclusion follows not only from the Hohfeldian analysis, but also from H.L.A. Hart's famous critique of John Austin's jurisprudential theory. In one strand of that critique, Hart cogently argued that the nullity ensuing from an unsuccessful attempt to exercise a legal power is not equivalent to a sanction imposed for a violation of a legal obligation (Hart 1994, 33–5; Kramer 2018,

39–41). Yet, given that disabilities are not equivalent to duties, and given that the nullity which ensues from the implementation of a legal disability is not equivalent to a sanction which ensues from the enforcement of a legal duty, the role of nullity as a remedy for contraventions of the principle of freedom of expression at the level of general laws might seem problematic. After all, those contraventions are breaches of moral duties. How can the effectuation of a legal *disability* be a suitable remedy for a breach of a moral *duty*? Should not instead the suitable remedy be the enforcement of a legal duty?

Three replies to such a worry are apposite here. First, although Hart and Hohfeld were correct to highlight the logical differences between legal duties and legal disabilities, and although Hart was also correct to highlight the functional differences between them, there is a functional overlap between them in contexts where adjudicators are called upon to say whether the efforts of legislators to exercise law-making powers have been successful.[5] In such a context, the invalidation of a statute or an ordinance or some other law—though not equivalent to the levying of a sanction such as a fine—is quite a rebuke to the legislative body whose enactment has been annulled. Such a remedy undoes what the legislature has presumed to accomplish, and it in effect requires the members of that body to expend further time and effort if they wish to come up with some alternative to the enactment that has been nullified. A court that invalidates a law might forbear from using any reproachful language in its presentation of its judgment on the matter, but that judgment does function as a reproach implicitly if not explicitly.

Second, although a general law that clashes with the principle of freedom of expression should normally be invalidated by the courts without the imposition of legal sanctions, there can be exceptional circumstances in which the imposition of such sanctions on a legislative body would be morally suitable and indeed morally requisite. Suppose for example that a local government enacts a succession of nearly identical ordinances, each of which is glaringly in contravention of the principle of freedom of expression (and glaringly in contravention of a constitutional guarantee which corresponds to that principle). After constitutional challenges to several of the successive editions of the ordinance have resulted in the invalidation of all of them, a court will be morally warranted in issuing an injunction that forbids the local government to continue to enact versions of the ordinance that are nearly identical to those which have already been annulled. Such an injunction will place the local government under a legal duty to desist from its cynical pattern of behavior. Under the terms of the injunction, any subsequent enactments must differ from the invalidated versions of the ordinance in ways that duly take account

[5] My references to legislators and legislative bodies are to be understood expansively here. Such references encompass any organs of governance that establish general laws, including not only any straightforwardly legislative institutions such as the U.S. Congress and the U.K. Parliament but also—among others—any administrative agencies that promulgate regulations and any local authorities that enact ordinances or by-laws.

of the unconstitutionality of those previous versions. Any enactment by the local government that defies the terms of the injunction will trigger the levying of a sanction such as a fine. In the circumstances envisaged here, where the local government has displayed flagrantly bad faith by declining to heed its constitutional limitations and its moral obligations, the placing of it under a legal duty through the issuance of an injunction can be morally justified. Likewise, of course, the application of sanctions against the local authorities in the event of their noncompliance with that duty can be morally justified.

Third, in the absence of circumstances in which a legislative body has exhibited arrantly bad faith or gross remissness, the effectuation of a legal disability through the nullification of an enactment is the fitting remedy for a transgression of the principle of freedom of expression at the level of a general law. As has been argued, although such a remedy is not a sanction, its function in the context of its occurrence is partly that of a sanction. Moreover, in the absence of egregiously bad faith or gross remissness on the part of a legislative body, the employment of such a remedy avoids both excessive confrontationality and excessive deference. Measures suitable for rectifying transgressions of the principle of freedom of expression have to be responsive to the requirements of other major moral precepts such as the principle of democratic legitimacy. Although that latter principle is obviously not something that can be expounded in any depth here, its requirement of respect for the operations of a democratically elected legislative body is binding as a constraint on any remedial response to a violation of the principle of freedom of expression. In the absence of strikingly bad faith or blatant remissness in those operations, the respect due is not shown if a legislative body is subjected to legal sanctions when its enactments collide with the principle of freedom of expression. In the event of a clash between an enactment and that principle, the invalidation of the enactment serves the ideal of freedom of expression while also serving the ideal of democratic legitimacy by keeping a legislative body within the ambit of its authority.

7.2.3 The Avoidance of Contraventions through Anticipatory Measures

A conspectus of remedies can be somewhat misleading, for the measures delineated in such a conspectus are reactive to what has already occurred. Crucial though such remedies are as means of rectifying any transgressions of the principle of freedom of expression that have indeed taken place, they are ancillary to the anticipatory steps through which the occurrence of transgressions can be averted. As Hart observed in his critique of Austin, the role of remedies in any system of governance is activated only when the main functioning of the system has failed in some respect.[6] In any robustly liberal-democratic system of governance, the main functioning includes an array of approaches—like those contemplated in Chapters 4 to 6—which cultivate and maintain a hardy societal ethos suffused with the values of liberal democracy. As has been emphasized in the chapters just mentioned, the sustainment of such an ethos is not only morally obligatory in itself but is also invaluable in facilitating the fulfillment of other moral obligations that are binding on any system of governance. Among the other obligations, of course, are those which are imposed by the principle of freedom of expression. When a system of governance has brought about a sturdy ethos of the kind envisaged here, its officials are securely in a position to comply with the principle of freedom of expression by refraining from the imposition of legal restrictions on pornographic materials and hateful utterances that are not constitutive of communication-independent misdeeds. We have seen as much in the preceding three chapters. Accordingly, the exertions through which such an ethos materializes can avert breaches of the principle of freedom of expression and can thereby obviate remedies for those breaches. In a phrase that might seem oxymoronic, such exertions are informatively characterizable as "anticipatory remedies" (somewhat akin to anticipatory injunctions). Such "remedies" deal with contraventions not by rectifying them but by forestalling them.

7.3 Overdemandingness?

As has been observed in the opening portion of this chapter, the legislative and administrative and adjudicative officials who have to come to grips with problems and controversies are sometimes confronted with moral conflicts and are often in the domain of non-ideal theory. Some contraventions of the principle of freedom of expression occur in such contexts. Given as much, certain readers may worry that an insistence on legally remedying those contraventions is unreasonably demanding. Anyone faced with a moral conflict cannot avoid the perpetration of wrongdoing in one direction or the other. If officials confronted with such a conflict are not morally responsible for its emergence, and if they breach the less stringent moral duty-not-to-φ only in order to comply with the more stringent moral duty-to-φ, then an insistence on legally rectifying their breach of the moral duty-not-to-φ may seem decidedly unfair to them—in a situation where their fulfillment of that duty (and their consequent breach of the duty-to-φ) would have been morally worse. Worries of this sort have often been voiced by philosophers who doubt the actuality, or at least the frequency, of the occurrence of moral conflicts. Michael Moore, for example, has opined that

6 Hart 1994, 38–40. Hart made this point specifically about sanctions, but it applies also to remedies that are not sanctions.

> it would be unfortunate for us in the extreme if morality often confronted us with choices where we will be "damned if we do and damned if we don't." The distinctions we shall examine hold out the possibility of so limiting our stringent obligations as to minimize or even eliminate such situations of moral conflict. (Moore 2007, 37–8)

In several of my earlier writings on moral conflicts (Kramer 2004, 249–94; 2014, 2–19; 2016; 2019c), I have replied at length to concerns of the type articulated by Moore. Those earlier replies have pertained to moral conflicts in general, without any specific reference to the principle of freedom of expression. This section of the present chapter will first provide a highly compressed distillation of the gist of those earlier general replies, and will then comment more specifically on moral conflicts that involve the requirements imposed by the principle of freedom of expression.

7.3.1 Drawing the Apt Conclusion

Moore's ambition to establish the infrequency of moral conflicts is centered on the onerousness or unfairness of a world in which someone often finds that every mode of conduct open to her is morally wrong. Such a worry is pertinent, of course, but Moore draws an inapt conclusion from it. Instead of trying to expound the general structure of morality in a manner that whisks most moral conflicts out of sight, we should quite frequently seek to act in ways—and to arrange our institutions in ways—that will reduce the incidence of such conflicts. Acting in conformity to a practically oriented conclusion of that kind is the best means of allaying the anxiety felt by Moore and others about the prospect of unavoidable wrongness. To act in such a fashion, one needs to be alert to the possibility and actuality of moral conflicts in a diversity of settings.

In other words, the consternation engendered by the specter of unavoidable wrongness should prompt us to do the opposite of what Moore recommends. Far from trying to limn the contours of morality so as to obscure the emergence of moral conflicts, we should be seeking to grasp those contours with keen sensitivity to the likelihood of such conflicts. Only thus can we informedly fix upon the practical steps that are best suited to avert predicaments of unavoidable wrongness (insofar as they can and should be averted).

7.3.2 Moral Conflicts and the Principle of Freedom of Expression

My general conclusion in response to Moore is particularly germane with regard to contraventions of the principle of freedom of expression. As has been observed in Chapters 4 to 6, many of the settings where the officials in liberal-democratic systems of governance incline most strongly toward such contraventions are quandaries in which the officials ponder how to handle pernicious modes of communication such as pornography and bigoted declamations. Although the principle of freedom of expression is of course consistent with the imposition of legal restrictions on any types or instances of those modes of communication that are constitutive of communication-independent misconduct, it forbids the imposition of legal restrictions on any types or instances of those modes of communication that are not constitutive of such misconduct. Yet, like Rae Langton and Catharine MacKinnon and Jeremy Waldron, the officials in a liberal-democratic system of governance may feel gravely concerned about the distinctively communicative effects of pornography and hatemongering. Such concerns are reasonable and urgent, as I have readily accepted in the past few chapters. With reference to a non-ideal situation where the officials plausibly conclude that the most effective way of addressing those concerns is to clamp legal curbs on pornography or hatemongering as a mode of communication, some readers may balk at the notion that the officials are morally duty-bound to abstain from introducing such curbs. In the eyes of these readers, any duties to abstain would be grievously unfair to officials who are earnestly endeavoring to carry out moral responsibilities. Recoiling from the idea that the officials are somehow morally obligated not to safeguard women and the members of vulnerable minority groups against the harms that can ensue from the marketing of pornography or the advocacy of venomous creeds, these readers would be voicing unease roughly in line with that articulated by Moore—and they would be doing so specifically in connection with contraventions of the principle of freedom of expression.

The fatal misconception in such unease should be apparent from the past three chapters. Although legal-governmental officials are morally duty-bound not to impose legal restrictions on any pornographic materials or hateful tirades qua modes of communication, they are also morally duty-bound to protect women and the members of vulnerable minority groups against the noxious effects of those modes of communication. As the past few chapters have emphasized, any system of governance is failing in its moral responsibilities unless it has plied numerous techniques that furnish the requisite protection. Many of those techniques are aimed at gaining very widespread currency for the values of liberal democracy among the citizens over whom the system presides. When a robust societal ethos replete with those values has become entrenched, and when various other measures are also undertaken to counter the perniciousness of pornography and hatemongering, legal-governmental officials will have enabled themselves to sustain with confidence a posture of legal toleration toward the activities of pornographers and hatemongers (where those activities do not constitute any communication-independent misdeeds).

Thus, when the officials in a system of governance are reaching decisions in non-ideal circumstances where the allegiance of citizens to the values of liberal democracy is tenuous, the non-ideal character of the circumstances in that very respect is a product of the failure of the officials to fulfill a major moral responsibility incumbent on their system of governance. Had the duty to cultivate a hardy ethos of liberal-democratic values been carried out, the officials would not now face a situation where their compliance with the principle of freedom of expression (in application to pornography or to hateful utterances) might be morally perilous. In this connection, we should note three points that are directly responsive to the complaint which I am seeking here to rebut: that is, the complaint about the putative unfairness of the fact that the officials in the non-ideal situation just broached are morally obligated to abide by the principle of freedom of expression.

First, as has been emphasized in the past three chapters, the moral duty of every system of governance to maintain a robust liberal-democratic ethos in its society is not preposterously utopian. On the contrary, such a duty is realistically fulfillable—with sufficient diligence—in any society where all or most citizens are reasonably well-educated. (Educational programs of multiple kinds are, of course, foremost among the measures that are vital for the nurturing of a stout ethos of liberal-democratic values.) Given that the performance of that duty is not fancifully demanding, the absence of the resultant ethos in a given society is a serious moral failing for which the regnant system of governance and its officials can justly be held accountable. To be sure, as I have argued elsewhere at length (Kramer 2004, 249-94), some moral responsibilities incumbent on any system of governance are entirely fair even when they are not satisfiable through all feasible precautions and efforts. However, a complaint about unfairness is especially inapt when the moral duties to which it pertains are such that they could have been fulfilled quite straightforwardly if some other realistically satisfiable moral duties had been fulfilled. Legal-governmental officials who encounter circumstances like those envisaged by such a complaint may be in a difficult plight, but the plight is something for which the officials' system of governance is at fault. Accordingly, if the officials in their predicament are confronted with a conflict between moral duties that are binding upon them, the fact that they will breach a moral duty regardless of what they do is not unfair to them. Their quandary derives from the failure of their system of governance to execute its moral responsibilities.

Second, save in cases where any officials have individually engaged in abuses of their positions as officials, the moral responsibility for contraventions of the principle of freedom of expression in any society attaches to officials collectively (that is, to their overall system of governance) rather than to one or more of the officials individually. Likewise, the legal remedies that serve as responses to the violations of that moral principle—remedies that are grounded in constitutional guarantees which correspond more or less closely to that principle—are applicable at the collective level rather than at the individual level. They apply to a system of governance as a whole or to particular institutions or bodies within it. Hence, although the freedom-of-expression moral obligations that bind officials in the circumstances envisioned by proponents of bans on pornography or on hateful utterances would doubtless be unfair to the officials if the obligations were borne by them as discrete individuals, those moral obligations are in fact shouldered by the officials collectively as participants in the enterprise of running a system of governance. Borne collectively, the obligations are not unfair to anyone.

Third—as has been discussed in §7.2.2 above—when a transgression of the principle of freedom of expression is at the level of a general law, the suitable legal remedy is normally the invalidation of that law. Such a remedy shares some of the functional properties of a sanction (as §7.2.2 has explained), but its normative upshot consists in keeping a system of governance from exceeding the boundaries of the legal powers and moral powers with which that system is endowed. A remedy with that upshot, applicable at the systemic level to which it pertains, is not unfair in any respect. Ergo, the moral duty effectuated by the remedy of legal invalidation is not unfair in any regard. The fact that such a duty is always borne by every system of governance—even in the extreme circumstances where the duty comes into conflict with an urgently countervailing moral obligation—does not warrant any complaints about overdemandingness. A complaint of that kind, at least in this context, would amount to an end-justifies-the-means line of reasoning. Deontological duties such as those established by the principle of freedom of expression are impervious to any end-justifies-the-means calculations, even when the duties are locked in conflicts with other pressing moral obligations. No such conflict ever negates or suspends either of the moral duties which it comprises.

7.4 Prescinding from Details of Implementation

Although this book is fairly long, it should conclude by pointing out that it has prescinded from quite a few topics that would have to be examined carefully in a full treatment of the principle of freedom of expression. In particular, as has been suggested near the outset of §7.2 above, I have pretermitted most of the procedural issues that figure saliently in the efforts of jurists and other officials to implement constitutional free-speech guarantees. To be sure, the present chapter has touched upon the matter of legal remedies for violations of the principle of freedom of expression. However, even that topic has been contemplated only briskly and selectively, as many of the involuted controversies pertaining to remedies have been left aside. Numerous other aspects of the processes through which the principle of freedom of expression is implemented (via the implementation of the constitutional guarantees which correspond more or less closely to that principle) have not received any attention in this book heretofore.

As has been indicated in the opening portion of §7.2, my disregard of procedural issues has not been inadvertent. Any significant engagement with those issues would have diverted this book from its main objective: the objective of elucidating and defending the moral principle of freedom of expression. Although the implementation of that principle through constitutional or statutory guarantees and through various ancillary legal devices and procedures is of enormous importance, an exploration of the intricacies of that implementation is a project for a separate book. Such a book (unlike the present volume) would not be entirely philosophical, since the complexities probed by it would not all be resolvable at a philosophical level of abstraction. Some of them would have to be addressed in a jurisdiction-specific fashion that takes account of the peculiarities of history.

By contrast, the present volume has sought to vindicate the principle of freedom of expression in a jurisdiction-transcendent fashion through philosophical reasoning. I have endeavored to expound rigorously the content of that moral principle, and I have considered at some length the implications of its content in order to pin down what it allows and what it disallows. Equally important, this book has plumbed the moral foundations of the principle of freedom of expression and has thereby accounted for the status of that principle as a moral absolute that is binding on systems of governance always and everywhere. My justification of the principle has extended into Chapters 5 and 6, where I have upheld the ideal of freedom of expression in rejoinders to some powerful arguments that have been marshaled against it during the past few decades. All of these strands in my vindication of the principle of freedom of expression have been brought together without my having to reflect more than fleetingly on the procedural gnarls involved in the implementation of that principle through the workings of a legal system. By keeping the focus of this book trained on substantive matters, I have facilitated its accomplishment of what it has set out to accomplish.

Still, given the importance of many of the procedural cruxes from which this book has prescinded, and given the blurriness of the procedure/substance distinction at a number of points, this chapter will conclude by glancing at a couple of the issues that have been omitted from my discussions heretofore. One of those issues has arisen quite often in litigation under the First Amendment to the American Constitution, and the other one is a deeper concern that has been debated vigorously among philosophers and legal theorists in most liberal democracies. A few pithy remarks may help to reveal that, although these matters and other procedural conundrums have rightly been left aside in this volume, the implementation of the principle of freedom of expression through the workings of a legal system is a complicatedly and fascinatingly multidimensional topic.

7.4.1 Burdens of Proof

When the principle of freedom of expression is given effect through the operations of a legal system, questions about the placement and onerousness of the burden of proof in administrative or adjudicative proceedings are frequently of pivotal importance. In controversies pursued through litigation under the First Amendment, those questions have oft loomed large. One relevant area is the law of defamation, which is of byzantine complexity in the United States even more than in most other countries. Among the chief dichotomies in that province of American law is the distinction between public figures (such as celebrities and politicians) and ordinary private individuals.[7] When a lawsuit for defamation is undertaken by a public figure, the burden of proof lies on the plaintiff to establish that the defendant proceeded with actual malice when uttering or writing or publishing some false and pejorative allegation(s) about the plaintiff. In this context, the phrase "actual malice" denotes either the defendant's awareness of the falsity of the allegation(s) or the defendant's reckless unconcern for the truth or falsity thereof. Because of the placement and onerousness of the burden of proof in defamation lawsuits brought by public figures, the prospects of success for such plaintiffs in the United States are far lower than in a number of other jurisdictions.[8] What is worth noting here is that the distinction between public figures and ordinary individuals has itself become formidably knotty, as some people are deemed to be public figures in all contexts whereas some other people are deemed to be public figures in certain limited contexts only. These classificatory involutions are naturally of central importance in the instances of litigation that hinge on them, but my endeavor to vindicate the principle of freedom of expression—which has concentrated on more general substantive matters such as the question whether the outlawing of defamatory statements is morally permissible at all—has been able to abstract from such tangles quite safely.

The category of "true threats," which we have examined in §3.2.8 of Chapter 3, is another precinct of the law of the First Amendment in which some issues about the placement and onerousness of the burden of proof in litigation have been conspicuous. In the 2003 case of *Virginia v Black*, the U.S. Supreme Court had to pass judgment on the constitutionality of a Virginia statute which prohibited any burning of a cross with an intention to intimidate some person or group of persons. In a rather unwieldy array of opinions, a majority of the Justices on the

[7] The seminal case on this distinction in the American law of defamation is, of course, *New York Times v Sullivan*, 376 U.S. 254 (1964). For one of the numerous discussions of the matter, see Shiffrin 2016, 119–22.

[8] Even so, the costs of being sued for defamation—notwithstanding the high likelihood of prevailing against a public-figure plaintiff—can deter newspapers and broadcasters from carrying certain reports about famous people. See Acheson and Wohlschlegel 2018, 355–68. Thus, another crucial procedural matter in this area of the law is how the costs of litigation should be apportioned between the parties.

Court agreed that the main substance of the statute could be in keeping with the requirements of the American Constitution. However, they held that a provision in the statute pertaining to the burden of proof was inconsistent with those requirements.[9] Under that provision, any burning of a cross on the property of someone else or in a public place would amount to *prima facie* evidence of an intention to intimidate some person or group of persons. Accordingly, the provision in effect placed the burden of proof on a defendant to establish that he or she did not harbor such an intention when he or she engaged in the burning of a cross. Although the Justices of the Court in the majority were divided on the question whether the impugned provision could be salvaged if it were reconstrued by the Virginia judiciary, they agreed that the provision as it had been interpreted was at odds with the U.S. Constitution. Now, although the conclusion reached by those Justices about the unconstitutionality of the burden-of-proof provision is parallel to the conclusion that should be reached by anyone who needs to gauge whether the provision would be consistent with the principle of freedom of expression, this book in its exploration and vindication of that principle has been able to attain its purposes without becoming entangled in these procedural thickets. *A fortiori*, this book has been able to attain its purposes without becoming immersed in the further minutiae about which the Justices in the Court's majority were divided among themselves. Still, such procedural details are very often the foci for the determinations that have to be rendered by judges and other legal-governmental officials in their implementation of constitutional or statutory free-speech protections that correspond (more or less closely) to the principle of freedom of expression.

7.4.2 Who Decides?

An even more contentious and profound matter in the implementation of the principle of freedom of expression is the location of the legal authority to arrive at the decisions through which the implementation takes place. Among philosophers and constitutional theorists in the United States and in other liberal democracies, controversies over this topic have most often centered on the question whether courts should be legally empowered to invalidate any enactments of legislative bodies which the courts deem to be unconstitutional.[10] That question with

[9] Three of the Justices (Souter, Kennedy, and Ginsburg) argued that the main substance of the Virginia statute was unconstitutionally viewpoint-specific. As is evident from my exposition of the principle of freedom of expression in the foregoing chapters of this book, I concur with their assessment of the statute's substance. Nevertheless, the provision concerning the burden of proof—on which the outcome of the case hinged—would have posed an important problem even if the provision itself and the statute as a whole had been viewpoint-neutral.

[10] For my previous discussions of this matter, see Kramer 2008, 421–7; 2012, 130–2. For a few of the multitudinous powerful writings on this topic, see Allan 2001; Brink 1988; Dworkin 1996, 1–38; Fallon 2008; Freeman 1990; Harel 2014, 191–224; Tribe, Waldron, and Tushnet 2005; Waldron 1999, Part III; 2006; Waluchow 2005; 2007.

its many ramifications obviously extends well beyond the implementation of the principle of freedom of expression. Nonetheless, cases that do involve the constitutional or statutory guarantees which correspond (more or less closely) to that principle are among the most prominent settings in which the remedy of invalidation is suitably employed.

This chapter's meditations on remedies may have seemed to take as given that the judicial branch in any liberal-democratic system of governance will be vested—or should be vested—with legal powers to invalidate any enactments by legislative bodies that run athwart constitutional or statutory free-speech guarantees. However, the matter is more subtle than it might at first appear to be. Salutary though the institution of judicial review typically is in the liberal democracies where it is operative, the assignment to the judiciary of the legal authority to invalidate the enactments of legislative bodies is not indispensable as a hallmark of liberal-democratic systems of governance. Moreover, even when such authority is indeed located in the judiciary, it can produce its effects through a multiplicity of routes. Let us very briefly consider each of these two points.

First, on the one hand—as has been stated—the institution of judicial review is frequently salutary as a check on overreaching by legislative bodies. Furthermore, some such check is essential for the implementation of the principle of freedom of expression and for the sustainment of the liberal-democratic character of a system of governance more generally. On the other hand, the legal power to invalidate legislative enactments in order to terminate contraventions of the principle of freedom of expression does not have to be vested in the judiciary. It could instead be assigned to a special chamber or committee of the topmost legislature in a system of governance, or it could be assigned to the executive branch (at least where that branch is quite plainly distinct from the legislature, as is the case in the American system of governance). It could even be vested in a council of constitutional-law experts, whose sole quasi-judicial function would be to appraise laws for their consistency with the main principles of liberal democracy. In any system of governance that aspires to uphold those principles, one or more of these institutional arrangements could play the role that is performed by judicial review in many contemporary liberal democracies. Hence, although some of this chapter's discussions have indeed assumed that legal powers to invalidate the enactments of legislative bodies will be located in the courts, that assumption has been made because such an allocation of authority is familiar rather than because it is perceived here as inevitable.

Second, even when the legal authority to assess the constitutionality of the enactments of legislative bodies is wielded through the practice of judicial review, there is no canonical form which that practice has to take. It can proceed along a number of different paths. We are able to discern as much not only through abstract speculation but also by investigating the sundry incarnations of the practice of judicial review in the liberal democracies where it has been embraced. At one end of the spectrum, associated most saliently with the American system of governance, the courts are authorized to invalidate the enactments of legislative bodies by invoking constitutional provisions that correspond (more or less closely) to the principle of freedom of expression and the other major principles of liberal democracy. Unless the instances of invalidation are subsequently reversed by the courts, the only way of overturning them is to procure some constitutional amendments. At the other end of the spectrum, associated most notably with the system of governance in England until quite recently, the courts are not authorized to invalidate any of the enactments of the supreme legislative body such as the British Parliament. Between those two extremes are diverse alternatives, some of which are instantiated in countries such as Canada and New Zealand (Waluchow 2005, 211 n7; 2007, 129–30). For example, the courts in a given country can be authorized to pronounce upon the constitutionality of the enactments of legislative bodies even if the courts are not authorized to decline to give effect to the enactments which they have deemed to be unconstitutional. Similarly, the courts can be authorized to bid legislative bodies to reconsider any enactments which the courts have deemed to be constitutionally dubious; unless the legislative body responsible for some contested enactment has formally reapproved it within a certain span of time, the enactment in question will have become legally invalid. Yet another possibility is that the courts are authorized to invalidate the enactments of legislative bodies on grounds of unconstitutionality, but only for a limited period of time in each case. If an invalidated enactment has not been repealed by the relevant legislative body within the specified period of time, then it regains its legal validity and is therefore once again a law to which the courts are legally obligated to give effect. These possibilities and many other possible arrangements lie between the American and English ends of the spectrum. Participants in the debates about the morality of judicial review sometimes lose sight of the multifariousness of the approaches that are feasible, but that multifariousness should be kept in mind by anybody who is assessing the cogency of the contributions to those debates. Even among societies whose systems of governance all invest judges with the authority to appraise the constitutionality of the enactments of legislative bodies, myriad variations are possible.

My point in the foregoing paragraph has not been to suggest that every feasible arrangement for monitoring the constitutionality of legislative enactments is suitable for the implementation of the principle of freedom of expression. As can be inferred from this chapter's musings on remedies, a practice of invalidation at or near the American end of the spectrum (whether located in the judiciary or elsewhere) is requisite for the satisfactory implementation of that principle. Still, vital though such a practice of invalidation is, the point of the preceding paragraph is to indicate why this book has forborne from becoming engrossed with these anfractuous procedural matters. Controversies over the legitimacy of judicial review bear quite importantly on the topic of freedom of expression, but any participation in those controversies would have led this book far afield from its project of expounding and justifying the principle of freedom of expression—for such participation would have had to engage with numerous issues that are only tenuously related to that project. Hence, worthy of attention though the procedural intricacies are, the omission of them from this volume has sharpened its focus on the substantive ideal of freedom of expression. That ideal is the realization of a type of self-restraint that is unforgoable in the striving by any system of governance to discharge the paramount moral responsibility incumbent upon it.

References

Abrams, Floyd. 2012. “On American Hate Speech Law.” In Michael Herz and Peter Molnar (eds), *The Content and Context of Hate Speech*. Cambridge: Cambridge University Press, pp 116–26.

Abrams, Floyd. 2019. “*Citizens United*: Predictions and Reality.” In Lee Bollinger and Geoffrey Stone (eds), *The Free Speech Century*. Oxford: Oxford University Press, pp 81–94.

Acheson, David and Wohlschlegel, Ansgar. 2018. “The Economics of Weaponized Defamation Lawsuits.” 47 *Southwestern Law Review* 335–83.

Adams, Matthew. 2020. “The Value of Ideal Theory.” In Jon Mandle and Sarah Roberts-Cady (eds), *John Rawls: Debating the Major Questions*. Oxford: Oxford University Press, pp 73–85.

Alexander, Larry. 2005. *Is There a Right of Freedom of Expression?* Cambridge: Cambridge University Press.

Alfange Jr, Dean. 1968. “Free Speech and Symbolic Conduct: The Draft-Card Burning Case.” 1968 *Supreme Court Review* 1–52.

Allan, Trevor. 2001. *Constitutional Justice*. Oxford: Oxford University Press.

Almog, Shmuel. 1987. *Zionism and History*. New York: St Martin's Press.

Altman, Andrew. 2004. “Equality and Expression: The Radical Paradox.” In Ellen Frankel Paul, Fred Miller Jr, and Jeffrey Paul (eds), *Freedom of Speech*. Cambridge: Cambridge University Press, pp 1–22.

American Booksellers Association v Hudnut. 1985. United States Circuit Court of Appeals for the Seventh Circuit. 771 *US Federal Reporter, Second Series*, pp 323–33.

Antony, Louise. 2011. “Against Langton's Illocutionary Treatment of Pornography.” 2 *Jurisprudence* 387–401.

Antony, Louise. 2017. “Be What I Say: Authority versus Power in Pornography.” In Mari Mikkola (ed.), *Beyond Speech*. Oxford: Oxford University Press, pp 59–87.

Appiah, Kwame Anthony. 2012. “What's Wrong with Defamation of Religion?” In Michael Herz and Peter Molnar (eds), *The Content and Context of Hate Speech*. Cambridge: Cambridge University Press, pp 164–82.

Austin, J.L. 1975. *How to Do Things with Words*. Second Edition. Edited by J.O. Urmson and Marina Sbisà. Cambridge, MA: Harvard University Press.

Avineri, Shlomo. 1981. *The Making of Modern Zionism*. New York: Basic Books.

Badamchi, Devrim Kabasakal. 2015. “Justifications of Freedom of Speech: Towards a Double-Grounded Non-Consequentialist Approach.” 41 *Philosophy and Social Criticism* 907–27.

Baer, Ulrich. 2019. *What Snowflakes Get Right: Free Speech, Truth, and Equality on Campus*. Oxford: Oxford University Press.

Baker, C. Edwin. 1978. “Scope of the First Amendment Freedom of Speech.” 25 *UCLA Law Review* 964–1040.

Baker, C. Edwin. 1989. *Human Liberty and Freedom of Speech*. Oxford: Oxford University Press.

Baker, C. Edwin. 1994. *Advertising and a Democratic Press*. Princeton, NJ: Princeton University Press.

Baker, C. Edwin. 2012. "Hate Speech." In Michael Herz and Peter Molnar (eds), *The Content and Context of Hate Speech*. Cambridge: Cambridge University Press, pp 57–80.

Ballam, Deborah. 1989. "The Expanding Scope of the Tort of Negligent Misrepresentation: Are Publishers Next?" 22 *Loyola of Los Angeles Law Review* 761–89.

Bambauer, Derek. 2006. "Shopping Badly: Cognitive Biases, Communications, and the Fallacy of the Marketplace of Ideas." 77 *University of Colorado Law Review* 649–710.

Barendt, Eric. 2005. *Freedom of Speech*. Second Edition. Oxford: Oxford University Press.

Barnum, David. 1981. "Freedom of Assembly and the Hostile Audience in Anglo-American Law." 29 *American Journal of Comparative Law* 59–96.

Barry, Bruce. 2007. *Speechless: The Erosion of Free Expression in the American Workplace*. San Francisco, CA: Berrett-Koehler.

Benton-Evans, Ray. 1997. "Just Before You Close the Book on Keegstra ... Does He Exist in Every Classroom?" 31 *Journal of Educational Thought* 123–36.

BeVier, Lillian. 2004. "Copyright, Trespass, and the First Amendment: An Institutional Perspective." In Ellen Frankel Paul, Fred Miller Jr, and Jeffrey Paul (eds), *Freedom of Speech*. Cambridge: Cambridge University Press, pp 104–47.

Bhagwat, Ashutosh. 2019. "Free Speech Categories in the Digital Age." In Susan Brison and Katharine Gelber (eds), *Free Speech in the Digital Age*. Oxford: Oxford University Press, pp 88–103.

Black, Hugo and Cahn, Edmond. 1962. "Justice Black and First Amendment 'Absolutes': A Public Interview." 37 *New York University Law Review* 549–63.

Blasi, Vincent. 1977. "The Checking Value in First Amendment Theory." 1977 *American Bar Foundation Research Journal* 521–649.

Blasi, Vincent. 2004. "Holmes and the Marketplace of Ideas." 2004 *Supreme Court Review* 1–46.

Bodney, David. 2009. "Extreme Speech and American Press Freedoms." In Ivan Hare and James Weinstein (eds), *Extreme Speech and Democracy*. Oxford: Oxford University Press, pp 598–607.

Bollinger, Lee. 1986. *The Tolerant Society*. Oxford: Oxford University Press.

Bollinger, Lee and Stone, Geoffrey (eds). 2019. *The Free Speech Century*. Oxford: Oxford University Press.

Bork, Robert. 1971. "Neutral Principles and Some First Amendment Problems." 47 *Indiana Law Journal* 1–35.

Brandenburg v Ohio. 1969. United States Supreme Court. 395 *United States Reports*, pp 444–54.

Brennan, Tad. 2005. *The Stoic Life*. Oxford: Oxford University Press.

Brettschneider, Corey. 2012. *When the State Speaks, What Should It Say?* Princeton, NJ: Princeton University Press.

Brietzke, Paul. 1997. "How and Why the Marketplace of Ideas Fails." 31 *Valparaiso University Law Review* 951–70.

Brink, David. 1988. "Legal Theory, Legal Interpretation, and Judicial Review." 17 *Philosophy and Public Affairs* 105–48.

Brison, Susan. 1998. "The Autonomy Defense of Free Speech." 108 *Ethics* 312–39.

Brison, Susan and Gelber, Katharine (eds). 2019. *Free Speech in the Digital Age*. Oxford: Oxford University Press.

Buchanan, Allen. 1979. "Autonomy and Categories of Expression: A Reply to Professor Scanlon." 40 *University of Pittsburgh Law Review* 551–9.

Carter, Ian. 1999. *A Measure of Freedom*. Oxford: Oxford University Press.

Carter, Ian; Kramer, Matthew; and Steiner, Hillel (eds). 2007. *Freedom: A Philosophical Anthology*. Oxford: Blackwell.

Chahboun, Naima. 2015. "Nonideal Theory and Compliance—A Clarification." 14 *European Journal of Political Theory* 229–45.

Citron, Danielle Keats. 2019. "Restricting Speech to Protect It." In Susan Brison and Katharine Gelber (eds), *Free Speech in the Digital Age*. Oxford: Oxford University Press, pp 122–36.

Coenen, Dan. 2017. "Freedom of Speech and the Criminal Law." 97 *Boston University Law Review* 1533–1605.

Cohen, G.A. 2008. *Rescuing Justice and Equality*. Cambridge, MA: Harvard University Press.

Cohen, Joshua. 1996. "Freedom, Equality, Pornography." In Austin Sarat and Thomas Kearns (eds), *Justice and Injustice in Law and Legal Theory*. Ann Arbor: University of Michigan Press, pp 99–138.

Cotler, Irwin. 2012. "State-Sanctioned Incitement to Genocide: The Responsibility to Prevent." In Michael Herz and Peter Molnar (eds), *The Content and Context of Hate Speech*. Cambridge: Cambridge University Press, pp 430–55.

Crane, Paul. 2006. "True Threats and the Issue of Intent." 92 *Virginia Law Review* 1225–78.

Darwall, Stephen. 1977. "Two Kinds of Respect." 88 *Ethics* 36–49.

Darwall, Stephen. 2009. "Authority and Second-Personal Reasons for Acting." In David Sobel and Steven Wall (eds), *Reasons for Action*. Cambridge: Cambridge University Press, pp 134–54.

Darwall, Stephen. 2010. "Authority and Reasons for Acting: Exclusionary and Second Personal." 120 *Ethics* 257–78.

Davidson, Donald. 2001. *Inquiries into Truth and Interpretation*. Second Edition. Oxford: Oxford University Press.

Deb, Sopan. 2019. "Chinese State Media Vows 'Retribution' Against Silver." *New York Times*, October 20: §SP, p 7.

DeCew, Judith Wagner. 2004. "Free Speech and Offensive Expression." In Ellen Frankel Paul, Fred Miller Jr, and Jeffrey Paul (eds), *Freedom of Speech*. Cambridge: Cambridge University Press, pp 81–103.

De Montigny, Yves. 1992. "The Difficult Relationship between Freedom of Expression and Its Reasonable Limits." 55 *Law and Contemporary Problems* 35–52.

Donohue, Laura. 2008. *The Cost of Counterterrorism*. Cambridge: Cambridge University Press.

Douglas, Lawrence. 1995. "The Force of Words: Fish, Matsuda, MacKinnon, and the Theory of Discursive Violence." 29 *Law and Society Review* 169–90.

DuVal Jr, Benjamin. 1972. "Free Communication of Ideas and the Quest for Truth: Toward a Teleological Approach to First Amendment Adjudication." 41 *George Washington Law Review* 161–259.

Dworkin, Ronald. 1978. *Taking Rights Seriously*. Cambridge, MA: Harvard University Press.

Dworkin, Ronald. 1985. *A Matter of Principle*. Oxford: Oxford University Press.

Dworkin, Ronald. 1986. *Law's Empire*. London: Fontana Press.

Dworkin, Ronald. 1994. "A New Map of Censorship." 23 *Index on Censorship* 9–15.

Dworkin, Ronald. 1996. *Freedom's Law*. Oxford: Oxford University Press.

Dworkin, Ronald. 2000. *Sovereign Virtue*. Cambridge, MA: Harvard University Press.

Dworkin, Ronald. 2009. "Foreword." In Ivan Hare and James Weinstein (eds), *Extreme Speech and Democracy*. Oxford: Oxford University Press, pp v–ix.

Edgar, Harold and Schmidt Jr, Benno. 1973. "The Espionage Statutes and Publication of Defense Information." 73 *Columbia Law Review* 929–1087.

Edwards III, George. 2020. "The Bully in the Pulpit." 50 *Presidential Studies Quarterly* 286–324.

Ely, John Hart. 1975. "Flag Desecration: A Case Study in the Roles of Categorization and Balancing in First Amendment Analysis." 88 *Harvard Law Review* 1482–1508.

Ely, John Hart. 1980. *Democracy and Distrust*. Cambridge, MA: Harvard University Press.

Emerson, Thomas. 1963. "Toward a General Theory of the First Amendment." 72 *Yale Law Journal* 877–956.

Emerson, Thomas. 1970. *The System of Freedom of Expression*. New York: Random House.

Endicott, Timothy. 2000. *Vagueness in Law*. Oxford: Oxford University Press.

Epstein, Richard. 1992. "Property, Speech, and the Politics of Distrust." 59 *University of Chicago Law Review* 41–89.

Fallon, Richard. 2008. "The Core of an Uneasy Case *for* Judicial Review." 121 *Harvard Law Review* 1693–1736.

Farrelly, Colin. 2020. "The 'Focusing Illusion' of Rawlsian Ideal Theory." In Jon Mandle and Sarah Roberts-Cady (eds), *John Rawls: Debating the Major Questions*. Oxford: Oxford University Press, pp 61–72.

Finnis, John. 1980. *Natural Law and Natural Rights*. Oxford: Oxford University Press.

Frantz, Laurent. 1962. "The First Amendment in the Balance." 71 *Yale Law Journal* 1424–50.

Frantz, Laurent. 1963. "Is the First Amendment Law? A Reply to Professor Mendelson." 51 *California Law Review* 729–54.

Freeman, Samuel. 1990. "Constitutional Democracy and the Legitimacy of Judicial Review." 9 *Law and Philosophy* 327–70.

Fuller, Lon. 1969. *The Morality of Law*. Revised Edition. New Haven, CT: Yale University Press.

Fuller, P. Brooks. 2016. "The Angry Pamphleteer: True Threats, Political Speech, and Applying *Watts v United States* in the Age of Twitter." 21 *Communication Law and Policy* 87–128.

Gans, Chaim. 2008. *A Just Zionism*. Oxford: Oxford University Press.

Gelber, Katharine. 2012a. "Reconceptualizing Counterspeech in Hate Speech Policy (with a Focus on Australia)." In Michael Herz and Peter Molnar (eds), *The Content and Context of Hate Speech*. Cambridge: Cambridge University Press, pp 198–216.

Gelber, Katharine. 2012b. "'Speaking Back': The Likely Fate of Hate Speech Policy in the United States and Australia." In Ishani Maitra and Mary Kate McGowan (eds), *Speech and Harm*. Oxford: Oxford University Press, pp 50–71.

Gelber, Katharine and Brison, Susan. 2019. "Digital Dualism and the 'Speech as Thought' Paradox." In Susan Brison and Katharine Gelber (eds), *Free Speech in the Digital Age*. Oxford: Oxford University Press, pp 12–32.

Gellman, Susan. 1992. "'Brother, You Can't Go to Jail for What You're Thinking': Motives, Effects, and 'Hate Crime' Laws." 11(2) *Criminal Justice Ethics* 24–9.

Gerber, Scott. 2004. "The Politics of Free Speech." In Ellen Frankel Paul, Fred Miller Jr, and Jeffrey Paul (eds), *Freedom of Speech*. Cambridge: Cambridge University Press, pp 23–47.

Gey, Steven. 2000. "The *Nuremberg Files* and the First Amendment Value of Threats." 78 *Texas Law Review* 541–98.

Goldberg, Erica. 2016. "Free Speech Consequentialism." 116 *Columbia Law Review* 687–756.

Goldman, Alvin and Cox, James. 1996. "Speech, Truth, and the Free Market for Ideas." 2 *Legal Theory* 1–32.

Goodin, Robert and Reeve, Andrew. 1989. "Do Neutral Institutions Add Up to a Neutral State?" In Robert Goodin and Andrew Reeve (eds), *Liberal Neutrality*. London: Routledge, pp 193–210.

Gourevitch, Philip. 1998. *We Wish to Inform You that Tomorrow We will be Killed with Our Families*. New York: Farrar, Strauss, and Giroux.

Greenawalt, Kent. 1989. *Speech, Crime, and the Uses of Language*. Oxford: Oxford University Press.

Greenawalt, Kent. 1995. *Fighting Words: Individuals, Communities, and Liberties of Speech*. Princeton, NJ: Princeton University Press.

Greenawalt, Kent. 2016. *From the Bottom Up: Selected Essays*. Oxford: Oxford University Press.

Greene, Jamal. 2012. "Hate Speech and the Demos." In Michael Herz and Peter Molnar (eds), *The Content and Context of Hate Speech*. Cambridge: Cambridge University Press, pp 92–115.

Greer, Tanner. 2020. "China's Plans to Win Control of the Global Order." *Tablet Magazine*, May 18, 2020. https://www.tabletmag.com/sections/news/articles/china-plans-global-order

Griffiths, Leanne. 2005. "The Implied Freedom of Political Communication: The State of the Law Post *Coleman* and *Mulholland*." 12 *James Cook University Law Review* 93–111.

Hamlin, Alan and Stemplowska, Zofia. 2012. "Theory, Ideal Theory, and the Theory of Ideals." 10 *Political Studies Review* 48–62.

Hare, Ivan and Weinstein, James (eds). 2009. *Extreme Speech and Democracy*. Oxford: Oxford University Press.

Harel, Alon. 2012. "Hate Speech and Comprehensive Forms of Life." In Michael Herz and Peter Molnar (eds), *The Content and Context of Hate Speech*. Cambridge: Cambridge University Press, pp 306–26.

Harel, Alon. 2014. *Why Law Matters*. Oxford: Oxford University Press.

Harpin, Lee. 2019. "Police Investigate Labour Member Who Wrote 'I Hate Jews!' on Facebook." *Jewish Chronicle*, June 4. https://www.thejc.com/news/uk-news/police-investigate-labour-member-who-wrote-i-hate-jews-on-facebook-1.485084

Hart, H.L.A. 1994. *The Concept of Law*. Second Edition. Oxford: Oxford University Press.

Heinze, Eric. 2009. "Cumulative Jurisprudence and Hate Speech: Sexual Orientation and Analogies to Disability, Age, and Obesity." In Ivan Hare and James Weinstein (eds), *Extreme Speech and Democracy*. Oxford: Oxford University Press, pp 265–85.

Heinze, Eric. 2016. *Hate Speech and Democratic Citizenship*. Oxford: Oxford University Press.

Henkin, Louis. 1971. "The Right to Know and the Duty to Withhold: The Case of the Pentagon Papers." 120 *University of Pennsylvania Law Review* 271–80.

Hershovitz, Scott. 2003. "Legitimacy, Democracy, and Razian Authority." 9 *Legal Theory* 201–20.

Hershovitz, Scott. 2011. "The Role of Authority." 11(7) *Philosophers' Imprint* 1–19.

Herzog, Lisa. 2012. "Ideal and Non-ideal Theory and the Problem of Knowledge." 29 *Journal of Applied Philosophy* 271–88.

Heyman, Steven. 2009. "Hate Speech, Public Discourse, and the First Amendment." In Ivan Hare and James Weinstein (eds), *Extreme Speech and Democracy*. Oxford: Oxford University Press, pp 158–81.

Himma, Kenneth. 2007. "Just 'Cause You're Smarter than Me Doesn't Give You a Right to Tell Me What to Do: Legitimate Authority and the Normal Justification Thesis." 27 *Oxford Journal of Legal Studies* 121–50.

Hirsh, David. 2018. *Contemporary Left Antisemitism*. London: Routledge.

Ho, Daniel and Schauer, Frederick. 2015. "Testing the Marketplace of Ideas." 90 *New York University Law Review* 1160–1228.

Hohfeld, Wesley. 1923. *Fundamental Legal Conceptions*. Edited by Walter Wheeler Cook. New Haven, CT: Yale University Press.

Holmes, Stephen. 2012. "Waldron, Machiavelli, and Hate Speech." In Michael Herz and Peter Molnar (eds), *The Content and Context of Hate Speech*. Cambridge: Cambridge University Press, pp 345–51.

Hopkins, Daniel and Washington, Samantha. 2020. "The Rise of Trump, the Fall of Prejudice? Tracking White Americans' Racial Attitudes 2008-2018 via a Panel Survey." *Public Opinion Quarterly* (advance publication on June 11, 2020). https://doi.org/10.1093/poq/nfaa004

Hornsby, Jennifer. 1994. "Illocution and Its Significance." In Savas Tsohatzidis (ed.), *Foundations of Speech Act Theory*. London: Routledge, pp 187–207.

Hornsby, Jennifer. 2011. "Subordination, Silencing, and Two Ideas of Illocution." 2 *Jurisprudence* 379–85.

Horton, John. 1992. *Political Obligation*. London: Macmillan.

Horwitz, Paul. 2012. "The First Amendment's Epistemological Problem." 87 *Washington Law Review* 445–94.

Ingber, Stanley. 1984. "The Marketplace of Ideas: A Legitimizing Myth." 1984 *Duke Law Journal* 1–91.

Inwood, Brad. 1985. *Ethics and Human Action in Early Stoicism*. Oxford: Oxford University Press.

Inwood, Brad (ed.). 2003. *The Cambridge Companion to the Stoics*. Cambridge: Cambridge University Press.

Jacobson, Arthur and Schlink, Bernhard. 2012. "Hate Speech and Self-Restraint." In Michael Herz and Peter Molnar (eds), *The Content and Context of Hate Speech*. Cambridge: Cambridge University Press, pp 217–41.

Jacobson, Daniel. 1995. "Freedom of Speech Acts? A Response to Langton." 24 *Philosophy and Public Affairs* 64–79.

Jacobson, Daniel. 2004. "The Academic Betrayal of Free Speech." In Ellen Frankel Paul, Fred Miller Jr, and Jeffrey Paul (eds), *Freedom of Speech*. Cambridge: Cambridge University Press, pp 48–80.

Jenkins, Katharine. 2017. "What Women are For: Pornography and Social Ontology." In Mari Mikkola (ed.), *Beyond Speech*. Oxford: Oxford University Press, pp 91–111.

Jubb, Robert. 2019. "Disaggregating Political Authority: What's Wrong with Rawlsian Civil Disobedience?" 67 *Political Studies* 955–71.

Kagan, Elena. 1992. "The Changing Faces of First Amendment Neutrality: *R.A.V. v St Paul, Rust v Sullivan*, and the Problem of Content-Based Underinclusion." 1992 *Supreme Court Review* 29–77.

Kagan, Elena. 1993. "Regulation of Hate Speech and Pornography after *R.A.V.*" 60 *University of Chicago Law Review* 873–902.

Kagan, Elena. 1996a. "Private Speech, Public Purpose: The Role of Governmental Motive in First Amendment Doctrine." 63 *University of Chicago Law Review* 413–517.

Kagan, Elena. 1996b. "When a Speech Code is a Speech Code: The Stanford Policy and the Theory of Incidental Restraints." 29 *University of California at Davis Law Review* 957–69.

Kalven Jr, Harry. 1971. "Foreword: Even When a Nation is at War." 85 *Harvard Law Review* 3–36.

Kamm, Frances. 2007. *Intricate Ethics*. Oxford: Oxford University Press.

Keil, Geert and Poscher, Ralf (eds). 2016. *Vagueness and Law*. Oxford: Oxford University Press.
Kenyon, Andrew. 2014. "Assuming Free Speech." 77 *Modern Law Review* 379–408.
Knowles, Dudley. 2010. *Political Obligation*. London: Routledge.
Koppelman, Andrew. 1996. *Antidiscrimination Law and Social Equality*. New Haven, CT: Yale University Press.
Kramer, Matthew. 1998. "Rights without Trimmings." In Matthew Kramer, N.E. Simmonds, and Hillel Steiner, *A Debate over Rights*. Oxford: Oxford University Press, pp 7–111.
Kramer, Matthew. 1999. *In Defense of Legal Positivism*. Oxford: Oxford University Press.
Kramer, Matthew. 2001. "Getting Rights Right." In Matthew Kramer (ed.), *Rights, Wrongs, and Responsibilities*. Basingstoke: Palgrave Macmillan, pp 28–95.
Kramer, Matthew. 2003. *The Quality of Freedom*. Oxford: Oxford University Press.
Kramer, Matthew. 2004. *Where Law and Morality Meet*. Oxford: Oxford University Press.
Kramer, Matthew. 2005. "Moral Rights and the Limits of the 'Ought'-Implies-'Can' Principle: Why Impeccable Precautions are No Excuse." 48 *Inquiry* 307–355.
Kramer, Matthew. 2007. *Objectivity and the Rule of Law*. Cambridge: Cambridge University Press.
Kramer, Matthew. 2008. "Rights in Legal and Political Philosophy." In Keith Whittington, Daniel Kelemen, and Gregory Caldeira (eds), *The Oxford Handbook of Law and Politics*. Oxford: Oxford University Press, pp 414–27.
Kramer, Matthew. 2009. *Moral Realism as a Moral Doctrine*. Oxford: Wiley-Blackwell.
Kramer, Matthew. 2010. "Freedom and the Rule of Law [Meador Lecture on Freedom]." 61 *Alabama Law Review* 805–23.
Kramer, Matthew. 2011. *The Ethics of Capital Punishment*. Oxford: Oxford University Press.
Kramer, Matthew. 2012. "What is Legal Philosophy?" 43 *Metaphilosophy* 125–34.
Kramer, Matthew. 2014. *Torture and Moral Integrity*. Oxford: Oxford University Press.
Kramer, Matthew. 2016. "Moral Conflicts, the 'Ought Implies Can' Principle, and Moral Demandingness." In Marcel van Ackeren and Michael Kühler (eds), *The Limits of Moral Obligation*. London: Routledge, pp. 163–84.
Kramer, Matthew. 2017. *Liberalism with Excellence*. Oxford: Oxford University Press.
Kramer, Matthew. 2018. *H.L.A. Hart: The Nature of Law*. Cambridge: Polity Press.
Kramer, Matthew. 2019a. "On No-Rights and No Rights." 64 *American Journal of Jurisprudence*.
Kramer, Matthew. 2019b. "Shakespeare, Moral Judgements, and Moral Realism." In Craig Bourne and Emily Caddick Bourne (eds), *The Routledge Companion to Shakespeare and Philosophy*. London: Routledge, pp 234–45.
Kramer, Matthew. 2019c. "The Demandingness of Deontological Duties: Is the Absolute Impermissibility of Placatory Torture Irrational?" 6 *Moral Philosophy and Politics* 9–40.
Krotoszynski Jr, Ronald. 2015. "Free Speech Paternalism and Free Speech Exceptionalism: Pervasive Distrust of Government and the Contemporary First Amendment." 76 *Ohio State Law Journal* 659–90.
Lakier, Genevieve. 2015. "The Invention of Low-Value Speech." 128 *Harvard Law Review* 2166–2233.
Lane Jr, Daniel McNeel. 1988. "Publisher Reliability for Material that Invites Reliance." 66 *Texas Law Review* 1155–94.
Langton, Rae. 2009. *Sexual Solipsism*. Oxford: Oxford University Press.
Langton, Rae. 2011. "Response." 2 *Jurisprudence* 425–40.

Langton, Rae. 2012. "Beyond Belief: Pragmatics in Hate Speech and Pornography." In Ishani Maitra and Mary Kate McGowan (eds), *Speech and Harm*. Oxford: Oxford University Press, pp 72–93.

Langton, Rae. 2016. "Hate Speech and the Epistemology of Justice." 10 *Criminal Law and Philosophy* 865–73.

Langton, Rae. 2017. "Is Pornography Like the Law?" In Mari Mikkola (ed.), *Beyond Speech*. Oxford: Oxford University Press, pp 23–38.

Langton, Rae. 2018a. "The Authority of Hate Speech." In John Gardner, Leslie Green, and Brian Leiter (eds), *Oxford Studies in Philosophy of Law, Volume 3*. Oxford: Oxford University Press, pp 123–52.

Langton, Rae. 2018b. "Blocking as Counter-Speech." In Daniel Fogal, Daniel Harris, and Matt Moss (eds), *New Work on Speech Acts*. Oxford: Oxford University Press, pp 144–64.

Langton, Rae and West, Caroline. 1999. "Scorekeeping in a Pornographic Language Game." 77 *Australasian Journal of Philosophy* 303–19.

Lawrence III, Charles. 1990. "If He Hollers Let Him Go: Regulating Racist Speech on Campus." 1990 *Duke Law Journal* 431–83.

Leanza, Cheryl. 2007. "Heckler's Veto Case Law as a Resource for Democratic Discourse." 35 *Hofstra Law Review* 1305–19.

Lee, Gia. 2009. "First Amendment Enforcement in Government Institutions and Programs." 56 *UCLA Law Review* 1691–1774.

Leiter, Brian. 2016. "The Case against Free Speech." 38 *Sydney Law Review* 407–39.

Lepoutre, Maxime. 2017. "Hate Speech in Public Discourse: A Pessimistic Defense of Counterspeech." 43 *Social Theory and Practice* 851–83.

Lepoutre, Maxime. 2019. "Hate Speech Laws: Expressive Power is not the Answer." 25 *Legal Theory* 272–96.

Lewis, Anthony. 2007. *Freedom for the Thought That We Hate*. New York: Basic Books.

Linde, Hans. 1969. "Book Review (*Rights of the Person* by Bernard Schwartz)." 67 *Michigan Law Review* 1282–8.

Linde, Hans. 1970. "'Clear and Present Danger' Reexamined: Dissonance in the *Brandenburg* Concerto." 22 *Stanford Law Review* 1163–86.

MacKinnon, Catharine. 1987. *Feminism Unmodified*. Cambridge, MA: Harvard University Press.

MacKinnon, Catharine. 1993. *Only Words*. Cambridge, MA: Harvard University Press.

Maitra, Ishani. 2012. "Subordinating Speech." In Ishani Maitra and Mary Kate McGowan (eds), *Speech and Harm*. Oxford: Oxford University Press, pp 94–120.

Maitra, Ishani and McGowan, Mary Kate. 2007. "The Limits of Free Speech: Pornography and the Question of Coverage." 13 *Legal Theory* 41–68.

Maitra, Ishani and McGowan, Mary Kate. 2010. "On Racist Hate Speech and the Scope of a Free Speech Principle." 23 *Canadian Journal of Law and Jurisprudence* 343–72.

Malik, Kenan and Molnar, Peter. 2012. "Interview with Kenan Malik." In Michael Herz and Peter Molnar (eds), *The Content and Context of Hate Speech*. Cambridge: Cambridge University Press, pp 81–91.

Matsuda, Mari. 1989. "Public Response to Racist Speech: Considering the Victim's Story." 87 *Michigan Law Review* 2320–81.

McBride, Nicholas and Bagshaw, Roderick. 2012. *Tort Law*. Fourth Edition. Harlow: Pearson Education.

McGaffey, Ruth. 1973. "The Heckler's Veto: A Reexamination." 57 *Marquette Law Review* 39–64.

McGowan, Mary Kate. 2003. "Conversational Exercitives and the Force of Pornography." 31 *Philosophy and Public Affairs* 155–89.

McGowan, Mary Kate. 2012. "On 'Whites Only' Signs and Racist Hate Speech: Verbal Acts of Racial Discrimination." In Ishani Maitra and Mary Kate McGowan (eds), *Speech and Harm*. Oxford: Oxford University Press, pp 121–47.

McGowan, Mary Kate. 2017. "On Multiple Types of Silencing." In Mari Mikkola (ed.), *Beyond Speech*. Oxford: Oxford University Press, pp 39–58.

Meiklejohn, Alexander. 1948. *Free Speech and its Relation to Self-Government*. New York: Harper & Brothers.

Meiklejohn, Alexander. 1961. "The First Amendment is an Absolute." 1961 *Supreme Court Review* 245–66.

Mengistu, Yared Legesse. 2012. "Shielding Marginalized Groups from Verbal Assaults without Abusing Hate Speech Laws." In Michael Herz and Peter Molnar (eds), *The Content and Context of Hate Speech*. Cambridge: Cambridge University Press, pp 352–77.

Merrill, Lisa. 1998. "Spectatorship and Complicity: Who is the 'Accused' in Popular Film Depictions of Gender and Violence?" In Linda Longmire and Lisa Merrill (eds), *Untying the Tongue: Gender, Power, and the Word*. Westport, CT: Greenwood Press, pp 91–102.

Mill, John Stuart. 1956. *On Liberty*. Edited by Currin Shields. Indianapolis, IN: Bobbs-Merrill [originally published 1859].

Mills, Charles. 2005. "'Ideal Theory' as Ideology." 20 *Hypatia* 165–84.

Minow, Martha. 2000. "Regulating Hatred: Whose Speech, Whose Crimes, Whose Power? An Essay for Kenneth Karst." 47 *UCLA Law Review* 1253–77.

Molnar, Peter. 2012. "Responding to 'Hate Speech' with Art, Education, and the Imminent Danger Test." In Michael Herz and Peter Molnar (eds), *The Content and Context of Hate Speech*. Cambridge: Cambridge University Press, pp 183–97.

Moore, Michael. 2007. "Patrolling the Borders of Consequentialist Justifications: The Scope of Agent-Relative Restrictions." 27 *Law and Philosophy* 35–96.

Nehushtan, Yossi. 2015. *Intolerant Religion in a Tolerant-Liberal Democracy*. Oxford: Hart Publishing.

Nelson, Louis and Harold, Claudrena (eds). 2018. *Charlottesville 2017: The Legacy of Race and Inequity*. Charlottesville: University of Virginia Press.

Nussbaum, Martha. 1994. *The Therapy of Desire*. Princeton, NJ: Princeton University Press.

Oster, Jan. 2015. *Media Freedom as a Fundamental Right*. Cambridge: Cambridge University Press.

Parekh, Bhikhu. 2012. "Is There a Case for Banning Hate Speech?" In Michael Herz and Peter Molnar (eds), *The Content and Context of Hate Speech*. Cambridge: Cambridge University Press, pp 37–56.

Parfit, Derek. 1984. *Reasons and Persons*. Oxford: Oxford University Press.

Peel, Edwin and Goudkamp, James. 2014. *Winfield and Jolowicz on Tort*. Nineteenth Edition. London: Sweet & Maxwell.

Perry, Stephen. 2013. "Political Authority and Political Obligation." 2 *Oxford Studies in Philosophy of Law* 1–74.

Piety, Tamara. 2007. "Market Failure in the Marketplace of Ideas: Commercial Speech and the Problem that Won't Go Away." 41 *Loyola of Los Angeles Law Review* 181–226.

Post, Robert. 1997. "Equality and Autonomy in First Amendment Jurisprudence." 95 *Michigan Law Review* 1517–41.

Post, Robert. 2000. "Reconciling Theory and Doctrine in First Amendment Jurisprudence." 88 *California Law Review* 2353–74.

Post, Robert. 2011. "Participatory Democracy and Free Speech." 97 *Virginia Law Review* 477–89.

Post, Robert. 2019. "The Classic First Amendment Tradition Under Stress: Freedom of Speech and the University." In Lee Bollinger and Geoffrey Stone (eds), *The Free Speech Century*. Oxford: Oxford University Press, pp 106–22.

Post, Robert and Molnar, Peter. 2012. "Interview with Robert Post." In Michael Herz and Peter Molnar (eds), *The Content and Context of Hate Speech*. Cambridge: Cambridge University Press, pp 11–36.

Pozen, David. 2013. "The Leaky Leviathan: Why the Government Condemns and Condones Unlawful Disclosures of Information." 127 *Harvard Law Review* 512–635.

Price, Zachary. 2018. "Our Imperiled Absolutist First Amendment." 20 *Journal of Constitutional Law* 817–44.

Quong, Jonathan. 2011. *Liberalism without Perfection*. Oxford: Oxford University Press.

Rawls, John. 1993. *Political Liberalism*. New York: Columbia University Press.

Rawls, John. 1999. *A Theory of Justice*. Revised Edition. Oxford: Oxford University Press.

Rawls, John. 2001. *Justice as Fairness: A Restatement*. Cambridge, MA: Harvard University Press.

Raz, Joseph. 1986. *The Morality of Freedom*. Oxford: Oxford University Press.

Raz, Joseph. 1994. *Ethics in the Public Domain*. Oxford: Oxford University Press.

Raz, Joseph. 2009a. *The Authority of Law*. Second Edition. Oxford: Oxford University Press.

Raz, Joseph. 2009b. *Between Authority and Interpretation*. Oxford: Oxford University Press.

Redish, Martin. 1992. "Freedom of Thought as Freedom of Expression: Hate Crime Sentencing Enhancement and First Amendment Theory." 11(2) *Criminal Justice Ethics* 29–42.

Rich, Dave. 2018. *The Left's Jewish Problem: Jeremy Corbyn, Israel, and Anti-Semitism*. Updated Edition. London: Biteback.

Robeyns, Ingrid. 2008. "Ideal Theory in Theory and Practice." 34 *Social Theory and Practice* 341–62.

Rosenfeld, Michel. 2012. "Hate Speech in Constitutional Jurisprudence: A Comparative Analysis." In Michael Herz and Peter Molnar (eds), *The Content and Context of Hate Speech*. Cambridge: Cambridge University Press, pp 242–89.

Rothman, Jessica. 2001. "Freedom of Speech and True Threats." 25 *Harvard Journal of Law and Public Policy* 283–367.

Rotunda, Ronald. 2004. "Current Proposals for Media Accountability in Light of the First Amendment." In Ellen Frankel Paul, Fred Miller Jr, and Jeffrey Paul (eds), *Freedom of Speech*. Cambridge: Cambridge University Press, pp 269–309.

Rubenfeld, Jed. 2001. "The First Amendment's Purpose." 53 *Stanford Law Review* 767–832.

Rubenfeld, Jed. 2002a. "The Freedom of Imagination: Copyright's Constitutionality." 112 *Yale Law Journal* 1–60.

Rubenfeld, Jed. 2002b. "A Reply to Posner." 54 *Stanford Law Review* 753–67.

Sachs, Albie. 2019. "Reflections on the Firstness of the First Amendment in the United States." In Lee Bollinger and Geoffrey Stone (eds), *The Free Speech Century*. Oxford: Oxford University Press, pp 179–92.

Sadurski, Wojciech. 1999. *Freedom of Speech and Its Limits*. Dordrecht: Kluwer Academic.

Sbisà, Marina. 2009. "Uptake and Conventionality in Illocution." 5 *Lodz Papers in Pragmatics* 33–52.

Scanlon, Thomas. 1972. "A Theory of Freedom of Expression." 1 *Philosophy and Public Affairs* 204–26.

Scanlon, Thomas. 1979. "Freedom of Expression and Categories of Expression." 40 *University of Pittsburgh Law Review* 519–50.
Scanlon, Thomas. 2003. *The Difficulty of Tolerance*. Cambridge: Cambridge University Press.
Scanlon, Thomas. 2017. "Thinkers, Lies, and Freedom of Speech." 23 *Legal Theory* 132–40.
Schauer, Frederick. 1979. "Speech and 'Speech'—Obscenity and 'Obscenity': An Exercise in the Interpretation of Constitutional Language." 67 *Georgetown Law Journal* 899–933.
Schauer, Frederick. 1981. "Categories and the First Amendment: A Play in Three Acts." 34 *Vanderbilt Law Review* 265–307.
Schauer, Frederick. 1982. *Free Speech*. Cambridge: Cambridge University Press.
Schauer, Frederick. 1992. "Uncoupling Free Speech." 92 *Columbia Law Review* 1321–57.
Schauer, Frederick. 1998. "Principles, Institutions, and the First Amendment." 112 *Harvard Law Review* 84–121.
Schauer, Frederick. 2003. "Intentions, Conventions, and the First Amendment: The Case of Cross-Burning." 2003 *Supreme Court Review* 197–230.
Schauer, Frederick. 2008. "Hohfeld's First Amendment." 76 *George Washington Law Review* 914–32.
Schauer, Frederick. 2010. "Facts and the First Amendment." 57 *UCLA Law Review* 897–920.
Schauer, Frederick. 2012. "Social Epistemology, Holocaust Denial, and the Post-Millian Calculus." In Michael Herz and Peter Molnar (eds), *The Content and Context of Hate Speech*. Cambridge: Cambridge University Press, pp 129–43.
Schauer, Frederick. 2017. "Free Speech, the Search for Truth, and the Problem of Collective Knowledge." 70 *SMU Law Review* 231–51.
Schauer, Frederick. 2019a. "Every Possible Use of Language?" In Lee Bollinger and Geoffrey Stone (eds), *The Free Speech Century*. Oxford: Oxford University Press, pp 33–47.
Schauer, Frederick. 2019b. "Costs and Challenges of the Hostile Audience." 94 *Notre Dame Law Review* 1671–98.
Shakespeare, William. 1974. *The Riverside Shakespeare*. Edited by G. Blakemore Evans. Boston, MA: Houghton Mifflin.
Shaw, Theodore and Molnar, Peter. 2012. "Interview with Theodore Shaw." In Michael Herz and Peter Molnar (eds), *The Content and Context of Hate Speech*. Cambridge: Cambridge University Press, pp 399–413.
Sher, George. 1997. *Beyond Neutrality*. Cambridge: Cambridge University Press.
Shiffrin, Seana. 2014. *Speech Matters*. Princeton, NJ: Princeton University Press.
Shiffrin, Steven. 2016. *What's Wrong with the First Amendment?* Cambridge: Cambridge University Press.
Shipp, E.R. 1984. "Tape Contradicts Disavowal of 'Gutter Religion' Attack." *New York Times*, June 29, p 12.
Silverman, Matthew. 2003. "National Security and the First Amendment: A Judicial Role in Maximizing Public Access to Information." 78 *Indiana Law Journal* 1101–29.
Simmons, A. John. 2010. "Ideal and Nonideal Theory." 38 *Philosophy and Public Affairs* 5–36.
Skillen, Anthony. 1982. "Freedom of Speech." In Keith Graham (ed.), *Contemporary Political Philosophy: Radical Studies*. Cambridge: Cambridge University Press, pp 139–59.
Smolla, Rodney. 1992. *Free Speech in an Open Society*. New York: Vintage Books.
Somerville, Keith. 2012. "Rwanda: Genocide, Hate Radio and the Power of the Broadcast Word." In *Radio Propaganda and the Broadcasting of Hatred*. Basingstoke: Palgrave Macmillan, pp 152–207.
Sorabji, Richard. 2000. *Emotion and Peace of Mind*. Oxford: Oxford University Press.
Spellman, Robert. 1988. "The First Amendment Defense to Negligent Misstatement." 10 *Communications and the Law* 59–72.

Stalnaker, Robert. 1973. "Presuppositions." 2 *Journal of Philosophical Logic* 447–57.
Stanner, Andrew. 2006. "Toward an Improved Threat Doctrine for Student Speakers." 81 *New York University Law Review* 385–417.
Stemplowska, Zofia. 2008. "What's Ideal about Ideal Theory?" 34 *Social Theory and Practice* 319–40.
Stemplowska, Zofia and Swift, Adam. 2012. "Ideal and Nonideal Theory." In David Estlund (ed.), *Oxford Handbook of Political Philosophy*. Oxford: Oxford University Press, pp 373–89.
Stone, Geoffrey. 1983. "Content Regulation and the First Amendment." 25 *William and Mary Law Review* 189–252.
Stone, Geoffrey. 1993. "Autonomy and Distrust." 64 *University of Colorado Law Review* 1171–8.
Stone, Geoffrey. 1994. "Hate Speech and the U.S. Constitution." 3 *East European Constitutional Review* 78–82.
Stone, Geoffrey. 2007a. "Government Secrecy vs. Freedom of the Press." 1 *Harvard Journal of Law and Public Policy* 185–217.
Stone, Geoffrey. 2007b. "Prosecuting the Press for Publishing Classified Information." 2 *Florida International University Law Review* 93–6.
Strauss, David. 2019. "Keeping Secrets." In Lee Bollinger and Geoffrey Stone (eds), *The Free Speech Century*. Oxford: Oxford University Press, pp 123–39.
Strossen, Nadine. 1990. "Regulating Racist Speech on Campus: A Modest Proposal." 1990 *Duke Law Journal* 484–573.
Strossen, Nadine. 2001. "Incitement to Hatred: Should There be a Limit?" 25 *Southern Illinois University Law Journal* 243–80.
Strossen, Nadine. 2018. *Hate: Why We Should Resist It with Free Speech, Not Censorship*. Oxford: Oxford University Press.
Strossen, Nadine and Molnar, Peter. 2012. "Interview with Nadine Strossen." In Michael Herz and Peter Molnar (eds), *The Content and Context of Hate Speech*. Cambridge: Cambridge University Press, pp 378–98.
Suk, Julie. 2012. "Denying Experience: Holocaust Denial and the Free-Speech Theory of the State." In Michael Herz and Peter Molnar (eds), *The Content and Context of Hate Speech*. Cambridge: Cambridge University Press, pp 144–63.
Sunstein, Cass. 1992. "Free Speech Now." 59 *University of Chicago Law Review* 255–316.
Sunstein, Cass. 2019. "Does the Clear and Present Danger Test Survive Cost-Benefit Analysis?" In Lee Bollinger and Geoffrey Stone (eds), *The Free Speech Century*. Oxford: Oxford University Press, pp 162–76.
Swift, Adam. 2008. "The Value of Philosophy in Nonideal Circumstances." 34 *Social Theory and Practice* 363–87.
Tabarovsky, Izabella. 2019. "Soviet Anti-Zionism and Contemporary Left Antisemitism." 22 *Fathom*, May 2019. http://fathomjournal.org/soviet-anti-zionism-and-contemporary-left-antisemitism/
Tribe, Laurence. 1978. *American Constitutional Law*. Mineola, NY: Foundation Press.
Tribe, Laurence; Waldron, Jeremy; and Tushnet, Mark. 2005. "On Judicial Review." 52(3) *Dissent* 81–6.
Tsesis, Alexander. 2016. "Balancing Free Speech." 96 *Boston University Law Review* 1–54.
Valentini, Laura. 2009. "On the Apparent Paradox of Ideal Theory." 17 *Journal of Political Philosophy* 332–55.
Volacu, Alexandru. 2018. "Bridging Ideal and Non-ideal Theory." 66 *Political Studies* 887–902.

Waldron, Jeremy. 1999. *Law and Disagreement*. Oxford: Oxford University Press.
Waldron, Jeremy. 2006. "The Core of the Case against Judicial Review." 115 *Yale Law Journal* 1346–1406.
Waldron, Jeremy. 2012. *The Harm in Hate Speech*. Cambridge, MA: Harvard University Press.
Waluchow, W.J. 2005. "Constitutions as Living Trees: An Idiot Defends." 18 *Canadian Journal of Law and Jurisprudence* 207–47.
Waluchow, W.J. 2007. *A Common Law Theory of Judicial Review*. Cambridge: Cambridge University Press.
Wechsler, Herbert; Jones, William; and Korn, Harold. 1961. "The Treatment of Inchoate Crimes in the Model Penal Code of the American Law Institute: Attempt, Solicitation, and Conspiracy (Part One)." 61 *Columbia Law Review* 571–628.
Weingarten, Steven. 1984. "Tort Liability for Nonlibelous Negligent Statements: First Amendment Considerations." 93 *Yale Law Journal* 744–62.
Weinstein, James. 1992. "First Amendment Challenges to Hate Crime Legislation: Where's the Speech?" 11(2) *Criminal Justice Ethics* 6–20.
Weinstein, James. 2009. "Extreme Speech, Public Order, and Democracy: Lessons from *The Masses*." In Ivan Hare and James Weinstein (eds), *Extreme Speech and Democracy*. Oxford: Oxford University Press, pp 23–61.
Weinstein, James. 2011. "Participatory Democracy as the Central Value of American Free Speech." 97 *Virginia Law Review* 491–514.
Weinstein, James. 2019. "Cyber Harassment and Free Speech: Drawing the Line Online." In Susan Brison and Katharine Gelber (eds), *Free Speech in the Digital Age*. Oxford: Oxford University Press, pp 52–73.
Weiss, Lori. 2004. "Is the True Threats Doctrine Threatening the First Amendment? *Planned Parenthood of the Columbia/Williamette, Inc. v American Coalition of Life Activists* Signals the Need to Remedy an Inadequate Doctrine." 72 *Fordham Law Review* 1283–1340.
Wellington, Harry. 1979. "On Freedom of Expression." 88 *Yale Law Journal* 1105–42.
Welshon, Rex. 2020. "Hate Speech on Campus: What Public Universities Can and Should Do to Counter Weaponized Intolerance." 26 *Res Publica* 45–66.
Wright, R. George. 2017. "The Heckler's Veto Today." 68 *Case Western Reserve Law Review* 159–88.

Index

For the benefit of digital users, indexed terms that span two pages (e.g., 52–53) may, on occasion, appear on only one of those pages.

N.B. In this Index, the phrase "the principle of freedom of expression" has been shortened to "PFE."